KB084800

적중 100

영어 기출 문제집

중 **2**

시사 | 송미정

Best Collection

구성과 특징

교과서의 주요 학습 내용을 중심으로 학습 영역별 특성에 맞춰 단계별로 다양한 학습 기회를 제공하여
단원별 학습능력 평가는 물론 중간 및 기말고사 시험 등에 완벽하게 대비할 수 있도록 내용을 구성

Words & Expressions

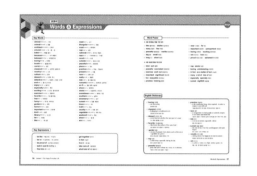

Step1   Key Words 단원별 핵심 단어 설명 및 풀이
           Key Expression 단원별 핵심 숙어 및 관용어 설명
           Word Power 반대 또는 비슷한 뜻 단어 배우기
           English Dictionary 영어로 배우는 영어 단어

Step2   실력평가 단원별 수시평가 대비 주관식, 객관식 문제풀이

Step3   서술형 대비 학업성취도 및 수행능력평가 대비 서술형 문제풀이

Conversation

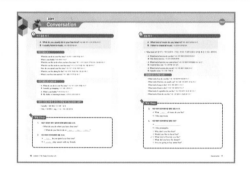

Step1   핵심 의사소통 소통에 필요한 주요 표현 방법 요약
           핵심 Check 기본적인 표현 방법 및 활용능력 확인

Step2   대화문 익히기 교과서 대화문 심층 분석 및 확인

Step3   교과서 확인학습 빈칸 채우기를 통한 문장 완성 능력 확인

Step4   기본평가 시험대비 기초 학습 능력 평가

Step5   실력평가 단원별 수시평가 대비 주관식, 객관식 문제풀이

Step6   서술형 대비 학업성취도 및 수행능력평가 대비 서술형 문제풀이

Grammar

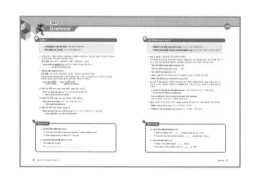

Step1   주요 문법 단원별 주요 문법 사항과 예문을 알기 쉽게 설명
           핵심 Check 기본 문법사항에 대한 이해 여부 확인

Step2   기본평가 시험대비 기초 학습 능력 평가

Step3   실력평가 단원별 수시평가 대비 주관식, 객관식 문제풀이

Step4   서술형 대비 학업성취도 및 수행능력평가 대비 서술형 문제풀이

Reading

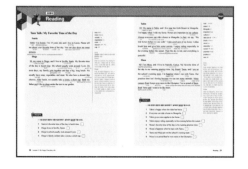

Step1   구문 분석 단원별로 제시된 문장에 대한 구문별 분석과 내용 설명
           확인문제 문장에 대한 기본적인 이해와 인지능력 확인

Step2   확인학습A 빈칸 채우기를 통한 문장 완성 능력 확인

Step3   확인학습B 제시된 우리말을 영어로 완성하여 작문 능력 키우기

Step4   실력평가 단원별 수시평가 대비 주관식, 객관식 문제풀이

Step5   서술형 대비 학업성취도 및 수행능력평가 대비 서술형 문제풀이
           교과서 구석구석 교과서에 나오는 기타 문장까지 완벽 학습

Composition

|영역별 핵심문제|

단어 및 어휘, 대화문, 문법, 독해 등 각 영역별 기출문제의 출제 유형을 분석하여 실전에 대비하고 연습할 수 있도록 문제를 배열

|단원별 예상문제|

기출문제를 분석한 후 새로운 시험 출제 경향을 더하여 새롭게 출제될 수 있는 문제를 포함하여 시험에 완벽하게 대비할 수 있도록 준비

|서술형 실전 및 창의사고력 문제|

학교 시험에서 점차 늘어나는 서술형 시험에 집중 대비하고 고득점을 취득하는데 만전을 기하기 위한 학습 코너

|단원별 모의고사|

영역별, 단계별 학습을 모두 마친 후 실전 연습을 위한 모의고사

교과서 파헤치기

- **단어Test1~3** 영어 단어 우리말 쓰기, 우리말을 영어 단어로 쓰기, 영영풀이에 해당하는 단어와 우리말 쓰기
- **대화문Test1~2** 대화문 빈칸 완성 및 전체 대화문 쓰기
- **본문Test1~5** 빈칸 완성, 우리말 쓰기, 문장 배열연습, 영어 작문하기 복습 등 단계별 반복 학습을 통해 교과서 지문에 대한 완벽한 습득
- **구석구석지문Test1~2** 지문 빈칸 완성 및 전문 영어로 쓰기

Contents

Lesson 1

My Bucket List

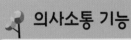 **의사소통 기능**

- 바람, 소망 말하기

  A: I hope I can travel to Europe this summer.

  B: That sounds great.

- 계획 묻고 답하기

  A: What are you planning to do at the school festival?

  B: I'm planning to sell snacks.

언어 형식

- 최상급

  I think the guitar has **the most beautiful** sound of all musical instruments.

- to부정사의 부사적 용법(목적)

  I will put more effort into studying math **to overcome** my weakness.

Words & Expressions

교과서

Key Words

- ☐ **adopt** [ədápt] 동 입양하다
- ☐ **band** [bænd] 명 밴드
- ☐ **book fair** 도서 박람회
- ☐ **bucket list** 버킷 리스트(달성하고 싶은 일들을 적은 목록)
- ☐ **by** [bai] 전 ~까지(는)
- ☐ **can** [kæn] 조 ~할 수 있다
- ☐ **cartoon** [kɑːrtúːn] 명 만화
- ☐ **challenging** [tʃælindʒiŋ] 형 도전적인, 힘든, 간단하지 않은
- ☐ **Chinese** [tʃàiníːz] 명 중국어 형 중국의
- ☐ **complete** [kəmplíːt] 동 완료하다, 완결하다
- ☐ **concert** [kɑ́ːnsərt] 명 콘서트
- ☐ **detective** [ditéktiv] 명 탐정, 형사
- ☐ **drama** [drɑ́ːmə] 명 드라마
- ☐ **draw** [drɔː] 동 그리다
- ☐ **Europe** [júərəp] 명 유럽, 유럽 대륙
- ☐ **exercise** [éksərsàiz] 동 운동하다 명 운동
- ☐ **experience** [ikspíəriəns] 동 경험하다 명 경험
- ☐ **famous** [féiməs] 형 유명한, 잘 알려진
- ☐ **favor** [féivər] 명 호의, 친절
- ☐ **favorite** [féivərit] 형 아주 좋아하는
- ☐ **festival** [féstəvəl] 명 축제
- ☐ **finally** [fáinəli] 부 마지막으로
- ☐ **freely** [fríːli] 부 자유롭게
- ☐ **fully** [fúlli] 부 완전히
- ☐ **goal** [goul] 명 목표
- ☐ **hope** [houp] 동 희망하다, 바라다 명 희망

- ☐ **introduce** [intrədjúːs] 동 소개하다
- ☐ **missing** [mísiŋ] 형 없어진, 분실한
- ☐ **most** [moust] 부 가장
- ☐ **musical instrument** 악기
- ☐ **national** [næʃənl] 형 국가의, 국민의
- ☐ **overcome** [ouvərkám] 동 극복하다
- ☐ **plan** [plæn] 명 계획 동 계획하다
- ☐ **pleased** [plíːzd] 형 기쁜
- ☐ **ride** [raid] 동 타다
- ☐ **right** [rait] 부 바로
- ☐ **save** [seiv] 동 구하다, 아끼다
- ☐ **sell** [sel] 동 팔다, 판매하다
- ☐ **someday** [sámdei] 부 언젠가
- ☐ **special** [spéʃəl] 형 특별한
- ☐ **spend** [spend] 동 쓰다, 소비하다
- ☐ **start** [stɑːrt] 동 시작하다
- ☐ **stay** [stei] 동 머무르다, 지내다
- ☐ **subject** [sábdʒikt] 명 과목
- ☐ **surprise** [sərpráiz] 동 놀라게 하다
- ☐ **talk** [tɔːk] 동 말하다
- ☐ **walk** [wɔːk] 동 걷게 하다, 데리고 가다
- ☐ **wash** [waʃ] 동 씻다
- ☐ **weak** [wiːk] 형 약한
- ☐ **weakness** [wíːknis] 명 약점
- ☐ **worry** [wə́ːri] 동 걱정하다
- ☐ **writer** [ráitər] 명 작가

Key Expressions

- ☐ **ask for help**: 도움을 청하다
- ☐ **be planning to** 동사원형: ~할 계획이다
- ☐ **be ready to** 동사원형: ~할 준비가 되다
- ☐ **be willing to** 동사원형: 기꺼이 ~하다
- ☐ **by the end of** ~: ~ 말까지
- ☐ **do a favor**: 호의를 베풀다
- ☐ **for a while**: 잠깐
- ☐ **get better**: (병·상황 등이) 나아지다
- ☐ **get interested in**: ~에 관심을 갖게 되다
- ☐ **get into**: ~에 흥미를 갖게 되다
- ☐ **get one's hair cut**: ~의 머리를 자르다
- ☐ **go back to** ~: ~으로 돌아가다

- ☐ **go on a tour**: 관광하다, 여행을 떠나다
- ☐ **how to** 동사원형: ~하는 방법
- ☐ **make a friend**: 친구를 사귀다
- ☐ **make an effort**: 노력하다
- ☐ **put effort into** ~: ~에 노력을 들이다, 힘들이다
- ☐ **share A with B**: A를 B와 나누다[공유하다]
- ☐ **stand in line**: 줄을 서서 기다리다
- ☐ **take a picture with**: ~와 사진을 찍다
- ☐ **take care of**: ~을 돌보다
- ☐ **throw away**: ~을 버리다, ~을 던지다
- ☐ **would like to** 동사원형: ~하고 싶다

Word Power

※ 서로 반대되는 뜻을 가진 단어
- [ ] **sell** (팔다) ↔ **buy** (사다)
- [ ] **weak** (약한) ↔ **strong** (강한)
- [ ] **special** (특별한) ↔ **general** (일반적인)

- [ ] **finish** (끝내다) ↔ **begin** (시작하다)
- [ ] **weakness** (약함, 약점) ↔ **strength** (힘, 강점)
- [ ] **hope** (희망) ↔ **despair** (절망)

※ 서로 비슷한 뜻을 가진 단어
- [ ] **complete** (완료하다, 완결하다) = **finish** (끝내다)
- [ ] **finally** (마지막으로) = **lastly** (마지막으로, 끝으로)
- [ ] **goal** (목표) = **aim** (목표)
- [ ] **pleased** (기쁜) = **glad** (기쁜)

- [ ] **famous** (유명한, 잘 알려진) = **well-known** (유명한, 잘 알려진)
- [ ] **fully** (완전히) = **completely** (완전히, 완벽하게)
- [ ] **missing** (없어진, 행방불명의) = **lost** (잃은, 분실한)
- [ ] **start** (시작하다) = **begin** (시작하다)

English Dictionary

- [ ] **book fair** 도서 박람회
  → an event at which people or businesses show and sell their books
  사람들이나 기업들이 그들의 책을 보여주고 파는 행사

- [ ] **band** 밴드
  → a group of musicians, especially a group that plays popular music
  음악가들의 그룹, 특히 대중적인 음악을 연주하는 그룹

- [ ] **challenging** 도전적인
  → difficult in an interesting or enjoyable way
  흥미롭거나 재미있는 방식으로 어려운

- [ ] **complete** 완료하다, 완결하다
  → to finish doing or making something, especially when it has taken a long time
  특히 긴 시간이 걸릴 때 무엇인가를 하거나 만드는 행위를 끝내다

- [ ] **detective** 탐정
  → someone whose job is to discover what has happened in a crime or other situation and to find the people involved
  범죄나 다른 상황에서 무슨 일이 일어났는지 발견하고 관련된 사람들을 찾는 것이 직업인 사람

- [ ] **draw** 그리다
  → to produce a picture of something using a pencil, pen, etc.
  연필이나 펜을 사용해서 어떤 것의 그림을 만들다

- [ ] **favor** 호의, 친절
  → something that you do for someone in order to help them or be kind to them
  누군가를 돕거나 친절하게 하기 위해서 하는 어떤 것

- [ ] **freely** 자유롭게
  → without anyone stopping or limiting something
  어떤 것을 멈추거나 제한하는 사람 없이

- [ ] **fully** 완전히
  → completely
  완전히

- [ ] **goal** 목표
  → something that you hope to achieve in the future
  미래에 달성하기를 바라는 어떤 것

- [ ] **most** 가장
  → to a greater degree or more times than anything else
  다른 어떤 것보다 더 많은 정도나 더 많은 횟수

- [ ] **overcome** 극복하다
  → to successfully control a feeling or problem
  감정이나 문제를 성공적으로 통제하다

- [ ] **right** 바로
  → exactly in a particular position or place
  정확히 특정한 위치나 장소에

- [ ] **save** 구하다, 살리다
  → to make someone or something safe from danger, harm, or destruction
  위험, 해 또는 파괴로부터 어떤 사람이나 사물을 안전하게 만들다

- [ ] **someday** 언젠가
  → at an unknown time in the future, especially a long time in the future
  미래 특히 긴 시간 후의 미래의 이떤 알지 못하는 시기에

- [ ] **spend** 쓰다, 소비하다
  → to use your money to pay for goods or services
  상품이나 서비스에 돈을 사용하다

01 다음 문장의 빈칸에 알맞은 것은?

> They were recommended to _____ dogs from animal shelters instead of buying them from pet stores.

① adopt　　　　② adapt
③ accompany　　④ admit
⑤ acquire

02 밑줄 친 부분의 의미가 나머지 넷과 다른 하나는?

① Mike wants to learn Chinese.
② This Chinese food matches well with chicken soup.
③ The number of schools which teach Chinese is increasing.
④ His name means "orange" in Chinese.
⑤ I study Chinese day and night.

03 다음 제시된 단어를 사용하여 자연스러운 문장을 만들 수 없는 것은?

> bucket list　band　overcome　introduce

① She can _____ herself in Spanish.
② I want to see my favorite _____ in a concert.
③ Did you complete your _____ for this year?
④ A woman _____ two cats.
⑤ I hope I can _____ my weakness.

04 서답형 다음 빈칸에 들어갈 알맞은 단어를 〈보기〉에서 찾아 쓰시오.

> ┤ 보기 ├
> in　to　for　of

(1) I talked with my friends _____ a while.
(2) People are standing _____ line to buy tickets.

05 중요 다음 중 밑줄 친 부분의 뜻풀이가 바르지 않은 것은?

① She was standing right in the middle of the room. (오른쪽에)
② The band was playing old Beatles songs. (밴드)
③ It's important to exercise regularly. (운동하다)
④ What's your favorite color? (아주 좋아하는)
⑤ Christmas is one of the famous festivals. (축제)

06 밑줄 친 부분과 의미가 가장 가까운 것은?

> Teamwork is required in order to achieve the aim.

① effort　　　② turn
③ cause　　　④ goal
⑤ result

07 서답형 다음 주어진 우리말에 맞게 빈칸을 채우시오.

(1) Could you do me _____ _____?
(부탁 좀 들어줄래?)
(2) I _____ the cake _____ _____.
(나는 케이크를 그들과 나누었다.)

01 다음 빈칸에 알맞은 단어를 〈보기〉에서 골라 쓰시오. (형태 변화 가능)

> ── 보기 ──
> ask   get   take   make

(1) I know you don't like her, but please _____ an effort to be polite.

(2) Who's _____ care of the dog while you're away?

(3) Sheila _____ interested in starting her own business these days.

(4) Some people think it is difficult to _____ for help.

02 다음 대화의 빈칸에 우리말과 일치하도록 알맞은 말을 쓰시오.

> A: What's wrong? You look worried.
> B: My son is sick. He is in the hospital.
> A: I _____ _____ son _____ better soon.
> (나는 너의 아들이 곧 나아지기를 바라.)

03 우리말에 맞게 주어진 단어를 바르게 배열하시오.

(1) 나는 그가 하는 말을 완전히 인정한다.
(accept, he, I, says, what, fully)
➡ _____

(2) 그 집은 바로 너의 앞에 있다.
(is, right, of, the house, front, you, in)
➡ _____

(3) 그것은 오직 특별한 상황에서만 사용되었다.
(only, situations, was, special, it, on, used)
➡ _____

(4) 좋지 못한 빛은 약한 식물을 만든다.
(weak, poor, plants, produces, light)
➡ _____

[04~05] 다음 영영풀이에 해당하는 말을 주어진 철자로 시작하여 쓰시오.

04
> f_____ : without anyone stopping or limiting something

05
> c_____ : difficult in an interesting or enjoyable way

06 다음 빈칸에 공통으로 들어갈 말을 쓰시오.

> • How much are they willing _____ pay?
> • He was always ready _____ help us.

07 다음 〈보기〉에서 빈칸에 공통으로 들어갈 단어를 골라 쓰시오.

> ── 보기 ──
> experience   effect   exercise   enjoy

(1) • I _____ for half an hour in the morning.
    • Most people need to do more _____ .

(2) • Children need to _____ things for themselves in order to learn from them.
    • I had some _____ in fashion design.

교과서

Conversation

> **A** I hope I can travel to Europe this summer. 나는 이번 여름에 유럽 여행을 할 수 있기를 바라.
> **B** That sounds great. 그거 좋은데.

■ 'I hope (that) 주어+동사'로 소망을 표현할 수 있다. 어떤 일이 일어나기를 바랄 때, 동사 hope를 사용하여 소망을 표현할 수 있다.

바람, 소망 말하기

- I hope (that) 주어 (can) 동사 ~.
- I hope to 동사원형 ~. (나는 ~하기를 바란다.)
- I hope for 명사 ~. (나는 ~을 바란다.)
- I want to 동사원형 ~. (나는 ~하기를 원한다.)
- I want 목적어 to 동사원형 ~. (나는 목적어가 ~하기를 원한다.)

- I hope to get a good score. (나는 좋은 점수를 받기를 바라.)
- I'm hoping for good weather. (나는 좋은 날씨를 바라고 있어.)
- I want to wake up early. (나는 일찍 일어나기를 원해.)
- I want you to keep a diary every day. (나는 네가 매일 일기 쓰기를 원해.)

핵심 Check

1. 다음 우리말과 일치하도록 빈칸에 알맞은 말을 쓰시오.

   G: What's your plan for this year? (올해 뭐 할 계획이니?)

   B: I _____ that _____ many books. (나는 많은 책을 읽을 수 읽기를 바라.)

   G: _____ year. (나는 올해는 좋은 성적을 얻기를 바라.)

   B: You will. Don't worry. (그럴 거야. 걱정하지 마.)

2. 다음 주어진 단어를 이용하여 대화를 완성하시오.

   A: _____ (learn, hope, how, swim, to, can)

   B: That sounds great.

   A: I have a lot of homework.

   B: _____ (it, that, hope, soon, finish)

② 계획 묻고 답하기

> **A** What are you planning to do at the school festival? 학교 축제에서 뭐 할 계획이니?
> **B** I'm planning to sell snacks. 간식을 팔 계획이야.

■ 'I'm planning to 동사원형 ~.'은 '~할 계획이다'라는 뜻으로, 앞으로의 계획이나 의도에 대해 말할 때 사용하는 표현으로 to 다음에는 동사원형이 온다.

계획 말하기

- I'm planning to 동사원형 ~. (나는 ~할 계획이야.)
- I'm going to 동사원형 ~. (나는 ~할 거야.)
- I'll 동사원형 ~. (나는 ~할 거야.)

- A: I'll go to the party tonight. (나는 오늘 밤 파티에 갈 거야.)
  B: Me, too. I'm going to wear a yellow dress. (나도 그래. 나는 노란색 드레스를 입을 거야.)

계획 묻기

- Be동사 주어 planning to 동사원형 ~?
- 의문사 be동사 주어 planning to 동사원형 ~?
- Be 동사 주어 going to 동사원형 ~?
- 의문사 be동사 주어 going to 동사원형 ~?
- Will 주어 동사원형 ~?
- 의문사 will 주어 동사원형 ~?

- A: Are you planning to eat out tonight? (너 오늘 밤 외식할 거니?)
  B: Yes, I am. (응. 그래.)
- A: Where are you planning to eat out tonight? (너 오늘 밤 어디서 외식할 거니?)
  B: I am planning to go to the Italian restaurant. (나는 이탈리아 식당에 갈 거야.)

핵심 Check

3. 다음 주어진 단어를 이용하여 대화를 완성하시오.

   A: I'm going to go to the zoo this Saturday. How about you?

   B: _____ (planning, games, friends)

4. 다음 주어진 단어를 배열하여 대화를 완성하시오.

   A: _____ (meet, where, they, are, to, planning)

   B: They are planning to meet at the airport.

Listen and Speak 1-B

B: Hana, ❶it's your birthday today. Happy birthday!

G: Thank you.

B: ❷What do you want ❸for your birthday?

G: ❹I hope I get a new computer.

B: 하나야, 오늘은 너의 생일이
야. 축하해!

G: 고마워.

B: 생일 선물로 뭘 원하니?

G: 새 컴퓨터를 받길 바라.

❶ it: 날짜를 나타내는 비인칭 주어 / 날씨, 시간, 요일, 날짜, 거리, 명암 등을 나타낼 때 it을 주어로 사용.

❷ What: '무엇'의 의미로 의문대명사 / want는 '원하다'라는 의미의 일반동사로, '의문사+do[does/did]+주어+동사원형 ～?'으로 의문문 형식
이 사용됨

❸ for: ～을 위한

❹ I hope (that) I get a new computer. / get: 얻다, 획득하다

Check(√) True or False

(1) Today is Hana's birthday.　　　　　　　　　　　　　　　　　T ☐ F ☐

(2) She wants to get a new computer for her birthday present.　　T ☐ F ☐

B: Kate, do you have any special plans for the new school year?

G: ❶I'm planning to study one new Chinese word every day.

B: I didn't know you ❷were interested in Chinese. When did you start
studying Chinese?

G: Only last month. But now I can introduce ❸myself in Chinese.

B: That's amazing! How did you ❹get so into Chinese?

G: It's because I'm a big fan of Chinese dramas. I hope I can soon watch
them in Chinese and understand what they're saying.

B: Well, ❺keep studying hard, and I'm sure you'll be able to do it
someday.

G: I hope so. What about you? What are your plans for this year?

B: Let me think. Hmm.... Getting a good grade in every subject? As
usual.

G: Hahaha.

B: Kate, 새 학년을 맞이하여 특
별한 계획이 있니?

G: 나는 매일 새로운 중국어 단
어 하나를 공부할 계획이야.

B: 나는 네가 중국어에 관심이
있는지 몰랐어. 언제 중국어
공부를 시작했니?

G: 겨우 지난달에. 그러나 지금
은 중국어로 내 소개를 할 수
있어.

B: 놀라워! 어떻게 중국어에 그
토록 관심을 가지게 되었어?

G: 중국 드라마의 열렬한 팬이기
때문이야. 나는 곧 드라마를
중국어로 보고, 무슨 말을 하
는지 이해할 수 있기를 바라.

B: 음, 계속 열심히 공부하면 언
젠가는 그렇게 할 수 있을 거
야.

G: 그랬으면 좋겠어. 너는 어때?
올해 계획이 뭐니?

B: 생각 좀 해보고. 음.... 모든 과
목에서 좋은 성적 얻기? 평소
처럼.

G: 하하하.

❶ be planning to 동사원형: ～할 계획이다

❷ be interested in 명사/동명사: ～에 흥미[관심]가 있다 / Chinese: 중국어; 중국의

❸ 주어(I)와 목적어가 같기 때문에 재귀대명사 myself를 사용함.

❹ get into: ～에 관심을 갖게 되다

❺ keep Ving: ～을 계속하다, 유지하다

Check(√) True or False

(3) Kate started studying Chinese last year.　　　　　T ☐ F ☐

(4) Kate likes to see Chinese movies.　　　　　　　　T ☐ F ☐

Listen and Speak 1

G: ❶What are you doing?

B: ❷I'm making my wish list for the new school year.

G: That ❸sounds cool! What's the first thing on your list?

B: I hope I ❹ make a lot of new friends.

❶ 무엇을 하고 있는지 묻는 표현
❷ be+동사원형ing: ~하는 중이다
❸ sound+형용사: ~하게 들리다
❹ make friends: 친구를 사귀다 / a lot of: 많은 (= lots of = many)

Listen and Speak 1

G: ❶How was your English class?

B: ❷It was fun! We ❸wrote down our dreams for the future.

G: Oh, did you? So tell me. What's ❹yours?

B: Well, first. ❺I hope I become a rock star someday.

❶ How was ~?: '~은 어땠니?'라는 의미로, 과거의 경험에 대해 느낀 점을 묻는 표현
❷ It은 앞 문장의 your English class를 받는 인칭대명사
❸ write down: ~을 적다
❹ yours = your dream for the future
❺ I hope (that) 주어 동사: 주어가 ~하는 것을 바라다 / become+명사: ~가 되다 / someday: 언젠가

Listen and Speak 2

B: ❶What are you planning to do tomorrow?

G: I'm planning to go to ❷the book fair with Jimmy. ❸Would you like to join us?

B: Sure. ❹What time are you going to meet?

G: ❺At 3:00 in front of the school cafeteria.

❶ What are you planning to 동사원형 ~?: 너는 무엇을 할 계획이니?
❷ book fair: 도서 박람회 / with: ~와 함께
❸ would like to 동사원형: ~하고 싶다, ~하기를 바라다(= want to 동사원형)
❹ What time: 몇 시에 / be going to 동사원형: ~할 것이다, ~할 예정이다
❺ at+시간: ~시에 / in front of+명사: ~ 앞에서 / cafeteria: 카페테리아, 구내식당

Listen and Speak 2

G: ❶What are you planning to do tomorrow?

B: Well, I'm not ❷sure.

G: Then ❸ how about going to a movie with me?

B: That sounds wonderful.

❶ 미래의 계획을 묻는 표현 (= What are you going to do tomorrow? = What will you do tomorrow?)
❷ sure: 확실한
❸ How about 동사원형ing ~?: '~하는 건 어때?'라는 의미로 권유할 때 사용 (= What about 동사원형ing) ~?/ go to a movie: 영화를 보러 가다

Listen and Speak 2

G: Jack! ❶Can you do me a favor?

B: Yes, what is ❷it?

G: ❸I'm planning to buy a new bike tomorrow. Can you ❹help me choose one?

B: Sure, I'd love to.

❶ 부탁하는 표현 / favor: 부탁
❷ it은 앞 문장의 a favor를 받는 인칭대명사
❸ be planning to 동사원형 ~?: ~할 계획이다(= be going to 동사원형 = will 동사원형)
❹ help 목적어 (to)동사원형: 목적어가 ~하는 것을 돕다

Wrap Up

G: Hi, Brian.

B: Hi, Somin. It's Friday! Are you planning to do ❶anything special this weekend?

G: Well, I'm planning to ❷visit my grandmother. She is sick.

B: Oh, ❸I'm sorry to hear that. I hope she ❹gets better soon.

G: Thank you. What about you? What's your plan?

B: I'm planning to ❺wash my dog.

❶ -thing, -one, -body로 끝나는 부정대명사는 형용사가 후치 수식 / this weekend: 이번 주말에
❷ visit: 방문하다
❸ 상대방에게 유감을 나타내는 표현
❹ get better: (병·상황 등이) 나아지다
❺ wash: 씻기다

다음 우리말과 일치하도록 빈칸에 알맞은 말을 쓰시오.

Listen & Speak 1 A

G: I _____ I _____ good grades this year.

B: You will. Don't _____.

1. G: 난 올해 좋은 성적을 얻길 바라.
   B: 그럴 거야. 걱정하지 마.

Listen & Speak 1 B

1. B: Hana, _____ your birthday today. Happy birthday!

   G: Thank you.

   B: _____ do you _____ _____ your birthday?

   G: _____ _____ _____ a new computer.

2. G: _____ are you doing?

   B: _____ _____ my wish list for the new school year.

   G: That sounds cool! What's _____ _____ thing on your list?

   B: I _____ I _____ a lot of new friends.

3. G: _____ was your English class?

   B: _____ _____ fun! We _____ down our dreams _____ the future.

   G: Oh, did you? So _____ me. What's _____?

   B: Well, first, I _____ _____ become a rock star _____.

1. B: 하나야. 오늘은 너의 생일이야. 축하해!
   G: 고마워.
   B: 생일 선물로 뭘 원하니?
   G: 새 컴퓨터를 받길 바라.

2. G: 뭐 하고 있니?
   B: 나는 새 학년을 맞이하여 소원 목록을 만들고 있어.
   G: 멋지다! 목록의 첫 번째는 뭐니?
   B: 나는 새로운 친구들을 많이 사귈 수 있기를 바라.

3. G: 영어 수업은 어땠니?
   B: 재밌었어! 우리는 미래에 대한 꿈을 적었어.
   G: 오, 그랬니? 나에게 말해줘. 너의 꿈은 뭐니?
   B: 음, 우선, 나는 내가 언젠가 록 스타가 되길 바라.

Listen & Speak 1 C

1. A: I _____ _____ can travel to Europe _____ summer.

   B: That _____ great.

2. A: I hope I can see my grandmother.

   B: That _____ great.

3. A: I _____ _____ _____ _____ how _____ swim.

   B: That sounds great.

1. A: 나는 이번 여름에 유럽으로 여행을 할 수 있기를 바라.
   B: 좋은데.

2. A: 나는 할머니를 뵐 수 있기를 바라.
   B: 좋은데.

3. A: 나는 수영하는 법을 배울 수 있기를 바라.
   B: 좋은데.

Everyday English 2. A Function Practice 2

G: _____ _____ _____ _____ _____ _____ do tomorrow?

B: I'm _____ _____ _____ my hair cut.

Everyday English 2 – B Listening Activity

1. B: What are you _____ _____ _____ _____?

   G: _____ _____ to go to the _____ _____ _____

   Jimmy. Would you _____ _____ join us?

   B: Sure. _____ _____ are you going to meet?

   G: _____ 3:00 _____ _____ _____ the school cafeteria.

2. G: What _____ _____ _____ to do tomorrow?

   B: Well, I'm _____ sure.

   G: Then how _____ _____ to a movie _____ me?

   B: That sounds wonderful.

3. G: Jack! _____ you do me _____ _____?

   B: Yes, what is it?

   G: I'm planning _____ _____ a new bike _____. Can you

   _____ me _____ _____?

   B: Sure, I'd love to.

1. B: 내일 뭐 할 거니?
   G: 지미랑 도서 박람회에 갈 계획이야. 같이 갈래?
   B: 물론이지. 몇 시에 만날 거니?
   G: 학교 식당 앞에서 3시에.

2. G: 내일 뭐 할 계획이니?
   B: 글쎄, 잘 모르겠어.
   G: 그럼, 나랑 영화 보러 가는 게 어때?
   B: 좋아.

3. G: 잭! 부탁 좀 들어줄래?
   B: 응, 뭔데?
   G: 내일 새 자전거를 살 계획이야. 하나 고르는 걸 도와줄 수 있니?
   B: 좋아. 그러고 싶어.

Listen & Speak 2 C

1. A: What are you planning to _____ _____ the school festival?

   B: I'm planning _____ _____ snacks.

2. A: What _____ _____ _____ _____ do at the school

   festival?

   B: I'm planning _____ _____ _____ _____ _____ show.

3. A: _____ _____ _____ _____ _____ to do at the school

   festival?

   B: I'm planning _____ _____ _____ _____ _____.

1. A: 학교 축제에서 뭐 할 계획이니?
   B: 간식을 팔 계획이야.

2. A: 학교 축제에서 뭐 할 계획이니?
   B: 마술 쇼를 할 계획이야.

3. A: 학교 축제에서 뭐 할 계획이니?
   B: 그룹으로 춤 출 계획이야.

01 다음 대화의 빈칸에 공통으로 들어갈 말은?

> A: What are you _____ do at the school festival?
> B: I'm _____ sell snacks.

① planning   ② making   ③ going

④ planning to   ⑤ taking to

[02~03] 다음 대화를 읽고 물음에 답하시오.

> B: Hana, it's your birthday today. Happy birthday!
> B: Thank you.
> B: _____ do you want for your birthday?
> G: I hope I get a new computer.

02 위 대화의 빈칸에 알맞은 것을 고르시오.

① What   ② What computer   ③ When

④ How   ⑤ What time

03 위 대화의 밑줄 친 부분과 바꾸어 쓸 수 없는 것을 모두 고르시오.

① I hope that I get a new computer.

② I hope to get a new computer.

③ I hope getting a new computer.

④ I want to get a new computer.

⑤ I want you to get a new computer.

04 다음 대화의 빈칸에 알맞은 것을 고르시오.

> A: _____
> B: I'm planning to dance in a group.

① What are you doing at the school festival?

② What are you planning to do at the school festival?

③ What did you do at the school festival?

④ What can you do at the school festival?

⑤ What are you looking for at the school festival?

01 주어진 문장 다음에 이어질 문장의 순서로 알맞은 것은?

> Hi, Somin. It's Friday! Are you planning to do anything special this weekend?

> (A) Thank you. What about you? What's your plan?
> (B) Well, I'm planning to visit my grandmother. She is sick.
> (C) Oh, I'm sorry to hear that. I hope she gets better soon.

① (A) - (C) - (B)　　② (B) - (A) - (C)
③ (B) - (C) - (A)　　④ (C) - (A) - (B)
⑤ (C) - (B) - (A)

[02~03] 다음 대화를 읽고 물음에 답하시오.

> G: What are you doing?
> B: I (A)_____ my wish list for the new school year.
> G: That sounds (B)_____! What's the first thing on your list?
> B: (C)I hope making lot of new friends.

02 빈칸 (A)와 (B)에 알맞은 것으로 짝지어진 것을 고르시오.

① make – cool
② make – well
③ am making – cool
④ am making – well
⑤ was making – cool

03 밑줄 친 (C)에서 어색한 부분을 찾아 고치시오. (2개)

➡ (1) _____
　 (2) _____

04 대화의 순서를 바르게 배열하시오.

> (A) At 3:00 in front of the school cafeteria.
> (B) What are you planning to do tomorrow?
> (C) I'm planning to go to the book fair with Jimmy. Would you like to join us?
> (D) Sure. What time are you going to meet?

➡ _____

[05~07] 다음 대화를 읽고 물음에 답하시오.

> G: (A)_____
> B: ①It was fun! ②We wrote down our dreams for the future.
> G: ③Oh, did you? ④So tell me. ⑤What's your?
> B: Well, first. (B)나는 내가 언젠가 록 스타가 되길 바라. (become, hope, someday)

05 위 대화의 빈칸 (A)에 알맞은 것은?

① How was your English class?
② What do you want to be?
③ Will you write down your dream?
④ Did you make your list?
⑤ How about taking an English class?

06 위 대화의 ①~⑤ 중 어색한 부분을 찾아 번호를 쓰고 고치시오.

_____　➡　_____

서답형
07 위 대화의 밑줄 친 우리말 (B)를 주어진 단어를 이용해 영작하시오.

➡ _____

[08~11] 다음 대화를 읽고 물음에 답하시오.

B: Kate, do you have any special plans for the new school year? (①)
G: (A)나는 매일 새로운 중국어 단어 하나를 공부할 계획이야.(every day, to, Chinese, study, one, planning)
B: I didn't know you were interested in Chinese. (②)
G: Only last month. But now I can introduce myself in Chinese. (③)
B: That's amazing! How did you get so into Chinese?
G: It's because I'm a big fan of Chinese dramas. I hope I can soon watch them in Chinese and understand (B)[that / what] they're saying. (④)
B: Well, keep (C)[studying / to study] hard, and I'm sure you'll be able to do it someday. (⑤)
G: I hope so. What about you? (D)_____
B: Let me think. Hmm.... Getting a good grade in every subject? As usual.
G: Hahaha.

중요
08 위 대화의 ①~⑤ 중 다음 주어진 말이 들어갈 알맞은 곳은?

When did you start studying Chinese?

①　　　②　　　③　　　④　　　⑤

서답형
09 밑줄 친 (A)의 우리말을 주어진 단어를 이용해 영작하시오.

➡ _____

서답형
10 괄호 (B)와 (C)에서 알맞은 말을 고르시오.

➡ _____

중요
11 빈칸 (D)에 알맞은 말을 고르시오.

① Did you get a good grade?
② Are you going to make plans?
③ What was your plan for last month?
④ What are your plans for this year?
⑤ Where are you planning to go?

[12~13] 다음 대화를 읽고 물음에 답하시오.

B: Hana, it's your birthday today. Happy birthday!
G: Thank you.
B: 생일 선물로 뭘 원하니?
G: I hope I get a new computer.

서답형
12 주어진 우리말과 같도록 영작할 때 두 번째와 다섯 번째에 오는 단어를 쓰시오. (총 7단어)

➡ _____

13 위의 대화에서 알 수 없는 것을 고르시오. (2개)

① Is it Hana's birthday today?
② What does the boy want to get?
③ What did the boy plan to buy as Hana's present?
④ Whose birthday is today?
⑤ What does the girl hope to get?

01 다음 그림을 보고 주어진 단어를 이용하여 답하시오.

(1) What are you planning to do at the school festival? (in, planning, to, a group)

➡ _____

(2) What's your dream for this year? (summer, hope, travel, to, can, Europe)

➡ _____

[02~03] 다음 대화를 읽고 물음에 답하시오.

A: Do you have any special plans for this year?
B: I hope I can take pictures with my favorite singer.
A: How do you plan to (A)do that?
B: I'm planning go to one of his concert.

02 (A)가 가리키고 있는 내용을 본문에서 찾아 영어로 쓰시오.

➡ _____

03 밑줄 친 문장에서 어색한 부분을 찾아 고치시오. (2개)

➡ _____ , _____

[04~06] 다음 대화를 읽고 물음에 답하시오.

B: ①Kate, did you have any special plans for the new school year?
G: ②I'm planning to study one new Chinese words every day.
B: 나는 네가 중국어에 관심이 있는지 몰랐어, (in, didn't, interested) ③When did you start studying Chinese?
G: ④Only last month. ⑤But now I can introduce myself in Chinese.

04 위 대화의 ①~⑤ 중 어색한 부분을 찾아 쓰고 고치시오.

_____ ➡ _____

05 밑줄 친 우리말을 주어진 단어를 이용해 영작하시오. (8 words)

➡ _____

06 위 대화의 내용과 일치하도록 빈칸을 채우시오.

Kate _____ _____ to study one new Chinese _____ every day. She started _____ _____ Chinese _____ month. She can _____ introduce _____ _____ Chinese.

Grammar 교과서

① 최상급

> This is **the largest** room in the house. 이것이 그 집에서 가장 큰 방이다.
> Harry is **the tallest** player in my team. Harry는 내 팀에서 가장 키가 큰 선수이다.

■ 최상급

- 비교급은 서로 다른 두 대상이 가진 공통된 특징을 비교하는 표현인데 반하여 최상급은 여러 비교 대상 중에서 (셋 이상을 비교) 어떤 성질이 가장 뛰어나다는 것을 나타낸다.
- '최상급+명사'의 형태로 '~중 가장 …한'으로 해석하며 일반적으로 '~에서'라고 범위를 나타내는 말을 함께 쓴다.
- 형용사의 최상급은 정관사 the를 사용하지만, 부사의 최상급에서는 정관사 the를 생략하는 것이 일반적이며 범위를 나타낼 때에는 보통 'of+비교 대상의 복수 명사' 또는 'in+장소, 단체 등의 단수 명사'를 사용한다.

• 비교급 · 최상급 만드는 법

조건	비교급	최상급	예시
대부분의 1음절, 2음절 형용사 / 부사	원급 + -er	원급 + -est	long - longer- longest tall - taller - tallest
'-e'로 끝나는 단어	원급 + -r	원급 + -st	large - larger - largest
'자음+y'로 끝나는 2음절 단어	y → i + -er	y → i + -est	busy - busier - busiest early - earlier - earliest
'단모음+단자음'으로 끝나는 1음절 단어	마지막 자음을 한 번 더 쓰고 -er	마지막 자음을 한 번 더 쓰고 -est	big - bigger - biggest hot - hotter - hottest
3음절 이상의 단어 및 '-ing, -ous, -ful' 등으로 끝나는 단어	more + 원급	most + 원급	famous - more famous – most famous
불규칙하게 변하는 단어 (불규칙 변화형)	many - more - most little - less - least good - better - best bad - worse - worst well - better - best		

Anne is **the cleverest** daughter. (Anne이 가장 영리한 딸이다.)

It was **the best** movie. (그것은 최고의 영화였다.)

핵심 Check

1. 괄호 안에서 알맞은 단어를 고르시오.

   (1) He is (the tallest / tallest) student in his class.

   (2) It's the (longer / longest) bridge in the world.

   (3) Olivia wants to have (the coolest / the most cool) smartphone.

❷ to부정사의 부사적 용법 (목적)

> Jack went to the library **to borrow** some books.
>
> Jack은 책을 몇 권 빌리러 도서관에 갔다.
>
> He went to the gym **to exercise**. 그는 운동하기 위해 체육관에 갔다.

■ 'to+동사원형' 형태의 to부정사가 부사처럼 쓰여, 목적의 의미를 나타내며 '~하기 위해서, ~하러'라는 의미를 갖는다. 이외에도 부사적 용법의 to부정사는 '(감정의) 원인', '조건', '결과', '이유나 판단의 근거' 등을 나타내며 형용사를 수식한다.

■ 목적의 뜻을 보다 분명하게 하기 위하여 to부정사 앞에 in order나 so as를 쓰기도 한다.

■ **to부정사의 부사적 용법**

(1) 원인

Harry was happy **to win** the contest. (Harry는 그 대회에서 우승을 해서 기뻤다.) (to win the contest가 was happy의 원인을 나타낸다.)

(2) 이유나 판단의 근거

Mike must be foolish **to do** such a thing. (그런 짓을 하다니 Mike는 멍청함에 틀림없다.) (to do such a thing 이 be foolish로 판단하는 근거를 나타낸다.)

(3) 결과

Her grandmother lived **to be** 100. (그녀의 할머니는 100세까지 사셨다.) (to be 100이 동사 lived의 결과를 나타낸다.)

(4) 형용사 수식

Advertisements should be easy **to understand**. (광고는 이해하기 쉬워야 한다.) (to understand가 형용사 easy를 수식한다.)

핵심 Check

2. 괄호 안에서 알맞은 것을 고르시오.

(1) She waved her hand (to say / say) good bye.

(2) Lindsey turned on her computer (doing / to do) her homework.

(3) John visited Korea (to write / writes) a report on K-pop.

3. 다음 우리말에 맞게 괄호 안의 단어를 바르게 배열하시오.

• 그는 과학자가 되기 위해 과학을 열심히 공부한다.

(he, to, very, a scientist, hard, science, be, studies)

➡ _____

01 다음 문장에서 어법상 어색한 부분을 찾아 바르게 고쳐 쓰시오.

(1) Mt. Halla is highest mountain in South Korea.

_____ ➡ _____

(2) This sparrow is the most small bird at this park.

_____ ➡ _____

(3) You have to be diligent being a cook.

_____ ➡ _____

(4) She exercises hard in order to not gain weight.

_____ ➡ _____

02 다음 〈보기〉의 단어를 이용하여 문장을 완성하시오.

┌─ 보기 ─┐
order   cheap   boring   meet   thin   healthy

(1) This is _____ _____ wallet of all.

(2) It is _____ _____ _____ book I've read.

(3) How much is _____ _____ laptop here?

(4) My mother went to the school _____ _____ my English teacher.

(5) We need to relax _____ _____ _____ _____ healthy.

03 다음 우리말에 맞게 주어진 단어를 바르게 배열하시오. (필요하면 어형을 바꿀 것)

(1) 세 자매 중에서 Alice가 가장 예쁘다. (pretty / three / Alice / the / sisters / of / the / is)

➡ _____

(2) 일 년 중에 가장 바쁜 날이 언제인가요? (year / when / day / of / busy / the / the / is)

➡ _____

(3) 그는 한국 TV 드라마를 보기 위해 한국어를 열심히 공부한다. (Korean / Korean / as / he / TV dramas / so / hard / watch / study / to)

➡ _____

(4) 나는 첫 기차를 놓치지 않으려고 일찍 일어났다. (early / train / I / to / not / get up / the / in / miss / first / order)

➡ _____

01 다음 빈칸에 알맞은 것은?

> This is _____ one of my blouses.

① expensive
② expensiver
③ more expensive
④ most expensive
⑤ the most expensive

 02 다음 문장의 빈칸에 들어갈 수 <u>없는</u> 것은?

> This hamburger is _____ one of all the hamburgers.

① the cheapest
② the thickest
③ the most special
④ the most largest
⑤ the most delicious

03 다음 빈칸에 알맞은 말이 바르게 짝지어진 것은?

> • That is _____ one of the programs.
> • He was _____ player in this team.

① the most silliest - the most valuable
② the silliest – the most valuable
③ the silliest – the valuablest
④ silliest – valuablest
⑤ silly – valuable

서답형
04 다음 문장에서 어법상 <u>틀린</u> 부분을 바르게 고쳐 다시 쓰시오.

> He is a fastest swimmer in my team.

➡ _____

서답형
05 괄호 안에서 알맞은 것을 고르시오.

(1) This is going to be (the most / most) interesting event today.
(2) He was one of the greatest men (in / of) the world.
(3) What can we do (to celebrate / celebrate) her?
(4) We met yesterday (to go / going) shopping together.
(5) His father lived (be / to be) 90.
(6) Einstein grew up (be / to be) a world famous scientist.

06 다음 〈보기〉의 밑줄 친 부분과 용법이 <u>다른</u> 하나는?

> ┤ 보기 ├
> Mom went to the department store <u>to buy</u> holiday gifts.

① Mom has enough time <u>to make</u> chocolate cake for me.
② He studied very hard not <u>to fail</u> the exam.
③ She bought hiking boots <u>to climb</u> the mountain.
④ I dropped by the bank <u>to save</u> my money.
⑤ Mom had a party <u>to celebrate</u> my middle school graduation.

07 다음 빈칸에 공통으로 알맞은 말은?

> • He turned on his computer _____ check his email.
> • She bought a fishbowl _____ raise some gold fish.

① in order that ② in order to
③ so as that ④ so long as
⑤ as long as

서답형

08 다음 대화의 빈칸에 들어갈 알맞은 말을 쓰시오.

> A: Do you like this red dress?
> B: Yes. It is _____ _____ dress that I've ever seen.

중요

09 다음 우리말에 맞게 영작한 것을 고르시오.

> Stephanie는 나를 깨우기 위해서 아침 일찍 전화했다.

① Stephanie called me waking me up early in the morning.
② Stephanie called me to wake me up early in the morning.
③ Stephanie called me woke me up early in the morning.
④ Stephanie called me wakes me up early in the morning.
⑤ Stephanie called me to waking me up early in the morning.

서답형

10 주어진 단어를 이용하여 빈칸에 들어갈 알맞은 말을 쓰시오.

> She was _____ (sad) woman in this village when she heard of his death.

중요

11 다음 중 밑줄 친 부분의 쓰임이 다른 두 개는?

① I don't have enough time to do my homework.
② She flew to Korea to meet her father.
③ Her grandfather lived to be 90 years old.
④ My mother allowed us to stay up late tonight.
⑤ He was happy to help the children in need.

12 다음 우리말을 영작했을 때 빈칸에 적절하지 않은 것은?(2개)

> • 그는 교실을 청소하기 위해 이 빗자루를 샀다.
> = He bought this broom _____ our classroom.

① so as to clean ② cleaning
③ to cleaning ④ to clean
⑤ in order to clean

서답형

13 다음 문장에서 어법상 어색한 부분을 바르게 고쳐 다시 쓰시오.

(1) I want to win first prize surprising my mom.
➡ _____

(2) Jack used a compass found the right direction.
➡ _____

(3) I visited the museum to seeing the works of Gogh.
➡ _____

(4) Tom and Judy went to the restaurant so that to have lunch.
➡ _____

14 다음 중 어법상 올바른 문장을 <u>모두</u> 고르시오.

① Biggest fruit in this shop is that watermelon.
② The light bulb is one of the famousest inventions of the 19th century.
③ This is the thinnest laptop that the store has.
④ The most wisest man in the world was Gandhi.
⑤ One of the most beautiful mountains in Korea is Mt. Seorak.

서답형

15 다음 우리말과 일치하도록 주어진 단어를 이용하여 빈칸에 알맞은 말을 쓰시오.

(1) George는 친구들과 농구를 하기 위해 공원으로 갔다.
➡ George went to the park _____ _____ _____ with his friends. (play)

(2) Bella는 공부하기 위해서 영어 책을 펼쳤다.
➡ Bella _____ the English book _____ _____. (open, study)

(3) Clint는 어젯밤에 축구 경기를 보기 위해 TV를 켰다.
➡ Clint _____ _____ the TV _____ _____ the soccer game last night. (turn, watch)

(4) 어제는 이번 겨울 들어 가장 추운 날이었다.
➡ Yesterday was _____ _____ day of this winter. (cold)

(5) 네 친구들 중에서 누가 가장 똑똑한 학생이니?
➡ Who is _____ _____ student among your friends? (clever)

(6) 이 영화는 금년의 모든 영화 중에서 최악이다.
➡ This movie is _____ _____ _____ all the movies of this year. (bad)

16 다음 표의 내용에 맞게 설명한 것을 고르시오.

	age	height	weight
giraffe	5	350cm	520kg
kangaroo	9	212cm	110kg
flamingo	7	120cm	4kg

① The giraffe is not the youngest of all.
② The kangaroo is not the oldest of all.
③ The flamingo is the tallest of all.
④ The kangaroo is the heaviest of all.
⑤ The flamingo is the smallest of all.

서답형

17 다음 주어진 두 문장을 한 문장으로 만들 때, 빈칸에 알맞은 말을 쓰시오.

(1) • Steve studies math very hard.
　• He wishes to be a math teacher.
　➡ Steve studies math very hard _____ _____ _____ _____.

(2) • Vivian visited the shopping mall.
　• She wanted to buy a dress.
　➡ Vivian visited the shopping mall _____ _____ _____ _____.

(3) • Lincoln took a taxi in a hurry.
　• He didn't want to be late for the meeting.
　➡ Lincoln took a taxi in a hurry _____ _____ _____ for the meeting.

서답형

18 다음 문장에서 어법상 바르지 <u>못한</u> 것을 찾아 고쳐 쓰시오.

> We don't know which star is truly the most brightest. Some scientists say Deneb may be the most brightest star but some other bright stars have been seen in the night sky.

_____ ➡ _____

01 다음 글에서 문맥이나 어법상 잘못 쓰인 것을 찾아 알맞게 고치시오.

> Do you want to be a fast runner? These shoes are a great pick for you. These are the best running shoes when you run long distance. You should wear heaviest shoes when you run a marathon.

_____ ➡ _____

02 주어진 문장과 같은 뜻이 되도록 다음 빈칸에 알맞은 말을 쓰시오.

• Sue went to the library to return the books.
(1) Sue went to the library _____ _____ _____ return the books.
(2) Sue went to the library _____ _____ return the books.
(3) Sue went to the library _____ _____ _____ she _____ return the books.

03 주어진 다음 문장과 같은 뜻이 되도록 빈칸에 알맞은 말을 쓰시오.

• This is the heaviest bag in this shop.
(1) This is _____ _____ any other _____ in this shop.
(2) _____ other bag in this shop is _____ this.
(3) _____ other bag in this shop is _____ _____ as this.

04 다음 두 문장을 한 문장으로 만드시오.

(1) • Arthur was pleased.
   • He got a good grade in science.
   ➡ _____
(2) • Sue went out at night.
   • She had to buy some water.
   ➡ _____
(3) • Brenda went to Paris.
   • She wanted to study art.
   ➡ _____

05 다음 중 어법상 잘못된 것을 고쳐 문장을 다시 쓰시오.

(1) This is the most largest room in my house.
   ➡ _____
(2) John is the taller of the boys in his class.
   ➡ _____
(3) Marilyn studies English hard got good grades.
   ➡ _____
(4) I want to use my computer finding the information on the Internet.
   ➡ _____
(5) The most famous scientist, Isaac Newton, lived to being 74.
   ➡ _____

06 다음 문장을 to부정사를 이용하여 바꿔 쓸 때 빈칸에 알맞은 말을 쓰시오.

(1) Brian went to the bakery for some loaves of bread.

= Brian went to the bakery _____ _____ some loaves of bread.

(2) They set the table for dinner.

= They set the table _____ _____ dinner.

(3) Rob took a taxi to the restaurant because he didn't want to be late for dinner.

= Rob took a taxi to the restaurant _____ _____ _____ for dinner.

07 다음 우리말을 괄호 안에 주어진 어휘를 이용하여 영작하시오.

(1) 엄마는 내 옷을 사기 위하여 그 가게에 가셨다. (mom, the store, dress)

➡ _____

(2) 그녀는 딸의 머리를 빗기기 위해 머리빗을 사용했다. (use, a hairbrush, brush)

➡ _____

(3) Tom은 그녀가 Mike를 사랑하는 것을 알고 실망했다. (disappointed, find, that, love)

➡ _____

(4) Solomon은 세상에서 가장 현명한 사람들 중의 하나였다. (one, of, wise)

➡ _____

(5) 이 책은 내가 갖고 있는 모든 책들 중에서 가장 유용하다. (this book, useful, that, of)

➡ _____

08 다음 그림을 보고 주어진 어휘를 이용하여 빈칸에 알맞은 말을 쓰시오.

(1) Nick _____ _____ _____ shirt of the three. (wear, bright)

(2) Alex is _____ _____ person of the three. (heavy)

(3) Jay _____ _____ _____ hair of the three. (have, dark)

09 다음 〈보기〉의 어휘 중에서 골라 어법에 맞게 빈칸을 채우시오.

┌─ 보기 ┤

get   make   give
nice   pretty   long

(1) Laura bought _____ _____ dress in the shop _____ _____ it to her daughter.

(2) Hamilton used _____ _____ computer in his office _____ _____ the video.

(3) She spent _____ _____ night in her life _____ _____ the ticket.

10 다음 물음의 답에 있는 빈칸을 채워 자신의 답을 쓰시오.

(1) Q: Why did you buy the books?

A: I bought them _____.

(2) Q: Why do you want a new computer?

A: I want it _____.

My "Bucket List" for the New School Year

Hi, everyone. Today is the first day of our new school year.
<u>one</u>의 서수

I want to hear your <u>plans</u> and <u>hopes</u> for this year.
계획 희망

What do you want to do <u>most</u>? Think about three <u>things</u> you want to
가장 선행사 목적격 관계대명사 생략

do. And then, make a <u>bucket list</u> and <u>share</u> it with your friends.
죽기 전에 꼭 해야 할 일이나 달성하고 싶은 목표 리스트, 공유하다

bucket list 버킷 리스트
share 함께 쓰다, 공유하다
freely 자유롭게
musical instrument 악기
weakness 약함
subject 과목
overcome 극복하다
put effort into ~에 노력을 들이다

확인문제

● 다음 문장이 본문의 내용과 일치하면 T, 일치하지 <u>않으면</u> F를 쓰시오.

1 Today is the first day of the new school year. ☐

2 The writer wants to hear the plans and hopes for next year. ☐

3 You should think about four things you want to do. ☐

4 After making a bucket list, share it with your friends. ☐

Jinsu

Hi! I'm Jinsu. This is my bucket list for this year.

First, I want to <u>go on a bike tour</u> of Jejudo this summer.
자전거 여행을 떠나다

<u>I've been there before</u>, but I want to <u>experience</u> the <u>island</u> <u>more freely</u>
현재완료 'have[has]+p.p.' 경험 '~한 적이 있다' 경험하다 섬 freely의 비교급

on my bike <u>this time</u>. My second <u>goal</u> is to learn <u>how to play</u> the
이번에는 목표 how+to부정사 '~하는 방법'

guitar. I think the guitar has <u>the most</u> beautiful sound of all <u>musical</u>
형용사의 최상급. 3음절 이상의 단어 앞에 'the most'를 써서 최상급을 만듦

<u>instruments</u>. I hope I can play my <u>favorite</u> song on my guitar <u>by the</u>
악기 아주 좋아하는

<u>end of this year</u>. <u>Finally</u>, I want to get a good <u>grade</u> in <u>math</u>. Math is
올해 말쯤에는 마지막으로 성적 수학

my <u>weakest</u> <u>subject</u>. This year, I'll <u>put</u> more <u>effort into</u> studying math
최상급, '원급+est', 과목 ~에 노력을 기울이다

<u>to overcome</u> my <u>weakness</u>.
to부정사의 부사적 용법, 극복하다 약점

📎 **확인문제**

● 다음 문장이 본문의 내용과 일치하면 T, 일치하지 <u>않으면</u> F를 쓰시오.

1 Jinsu wants to go on a bike tour of Jejudo this summer. ☐

2 Jinsu has never been to Jejudo before. ☐

3 Math is Jinsu's weakest subject. ☐

4 Jinsu will put more effort into teaching math. ☐

Somi

Hi! My name is Somi. First, I want to see a concert of my favorite
band right in front of the stage. I'm willing to stand in line all night to
enter the front area. Second, I want to adopt a puppy.
I've always wanted a puppy. I think I'm fully ready to take care of a
pet now. My last goal is a little more challenging. I'd like to read all of
the Sherlock Holmes stories. I became a big fan of this detective series
last year, so I don't want to miss a single one.

band (가수를 중심으로 한) 밴드
in front of ~ 앞에서
be ready to ~할 준비가 되다
adopt 입양하다
puppy 강아지
challenging 도전적인
detective 탐정, 형사
miss 놓치다
single 단일의, 하나의

📎 **확인문제**

● 다음 문장이 본문의 내용과 일치하면 T, 일치하지 <u>않으면</u> F를 쓰시오.

1 Somi wants to see a concert of her favorite band right in front of the stage. ☐

2 Somi will not stand in line all night to enter the front area. ☐

3 Somi doesn't think she is fully ready to take care of a pet now. ☐

4 Somi became a big fan of the Sherlock Holmes stories last year. ☐

● 우리말을 참고하여 빈칸에 알맞은 말을 쓰시오.

1 My "Bucket List" _____ _____ _____ _____ _____

2 _____, everyone.

3 Today is _____ _____ _____ of our new school year.

4 I want to hear your plans and hopes _____ _____ _____.

5 What do you want to do _____?

6 Think about three things _____ _____ _____ _____.

7 And then, _____ _____ _____ _____ and _____ it _____ your friends.

8 Hi! _____ Jinsu.

9 _____ _____ my bucket list for this year.

10 First, I want to _____ _____ _____ _____ _____ of Jejudo this summer.

11 _____ _____ _____ _____, but I want to experience the island more freely _____ _____ _____ this time.

12 My second goal is to learn _____ _____ _____ the guitar.

13 I think the guitar has _____ _____ _____ _____ of all musical instruments.

14 I hope I can play my favorite song _____ my guitar _____ _____ _____ this year.

15 _____, I want to get a good grade in math.

16 Math is my _____ _____.

17 This year, I'll _____ more effort _____ studying math _____ _____ my weakness.

18 Hi! _____ _____ _____ Somi.

19 First, I want to see a concert of my favorite band _____ _____ _____ _____ the stage.

20 I'm _____ to _____ _____ _____ all night to enter the front area.

21 Second, I want to _____ _____ _____.

22 _____ always _____ a puppy.

23 I think _____ fully _____ _____ take care of a pet now.

24 My last goal is _____ _____ _____ _____.

25 _____ _____ _____ read all of the Sherlock Holmes stories.

26 I became _____ _____ _____ of this detective series last year, so I don't want to miss _____ _____ _____.

17 올해는 제 약점을 극복하기 위해 수학 공부에 좀 더 노력을 기울일 거예요.

18 안녕하세요! 제 이름은 소미예요.

19 우선, 저는 제가 가장 좋아하는 밴드의 공연을 무대 바로 앞에서 보고 싶어요.

20 앞자리에 들어가기 위해 저는 기꺼이 밤새 줄을 서서 기다릴 거예요.

21 두 번째로, 강아지를 입양하고 싶어요.

22 저는 항상 강아지를 원해 왔어요.

23 이제는 제가 애완동물을 돌볼 준비가 완벽히 되었다고 생각해요.

24 제 마지막 목표는 좀 더 도전적이에요.

25 저는 셜록 홈스 이야기들을 모두 읽고 싶어요.

26 저는 작년에 이 탐정 시리즈의 열성 팬이 되었어요. 그래서 저는 단 하나도 놓치고 싶지 않아요.

● 우리말을 참고하여 본문을 영작하시오.

1 나의 새 학년 버킷 리스트

➡ _____

2 모두들, 안녕.

➡ _____

3 오늘은 우리 새 학년의 첫날이에요.

➡ _____

4 저는 여러분들의 올해 계획과 희망을 듣고 싶어요.

➡ _____

5 여러분이 가장 원하는 것은 무엇인가요?

➡ _____

6 여러분이 원하는 것 세 가지를 생각해 보세요.

➡ _____

7 그리고 나서 버킷 리스트를 만들어 친구들과 공유해 봐요.

➡ _____

8 안녕하세요! 저는 진수예요.

➡ _____

9 이것은 올해 제 버킷 리스트예요.

➡ _____

10 우선, 저는 이번 여름에 제주도로 자전거 여행을 가고 싶어요.

➡ _____

11 저는 그곳을 전에 가 본 적이 있지만 이번에는 제 자전거를 타고 좀 더 자유롭게 그 섬을 경험해 보고 싶어요.

➡ _____

12 제 두 번째 목표는 기타 연주하는 법을 배우는 거예요.

➡ _____

13 저는 기타가 모든 악기 중에 가장 아름다운 소리를 낸다고 생각해요.

➡ _____

14 올해 말쯤에는 제가 가장 좋아하는 곡을 제 기타로 연주할 수 있으면 좋겠어요.

➡ _____

15 마지막으로 수학에서 좋은 점수를 받고 싶어요.

➡ _____

16 수학은 제가 가장 약한 과목이에요.

➡ _____

17 올해는 제 약점을 극복하기 위해 수학 공부에 좀 더 노력을 기울일 거예요.

➡ _____

18 안녕하세요! 제 이름은 소미예요.

➡ _____

19 우선, 저는 제가 가장 좋아하는 밴드의 공연을 무대 바로 앞에서 보고 싶어요.

➡ _____

20 앞자리에 들어가기 위해 저는 기꺼이 밤새 줄을 서서 기다릴 거예요.

➡ _____

21 두 번째로, 강아지를 입양하고 싶어요.

➡ _____

22 저는 항상 강아지를 원해 왔어요.

➡ _____

23 이제는 제가 애완동물을 돌볼 준비가 완벽히 되었다고 생각해요.

➡ _____

24 제 마지막 목표는 좀 더 도전적이에요.

➡ _____

25 저는 셜록 홈스 이야기들을 모두 읽고 싶어요.

➡ _____

26 저는 작년에 이 탐정 시리즈의 열성 팬이 되었어요. 그래서 저는 단 하나도 놓치고 싶지 않아요.

➡ _____

[01~03] 다음 글을 읽고 물음에 답하시오.

Hi, everyone. (①) Today is the first day of our new school year. (②) I want to hear your plans and hopes for this year. (③) What do you want ⓐto do most? (④) And then, make a bucket list and share ⓑit with your friends. (⑤)

01 위 글의 흐름으로 보아, 주어진 문장이 들어가기에 가장 적절한 곳은?

Think about three things you want to do.

①   ②   ③   ④   ⑤

02 (중요) 위 글의 밑줄 친 ⓐto do와 to부정사의 용법이 다른 것을 모두 고르시오.

① He has many friends to play with.
② My hope is to go to England.
③ He grew up to be a great doctor.
④ To get up early is good for the health.
⑤ I found it difficult to do so.

03 (서답형) 위 글의 밑줄 친 ⓑit이 가리키는 것을 본문에서 찾아 쓰시오.

➡ _____

[04~07] 다음 글을 읽고 물음에 답하시오.

Hi! I'm Jinsu. This is my bucket list for (A)[this / last] year. First, I want to go on a bike tour of Jejudo this summer. ⓐI've been there before, but I want to experience the island more freely on my bike this time. My second goal is to learn how to play the guitar. I think the guitar has the most beautiful sound of all musical instruments. I hope I can play my favorite song on my guitar ⓑ올해 말쯤에는. Finally, I want to get a good grade in math. Math is my (B)[strongest / weakest] subject. This year, I'll put more effort into studying math to overcome my (C)[strength / weakness].

04 위 글의 밑줄 친 ⓐ에 쓰인 현재완료와 용법이 같은 것을 모두 고르시오.

① She has been in Seoul since 2000.
② She has never eaten spaghetti.
③ I have lost my bag.
④ He has played baseball for two hours.
⑤ How many times have you seen it?

05 (서답형) 위 글의 괄호 (A)~(C)에서 문맥상 알맞은 낱말을 골라 쓰시오.

➡ (A)_____ (B)_____ (C)_____

06 (서답형) 위 글의 밑줄 친 ⓑ의 우리말을 6 단어로 쓰시오.

➡ _____

07 (중요) 위 글의 내용과 일치하지 않는 것은?

① 진수는 이번 여름에 제주도로 자전거 여행을 가고 싶어 한다.
② 진수는 전에 제주도에 가 본 적이 없다.
③ 진수는 올해 기타 연주하는 법을 배우고 싶어 한다.
④ 수학은 진수가 가장 약한 과목이다.
⑤ 진수는 수학 공부에 좀 더 노력을 기울일 것이다.

[08~10] 다음 글을 읽고 물음에 답하시오.

Hi! My name is Somi. First, I want to see a concert of my favorite band right in front of the stage. I'm willing to ⓐ줄을 서서 기다리다 all night to enter the front area. Second, I want to adopt a puppy. I've always wanted a puppy. I think I'm fully ready to take care of a pet now. My last goal is a little more challenging. I'd like to read all of the Sherlock Holmes stories. I became a big fan of this detective series last year, so I don't want to miss a single ⓑone.

서답형

08 위 글의 밑줄 친 ⓐ의 우리말에 맞게 3 단어로 영작하시오.

➡ _____

09 위 글의 밑줄 친 ⓑ와 문법적 쓰임이 같은 것을 고르시오.

① There's only one room for one person.
② I don't like this bag. Can you show me a cheaper one?
③ He's the one person I can trust.
④ One man's meat is another man's poison.
⑤ One must observe the rules.

중요
10 위 글의 주제로 알맞은 것을 고르시오.

① the difficulty of seeing a band's concert
② the reason Somi stands in line all night
③ the way Somi adopts a puppy
④ a challenging goal of reading all of the Sherlock Holmes stories
⑤ what Somi wants to do this year

[11~13] 다음 글을 읽고 물음에 답하시오.

My "Bucket List" for This Year
Here is my bucket list. First, I want to learn how to make cookies. I want to make (A)[it / them] to surprise my mom. Second, I want to ⓐlive a simple life. I will throw away things ⓑthat I do not need. The (B)[last / latest] thing is to study online English lessons (C)[everyday / every day]. At the end of this year, I will overcome my problems with my weakest subject, English.

서답형
11 위 글의 괄호 (A)~(C)에서 문맥이나 어법상 알맞은 낱말을 골라 쓰시오.

➡ (A)_____ (B)_____ (C)_____

12 위 글의 밑줄 친 ⓐlive와 바꿔 쓸 수 있는 말을 고르시오.

① take   ② put
③ leave   ④ have
⑤ bring

중요
13 위 글의 밑줄 친 ⓑthat과 문법적 쓰임이 다른 것을 고르시오.

① Where's the letter that came yesterday?
② The watch that you gave me keeps perfect time.
③ This is the book that I bought yesterday.
④ It's the best novel that I've ever read.
⑤ She said that the story was true.

[14~16] 다음 글을 읽고 물음에 답하시오.

Hi! I'm Jinsu. This is my bucket list for this year. First, I want to go on a bike tour of Jejudo this summer. I've been there before, but I want to experience the island more freely on my bike this time. My second goal is to learn how to play the guitar. I think the guitar has the most beautiful sound of all musical instruments. I hope I can play my favorite song on my guitar by the end of this year. ⓐ, I want to get a good grade in math. Math is my weakest subject. This year, I'll put more effort into studying math ⓑto overcome my weakness.

14 위 글의 제목으로 알맞은 것을 고르시오.

① Jinsu's Bucket List for This Year
② To Go on a Bike Tour of Jejudo
③ How to Experience Jejudo More Freely
④ Guitar Has the Most Beautiful Sound!
⑤ How to Get a Good Grade in Math

15 위 글의 빈칸 ⓐ에 들어갈 말을 모두 고르시오.

① After all   ② In addition
③ Finally   ④ Therefore
⑤ Lastly

16 아래 보기에서 위 글의 밑줄 친 ⓑto overcome과 to부정사의 용법이 다른 것의 개수를 고르시오.

┌─ 보기 ─────────────────┐
① I want a pen to write this letter with.
② We go to school to learn many things.
③ You have no need to go there.
④ It is wrong to tell a lie.
⑤ I went to the airport to see her off.
└────────────────────────┘

① 1개   ② 2개   ③ 3개   ④ 4개   ⑤ 5개

[17~19] 다음 글을 읽고 물음에 답하시오.

Hi! My name is Somi. First, I want to see a concert of my favorite band ⓐright in front of the stage. I'm ⓑ to stand in line all night to enter the front area. Second, I want to adopt a puppy. I've always wanted a puppy. I think I'm fully ready to take care of a pet now. My last goal is a little more challenging. I'd like to read all of the Sherlock Holmes stories. I became a big fan of this detective series last year, so I don't want to miss a single one.

17 위 글의 밑줄 친 ⓐright와 같은 의미로 쓰인 것을 고르시오.

① Mary was standing right behind Ted.
② I hope we're doing the right thing.
③ Is this the right way to the beach?
④ What gives you the right to do that?
⑤ Keep on the right side of the road.

서답형
18 주어진 영영풀이를 참고하여 빈칸 ⓑ에 철자 w로 시작하는 단어를 쓰시오.

┌────────────────────────┐
doing something fairly hard because one wants to do it rather than because one is forced to do it
└────────────────────────┘

➡ _____

19 위 글을 읽고 대답할 수 없는 질문은?

① What does Somi want to see?
② What does Somi want to adopt?
③ How was Somi able to be fully ready to take care of a pet?
④ What is Somi's last goal?
⑤ When did Somi become a big fan of Sherlock Holmes?

[20~21] 다음 글을 읽고 물음에 답하시오.

> This is the bucket list we bought.
> ___ⓐ___ , I hope I can meet my favorite actor.
> ___Ⓑ___ , I hope I can have dinner with my role model. ___©___ , I hope I can travel to ⓐ another countries. We spent ninety dollars to buy these items.

서답형
20 위 글의 빈칸 Ⓐ~©에 들어갈 알맞은 말을 쓰시오.

➡ (A)_____ (B)_____ (C)_____

서답형
21 위 글의 밑줄 친 ⓐ를 어법에 맞게 고치시오.

➡ _____

[22~24] 다음 글을 읽고 물음에 답하시오.

> I hope I can visit Bangkok. It is the ___ⓐ___ city ___ⓑ___ delicious food. I want to go there ©to take a cooking class.

서답형
22 위 글의 빈칸 ⓐ에 famous의 최상급을 쓰시오.

➡ _____

23 위 글의 빈칸 ⓑ에 들어갈 알맞은 전치사를 고르시오.

① to   ② by   ③ for
④ about   ⑤ in

24 위 글의 밑줄 친 ©와 의미가 <u>다른</u> 것을 고르시오.

① so as to take a cooking class
② in order that I can take a cooking class
③ so that I may take a cooking class
④ that I might not take a cooking class
⑤ in order to take a cooking class

[25~26] 다음 대화를 읽고 물음에 답하시오.

> Jinsu: Did you complete your bucket list for this year?
> Somi: Yes, I did.
> Jinsu: What is the first thing on your list?
> Somi: I want to see my favorite band in a concert, standing in front of the stage. ⓐWhat about you?
> Jinsu: The top thing on my list is a bike tour of Jejudo.

25 위 대화를 읽고 알 수 <u>없는</u> 것을 고르시오.

① Did Somi finish writing her bucket list for this year?
② Will Somi's bucket list come true?
③ What is Somi's first bucket list?
④ Does Somi want to see her favorite band sitting on the chair?
⑤ What is Jinsu's first bucket list?

서답형
26 위 대화의 밑줄 친 ⓐ가 물어보는 내용을 본문에서 찾아 쓰시오.

➡ _____

[01~03] 다음 글을 읽고 물음에 답하시오.

Hi, everyone. ⓐ오늘은 우리 새 학년의 첫날이에요. I want to hear your plans and hopes for this year. What do you want to do most? Think about three things you want to do. ⓑ And then, make a ⓒ_____ _____ and share it with your friends.

01 위 글의 밑줄 친 ⓐ의 우리말에 맞게 주어진 어휘를 이용하여 10 단어로 영작하시오.

first, school year

➡ _____

02 위 글의 밑줄 친 ⓑAnd then이 가리키는 내용을 주어진 단어로 시작하여 쓰시오. (8 단어, 동명사를 사용할 것.)

➡And after _____

_____

03 주어진 영영풀이를 참고하여 빈칸 ⓒ에 철자 b로 시작하는 단어를 쓰시오.

a list of things that people want to experience or achieve before they die

➡ _____

[04~06] 다음 글을 읽고 물음에 답하시오.

Hi! I'm Jinsu. This is my bucket list for this year. First, I want to go on a bike tour of Jejudo this summer. I've been there before, but I want to experience the island more freely on my bike this time. ⓐMy second

goal is to learn how to play guitar. ⓑ저는 기타가 모든 악기 중에 가장 아름다운 소리를 낸다고 생각해요. I hope I can play my favorite song on my guitar by the end of this year. Finally, I want to get a good grade in math. Math is my weakest subject. This year, I'll put more effort into studying math to overcome my weakness.

04 위 글의 밑줄 친 ⓐ에서 어법상 틀린 부분을 찾아 고치시오.

➡ _____

05 위 글의 밑줄 친 ⓑ의 우리말에 맞게 한 단어를 보충하여, 주어진 어휘를 알맞게 배열하시오.

musical instruments / most / sound / I / has / all / the guitar / beautiful / of / think

➡ _____

06 본문의 내용과 일치하도록 다음 빈칸 (A)와 (B)에 알맞은 말을 쓰시오.

Jinsu's last goal is (A) _____ _____ in math because math is his (B) _____.

[07~09] 다음 글을 읽고 물음에 답하시오.

Hi! My name is Somi. First, I want to see a concert of my favorite band right in front of the stage. I'm willing to stand in line all night to enter the front area. Second, I want to adopt a puppy. I've always wanted a puppy. I think I'm fully ready to ⓐtake care of a pet now. My last goal is a little more challenging. I'd like to read all of the Sherlock Holmes stories. I became a big fan of this detective series last year, so I don't want to miss a single ⓑ .

07 다음 문장에서 위 글의 내용과 <u>다른</u> 부분을 찾아서 고치시오.

> • Somi wants to see a concert of her favorite band right in front of the stage, so she is unwilling to stand in line all night to enter the front area.

➡ _____

08 위 글의 밑줄 친 ⓐ와 바꿔 쓸 수 있는 말을 쓰시오.

➡ _____

09 위 글의 빈칸 ⓑ에 들어갈 알맞은 말을 쓰시오.

➡ _____

[10~12] 다음 글을 읽고 물음에 답하시오.

Hi! I'm Jinsu. This is my bucket list for this year. First, I want to go on a bike tour of Jejudo this summer. ⓐ나는 그곳을 전에 가 본 적이 있다, but I want to experience the island more freely on my bike this time. My second goal is to learn ⓑhow to play the guitar. I think ⓒthe guitar has the most beautiful sound of all musical instruments. I hope I can play my favorite song on my guitar by the end of this year. Finally, I want to get a good grade in math. Math is my weakest subject. This year, I'll put more effort into studying math to overcome my weakness.

10 위 글의 밑줄 친 ⓐ의 우리말에 맞게 4 단어로 영작하시오.

➡ _____

11 위 글의 밑줄 친 ⓑhow to play와 같은 뜻이 되도록 빈칸에 들어갈 알맞은 말을 쓰시오. (2 단어)

➡ how _____ play

12 위 글의 밑줄 친 ⓒ를 비교급을 사용하여 고칠 때 빈칸에 알맞은 말을 쓰시오.

➡ the guitar has a more beautiful sound than any other _____ _____ does.

[13~15] 다음 글을 읽고 물음에 답하시오.

Hi! My name is Somi. First, I want to see a concert of my favorite band right in front of the stage. I'm willing to stand in line all (A)[night / nights] to enter the front area. Second, I want to adopt a puppy. I've always wanted a puppy. I think I'm fully ready (B)[taking / to take] care of a pet now. My last goal is a little more challenging. I'd like (C)[reading / to read] all of the Sherlock Holmes stories. I became a big fan of this detective series last year, so I don't want to miss a single one.

13 위 글의 괄호 (A)~(C)에서 어법상 알맞은 낱말을 골라 쓰시오.

➡ (A)_____ (B)_____ (C)_____

14 다음 질문에 대한 알맞은 대답을 주어진 단어로 시작하여 쓰시오. (5 단어)

> Q: Why does Somi want to read all of the Sherlock Holmes stories without missing a single one?
> A: Because _____ .

➡ _____

15 소미의 버킷 리스트 세 가지를 우리말로 쓰시오.

➡ (1) _____
　 (2) _____
　 (3) _____

Work Together Step 3

This is the bucket list we bought.
목적격 관계대명사 which나 that이 생략되어 있다.

First, I hope I can meet my favorite actor.
hope가 목적어로 that절을 받았다. hope 뒤에 that이 생략되어 있다.

Second, I hope I can have dinner with my role model.
식사하다

Third, I hope I can travel to other countries.

We spent ninety dollars to buy these items.
spend의 과거형   ~하기 위해서(부사적 용법의 목적)

구문해설 • role model: 역할 모델

이것은 우리가 산 버킷 리스트이다.
첫째, 나는 내가 좋아하는 배우를 만나기를 바란다.
둘째, 나는 나의 역할 모델과 식사할 수 있기를 바란다.
셋째, 나는 다른 나라들을 여행할 수 있기를 바란다.
이것들을 사기 위해 나는 90달러를 사용했다.

Writing Workshop

My "Bucket List" for This Year

Here is my bucket list. First, I want to learn how to make cookies. I want to
~이 있다   = I should

make them to surprise my mom.
= cookies   부사적 용법(목적)

Second, I want to live a simple life. I will throw away things that I do not
동족목적어   목적격 관계대명사

need. The last thing is to study online English lessons every day. At the end of
명사적 용법(보어)

this year, I will overcome my problems with my weakest subject, English.
동격을 나타내는 콤마

구문해설 • simple 간소한 • throw away: 버리다 • overcome: 극복하다 • weakest: 가장 약한

올해의 나의 "버킷 리스트"

여기에 나의 버킷 리스트가 있어. 먼저, 나는 쿠키 만드는 법을 배우고 싶어. 나는 엄마를 놀라게 하기 위해 그것들을 만들고 싶어. 두 번째로, 나는 간소한 삶을 살고 싶어. 나는 필요하지 않은 물건들을 버릴 거야. 마지막 것은 매일 온라인으로 영어 공부를 하는 거야. 올해 말에는 나는 가장 약한 과목인 영어에서의 문제를 극복할 거야.

Solve the Problem

Hi, I am Gijun. I hope I get good grades this year, but I sleep too much. Could
좋은 성적을 받다

you give me some advice?
'다소의, 약간(조금)의'

Why don't you go to bed on time and wake up early?
~하는 게 어때?   잠자리에 들다.

→ I think you need to go to bed early and sleep on a regular schedule to get

    better grades.

구문해설 • give advice: 조언을 하다 • on time: 시간을 어기지 않고, 정해진 시간에
          • regular: 규칙적인, 정기적인 • schedule: 일정

안녕, 나는 기준이야. 나는 올해 좋은 성적을 받길 바라, 하지만 나는 너무 많이 자. 나에게 조언을 좀 해주겠니?

정해진 시간에 자고 일찍 일어나는 게 어때?

나는 좋은 성적을 받기 위해서 네가 일찍 자고 규칙적으로 잘 필요가 있다고 생각해.

영역별 핵심문제

01 다음 〈보기〉와 같은 관계가 되도록 주어진 빈칸에 알맞은 말을 쓰시오.

┌─ 보기 ┌─
outside – inside

strength – _____

02 다음 중 밑줄 친 부분의 쓰임이 어색한 것은?

① Teaching young children is a <u>challenging</u> and rewarding job.
② They are looking for the <u>missing</u> child.
③ The restaurant is <u>full</u> booked this weekend.
④ The building took two years to <u>complete</u>.
⑤ I hope you made a really nice bucket <u>list</u>.

[03~05] 다음 빈칸에 공통으로 들어갈 말을 쓰시오.

03

• I want to _____ a good friend.
• I will _____ an effort to become a good person.

04

• I have to _____ back to Seoul this month.
• I want to _____ on a tour with friends.

05

• The cookies were made _____ me.
• It'll be on your desk _____ the end of this week.

06 다음 영영풀이에 해당하는 단어를 〈보기〉에서 골라 쓰시오.

┌─ 보기 ┌─
overcome challenge detective goal

(1) something that you hope to achieve in the future
➡ _____

(2) to successfully control a feeling or problem
➡ _____

07 다음 우리말과 일치하도록 괄호 안의 단어를 바르게 배열하시오.

(1) 그 개들은 사람들을 구하기 위해 더 빨리 달릴 수 있다.
(dogs, quickly, people, more, the, run, save, can, to)
➡ _____

(2) 이번이 나의 첫 유럽 방문이다.
(my, Europe, first, visit, to, this, is)
➡ _____

(3) 그 서점은 나의 회사 바로 옆에 있다.
(my, the, right, to, bookstore, next, is, company)
➡ _____

Conversation

08 다음 대화의 빈칸에 알맞은 것은?

> G: I hope I get good grades this year.
> B: _____

① I'm sorry to hear that.
② What about you? What's your plan?
③ Well, I'm not sure.
④ You will. Don't worry.
⑤ Yes, what is it?

[09~12] 다음 대화를 읽고 물음에 답하시오.

> G: Hi, Brian.
> B: Hi, Somin. It's Friday! (①) Are you (A) _____ (plan) to do anything special this weekend?
> G: Well, I'm (B)_____(plan) to visit my grandmother. She is sick. (②)
> B: Oh, I'm happy to hear that. I hope she got better soon. (③)
> G: Thank you. (④)
> B: I'm planning to wash my dog. (⑤)

09 위 대화의 ①~⑤ 중 다음 주어진 말이 들어갈 알맞은 곳은?

> What about you? What's your plan?

①   ②   ③   ④   ⑤

10 (A)와 (B) 빈칸에 공통으로 들어갈 말을 주어진 단어를 이용해 쓰시오.

➡ _____

11 밑줄 친 부분에서 어색한 부분을 찾아 고치시오. (2개)

➡ (1) _____ (B) _____

12 위 대화의 내용과 일치하지 않는 것을 고르시오.

① Brian is going to wash his dog this weekend.
② Somin's grandmother is sick.
③ Brian is sorry to hear that Somin's grandmother is sick.
④ Somin will visit her grandmother this Friday.
⑤ They are talking about the plan of this weekend.

[13~14] 다음 대화를 읽고 물음에 답하시오.

> B: What are you planning to do tomorrow?
> G: Jimmy랑 도서 박람회에 갈 계획이야.(plan, book fair) Would you like to join us?
> B: Sure. What time are you going to meet?
> G: At 3:00 in front of the school cafeteria.

13 밑줄 친 우리말을 주어진 단어를 이용해 영작하시오.

➡ _____

14 위 대화의 내용과 일치하도록 빈칸을 채우시오.

> The girl is planning _____ _____ to _____ _____ _____ _____ Jimmy _____. She suggests _____ _____ to the boy. They _____ meet _____ 3 o'clock _____ _____ _____ the school cafeteria.

15 형용사의 최상급 형태가 틀린 것은?

① brave – bravest
② happy – most happy
③ weak – weakest
④ hot – hottest
⑤ active – most active

16 보기의 밑줄 친 부분과 같은 용법으로 쓰인 것은?

┌─── 보기 ───┐
I took the subway <u>to arrive</u> there on time.
└────────────┘

① I want to learn how <u>to make</u> cookies.
② I want <u>to experience</u> the island more freely on my bike this time.
③ Nancy studied very hard <u>to become</u> a scientist.
④ The last thing is <u>to study</u> online English lessons every day.
⑤ I want something cold <u>to drink</u>.

17 다음 빈칸에 알맞은 말이 바르게 짝지어진 것은?

┌──────────────────────────────┐
│ • Which fruit is _____ in this grocery store?
│ • Turkey is not _____ country in the world.
└──────────────────────────────┘

① large – smallest
② largest – small
③ largest – the smallest
④ the largest – smallest
⑤ the largest – the smallest

18 다음 중 어법상 옳은 것은?

① I want getting a good grade in math.
② I'll put more effort into studying math overcome my weakness.
③ Arnold saved plenty of money bought a car.
④ She went to the theater to watch a movie with her friends.
⑤ William Shakespeare lived being fifty two.

19 다음 중 밑줄 친 부분의 쓰임이 어색한 것은?

① Garry is <u>the busiest</u> man in his company.
② Edga studies <u>hardest</u> in my school.
③ Emma is <u>kindest</u> girl in her school.
④ Math was <u>the most difficult</u> in the final exam.
⑤ Amanda is <u>the smartest</u> in her family.

20 괄호 안에 주어진 단어를 이용하여 다음을 영작하시오.

(1) Brian은 어제 Scarlet을 만나서 기뻤다. (pleased, 7 단어)
    ➡ _____

(2) Emily는 첫 기차를 타기 위해서 일찍 잠자리에 들었다. (go, bed, take, 10 단어)
    ➡ _____

(3) Audrey는 자라서 배우가 되었다. (grow up, be, actress, 7 단어)
    ➡ _____

(4) Wendy는 서울로 가서 결코 돌아오지 못했다. (go, never, return, 7 단어)
    ➡ _____

21 다음 두 문장의 의미가 같도록 빈칸에 들어갈 알맞은 말을 쓰시오.

> Nothing is more important than health in the world.
> = Health is ＿＿＿＿＿＿＿＿＿ thing in the world.

22 다음 문장을 to부정사를 이용한 문장으로 바꿔 쓰시오.

(1) • Ann wants to go to Korea.
　　• She wants to learn the Korean language.
　➡ ＿＿＿＿＿＿＿＿＿＿＿＿＿＿＿

(2) • Jane is planning to dance at the school festival.
　　• She wants to show her friends how well she dances.
　➡ ＿＿＿＿＿＿＿＿＿＿＿＿＿＿＿
　　＿＿＿＿＿＿＿＿＿＿＿＿＿＿＿

Reading

[23~24] 다음 글을 읽고 물음에 답하시오.

Hi, everyone. ①Today is the first day of our new school year. ②I want to hear your plans and hopes ＿ⓐ＿ this year. ③When students move to a higher grade, they spend much more time studying. ④What do you want to do most? ⑤Think about three things you want to do. And then, make a bucket list and share it ＿ⓑ＿ your friends.

23 위 글의 ①~⑤ 중에서 전체 흐름과 관계 없는 문장은?

① ② ③ ④ ⑤

24 위 글의 빈칸 ⓐ와 ⓑ에 들어갈 전치사가 바르게 짝지어진 것은?

① for - with ② to - by
③ on - from ④ for - to
⑤ at - with

[25~27] 다음 글을 읽고 물음에 답하시오.

Hi! I'm Jinsu. This is my bucket list for this year. First, I want to go on a bike tour of Jejudo this summer. I've been there before, but I want to experience the island more (A)[free / freely] on my bike this time. My ⓐ＿＿ goal is to learn (B)[how / what] to play the guitar. I think the guitar has ⓑ＿＿ ＿＿ ＿＿ ＿＿ of all musical instruments. I hope I can play my favorite song on my guitar by the end of this year. Finally, I want to get a good grade in math. Math is my weakest subject. This year, I'll put more effort into (C)[study / studying] math to overcome my weakness.

25 위 글의 괄호 (A)~(C)에서 어법상 알맞은 낱말을 골라 쓰시오.

➡ (A)＿＿＿＿ (B)＿＿＿＿ (C)＿＿＿＿

26 위 글의 빈칸 ⓐ에 들어갈 알맞은 말을 쓰시오.

➡ ＿＿＿＿＿＿＿＿＿＿＿

27 다음 문장과 같은 뜻이 되도록 위 글의 빈칸 ⓑ에 알맞은 말을 쓰시오.

> I think no other musical instrument has a more beautiful sound than the guitar does.

➡ ＿＿＿＿＿＿＿＿＿＿＿

[28~30] 다음 글을 읽고 물음에 답하시오.

Hi! My name is Somi. First, I want to see a concert of my favorite band right in front of the stage. I'm willing to stand in line all night to enter the front area. Second, I want to adopt a puppy. I've always wanted a puppy. I think I'm fully ready ⓐto take care of a pet now. My last goal is a little more challenging. I'd like to read all of the Sherlock Holmes stories. I became a big fan of ⓑthis detective series last year, so I don't want to miss a single one.

28 위 글의 밑줄 친 ⓐto take와 to부정사의 용법이 같은 것을 고르시오.

① He went abroad to study economics.
② I am sorry to hear that.
③ He lived to be one hundred years old.
④ He must be foolish to say so.
⑤ This book is easy to read.

29 위 글의 밑줄 친 ⓑ가 가리키는 것을 본문에서 찾아 쓰시오.

➡ _____

30 위 글의 내용과 일치하지 않는 것은?

① 소미는 자신이 가장 좋아하는 밴드의 공연을 무대 바로 앞에서 보고 싶어 한다.
② 소미는 강아지를 입양하고 싶어 한다.
③ 소미는 아직 애완동물을 돌볼 준비가 완전히 되어 있지는 않다.
④ 소미는 셜록 홈스 이야기를 모두 읽고 싶어 한다.
⑤ 소미는 작년에 셜록 홈스 시리즈의 열성 팬이 되었다.

[31~32] 다음 대화를 읽고 물음에 답하시오.

Jinsu: Did you complete your bucket list for this year?
Somi: Yes, I did.
Jinsu: What is the first thing on your list?
Somi: I want to see my favorite band in a concert, ⓐ _____ in front of the stage. What about you?
Jinsu: The ⓑtop thing on my list is a bike tour of Jejudo.

31 위 글의 빈칸 ⓐ에 stand를 알맞은 형태로 쓰시오.

➡ _____

32 위 대화의 밑줄 친 ⓑ와 바꿔 쓸 수 있는 단어를 본문에서 찾아 쓰시오.

➡ _____

[33~34] 다음 글을 읽고 물음에 답하시오.

My "Bucket List" for This Year
Here is my bucket list. First, I want to learn how to make cookies. I want to make them to surprise my mom. Second, I want to live a simple life. I will throw away things ⓐ _____ I do not need. The last thing is to study online English lessons every day. At the end of this year, I will overcome my problems with my weakest subject, English.

33 위 글의 빈칸 ⓐ에 들어갈 알맞은 말을 모두 고르시오.

① which   ② what   ③ who
④ that   ⑤ whom

34 다음 질문에 대한 알맞은 대답을 영어로 쓰시오. (1 단어)

Q: Is the writer good at English?

A: _____

출제율 90%

01 다음 짝지어진 두 단어의 관계가 같도록 주어진 철자로 시작하여 알맞은 말을 쓰시오.

(1) start : begin = finish : c_____
(2) initial : first = well-known : f_____
(3) in : out = before : a_____
(4) bright : smart = lost : m_____

출제율 100%

02 다음 빈칸에 알맞은 형태로 바르게 짝지어진 것은?

> • He is willing _____ your proposal.
> • I'll be ready _____ in about five minutes.

① accept – go
② accept – to go
③ to accept – go
④ to accept – to go
⑤ to accept – going

출제율 90%

03 다음 대화의 빈칸에 알맞은 것은?

> **A:** What do you want for your birthday?
> **B:** _____

① You will. Don't worry.
② That sounds great.
③ I'm planning to sell a new computer.
④ I hope I get a new computer.
⑤ I hope you get a new computer.

출제율 95%

04 다음 〈보기〉의 단어를 사용하여 자연스러운 문장을 만들 수 없는 것은?

> ┤ 보기 ├
> learn   plan   ride   surprise   walk

① I hope that you'll _____ your difficulties.
② What's the best way to _____ a language?
③ What they are saying doesn't _____ me.
④ He has never learned to _____ a bicycle.
⑤ We _____ to open a new office near the downtown area.

[05~06] 다음 대화의 순서를 바르게 배열하시오.

출제율 90%

05

> (A) I'm planning to buy a new bike tomorrow. Can you help me choose one?
> (B) Sure, I'd love to.
> (C) Yes, what is it?
> (D) Jack! Can you do me a favor?

➡ _____

출제율 85%

06

> (A) What are you planning to do tomorrow?
> (B) Then how about going to a movie with me?
> (C) Well, I'm not sure.
> (D) That sounds wonderful.

➡ _____

B: Kate, do you have any special plans for the new school year?

G: ①I'm planning to study one new Chinese word every day.

B: ②I didn't know you were interested in Chinese. (A)_____

G: Only last month. ③But now I can introduce me in Chinese.

B: That's amazing! (B)_____

G: It's because I'm a big fan of Chinese dramas. 나는 곧 그것들을 중국어로 보고, 무슨 말을 하는지 이해할 수 있기를 바라.

B: Well, ④keep studying hard, and I'm sure you'll be able to do it someday.

G: I hope so. ⑤What about you? What are your plans for this year?

B: Let me think. Hmm.... Getting a good grade in every subject? As usual.

G: Hahaha.

출제율 95%

07 What are they talking about?

① the way of learning Chinese
② the importance of studying hard
③ the way of making special plans
④ getting good grades for the new school year
⑤ the plans for the new school year

출제율 90%

08 빈칸 (A)와 (B)에 어울리는 질문을 보기에서 골라 쓰시오.

┌─ 보기 ─
• Do you like studying Chinese?
• When did you start studying Chinese?
• How many times did you visit China?
• How did you get so into Chinese?
• When are you going to start studying Chinese?
└─

➡ (A) _____
(B) _____

출제율 100%

09 위 대화의 밑줄 친 ①~⑤ 중 어법상 **틀린** 것은?

①   ②   ③   ④   ⑤

출제율 80%

10 밑줄 친 우리말에 맞게 주어진 단어를 알맞게 배열하시오.

┌─
hope, them, Chinese, saying, understand, I, I, and, they, what, are, soon, can, in, watch
└─

➡ _____
_____

출제율 90%

11 다음 중 어법상 올바른 문장은?

① Sumi is the tallest of my class.
② Today is the hottest day this summer.
③ A rabbit is one of fastest animal.
④ Bill is most hungry boy in this restaurant.
⑤ Steve is richest of the three gentlemen.

출제율 90%

12 밑줄 친 부분의 쓰임이 **다른** 하나를 고르시오.

① David went to the library to borrow some books.
② She went to the bus stop to take a bus.
③ To read in the plane, Morris took a book with him.
④ Sharon was very pleased to get the ticket at last.
⑤ Bruce lay on the sofa to take some sleep.

출제율 90%

13 다음 괄호 안의 단어를 빈칸에 알맞은 형태로 쓰시오.

(1) Who is the _____ girl in her class? (healthy)

(2) He is the _____ soccer player in his school. (good)

출제율 85%

14 다음 우리말과 같도록 주어진 단어를 바르게 배열하여 문장을 완성하시오.

> 비에 젖지 않게 우산을 가져가렴.
> (so / wet / to / get / as / not)

➡ Take your umbrella _____.

출제율 95%

15 어법상 잘못된 부분을 바르게 고쳐 문장을 다시 쓰시오.

(1) He is the better student in my class.

➡ _____

(2) Naomi is the most smartest girl of them all.

➡ _____

출제율 95%

16 다음 우리말을 주어진 어휘를 이용하여 영작하시오.

(1) 나는 Melanie에게 스마트폰을 사용해 전화를 했다. (use, my smartphone, call, 7 단어)

➡ _____

(2) Karen은 오늘 밤 그를 다시 보게 되어서 기뻤다. (glad, see, 8 단어)

➡ _____

[17~19] 다음 글을 읽고 물음에 답하시오.

Hi! I'm Jinsu. This is my bucket list for this year. First, ⓐ저는 자전거 여행을 가고 싶어요 this summer.(bike tour) I've been there before, but I want to experience the island more freely on my bike this time. My second ⓑgoal is to learn how to play the guitar. I think the guitar has the most beautiful sound of all musical instruments. I hope I can play my favorite song on my guitar by the end of this year. Finally, I want to get a good grade in math. Math is my ⓒ ____ subject. This year, I'll put more effort into studying math to overcome my weakness.

출제율 100%

17 위 글의 밑줄 친 ⓐ의 우리말을 주어진 어구를 써서 영어로 옮기시오.

➡ _____

출제율 95%

18 위 글의 밑줄 친 ⓑ와 뜻이 다른 말을 고르시오.

① target   ② object

③ end   ④ aim

⑤ subject

출제율 95%

19 위 글의 빈칸 ⓒ에 weak의 최상급을 쓰시오.

➡ _____

[20~22] 다음 글을 읽고 물음에 답하시오.

Hi! My name is Somi. First, I want to see a concert of my favorite band right in front of the stage. I'm (A)[willing / unwilling] to stand in line all night to enter the front area. Second, I want to (B)[adapt / adopt] a puppy. I've always wanted a puppy. I think I'm fully ready to take care of a pet now. My last goal is a little more (C)[challenging / relaxing]. I'd like to read all of the Sherlock Holmes stories. I became a big fan of this detective series last year, so I don't want to ⓐmiss a single one.

✏️ 출제율 95%

20 위 글의 괄호 (A)~(C)에서 문맥상 알맞은 낱말을 골라 쓰시오.

➡ (A)_____ (B)_____ (C)_____

✏️ 출제율 90%

21 위 글을 읽고 소미에 대해 알 수 <u>없는</u> 것을 고르시오.

① Where does she want to see a concert of her favorite band?

② Which does she want to adopt, a cat or a puppy?

③ Is she fully ready to take care of a pet now?

④ How many Sherlock Holmes stories did she read last year?

⑤ Why does she want to read all of the Sherlock Holmes stories?

✏️ 출제율 100%

22 위 글의 밑줄 친 ⓐmiss와 같은 의미로 쓰인 것을 고르시오.

① How did the train miss the accident?

② Don't miss next week's issue!

③ When you leave, I'll miss you.

④ When did you first miss the necklace?

⑤ A miss is as good as a mile.

[23~25] 다음 글을 읽고 물음에 답하시오.

My "Bucket List" for This Year
Here is my bucket list. First, I want to learn how to make cookies. I want to make ⓐthem to surprise my mom. Second, I want to live a simple life. I will throw away things that I do not need. The last thing is to study online English lessons every day. At the end of this year, I will overcome my problems with my weakest subject, English.

✏️ 출제율 85%

23 위 글의 밑줄 친 ⓐthem이 가리키는 것을 본문에서 찾아 쓰시오.

➡ _____

✏️ 출제율 95%

24 다음 질문에 대한 알맞은 대답을 빈칸에 쓰시오.

Q: Why does the writer want to make cookies?
A: In order to _____ his or her mom.

✏️ 출제율 90%

25 다음 중 글쓴이에 대한 내용으로 일치하지 <u>않는</u> 것을 고르시오.

① 쿠키 만드는 법을 배우고 싶어 한다.

② 간소한 삶을 살고 싶어 한다.

③ 필요하지 않은 물건들은 따로 보관할 것이다.

④ 매일 온라인으로 영어 공부를 할 것이다.

⑤ 영어가 가장 약한 과목이다.

서술형 실전문제

01 다음 대화의 밑줄 친 부분과 의미가 같도록 주어진 단어를 이용하여 영작하시오.

> A: What are you planning to do tomorrow?
> B: I'm planning to go to a movie with Toby.

➡ _____ (will)

➡ _____ (going)

02 괄호 안의 단어를 이용하여 우리말을 바르게 영작하시오.

(1) 나는 내년에 일본을 여행할 수 있기를 바란다.
(can, next, to, travel, 9단어)

➡ _____

(2) 내년에는, 나는 승자가 될 수 있기를 바란다.
(the winner, become, 9단어)

➡ _____

(3) 좋은 성적을 얻기 위해서, 나는 하루 종일 공부할 계획이다. (get, all day, planning, good, grades, 10단어)

➡ _____

03 다음 대화의 밑줄 친 부분에서 어색한 것을 모두 찾아 고치시오. (3개)

> B: ①Hi, Somin. Its Friday! ②Are you planning to do special anything this weekend?
> G: Well, I'm planning to visit my grandmother. She is sick.
> B: ③Oh, I'm sorry to hear that. I hope she gets better soon.
> G: Thank you. ④What about you? ⑤How is your plan?
> B: I'm planning to wash my dog.

➡ _____
_____

04 주어진 두 문장을 한 문장으로 만들 때, 빈칸에 알맞은 말을 쓰시오.

(1) • Johanna called Greg.
• Because she wanted to play tennis with him.
➡ Johanna called Greg _____ tennis with him.

(2) • Bob uses his computer.
• He sends emails to his friends.
➡ Bob uses his computer _____ emails to his friends.

05 다음 중 어법상 어색한 부분을 바르게 고치시오.

(1) The Golden Gate Bridge is one of the most famous bridge in the world.

➡ _____

(2) Dogs are popularest pet in America.

➡ _____

(3) I went to the store buying glasses.

➡ _____

(4) Natalie used to jog in the morning stayed healthy.

➡ _____

06 다음 두 문장의 의미가 같도록 빈칸 하나에 한 단어씩 쓰시오.

(1) Mt. Baekdu is the highest mountain in Korea.

= Mt. Baekdu is _____ _____

_____ _____ _____ in Korea.

(2) The Eiffel Tower is the most beautiful tower in the world.

= _____ other tower is _____

_____ than the Eiffel Tower in the world.

[07~09] 다음 글을 읽고, 물음에 답하시오.

Hi! I'm Jinsu. This is my bucket list for this year. First, I want to go on a bike tour of Jejudo this summer. I've been there before, but I want to experience the island more freely on my bike this time. ⓐMy second goal is to learn how to play the guitar. I think the guitar has the most beautiful sound of all musical instruments. I hope I can play my favorite song on my guitar by the end of this year. Finally, I want to get a good grade in math. Math is my weakest subject. ⓑThis year, I'll put more effort into studying math to greet my weakness.

07 위 글의 밑줄 친 ⓐ를 다음과 같이 바꿔 쓸 때 빈칸에 알맞은 말을 쓰시오.

➡ My second goal is _____ how to play the guitar.

08 위 글의 밑줄 친 ⓑ에서 흐름상 어색한 부분을 찾아 고치시오.

➡ _____

09 진수의 버킷 리스트 세 가지를 우리말로 쓰시오.

➡ (1) _____
(2) _____
(3) _____

[10~12] 다음 글을 읽고 물음에 답하시오.

Hi! My name is Somi. First, I want to see a concert of my favorite band right in front of the stage. I'm willing to stand in line all night to enter the front area. Second, I want to adopt a puppy. I've always wanted a puppy. I think I'm fully ready to take care of a pet now. ⓐMy last goal is a little more challenged. I'd like ⓑ _____ all of the Sherlock Holmes stories. I became a big fan of this detective series last year, so I don't want to miss a single one.

10 위 글의 밑줄 친 ⓐ에서 어법상 틀린 부분을 찾아 고치시오.

➡ _____

11 위 글의 빈칸 ⓑ에 read를 알맞은 형태로 쓰시오.

➡ _____

12 본문의 내용과 일치하도록 다음 빈칸 (A)와 (B)에 알맞은 단어를 쓰시오.

Somi's (A)_____ bucket list is to adopt a puppy. Actually she has always wanted a puppy and she thinks she's fully (B)_____ for taking care of a pet now.

01 다음 표에 제시된 정보를 보고, 계획을 묻고 대답하는 대화를 완성해 봅시다.

A

	Mon.	Tue.	Wed.	Thur.	Fri.	Sat.	Sun.
afternoon	go swimming	.	go swimming		go swimming.	read a book	play volleyball
evening			visit grandma	do exercise			

B

	Mon.	Tue.	Wed.	Thur.	Fri.	Sat.	Sun.
afternoon	read a book	.		draw cartoons	do exercise		go shopping
evening		walk the dog	visit the museum			draw cartoons	

A: What are you _____ on Wednesday evening?

B: I'm going _____. _____ going to do on Wednesday afternoon?

A: I'm planning _____.

02 자신이 열심히 하고 있는 것과 그 이유를 to부정사를 이용하여 두 문장 이상 쓰시오.

(1) _____

(2) _____

03 다음 버킷 리스트 경매에 관한 내용을 바탕으로 자신의 모둠에서 구매한 세 개의 버킷 리스트를 모아서 발표하는 글을 쓰시오.

A: I hope I can meet my favorite actor. How much will you pay for this bucket list? It starts at ten dollars.
B: Twenty dollars!
C: Thirty dollars!
A: Going once. Going twice. Sold.

<경매에 나온 버킷 리스트>
I hope I can meet my favorite actor.
I hope I can have dinner with my role model.
I hope I can travel to other countries.

This is the bucket list we (A)_____. First, I hope I can meet (B)_____. Second, I hope I can have dinner with (C)_____. Third, I hope I (D)_____ to other countries. We spent ninety dollars (E)_____ these items.

단원별 모의고사

01 다음 대화의 빈칸에 알맞은 단어를 고르시오.

> G: What are you planning to do tomorrow?
> B: I'm planning _____ my hair cut.

① do   ② to do   ③ to get
④ have   ⑤ got

02 〈보기〉의 단어를 사용하여 문장을 완성하시오.

> ┤ 보기 ├
> away at on into of to for

(1) The children are old enough to take care _____ themselves.
(2) Frank put a lot of effort _____ the exam.
(3) This could be used again. Don't throw it _____!
(4) My parents are going _____ a hiking tour.

03 다음 빈칸에 공통으로 들어갈 단어를 고르시오.

> • His _____ is to read two books a month.
> • When do you _____ to go to Europe?

① need   ② plan   ③ decide
④ ask   ⑤ get

04 빈칸에 공통으로 들어갈 단어를 주어진 철자로 시작하여 쓰시오.

> • This i_____ is used for cleaning and polishing teeth.
> • Are you learning a musical i_____ these days?

[05~08] 다음 대화를 읽고 물음에 답하시오.

> Jinsu: Did you ⓐ_____ your bucket list for this year?
> Somi: Yes, I did.
> Jinsu: What is the first thing on your list?
> Somi: I want ⓑ(see) my favorite band in a concert, ⓒ(stand) in front of the stage. What about you?
> Jinsu: <u>목록의 제일 위의 것은 제주도로 자전거 여행을 하는 거야.</u>

05 위 대화의 빈칸 ⓐ에 다음 영영풀이에 해당하는 단어를 주어진 철자로 시작하여 쓰시오.

> to finish doing or making something, especially when it has taken a long time

➡ c_____

06 ⓑ와 ⓒ에 알맞은 말을 괄호 안에 주어진 단어를 이용하여 쓰시오.

➡ ⓑ: _____ ⓒ: _____

07 밑줄 친 우리말과 의미가 같도록 주어진 단어를 이용해 문장을 완성하시오.

➡ _____
(Jejudo, a bike tour, top)

08 위 대화를 읽고, 알 수 없는 것을 고르시오.

① Does Somi have her favorite band?
② What does Jinsu want to do this year?
③ What are they talking about?
④ What is Somi's favorite band?
⑤ Where does Somi want to see the band in the concert?

[09~12] 다음 대화를 읽고 물음에 답하시오.

> B: Kate, 새 학년을 맞이하여 특별한 계획이 있니?
> G: ①I'm planning to study one new Chinese word every day.
> B: I didn't know you were interested ⓐ_____ Chinese. When did you start studying Chinese?
> G: Only last month. But now I can introduce myself ⓑ_____ Chinese.
> B: That's amazing! How did you get so ⓒ_____ Chinese?
> G: ②It's because I'm a big fan of Chinese dramas. I hope I can soon watch them in Chinese and understand what they're saying.
> B: ③Well, keep studying hard, and I'm not sure you'll be able to do it someday.
> G: ④I hope so. ⑤What about you? What are your plans for this year?
> B: Let me think. Hmm.... Getting a good grade in every subject? As usual.
> G: Hahaha.

09 밑줄 친 우리말과 의미가 같도록 주어진 단어를 이용해 문장을 완성하시오.

➡ _____

_____

(any, for, school, plans, have)

10 ⓐ~ⓒ에 알맞은 단어를 〈보기〉에서 찾아 쓰시오.

┌─── 보기 ───┐
at   for   in   into   to

➡ ⓐ: _____   ⓑ: _____   ⓒ: _____

11 ①~⑤ 중 흐름상 어색한 문장을 고르시오.

①   ②   ③   ④   ⑤

12 위 대화의 내용과 일치하는 것을 <u>모두</u> 고르시오.

① The boy usually gets a good grade.
② Kate isn't able to introduce herself in Chinese.
③ Kate has been studying Chinese since last month.
④ Kate doesn't have any plans for this year.
⑤ The boy likes to see Chinese dramas.

[13~14] 다음 대화를 읽고 물음에 답하시오.

> A: 이번 주말에 뭐 할 계획이니? (plan, are, do, this, what, weekend)
> B: I'm planning to _____ my hair cut.

13 괄호 안의 단어를 이용하여 우리말을 바르게 영작하시오. (형태 변형 가능)

➡ _____

14 빈칸에 알맞은 단어를 고르시오. (2개)

① have   ② make
③ take   ④ get
⑤ keep

[15~16] 다음 대화를 읽고 물음에 답하시오.

> A: Jack! Can you do me a ⓐ_____?
> B: Yes, what is it?
> A: I'm planning to buy a new bike tomorrow. Can you help me choose one?
> B: Sure, ⓑI'd love to.

15 위 대화의 빈칸 ⓐ에 다음 영영풀이에 해당하는 단어를 주어진 철자로 시작하여 쓰시오.

> something that you do for someone in order to help them or be kind to them

➡ f_____

16 밑줄 친 ⓑ의 문장 뒤에 생략된 부분을 대화에서 찾아 쓰시오. (4 단어)

➡ _____

17 다음 괄호 안의 단어의 형태로 알맞은 것끼리 바르게 짝지어진 것은?

> • That is the (dirty) pig we have ever seen.
> • The island is the (wet) one in the world.

① dirtyest – wetest
② dirtiest – wettest
③ most dirty – most wet
④ most dirtest – most wetest
⑤ most dirtiest – most wettest

18 다음 중 어법상 어색한 것을 고르시오.

① Tim is wearing the darkest shirt of the three.
② Diana was at a restaurant to has lunch.
③ I will overcome my problems with my weakest subject, English.
④ I want to learn how to make cookies.
⑤ I went to the hospital to meet my friend.

19 다음 두 문장의 의미가 같도록 빈칸 하나에 한 단어씩 쓰시오.

> • Mt. Everest is the highest mountain in the world.
> = _____ other mountain is _____ _____ as Mt. Everest in the world.

20 우리말과 일치하도록 괄호 안의 단어를 바르게 배열하시오.

(1) Sarah는 학교에 가기 위해 지하철을 탔다. (Sarah, the subway, school, took, go, to, to)

➡ _____

(2) 나는 쉬기 위해 나무 아래에 앉았다. (I, tree, rest, sat, take, a, a, under, to)

➡ _____

(3) Amy는 일어나서 그녀의 휴대폰이 침대 위에 있는 것을 발견했다. (Amy, her, bed, cellphone, woke, find, the, up, on, to)

➡ _____

[21~23] 다음 글을 읽고 물음에 답하시오.

Hi! I'm Jinsu. This is my bucket list for this year. First, I want to go ①on a bike tour of Jejudo this summer. I've been there before, but I want to experience the island more freely ②on my bike this time. My second goal is to learn how to play the guitar. I think the guitar has the most beautiful sound ③in all musical instruments. I hope I can play my favorite song ④on my guitar by the end of this year. Finally, I want to get a good grade in math. Math is my weakest ⓐsubject. This year, I'll put more effort ⑤into studying math to ⓑ overcome my weakness.

21 위 글의 밑줄 친 ①~⑤에서 전치사의 쓰임이 적절하지 않은 것을 찾아 알맞게 고치시오.

➡ _____

22 위 글의 밑줄 친 ⓐsubject와 같은 의미로 쓰인 것을 고르시오.

① We are all subject to the laws of nature.
② What subject do you teach at school?
③ Let's stop this unpleasant subject of conversation.
④ Focus the camera on the subject.
⑤ We need a male subject between the ages of 18 and 25 for the experiment.

23 위 글의 밑줄 친 ⓑovercome을 바꿔 쓸 때 빈칸에 알맞은 말을 쓰시오.

➡ _____ _____ my weakness

[24~26] 다음 글을 읽고 물음에 답하시오.

Hi! My name is Somi. First, I want to see a concert of my favorite band right in front of the stage. (①) I'm willing to stand in line all night ⓐto enter the front area. (②) Second, I want to adopt a puppy. I've always wanted a puppy. (③) ⓑI think I'm fully ready to take care of a pet now. (④) I'd like to read all of the Sherlock Holmes stories. (⑤) I became a big fan of this detective series last year, so I don't want to miss a single one.

24 위 글의 흐름으로 보아, 주어진 문장이 들어가기에 가장 적절한 곳은?

My last goal is a little more challenging.

①   ②   ③   ④   ⑤

25 위 글의 밑줄 친 ⓐ와 의미가 다른 것을 고르시오.

① so that I may enter the front area
② in order to enter the front area
③ that I may not enter the front area
④ in order that I can enter the front area
⑤ so as to enter the front area

26 위 글의 밑줄 친 ⓑ를 다음과 같이 바꿔 쓸 때 빈칸에 들어갈 알맞은 말을 쓰시오.

➡ I think I'm fully ready _____ taking care of a pet now.

[27~28] 다음 대화를 읽고, 물음에 답하시오.

Jinsu: Did you complete your bucket list for this year?
Somi: Yes, I ⓐdid.
Jinsu: What is the first thing on your list?
Somi: I want to see my favorite band in a concert, standing in front of the stage. ⓑWhat about you?
Jinsu: The top thing on my list is a bike tour of Jejudo.

27 위 대화의 밑줄 친 대동사 ⓐ가 가리키는 것을 영어로 쓰시오.

➡ _____

28 위 대화의 밑줄 친 ⓑ와 바꿔 쓸 수 있는 말을 쓰시오.

➡ _____

Let's Be Smart Smartphone Users

🎙 의사소통 기능

- 충고하기

  A: I'm always late for school. What should I do?

  B: You should set an alarm on your smartphone.

- 당부하기

  A: Can I eat this pizza?

  B: Sure. Just make sure you wash your hands first.

🎙 언어 형식

- to부정사의 형용사적 용법

  Here are some tips **to protect** your health.

- 사역동사

  It **makes your eyes feel** tired and dry to read small letters on a smartphone for a long time.

Words & Expressions

교과서

Key Words

- advice [ədváis] 명 충고
- avoid [əvɔ́id] 동 피하다
- back [bæk] 명 등
- bend [bend] 동 구부리다
- blink [bliŋk] 동 (눈을) 깜빡이다
- break [breik] 명 휴식
- cause [kɔːz] 동 초래하다, 야기하다
- check [tʃek] 동 확인하다
- crack [kræk] 명 금, 깨진 틈
- deserted [dizə́ːrtid] 형 버려진
- drop [drɑp] 동 떨어뜨리다
- hall [hɔːl] 명 복도
- historical [histɔ́ːrikəl] 형 역사적인
- hold [hould] 동 잡다
- hurt [həːrt] 동 다치게 하다, 아프다
- increase [inkríːs] 동 증가하다
- lean [liːn] 동 기대다
- letter [létər] 명 문자, 글자
- life jacket 구명 조끼

- lower [lóuər] 동 낮추다
- novel [návəl] 명 소설
- pain [pein] 명 고통
- pose [pouz] 명 자세
- pressure [préʃər] 명 압력
- prevent [privént] 동 예방하다, 막다
- protect [prətékt] 동 보호하다
- pull [pul] 동 당기다
- reduce [ridjúːs] 동 줄이다, 감소시키다
- rule [ruːl] 명 규칙
- service center 서비스 센터, 수리소
- text [tekst] 동 (휴대 전화로) 문자를 보내다
- tip [tip] 명 조언, 비법
- uncomfortable [ənkʌ́mfərbəl] 형 불편한
- under [ʌ́ndər] 전 ~ 아래에
- upset [ʌ́pset] 형 화난
- weather [wéðər] 명 날씨
- worse [wəːrs] 형 나쁜
- wrist [rist] 명 손목

Key Expressions

- a lot of 많은
- at least 적어도
- away from ~에서 떨어져서
- be good for ~에 좋다
- be late for ~에 늦다
- cut down on ~을 줄이다
- depend on ~에 의존하다
- do warm up exercise 준비운동을 하다
- from time to time 가끔, 이따금
- get in touch with ~와 연락[접촉]하다
- give back 돌려주다
- in front of ~ 앞에
- instead of ~ 대신에
- keep A from B A를 B로부터 막다

- keep in mind 명심하다
- make sure+주어+동사 반드시 ~하도록 하다, ~을 확실히 하다
- pay attention to ~에 주의를 기울이다
- put on ~을 늘리다, 더하다
- ride on ~을 타다
- right away 당장
- set an alarm 자명종 시계를 맞추다
- sleep over at (남의 집에) 묵다
- spend 시간[돈] Ving 시간[돈]을 ~하는 데 소비하다
- take a walk 산책하다
- turn off (불·라디오·텔레비전 등을) 끄다
- turn on (불·라디오·텔레비전 등을) 켜다
- watch out (for) (~을) 조심하다

Word Power

※ 서로 반대되는 뜻을 가진 단어
- □ **in front of**(~ 앞에) ↔ **behind**(~ 뒤에)
- □ **lower**(낮추다) ↔ **raise**(올리다)
- □ **turn on**([불·라디오·텔레비전 등을] 켜다) ↔ **turn off**([불·라디오·텔레비전 등을] 끄다)
- □ **under**(~ 아래에) ↔ **over**(~ 위에)
- □ **increase**(증가하다) ↔ **decrease**(감소하다), **reduce**(줄이다)
- □ **pull**(당기다) ↔ **push**(밀다)
- □ **worse**(더 나쁜) ↔ **better**(더 좋은)

※ 서로 비슷한 뜻을 가진 단어
- □ **rule**(규칙) : **law**(법, 규율), **regulation**(규정, 규제)
- □ **depend on**(~에 의존하다) : **rely on**(~에 의지[의존]하다)
- □ **turn on**([불·라디오·텔레비전 등을] 켜다) : **switch on**((전등 따위의) 스위치를 켜다)
- □ **reduce**(줄이다, 감소시키다) : **cut**(줄이다)

English Dictionary

- □ **advice** 충고
  → an opinion you give someone about what they should do
  누군가에게 그들이 해야 하는 것에 대해 당신이 주는 의견

- □ **avoid** 피하다
  → to prevent something bad from happening
  나쁜 일이 발생하지 않도록 막다

- □ **blink** (눈을) 깜빡이다
  → to shut and open your eyes quickly
  눈을 재빨리 감고 뜨다

- □ **break** 휴식
  → a period of time when you stop working in order to rest, eat, etc.
  쉬거나 먹기 위해서 일을 멈추는 일정한 시간

- □ **cause** 초래하다, 야기하다
  → to make something happen, especially something bad
  어떤 것, 특히 나쁜 것이 발생하도록 만들다

- □ **crack** 금, 깨진 틈
  → a thin line on the surface of something when it is broken but has not actually come apart
  어떤 것이 깨졌지만 실제로 분리되지는 않았을 때 표면에 생긴 얇은 선

- □ **deserted** 버려진
  → empty and quiet because no people are there
  사람들이 없어 비어 있고 조용한

- □ **drop** 떨어지다
  → to fall suddenly onto the ground or into something
  갑자기 땅 위로나 어떤 것 안으로 떨어지다

- □ **hall** 복도
  → the area just inside the door of a house or other building, that leads to other rooms
  집이나 다른 건물의 문 바로 안쪽에 있는, 다른 방으로 이어지는 지역

- □ **lower** 낮추다
  → to move something down from higher up
  더 높은 데서 무언가를 아래로 움직이다

- □ **novel** 소설
  → a long written story in which the characters and events are usually imaginary
  등장인물이나 사건이 보통 가상인 쓰여진 긴 이야기

- □ **prevent** 예방하다, 막다
  → to stop something from happening, or stop someone from doing something
  무엇인가가 발생하는 것을 막거나 누군가가 무엇을 하는 것을 막다

- □ **protect** 보호하다
  → to keep someone or something safe from harm, damage, or illness
  누군가 또는 무엇인가를 해, 손상, 질병으로부터 안전하게 유지시키다

- □ **reduce** 줄이다, 감소시키다
  → to make something smaller or less in size, amount, or price
  어떤 것을 크기, 양 또는 가격에서 작게 또는 보다 덜하게 만들다

- □ **text** (휴대 전화로) 문자를 보내다
  → to send someone a written message on a mobile phone
  휴대 전화로 쓰여진 메시지를 누군가에게 보내다

- □ **tip** 조언, 비법
  → a helpful piece of advice 도움이 되는 충고

- □ **uncomfortable** 불편한
  → not feeling physically comfortable, or not making you feel comfortable
  신체적으로 편하게 느끼지 못하거나 또는 당신이 편하게 느끼지 못하게 하는

- □ **upset** 화난
  → unhappy and worried because something unpleasant or disappointing has happened
  불쾌하거나 실망시키는 무엇인가가 발생해서 불행하거나 걱정스러워하는

서답형

01 다음 짝지어진 두 단어의 관계가 같도록 빈칸에 알맞은 단어를 쓰시오.

pull : push – _____ : decrease

중요

02 다음 빈칸에 공통으로 들어갈 말은?

• He walked along in front _____ me, holding the lantern.
• Could I have tuna instead _____ ham?

① to   ② with   ③ at
④ of   ⑤ from

[03~04] 다음 빈칸에 들어갈 말로 적절한 것은?

03

There were several small _____ in the glass.

① tips   ② cracks   ③ halls
④ lines   ⑤ pains

04

There's lots of _____ on baby care in the book.

① advice   ② center   ③ country
④ result   ⑤ level

05 다음 대화의 빈칸에 들어갈 말로 적절한 것은?

A: My phone doesn't work. What should I do?
B: You should take it to the _____.

① garage   ② service center
③ gallery   ④ factory   ⑤ bank

[06~07] 다음 밑줄 친 부분과 의미가 가장 가까운 것을 고르시오.

06

New York is planning to cut salt intake by at least 20 percent in 5 years.

① increase   ② lean   ③ hold
④ pull   ⑤ reduce

07

The old regulations were replaced by the new ones.

① tips   ② advices   ③ conditions
④ operations   ⑤ rules

중요

08 밑줄 친 부분의 의미가 잘못된 것은?

① It is important to look at the novel in its historical background. (역사적인)
② Don't say anything, you'll only make matters worse. (더 나쁜)
③ To avoid back problems, always bend your knees when you lift heavy objects. (뒤로)
④ A first rule in solving a mystery is to check the facts. (확인하다)
⑤ Let's take a ten-minute break. (휴식 시간)

서답형

09 다음 영영 풀이에 해당하는 단어를 주어진 철자로 시작하여 쓰시오.

to stop something from happening, or stop someone from doing something

➡ p_____

01 다음 〈보기〉와 같은 관계가 되도록 빈칸에 알맞은 말을 쓰시오.

┌─ 보기 ┐
small – big
└──────┘

(1) better – _____
(2) in front of – _____

02 다음 대화의 우리말과 일치하도록 빈칸에 알맞을 말을 쓰시오.

┌──────────────────────────┐
A: I'm _____ _____ _____ school.
(나는 항상 학교에 늦어.) What should I do?
B: You should set an alarm on your smartphone.
└──────────────────────────┘

03 다음 빈칸에 공통으로 들어갈 말을 쓰시오.

┌──────────────────────────┐
• The play was so boring that I couldn't keep myself _____ falling asleep.
• You need to relax _____ time to time.
└──────────────────────────┘

04 다음 빈칸에 알맞은 단어를 〈보기〉에서 골라 쓰시오. (형태 변화 가능)

┌─ 보기 ┐
bend   hurt   lean   lower
└──────────────────────────┘

(1) He was _____ on the bridge, watching the boats go by.
(2) Would you kindly _____ your voice a bit?
(3) Be careful you don't fall and _____ yourself.
(4) _____ your knees, but keep your back straight.

05 다음 주어진 우리말에 맞게 빈칸을 채우시오. (철자가 주어진 것도 있음)

(1) 내가 너에게 연락을 취할 경우를 대비해, 전화번호를 알려줄래?
➡ Can I have your phone number in case I need to g_____ with you?

(2) 이것은 너의 돈이 아니야, 너는 그것을 돌려줘야만 해.
➡ This isn't your money and you must _____.

(3) 물속으로 뛰어들기 전에 준비운동을 하세요.
➡ Before you dive into the water, _____.

(4) 나는 네가 말하는 것에 집중하지 않고 있었어.
➡ I wasn't _____ what you were saying.

06 다음 〈보기〉에서 빈칸에 공통으로 들어갈 단어를 골라 쓰시오.

┌─ 보기 ┐
at   in   on   from   to
└──────────────────────────┘

(1) • There's a train leaving for Seattle _____ 7 o'clock.
• _____ least once a week, he cleans his house at night.

(2) • The driver put _____ full speed to get to the station on time.
• Can I have a ride _____ your bike?

Conversation

교과서

1 충고하기

A I'm always late for school. What should I do? 나는 항상 학교에 늦어. 어떻게 해야 할까?

B You should set an alarm on your smartphone. 너는 스마트폰 알람을 맞춰야 해.

- 'What should I do?'는 '어떻게 해야 할까?'의 의미인데, 이에 대한 대답으로, 'You should + 동사원형'이나 'You had better + 동사원형'을 이용하여 충고나 조언을 할 수 있다.

- 'I think you should 동사원형 ~.'에서 think 다음에 접속사 that이 생략되어 있다. should는 도덕적 의무를 이야기할 때 사용하는 조동사로 must, have to에 비해 일상 회화 표현에서 자주 사용한다.

충고하기

- (I think) You should 동사원형 ~. 너는 ~해야 한다.
- Maybe you should 동사원형 ~. 아마 너는 ~해야 한다.
- You'd better + 동사원형. ~하는 것이 좋겠다.
- I advise you to 동사원형 ~. 네가 ~할 것을 충고한다.

충고의 말에 답하기

- That's a good idea. 그거 좋은 생각이다.
- I guess I should. 그래야 할 것 같아.
- OK, I will. Thanks. 그렇게 할게. 고마워.

핵심 Check

1. 괄호 안의 단어를 순서대로 배열하여 충고하는 말을 완성하시오.

   A: I have a test tomorrow. I'm not fully prepared it. What should I do?

   B: _____ (tonight, should, you, study)

   A: My dog doesn't eat anything and doesn't sleep well. What should I do?

   B: _____ (warm, you'd, better, him, keep)

2. 다음 우리말과 일치하도록 빈칸에 알맞은 말을 쓰시오.

   A: Let's eat hamburgers.

   B: You'd _____ _____ some vegetables. (너는 야채를 먹는 것이 좋겠다.)

   A: I got a poor grade.

   B: _____ harder. (너는 더 열심히 공부하는 편이 좋겠다.)

② 당부하기

A Can I eat this pizza? 이 피자를 먹어도 되나요?

B Sure. Just make sure you wash your hands first. 물론이죠. 반드시 손을 먼저 씻도록 하세요.

■ 'Make sure ~'는 '반드시 ~하도록 해라, ~을 확실히 해라'의 의미로, 상대방에게 당부할 때 사용하는 표현이다. 'make sure' 다음에 접속사 that을 생략할 수 있고 당부하고자 하는 내용을 주어와 동사를 갖춘 문장으로 쓴다.

• A: I think I caught a cold. (나 감기에 걸린 것 같아.)
  B: That's too bad. Make sure you take medicine and relax. (안됐구나. 꼭 약을 먹고 쉬도록 해.)

당부하기

• Make sure ~. (반드시 ~하도록 하세요.)
• You had better ~. (~하는 것이 좋겠다.)
• Don't forget to ~. (~할 것을 잊지 마.)
• Remember to ~. (~할 것을 기억해라.)

■ 'Make sure ~'에 대해서 응답을 할 때, 'Make sure ~' 다음에 대해 긍정이면 'OK. I will.'로 답하고, 부정이면 'OK. I won't.'로 답한다.

• A: Make sure you lock the door. (문을 꼭 잠그도록 해.)
  B: OK. I will. (알겠어요. 그럴게요.)
• A: Make sure you don't get wet. (꼭 젖지 않도록 해.)
  B: OK. I won't. (알겠어요. 젖지 않을게요.)

핵심 Check

3. 다음 우리말과 일치하도록 빈칸에 알맞은 말을 쓰시오.

A: Can I have the cookies on the table?

B: Sure. _____ leave some _____ your sister. (꼭 네 여동생 것을 좀 남기도록 하렴.)

A: _____ the artwork in the museum. (반드시 박물관에서 미술품을 만지지 않도록 하렴.)

B: OK. _____ touch the artwork. (알겠어요. 미술품을 만지지 않을게요.)

4. 다음 주어진 단어를 배열하여 대화를 완성하시오.

A: I'm not feeling well. I think I'm catching a cold. What should I do?

B: _____ (of, make, water, warm, you, sure, drink, a, lot)

Listen & Speak 1 A

G: Oh, no! I have dark circles ❶under my eyes.

M: ❷You should ❸get more sleep.

G: 오, 이런! 눈 밑에 다크서클이 있어요.
M: 너는 잠을 더 자야 한단다.

❶ under: ~ 아래에
❷ 상대방에게 조언을 할 때 '~해야 한다'라는 의미의 조동사 should를 이용하여 'You should 동사원형 ~.'의 형태로 표현할 수 있다. 좀 더 부드럽게 말하고 싶을 때에는 'I think (that) you should ~.'라고 말한다.
❸ get more sleep: 더 자다

Check(√) True or False

(1) The girl got too much sleep. T ☐ F ☐

(2) The girl has dark circles under her eyes. T ☐ F ☐

Listen & Speak 1 B-1

G: I ❶forgot Jenny's birthday!

B: Isn't she your best friend?

G: ❷Yes, she is. ❸What should I do?

B: ❹I think you should tell her you're very sorry.

G: 제니의 생일을 잊어버렸어!
B: 그녀는 너의 가장 친한 친구 아니니?
G: 응, 맞아. 어떻게 해야 할까?
B: 나는 네가 그녀에게 정말 미안하다고 말해야 한다고 생각해.

❶ forgot은 forget(잊다)의 과거형이다.
❷ 부정의문문의 질문에 대답할 때, 대답하는 내용이 긍정(그녀가 가장 친한 친구)이면 Yes로 대답한다.
❸ What should I do?: 어떻게 해야 할까?
❹ think와 you 사이에 접속사 that이 생략되어 있다. you should는 '너는 ~해야 한다'의 의미로 should가 조동사이므로 다음에는 동사원형이 온다는 점에 유의해야 한다.

Check(√) True or False

(3) The boy doesn't know Jenny. T ☐ F ☐

(4) The girl feels sorry for forgetting Jenny's birthday. T ☐ F ☐

Listen & Speak 1 B-2

B: I ❶feel down.

G: Why? What's the matter?

B: I ❷put on 5kg this winter. What should I do?

G: I think you should ❸cut down on snacks.

B: 기분이 우울해.
G: 왜? 무슨 일이니?
B: 이번 겨울에 5kg이 늘었어. 어떻게 해야 할까?
G: 나는 네가 간식을 줄여야 한다고 생각해.

❶ feel down: 기분이 우울하다 = feel depressed
❷ put on: ~을 늘리다, 더하다
❸ cut down on: ~을 줄이다

Check(√) True or False

(5) The boy is happy now. T ☐ F ☐

(6) The boy is too heavy now. T ☐ F ☐

Listen & Speak 2 A

W: ❶Make sure you ❷are home ❸by 12:00.

G: ❹Okay, I will.

❶ Make sure ~.는 '반드시 ~해라, ~을 확실히 해라.'라는 뜻으로 상대방에게 당부를 할 때 사용하는 표현이다.

❷ home은 명사 또는 부사로 사용될 수 있는데, 여기서는 부사로 사용되어 are가 '있다'의 의미로 해석된다. you are home 너는 '집에 있다'

❸ by+시간: ~까지

❹ Make sure 다음에 대해 긍정이면 OK. I will. '알겠어요, 그럴게요.'로 대답한다.

Listen & Speak 2 B-1

B: Mom, ❶may I ❷sleep over at Jinsu's house?

W: Did Jinsu's mom say it was okay?

B: Yes. ❸Jinsu said she would make pizza for us.

W: Okay. Make sure you ❹text me ❺when you get to Jinsu's house.

❶ May I ~?는 '~해도 될까요?'의 의미로, 상대방에게 허락을 구하는 표현이다. May 대신에 Can을 쓸 수도 있다.

❷ sleep over at ~: (남의 집에) 묵다

❸ said 뒤에 명사절을 이끄는 접속사 that이 생략되었다.

❹ text: (휴대전화로) 문자를 보내다

❺ when은 접속사로 '~할 때'의 의미로 사용되었다. get to + 장소: ~에 도착하다

Listen & Speak 2 B-2

G: Daniel, ❶what are you doing?

B: I'm reading a ❷novel on my smartphone.

G: Make sure you don't read ❸in the dark. ❹It's not good for your eyes.

B: Okay. I'll ❺turn the light on.

❶ 현재 무엇을 하고 있는지 물어보는 표현으로 'be동사의 현재형+동사ing'인 현재진행형을 사용하여 질문한다.

❷ novel: 소설

❸ in the dark: 어둠 속에서

❹ be good for: ~에 좋다

❺ turn on: [불·라디오·텔레비전 등을] 켜다

Listen & Speak 2 B-3

B: Oh, no! I didn't ❶bring my science book!

G: Ms. Lee ❷won't be happy about ❸that.

B: I know. Umm, can I ❹borrow your science book?

G: Okay. Just ❺make sure you give it back when you're done.

❶ bring: 가져오다

❷ won't는 will not의 줄임말이다.

❸ that의 내용은 과학책을 가져오지 않았다는 사실을 의미한다.

❹ borrow: 빌리다

❺ make sure 다음에 접속사 that이 생략되어 있다. give back: 돌려주다 give back은 이어동사인데, 이어동사의 목적어가 대명사인 경우는 그 목적어를 반드시 두 낱말 사이에 써야 한다.

Real-Life Zone A

G: What does your shirt say?

B: Oh, this? It says "No Cellphone ❶for 24 Hours."

G: No Cellphone? Why?

B: We ❷depend on our phones ❸too much these days.

G: That's true. ❹How often will you do this?

B: ❺I'm planning on doing it ❻once a month, but I'm not sure.

G: Try it first. Then, decide how often you should do it.

B: Okay. I'm going to ❼keep a diary of what I did without my phone for 24 hours. You should try it, too.

G: I'll think about it. Make sure you keep up with it.

B: I plan to. After I do it, I'll talk about my experience in class.

❶ for+숫자+시간 단위: ~ 동안 (during+기간 명사: ~ 동안, during summer vacation: 여름 방학 동안)

❷ depend on: ~에 의존하다, ~에 의지하다 (=rely on)

❸ too는 '너무'의 의미로 부정적인 의미를 가지고 있다.

❹ How often: 얼마나 자주

❺ be planning on ~ing: ~할 계획이다

❻ once[twice, three times, four times]+a+시간 단위[day, week, month] 여기서 a는 per(~당, ~에)의 의미로 사용된다. once a month: 한 달에 한 번

❼ keep a diary: 일기를 쓰다

● 다음 우리말과 일치하도록 빈칸에 알맞은 말을 쓰시오.

 해석

Listen & Speak 1 A

G: Oh, no! I have dark circles _____ my eyes.

M: You _____ _____ _____ _____.

1. G: 오, 이런! 눈 밑에 다크서클이 있어요.
   M: 너는 잠을 더 자야 한단다.

Listen & Speak 1 B

1. G: I _____ Jenny's birthday!

   B: Isn't she your best friend?

   G: _____, she is. _____ _____ _____ _____?

   B: _____ _____ _____ _____ _____ her you're very sorry.

2. B: I feel _____.

   G: Why? What's the matter?

   B: I _____ _____ 5 kg _____ winter. _____ _____ I do?

   G: I think you _____ _____ _____ _____ snacks.

1. G: 제니의 생일을 잊어버렸어!
   B: 그녀는 너의 가장 친한 친구 아니니?
   G: 응, 맞아. 어떻게 해야 할까?
   B: 나는 네가 그녀에게 정말 미안하다고 말해야 한다고 생각해.

2. B: 기분이 우울해.
   G: 왜? 무슨 일이니?
   B: 이번 겨울에 5kg이 늘었어. 어떻게 해야 할까?
   G: 나는 네가 간식을 줄여야 한다고 생각해.

Listen & Speak 1 C

1. A: I'm _____ _____ _____ school. What _____ _____ do?

   B: You should _____ _____ _____ on your smartphone.

2. A: I have a headache. _____ _____ _____ do?

   B: You _____ _____ _____ _____.

3. A: My phone doesn't work. _____ _____ _____ _____?

   B: You should _____ it to _____ _____ _____.

1. A: 나는 항상 학교에 늦어. 어떻게 해야 할까?
   B: 너는 스마트폰 알람을 맞춰야 해.
2. A: 두통이 있어. 어떻게 해야 할까?
   B: 너는 좀 쉬어야 해.
3. A: 내 휴대 전화가 작동하지 않아. 어떻게 해야 할까?
   B: 너는 그것을 서비스 센터에 가져가야 해.

Listen & Speak 2 A

W: _____ _____ you are home _____ 12:00.

G: Okay, I will.

W: 반드시 12까지는 집에 있도록 하세요.
G: 알겠어요, 그럴게요.

Listen & Speak 2 B

1. **B:** Mom, may I _____ _____ _____ Jinsu's house?

   W: Did Jinsu's mom say it was okay?

   B: Yes. Jinsu said she would _____ pizza for us.

   W: Okay. _____ _____ _____ _____ me when you _____ _____ Jinsu's house.

2. **G:** Daniel, _____ are you doing?

   B: I'm _____ a novel on my smartphone.

   G: Make sure you _____ _____ _____ _____ _____ . It's not _____ _____ your eyes.

   B: Okay. I'll _____ the light _____ .

3. **B:** Oh, no! I didn't _____ my science book!

   G: Ms. Lee _____ be happy about that.

   B: I know. Umm, can I _____ your science book?

   G: Okay. Just _____ _____ you _____ _____ _____ when you're done.

Listen & Speak 2 C

1. **A:** Can I eat this pizza?

   B: Sure. Just _____ _____ _____ wash your hands _____ .

2. **A:** _____ _____ use this computer?

   B: Sure. Just make sure you _____ _____ _____ _____ _____ _____ .

3. **A:** _____ _____ _____ _____ this boat?

   B: Sure. Just make sure you wear _____ _____ _____ .

[01~02] 다음 대화의 빈칸에 알맞은 말은?

01

> G: Oh, no! I have dark circles under my eyes.
> M: You _____ get more sleep.

① make ② should ③ can ④ will ⑤ do

02

> W: Make sure you are home by 12:00.
> G: _____

① Yes, I do. ② Yes, I am. ③ That's too bad.
④ OK. I will. ⑤ Okay. I won't.

03 자연스러운 대화가 되도록 순서대로 배열하시오.

> (A) Did Jinsu's mom say it was okay?
> (B) Yes. Jinsu said she would make pizza for us.
> (C) Mom, may I sleep over at Jinsu's house?
> (D) Okay. Make sure you text me when you get to Jinsu's house.

➡ _____

[04~05] 다음 대화를 읽고 물음에 답하시오.

> G: ①I forgot Jenny's birthday!
> B: ②Isn't she your best friend?
> G: ③No, she is. ④What should I do?
> B: ⑤I think you should tell her you're very sorry.

04 위 대화의 밑줄 친 ①~⑤ 중 어법상 어색한 것은?

① ② ③ ④ ⑤

05 위 대화를 읽고 답할 수 없는 질문은?

① Does the boy know Jenny?
② What advice does the boy give to the girl?
③ Is Jenny the girl's best friend?
④ Did the girl forget Jenny's birthday?
⑤ When is Jenny's birthday?

[01~02] 다음 대화를 읽고 물음에 답하시오.

> B: I feel (A)down.
> G: Why? What's the matter?
> B: I put (B)_____ 5kg this winter. What should I do?
> G: I think you should cut down (C)_____ snacks.

01 (A)와 바꿔 쓸 수 있는 말을 고르시오.

① disappointed　② excited
③ depressed　④ nervous
⑤ embarrassed

02 빈칸 (B)와 (C)에 공통으로 들어갈 말을 고르시오.

① in　② on　③ off
④ to　⑤ from

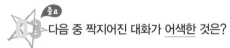다음 중 짝지어진 대화가 어색한 것은?

① A: I have a headache.
　B: I think you should go see a doctor.
② A: Can I borrow your science book?
　B: Of course not. Just make sure you give it back when you're done.
③ A: I forgot the test tomorrow. What should I do?
　B: You should start studying right away.
④ A: I think my dog has a stomachache. What should I do?
　B: You should take the dog to the animal hospital.
⑤ A: Can I ride on this boat?
　B: Sure. Just make sure you wear a life jacket.

04 다음 대화의 빈칸에 알맞은 말은?

> A: Can I eat this pizza?
> B: Sure. _____.

① You should get more ice cream.
② Just make sure you don't read in the dark.
③ Just make sure you wash your hands first.
④ I think you should get some rest.
⑤ Make sure you turn it off after using it.

[05~06] 다음 대화를 읽고 물음에 답하시오.

> A: (A)_____ Can you give me some advice?
> B: You should drink warm milk before bed. And (you, about, make, minutes, sure, take, for, a, walk, 30).

빈칸 (A)에 알맞은 말을 고르시오.

① I can't sleep well at night.
② We have a test tomorrow.
③ I didn't bring my science book.
④ I should practice more.
⑤ I should be home by 12:00.

06 서답형 괄호 안의 단어를 바르게 배열하시오.

➡ _____

밑줄 친 부분과 바꾸어 쓸 수 있는 문장을 모두 고르시오.

A: Can I ride on this boat?
B: Sure. <u>Just make sure you wear a life jacket.</u>

① I guess I should wear a life jacket.
② Don't forget to wear a life jacket.
③ Why don't we wear a life jacket?
④ You had better wear a life jacket.
⑤ Don't remember to wear a life jacket.

[08~09] 다음 대화를 읽고 물음에 답하시오.

B: Oh, no! I (A)_____ my science book!
G: Ms. Lee won't be happy about that.
B: I know. Umm, can I (B)_____ your science book?
G: Okay. <u>다 사용하면 반드시 다시 돌려주도록 해.</u>

08 빈칸 (A)와 (B)에 알맞은 것끼리 짝지어진 것을 고르시오.

	(A)	(B)
①	bring	borrow
②	bring	lend
③	didn't bring	lend
④	didn't bring	borrow
⑤	didn't bring	rent

09 밑줄 친 우리말과 같도록 주어진 단어를 이용해 영작하시오.

➡ _____

(back, just, do, give, make, when, sure)

[10~12] 다음 대화를 읽고, 물음에 답하시오.

G: What's the matter, Henry?
B: Look at my new cellphone. (①)
G: Oh, your phone screen has a crack. (②) Did you drop it?
B: Yes. (③) I'm so upset!
G: I think you should get a phone case. (④) It will protect your phone.
B: Okay. (⑤) I'll get one.

10 위 대화의 ①~⑤ 중 다음 주어진 말이 들어갈 알맞은 곳은?

I dropped it on the way here.

①　　②　　③　　④　　⑤

11 다음 영영풀이에 해당하는 단어를 대화에서 찾아 쓰시오.

a thin line on the surface of something when it is broken but has not actually come apart

➡ _____

12 위 대화의 내용과 일치하지 <u>않는</u> 것을 고르시오.

① A phone case can protect a phone.
② Henry is unhappy because his phone's screen has a crack.
③ Henry will buy a phone case.
④ Henry doesn't know how to use a new cellphone.
⑤ Henry bought a cellphone recently.

01 대화 속 괄호 안의 단어를 바르게 배열하시오.

> A: I have a headache. What should I do?
> B: (get, rest, you, some, should)

➡ _____

[02~03] 다음 대화를 읽고 물음에 답하시오.

> A: (A)무엇을 명심해야 하죠? (should, in mind)
> B: (B) _____ (the door, make, lean)

02 (A)에 주어진 어구를 이용하여 우리말을 영작하시오. (6 단어)

➡ _____

03 주어진 그림을 보고 빈칸 (B)를 괄호 안에 주어진 어구를 이용하여 채우시오.

➡ _____

04 대화의 ①~⑤ 중 어색한 부분을 찾아 바르게 고치시오.

> G: Daniel, ①what are you doing?
> B: ②I'm reading a novel on my smartphone.
> G: ③Make sure you don't read in the dark. ④It's not good for your eyes.
> B: Okay. ⑤I'll turn the light off.

➡ _____

05 자연스러운 대화가 되도록 순서대로 배열하시오.

> (A) I know. Umm, can I borrow your science book?
> (B) Oh, no! I didn't bring my science book!
> (C) Okay. Just make sure you give it back when you're done.
> (D) Ms. Lee won't be happy about that.

➡ _____

06 주어진 문장 다음에 이어질 대화의 순서를 바르게 배열하시오.

> What's the matter, Henry?

> (A) Yes. I dropped it on the way here. I'm so upset!
> (B) Okay. I'll get one.
> (C) I think you should get a phone case. It will protect your phone.
> (D) Oh, your phone screen has a crack. Did you drop it?
> (E) Look at my new cellphone.

➡ _____

07 대화의 흐름상 어색한 부분을 찾아 바르게 고치시오.

> G: Oh, no! I have dark circles under my eyes.
> M: You should get less sleep.

➡ _____

Grammar

1 to부정사의 형용사적 용법

> Here are some tips **to protect** your health. 여기 여러분의 건강을 지켜줄 몇 가지 조언이 있습니다.
> I needed a book **to read**. 나는 읽을 책이 필요했다.

■ to부정사는 'to+동사원형'의 형태로 명사, 형용사, 부사로 사용될 수 있다.
• **To visit** Rome is his dream. 〈명사〉 로마를 방문하는 것은 그의 꿈이다.
• I want something **to drink**. 〈형용사〉 나는 마실 것을 원해.
• The problem was difficult **to solve**. 〈부사〉 그 문제는 풀기에 어려웠다.

■ to부정사가 명사(구)나 대명사(구) 뒤에 놓여서 앞의 명사(구)나 대명사(구)를 수식하는 형용사와 같은 역할을 한다. 이때 보통 바로 앞에 위치한 명사를 꾸며준다.
• She had nothing **to wear**. 그녀는 입을 것이 없었다.

■ to부정사가 형용사 역할을 할 때 전치사를 동반한 경우 수식받는 명사가 전치사의 목적어로 사용되었으면 전치사를 생략하면 안 된다.
• I need a chair **to sit on**. 나는 앉을 의자가 필요해.

■ 수식받는 명사를 전치사 다음에 넣어 전치사의 목적어인지 아닌지 확인하는 것이 좋다.
• Mike needs a friend **to play with**.
  (play with a friend (○)) Mike는 함께 놀 친구가 필요하다.
  Mike needs a friend to play. (play a friend (×))

■ to부정사가 -thing, -body, -one으로 끝나는 부정대명사를 형용사와 함께 수식할 때는 '대명사+형용사+to부정사'의 어순임에 유의한다.
• I want something **cold to drink**. 나는 마실 차가운 것을 원해.
• We have somebody **new to meet**. 우리는 만나볼 새로 온 사람이 있어.

핵심 Check

1. 괄호 안에서 알맞은 것을 고르시오.
  (1) Dan wanted something (drink / to drink).
  (2) They need several teachers (to teach / teaching) Korean.
  (3) There was no spoon (to eat / to eat with).
  (4) I don't have anything (curious to ask / to ask curious).

② 사역동사

> My mom **made** me **clean** my room. 엄마는 내가 내 방을 청소하도록 시켰다.
>
> Susan **made** her daughter **play** the piano. Susan은 그녀의 딸이 피아노를 치도록 시켰다.

■ 사역동사는 '사역동사+목적어+목적격보어'의 형태로 '~을 하게 하다(하라고 시키다)'의 뜻을 가지며 사역동사에는 make, let, have가 있다.

• Mom **made** me **do** my homework. 엄마는 내게 숙제를 하라고 시켰다.

• **Let** me **introduce** myself. 제 소개를 하겠습니다.

■ 목적격보어로 동사원형이 오면 능동의 의미로 '~(목적어)가 …(목적격보어)을 하게 하다'의 뜻을 가지며, 과거분사가 오면 수동의 의미로 '~(목적어)가 …(목적격보어)을 당하게[되게] 하다'의 뜻을 갖는다.

• I **had** him **call** her. 〈능동〉 나는 그가 그녀에게 전화를 걸도록 시켰다. (전화를 거는 것으로 능동)

• I **had** my hair **cut**. 〈수동〉 나는 머리를 깎았다. (머리가 깎이는 것으로 수동)

■ help는 목적격보어로 동사원형이나 to부정사가 오며 뜻의 차이는 없다.

• Natalie **helped** her mom **prepare** dinner. Natalie는 엄마가 저녁 준비하는 것을 도왔다.
  = Natalie **helped** her mom **to prepare** dinner.

■ get도 '~하게 하다'라는 의미로 쓰일 수 있지만 목적격보어로 to부정사가 온다. 수동의 의미일 때는 사역동사와 마찬가지로 과거분사가 온다.

• Mom **got** me **to do** my homework. 〈능동〉 엄마는 내게 숙제를 하라고 시켰다.

• I **got** my hair **cut**. <수동> 나는 머리를 깎았다.

핵심 Check

2. 괄호 안에서 알맞은 것을 고르시오.

(1) Cartoons make me (laugh / to laugh).

(2) Nari had her computer (repairing / repaired).

(3) She helped me (to do / doing) my homework.

(4) I got him (paint / to paint) the wall.

01 다음 문장에서 어법상 <u>어색한</u> 부분을 바르게 고쳐 쓰시오.

(1) Give me a sheet of paper to write.

＿＿＿＿＿＿ ➡ ＿＿＿＿＿＿

(2) I want to make myself looking better in photos.

＿＿＿＿＿＿ ➡ ＿＿＿＿＿＿

(3) Do you have time play soccer?

＿＿＿＿＿＿ ➡ ＿＿＿＿＿＿

(4) He helped his brother doing his homework.

＿＿＿＿＿＿ ➡ ＿＿＿＿＿＿

02 다음 중 어법상 <u>틀린</u> 문장은?

① She didn't have any socks to wear.
② Mom made me do the dishes.
③ I have some pictures to show you.
④ Edan got me set the table.
⑤ What is the best way to learn Korean?

03 다음 우리말에 맞게 주어진 단어를 바르게 배열하시오. (필요하면 어형을 바꿀 것)

(1) 그는 모두가 늦게까지 일하게 시켰다.
(he / work / everyone / made / late)
➡ ＿＿＿＿＿＿＿＿＿＿＿＿

(2) 가을은 수확의 계절이다.
(is / harvest / season / autumn / the / to)
➡ ＿＿＿＿＿＿＿＿＿＿＿＿

(3) 그는 내가 무거운 상자를 옮기는 것을 도와주었다.
(he / me / box / carry / helped / the / heavy)
➡ ＿＿＿＿＿＿＿＿＿＿＿＿

(4) 나는 어젯밤에 할 일이 많았다.
(I / night / work / lot / do / had / a / last / to / of)
➡ ＿＿＿＿＿＿＿＿＿＿＿＿

01 다음 빈칸에 알맞은 것은?

> I need gloves _____ .

① put
② to put
③ putting
④ to put in
⑤ to put on

02 다음 문장의 빈칸에 들어갈 알맞은 것은?

> She made him _____ for her.

① wait
② waits
③ waited
④ waiting
⑤ to wait

03 다음 빈칸에 알맞은 말이 바르게 짝지어진 것은?

> • She had him _____ the boxes. (carry)
> • Jessica wants something _____ . (eat)

① carrying - eat
② carried - eating
③ carried - to eat
④ carry - eating
⑤ carry - to eat

04 다음 문장에서 어법상 틀린 부분을 찾아 바르게 고쳐 쓰시오.

> I want to buy something to wear nice.

_____ ➡ _____

05 괄호 안에서 알맞은 것을 고르시오.

(1) His jokes always make me (smile / to smile).

(2) Jake had the wall (paint / painted).

(3) Anna helped me (finding / to find) the way to the station.

(4) Nicole got her son (walk / to walk) the dog.

(5) It's time (checking / to check) the e-mails.

(6) Emily has two daughters (to take care / to take care of).

(7) Is there something (to correct wrong / wrong to correct)?

06 다음 〈보기〉의 밑줄 친 부분과 성격이 다른 하나는?

> ┤ 보기 ├
> You must bring something to eat.

① She will buy a pretty dress to wear to the party.

② He woke up to find himself famous.

③ We didn't have enough time to make cookies for them.

④ I had many files to copy.

⑤ Now it's my turn to take out the trash.

07 다음 중 밑줄 친 부분의 쓰임이 나머지 셋과 <u>다른 두 개</u>는?

① Do you have a book <u>to read</u>?

② I don't have enough money <u>to buy</u> the dress.

③ He was so surprised <u>to run</u> into a friend of his in New York.

④ My mother encouraged me <u>to study</u> history hard.

⑤ Nick needs a friend <u>to talk</u> with.

08 다음 중 어법상 <u>어색한</u> 것은?

① Can you help me to carry the boxes?

② He let the children cross the road.

③ I will have him call you back.

④ Mom let me go to the party.

⑤ My teacher made me to solve the difficult math problems.

09 다음 빈칸에 공통으로 알맞은 말은?

> • She helped me _____ the email.
> • She had a lot of emails _____.

① sending   ② to send   ③ sent
④ send   ⑤ sends

10 다음 문장의 빈칸에 알맞지 <u>않은</u> 것은?

> My brother _____ me do exercise every day.

① allowed   ② made   ③ let
④ helped   ⑤ had

11 다음 우리말에 맞게 영작한 것을 고르시오.

> 나의 부모님은 내가 밤늦게까지 밖에 있도록 하지 않으셨다.

① My parents didn't let me to stay out late at night.

② My parents didn't let me staying out late at night.

③ My parents didn't let me stay out late at night.

④ My parents didn't let me stayed out late at night.

⑤ My parents didn't let me to staying out late at night.

서답형
12 다음 문장에서 어법상 <u>어색한</u> 부분을 바르게 고쳐 다시 쓰시오.

(1) I want to make it happening during the school festival.

　➡ _____

(2) Is there anyone funny bring to the party?

　➡ _____

(3) I'll have all the files copy for the meeting.

　➡ _____

(4) Dominick bought his daughter a doll to play.

　➡ _____

(5) Amy got her sister do her homework by herself.

　➡ _____

13 다음 빈칸에 적절하지 **않은** 것을 고르시오.

> Her parents did not _____ her go to the concert.

① get ② have ③ let
④ make ⑤ help

14 다음 우리말을 영어로 바르게 옮긴 것은?

> Anna는 지난주에 살 집을 샀다.

① Anna bought a house lived last week.
② Anna bought a house lives last week.
③ Anna bought a house living last week.
④ Anna bought a house to live last week.
⑤ Anna bought a house to live in last week.

15 다음 밑줄 친 단어의 쓰임이 주어진 문장과 같은 것은?

> Using a smartphone too much <u>makes</u> my eyes feel dry and tired.

① You will <u>make</u> a lot of friends there.
② Ann often <u>makes</u> cookies for me.
③ The springshower <u>makes</u> the grass grow.
④ Mom <u>made</u> me a cheese cake.
⑤ Flowers <u>make</u> our rooms cheerful.

서답형
16 주어진 어구를 바르게 배열하여 문장을 완성하시오. (한 단어를 보충할 것.)

> Susan / T-shirt / the hiking / wants / wear / comfortable / during / a

➡ _____

_____

서답형
17 다음 우리말에 맞게 주어진 단어를 바르게 배열하시오.

> 저는 제가 잘생겨 보이게 해줄 어떤 멋진 것을 찾고 있어요.
> (I / me / something / looking / look / am / make / nice / good / for / to)

➡ _____

_____

서답형
18 다음 우리말과 일치하도록 주어진 단어를 이용하여 빈칸에 알맞은 말을 쓰시오.

(1) Chris는 진짜 가수가 될 기회를 얻었다.
➡ Chris got a chance _____ _____ a real singer. (become)

(2) 무엇이 Bella로 하여금 아침 전철에서 그 일을 하게 만들었을까?
➡ What made Bella _____ the work in a morning subway? (do)

(3) Ken은 Nicole을 기쁘게 하기 위하여 그녀에게 줄 선물을 샀다.
➡ Ken bought a present _____ _____ to Nicole _____ _____ her pleased. (give, make)

(4) 나는 그 보고서를 제시간에 끝내도록 하기 위해 최선을 다했다.
➡ I did my best to have the report _____ on time. (finish)

(5) 대화하기에 즐거운 사람은 항상 있다.
➡ There is always someone interesting _____ _____ _____. (talk, with)

(6) 선생님은 우리가 잠시 동안 함께 일하도록 하셨다.
➡ Our teacher got us _____ _____ together for a while. (work)

01 다음 글에서 어법상 잘못 쓰인 것을 찾아 알맞게 고치시오.

> If you don't wake up energized every morning to make your day an amazing one, you probably don't have life goals achieving.

_____ ➡ _____

02 다음 문장을 to부정사를 이용하여 한 문장으로 바꿔 쓰시오.

(1) • Angie has twin sisters.
   • She has to take care of them.

➡ _____

(2) • Allen knows many silly jokes.
   • The jokes make us laugh.

➡ _____

03 다음 중 어법상 잘못된 것을 고쳐 문장을 다시 쓰시오.

(1) Marilyn won't let her daughter to sleep over at her friend's.

➡ _____

(2) I don't know how she got him say yes.

➡ _____

(3) I asked him to have my computer repair.

➡ _____

(4) He helped her carrying her things.

➡ _____

04 주어진 어휘와 to부정사를 이용하여 자신의 문장을 쓰시오.

(1) want, ability, speak

➡ _____

(2) take, chance, become

➡ _____

(3) there, way, solve

➡ _____

05 다음 그림을 보고 주어진 어휘를 이용하여 빈칸에 알맞은 말을 쓰시오.

> **A:** My dog is sick.
> **B:** You should have him _____ to the animal hospital. (take)

06 다음 〈보기〉에 주어진 단어를 이용하여 문맥에 맞게 문장을 완성하시오.

┌─── 보기 ┌───
remember   decide   talk

(1) It is time _____ _____ our plan.

(2) We selected some interesting topics
_____ _____ _____.

(3) Harry received a list of names _____
_____.

07 다음 글에서 어법상 틀린 부분을 모두 찾아 바르게 고쳐 쓰시오.

> When I got a cold, my mom had me to eat chicken soup. It helped me feeling better.

➡ _____

08 다음 중 어법상 어색한 것을 바르게 고치시오.

(1) Here are some tips to protecting your health.

_____ ➡ _____

(2) Silvia needs someone to look her dog while she is away.

_____ ➡ _____

(3) Will you bring me a sheet of paper to write?

_____ ➡ _____

(4) Do you have important something to tell?

_____ ➡ _____

09 다음 문장을 make를 이용하여 비슷한 의미의 문장으로 바꿔 쓰시오.

(1) Our teacher told us to hand in our report by tomorrow.

➡ _____

(2) The police officer ordered them to leave immediately.

➡ _____

(3) My mom asked me to come home early today.

➡ _____

10 다음 우리말을 괄호 안에 주어진 어휘를 이용하여 영작하시오.

(1) 우리 선생님은 우리에게 수업에서 영어만 사용하도록 시키셨다. (make, only, in class)

➡ _____

(2) 그가 파리에 갔을 때 그가 의지할 사람은 아무도 없었다. (Paris, nobody, when, there, depend)

➡ _____

(3) Simon은 그의 컴퓨터를 검사받도록 했다. (have, check)

➡ _____

(4) 그들은 그들에게 영어를 가르칠 선생님이 필요했다. (need, a teacher, 8 단어)

➡ _____

(5) 나는 어제 저녁에 엄마가 식사를 준비하는 것을 도와드렸다. (Mom, prepare, dinner, 8 단어)

➡ _____

11 다음 두 문장의 뜻이 같도록 빈칸에 알맞은 말을 쓰시오.

(1) Neil got the car cleaned by the mechanic.
= Neil got the mechanic _____ the car.

(2) Sharon had Tom repair her bike.
= Sharon had her bike _____ by Tom.

Reading

교과서

Health Tips for Smartphone Users

Seongmin spends a lot of time using his smartphone.
> spend time + ~ing: ~하는 데 시간을 쓰다

He checks the news and weather.

He plays smartphone games.

He texts his friends.
> 문자를 보내다

He finds information on the Internet.
> 정보

He reads online comic books.
> 만화책

He watches movies.

Seongmin cannot take his hands off his smartphone all day long.
> cannot + 동사원형: ~할 수 없다   take ~ off: ~을 떼어 놓다   온종일

He does not know that using a smartphone too much can cause health
> 접속사 that (know의 목적어)   건강 문제

problems. Are you a heavy user of your smartphone like Seongmin? If
> 심한   ~처럼(전치사)   만일 그렇다면

so, here are some tips to protect your health.
> 여기 있다   to부정사의 형용사적 용법. tips를 수식

Vocabulary:
tip (실용적인) 조언
smartphone 스마트폰
spend (시간을) 보내다
text 문자를 보내다
information 정보
cause ~을 야기하다
protect 보호하다

● 다음 문장이 본문의 내용과 일치하면 T, 일치하지 않으면 F를 쓰시오.

1 Seongmin finds information on the Internet. ☐

2 Seongmin watches TV dramas on the Internet. ☐

3 Seongmin knows that using a smartphone too much can cause health problems. ☐

4. Seongmin is a heavy user of his smartphone. ☐

Watch your neck and back. When you read on your smartphone, you
> 목   등   시간의 접속사: ~할 때

usually bend your neck. This "text neck" pose increases the pressure
> 빈도 부사(동사 앞에 위치)   증가시키다   압력

on your neck and back. The best way to prevent this pressure is to
> ~에 대한   to부정사의 형용사적 용법. way를 수식

bring the phone up to the level of your eyes. Another way is to lower
> to부정사의 명사적 용법 (보어 역할)   ~까지   to부정사의 명사적 용법 (보어 역할)

your eyes instead of bending your neck.
> ~하는 대신에   동명사 (전치사 of의 목적어)

Vocabulary:
back 등, 척추
bend 굽히다, 숙이다
pose 포즈, 자세
increase 증가하다, 증가시키다
pressure 압력
prevent 막다, 예방하다
level 수준, 단계, 높이
lower 낮추다, 내리다
instead of ~ 대신에

Give your eyes a break. It makes your eyes feel tired and dry to read
small letters on a smartphone for a long time. Using a smartphone in
the dark or in a moving car makes this problem worse. To avoid this,
give your eyes a break from time to time.

Follow the 20-20-20 rules: Every 20 minutes, take a 20-second break
and look at something at least 20 feet away. Also, blink your eyes
often. This will keep your eyes from becoming dry.

dry 마른, 건조한
letter 글자, 문자
worse 더 나쁜
avoid 피하다
rule 규칙
blink 눈을 깜박이다

확인문제

● 다음 문장이 본문의 내용과 일치하면 T, 일치하지 않으면 F를 쓰시오.

1 This "text neck" pose increases the pressure on your neck and back. ☐

2 The best way to prevent the pressure on your neck and back is to lower your neck. ☐

3 You should give your eyes a break from time to time. ☐

4 You should follow the 20-20-20 rules. ☐

5 To blink your eyes often will make your eyes dry. ☐

Do you text a lot on your smartphone? Texting for a long time can hurt
your fingers and wrists. Try these exercises. They will help reduce the
pain in your fingers and wrists.
Pull on each finger of each hand.
Put the backs of your hands together with your arms out in front of you.
But remember. The best tip to prevent these health problems is to use
your smartphone less. Give yourself some rest from your smartphone.

a lot 많이
wrist 손목
reduce 줄이다
pain 아픔, 통증
pull 당기다

확인문제

● 다음 문장이 본문의 내용과 일치하면 T, 일치하지 않으면 F를 쓰시오.

1 Texting for a long time can hurt your fingers and wrists. ☐

2 Pull on each wrist of each hand. ☐

3 Put the palms of your hands together. ☐

4 Take some rest from your smartphone. ☐

● 우리말을 참고하여 빈칸에 알맞은 말을 쓰시오.

1 _____ _____ for Smartphone Users

2 Seongmin _____ a lot of time _____ his smartphone.

3 He _____ the news and weather.

4 He _____ smartphone _____.

5 He _____ his friends.

6 He _____ _____ on the Internet.

7 He reads _____ _____ _____.

8 He _____ movies.

9 Seongmin cannot _____ his hands _____ his smartphone all day long.

10 He does not know that using a smartphone too much can _____ _____ _____.

11 Are you _____ _____ _____ of your smartphone like Seongmin?

12 _____ _____, here are some tips _____ _____ your health.

13 _____ your neck and back.

14 When you read on your smartphone, you _____ _____ your neck.

15 This "_____ _____" _____ increases the pressure on your neck and back.

16 The best way _____ _____ this pressure is to bring the phone _____ _____ the level of your eyes.

1	스마트폰 사용자들을 위한 건강 조언
2	성민이는 스마트폰을 사용하는 데 많은 시간을 보냅니다.
3	그는 뉴스와 날씨를 확인합니다.
4	그는 스마트폰 게임을 합니다.
5	그는 친구들에게 문자 메시지를 보냅니다.
6	그는 인터넷에서 정보를 찾습니다.
7	그는 온라인 만화책을 읽습니다.
8	그는 영화를 봅니다.
9	성민이는 하루 종일 스마트폰에서 손을 뗄 수가 없습니다.
10	그는 스마트폰을 너무 많이 사용하는 것이 건강 문제를 일으킬 수 있다는 것을 모릅니다.
11	여러분은 성민이와 같은 스마트폰 과다 사용자인가요?
12	그렇다면, 여기 여러분의 건강을 지켜 줄 몇 가지 조언이 있습니다.
13	여러분의 목과 척추를 조심하세요.
14	스마트폰을 볼 때, 여러분은 보통 목을 구부립니다.
15	이 "거북목" 자세는 여러분의 목과 척추에 가해지는 압력을 증가시킵니다.
16	이러한 압력을 예방하는 가장 좋은 방법은 휴대 전화를 여러분의 눈높이까지 올리는 것입니다.

17 _____ _____ is to lower your eyes _____ _____ _____ your neck.

18 Give your eyes _____ _____.

19 It makes your eyes _____ _____ and dry to read small letters on a smartphone _____ _____ _____ _____.

20 Using a smartphone _____ _____ _____ or in a moving car makes this problem _____.

21 _____ _____ this, give your eyes a break _____ _____ _____ _____.

22 Follow the 20-20-20 rules: _____ 20 minutes, take _____ _____ _____ and look at something at least 20 _____ _____.

23 Also, _____ your eyes _____.

24 This will _____ your eyes _____ _____ dry.

25 Do you text a lot _____ _____ _____?

26 _____ for a long time can _____ your fingers and wrists.

27 _____ these exercises.

28 They will _____ _____ the pain in your fingers and wrists.

29 _____ _____ each finger of each hand.

30 _____ the backs of your hands _____ _____ _____ _____ out in front of you.

31 But _____.

32 _____ _____ ___ to prevent these health problems is _____ your smartphone _____.

33 Give yourself _____ _____ _____ your smartphone.

17 또 다른 방법은 여러분의 목을 구부리는 대신에 시선을 낮추는 것입니다.

18 눈을 쉬게 하세요.

19 오랫동안 스마트폰의 작은 글자를 읽는 것은 눈이 피곤해지고 건조하게 느끼도록 만듭니다.

20 어두운 곳이나 움직이는 차에서 스마트폰을 사용하는 것은 이러한 문제를 더욱 악화시킵니다.

21 이것을 피하려면, 눈을 때때로 쉬게 하세요.

22 20-20-20 규칙을 따르세요. 20분마다 20초의 휴식을 취하고 적어도 20피트 이상 떨어져 있는 사물을 바라보세요.

23 또한, 눈을 자주 깜박이세요.

24 이것은 여러분의 눈이 건조해지는 것을 막아 줄 것입니다.

25 스마트폰으로 문자 메시지를 많이 보내나요?

26 오랫동안 문자 메시지를 보내는 것은 여러분의 손가락과 손목을 상하게 할 수 있습니다.

27 이런 운동을 해 보세요.

28 그것은 여러분의 손가락과 손목의 통증을 줄이는 것을 도와줄 것입니다.

29 각 손의 각 손가락을 당기세요.

30 팔을 여러분 앞에서 벌린 채로 손등을 마주 놓으세요.

31 그러나 기억하세요.

32 이러한 건강 문제를 예방하는 가장 좋은 방법은 스마트폰을 덜 사용하는 것입니다.

33 여러분 자신에게 스마트폰으로부터 휴식을 주세요.

● 우리말을 참고하여 본문을 영작하시오.

1 스마트폰 사용자들을 위한 건강 조언

➡ _____

2 성민이는 스마트폰을 사용하는 데 많은 시간을 보냅니다.

➡ _____

3 그는 뉴스와 날씨를 확인합니다.

➡ _____

4 그는 스마트폰 게임을 합니다.

➡ _____

5 그는 친구들에게 문자 메시지를 보냅니다.

➡ _____

6 그는 인터넷에서 정보를 찾습니다.

➡ _____

7 그는 온라인 만화책을 읽습니다.

➡ _____

8 그는 영화를 봅니다.

➡ _____

9 성민이는 하루 종일 스마트폰에서 손을 뗄 수가 없습니다.

➡ _____

10 그는 스마트폰을 너무 많이 사용하는 것이 건강 문제를 일으킬 수 있다는 것을 모릅니다.

➡ _____

11 여러분은 성민이와 같은 스마트폰 과다 사용자인가요?

➡ _____

12 그렇다면, 여기 여러분의 건강을 지켜 줄 몇 가지 조언이 있습니다.

➡ _____

13 여러분의 목과 척추를 조심하세요.

➡ _____

14 스마트폰을 볼 때, 여러분은 보통 목을 구부립니다.

➡ _____

15 이 "거북목" 자세는 여러분의 목과 척추에 가해지는 압력을 증가시킵니다.

➡ _____

16 이러한 압력을 예방하는 가장 좋은 방법은 휴대 전화를 여러분의 눈높이까지 올리는 것입니다.

➡ _____

17 또 다른 방법은 여러분의 목을 구부리는 대신에 시선을 낮추는 것입니다.

➡ _____

18 눈을 쉬게 하세요.

➡ _____

19 오랫동안 스마트폰의 작은 글자를 읽는 것은 눈이 피곤해지고 건조하게 느끼도록 만듭니다.

➡ _____

20 어두운 곳이나 움직이는 차에서 스마트폰을 사용하는 것은 이러한 문제를 더욱 악화시킵니다.

➡ _____

21 이것을 피하려면, 눈을 때때로 쉬게 하세요.

➡ _____

22 20-20-20 규칙을 따르세요. 20분마다 20초의 휴식을 취하고 적어도 20피트 이상 떨어져 있는 사물을 바라보세요.

➡ _____

23 또한, 눈을 자주 깜박이세요.

➡ _____

24 이것은 여러분의 눈이 건조해지는 것을 막아 줄 것입니다.

➡ _____

25 스마트폰으로 문자 메시지를 많이 보내나요?

➡ _____

26 오랫동안 문자 메시지를 보내는 것은 여러분의 손가락과 손목을 상하게 할 수 있습니다.

➡ _____

27 이런 운동을 해 보세요.

➡ _____

28 그것은 여러분의 손가락과 손목의 통증을 줄이는 것을 도와줄 것입니다.

➡ _____

29 각 손의 각 손가락을 당기세요.

➡ _____

30 팔을 여러분 앞에서 벌린 채로 손등을 마주 놓으세요.

➡ _____

31 그러나 기억하세요.

➡ _____

32 이러한 건강 문제를 예방하는 가장 좋은 방법은 스마트폰을 덜 사용하는 것입니다.

➡ _____

33 여러분 자신에게 스마트폰으로부터 휴식을 주세요.

➡ _____

[01~03] 다음 글을 읽고 물음에 답하시오.

Seongmin cannot take his hands off his smartphone all day long. He does not know that using a smartphone too much can cause ⓐ____ problems. ⓑ여러분은 성민이와 같은 스마트폰 과다 사용자인가요? If so, here are some tips to protect your health.

01 위 글의 빈칸 ⓐ에 들어갈 알맞은 말을 고르시오.

① money   ② health
③ friend   ④ posture
⑤ grade

서답형
02 위 글의 밑줄 친 ⓑ의 우리말에 맞게 주어진 어휘를 이용하여 10 단어로 영작하시오.

heavy, like

➡ _____

_____

03 위 글의 뒤에 올 내용으로 가장 알맞은 것을 고르시오.

① 스마트폰 사용 시 당신의 건강을 해치는 여러 자세들
② 스마트폰 사용이 가져오는 여러 가지 장점들
③ 스마트폰 사용으로 인해 변하게 된 사람들의 일상
④ 스마트폰 사용 시 주의해야 할 내용들
⑤ 스마트폰 사용 시 여러분의 건강을 지켜 줄 몇 가지 조언

[04~06] 다음 글을 읽고 물음에 답하시오.

Watch your neck and back. When you read ⓐ____ your smartphone, you usually bend your neck. This "ⓑ____ ____" pose (A)[decreases / increases] the (B)[pleasure / pressure] ⓒ____ your neck and back. The best way to (C)[prevent / protect] this pressure is to bring the phone up to the level of your eyes. Another way is to lower your eyes instead of bending your neck.

04 위 글의 빈칸 ⓐ와 ⓒ에 공통으로 들어갈 알맞은 전치사를 고르시오.

① on   ② about
③ in   ④ for
⑤ from

서답형
05 주어진 영영풀이를 참고하여 빈칸 ⓑ에 철자 t로 시작하는 단어를 쓰시오.

the word to describe repeated stress, injury and pain in the neck resulting from excessive watching or texting on hand-held devices. It is also often known as turtle neck posture.

➡ _____

서답형
06 위 글의 괄호 (A)~(C)에서 문맥상 알맞은 낱말을 골라 쓰시오.

➡ (A)_____ (B)_____ (C)_____

[07~09] 다음 글을 읽고 물음에 답하시오.

Give your eyes a break. (①) Using a smartphone in the dark or in a moving car makes this problem worse. (②) To avoid this, give your eyes a break ⓐfrom time to time. (③) Follow the 20-20-20 rules: Every 20 minutes, take a 20-second break and look at something at least 20 feet away. (④) Also, blink your eyes often. (⑤) ⓑThis will keep your eyes from becoming dry.

07 위 글의 흐름으로 보아, 주어진 문장이 들어가기에 가장 적절한 곳은?

It makes your eyes feel tired and dry to read small letters on a smartphone for a long time.

①   ②   ③   ④   ⑤

08 위 글의 밑줄 친 ⓐfrom time to time과 바꿔 쓸 수 없는 말을 고르시오.

① sometimes   ② rarely
③ now and then   ④ at times
⑤ once in a while

서답형
09 위 글의 밑줄 친 ⓑThis가 가리키는 것을 본문에서 찾아 영어로 쓰시오.

➡ _____

[10~12] 다음 글을 읽고 물음에 답하시오.

Seongmin spends ⓐa lot of time ⓑ his smartphone.
He checks the news and weather.
He plays smartphone games.
He texts his friends.
He finds information on the Internet.
He reads online comic books.
He watches movies.

10 위 글의 밑줄 친 ⓐa lot of와 바꿔 쓸 수 없는 말을 고르시오.

① much   ② plenty of
③ lots of   ④ many
⑤ a great deal of

서답형
11 위 글의 빈칸 ⓑ에 use를 알맞은 형태로 쓰시오.

➡ _____

중요
12 위 글의 성민이의 스마트폰 사용에 관한 내용으로 일치하지 않는 것은?

① 스마트폰 사용에 많은 시간을 보낸다.
② 뉴스와 날씨를 확인한다.
③ 친구들에게 메일을 보낸다.
④ 인터넷에서 정보를 찾는다.
⑤ 온라인 만화책을 읽는다.

[13~15] 다음 글을 읽고 물음에 답하시오.

Do you text a lot on your smartphone? Texting for a long time can hurt your fingers and wrists. Try ⓐthese exercises. ⓑThey will help reduce the pain in your fingers and wrists.
Pull on each finger of each hand.
Put the backs of your hands together with your arms out in front of you.

서답형
13 다음 문장에서 위 글의 내용과 다른 부분을 찾아서 고치시오.

• To text for a long time can do harm to your eyes.

➡ _____

서답형
14 위 글의 밑줄 친 ⓐthese exercises를 하는 방법을 우리말로 설명하시오.

➡ (1) _____
    (2) _____

서답형

15 위 글의 밑줄 친 ⓑ를 다음과 같이 바꿔 쓸 때 빈칸에 알맞은 말을 쓰시오.

➡ They will help _____ _____ the pain in your fingers and wrists.

[16~18] 다음 글을 읽고 물음에 답하시오.

There are both good things and bad things about using a smartphone. First, I can get in touch with my friends right away. Also, I can easily get information I need. That is useful when I have a lot of homework to do. ⓐ , ⓑ스마트폰을 너무 많이 사용하는 것은 눈이 건조하고 피곤하게 만듭니다. Also, text messages and ads keep me from paying attention to my studies. So I need to use my smartphone intelligently.

 위 글의 제목으로 알맞은 것을 고르시오.

① Merits of Using a Smartphone
② Weakness of Using a Smartphone
③ How to Get Information Easily
④ Pay Attention to Your Studies
⑤ Merits and Demerits of a Smartphone

17 위 글의 빈칸 ⓐ에 들어갈 알맞은 말을 고르시오.

① In addition   ② On the other hand
③ Therefore   ④ For example
⑤ Similarly

서답형

18 위 글의 밑줄 친 ⓑ의 우리말에 맞게 한 단어를 보충하여, 주어진 어휘를 알맞게 배열하시오.

> my eyes / too much / dry and tired / makes / a smartphone / feel

➡ _____

_____

[19~21] 다음 글을 읽고 물음에 답하시오.

Give your eyes a break. ⓐIt makes your eyes feel tired and dry to read small letters on a smartphone for a long time. Using a smartphone in the dark or in a moving car makes this problem worse. To avoid this, give your eyes a break from time to time. Follow the 20-20-20 rules: Every 20 minutes, take a 20-second break and look at something at least 20 feet away. Also, blink your eyes often. This will keep your eyes ⓑ becoming dry.

19 위 글의 주제로 알맞은 것을 고르시오.

① the effective way to read small letters on a smartphone
② how to use a smartphone in the dark or in a moving car
③ the difficulty of following the 20-20-20 rules
④ how to prevent the eye problems when using a smartphone
⑤ the tips for keeping your eyes clean and moist

20 위 글의 밑줄 친 ⓐit과 문법적 쓰임이 같은 것을 고르시오.

① It is two miles from here to the beach.
② He took a stone and threw it.
③ It is impossible to get there in time.
④ Hello, Peter, it's Mike here.
⑤ I make it a rule to get up early.

서답형

21 위 글의 빈칸 ⓑ에 들어갈 알맞은 전치사를 쓰시오.

➡ _____

[22~24] 다음 스마트폰 사용 지수를 나타내는 표를 보고 물음에 답하시오.

	Always (2 points)	Sometimes (1 point)	Never (no point)
1. I use my smartphone when I eat breakfast.	✓		
2. I use my smartphone in a car.		✓	
3. I use my smartphone when I am walking.		✓	
4. I feel uncomfortable when I do not have my smartphone with me.	✓		
5. I use my smartphone in bed.	✓		

My score

⬤ 0-3 Smart! ◯ 4-6 Be careful! ⬤ 7-10 Danger!

서답형

22 위 표의 내용과 일치하도록 다음 빈칸에 알맞은 숫자를 쓰시오.

> The writer's score is _____.

➡ _____

서답형

23 위 표의 결과를 보고 다음 빈칸에 들어갈 알맞은 단어를 쓰시오.

➡ The writer is in the _____ situation in using the smartphone.

24 다음 글쓴이에 관한 설명 중 위 표의 내용과 일치하지 <u>않는</u> 것은?

① 아침을 먹으면서 항상 스마트폰을 사용한다.
② 차에서는 스마트폰을 사용하지 않는다.
③ 걸으면서 때때로 스마트폰을 사용한다.
④ 수중에 스마트폰이 없으면 항상 불편함을 느낀다.
⑤ 잠자리에서 항상 스마트폰을 사용한다.

[25~27] 다음 글을 읽고 물음에 답하시오.

A Smartphone & Me
There are both good things and bad things about using a smartphone. First, I can get in touch with my friends ⓐright away. Also, I can easily get information I need. ⓑThat is useful when I have a lot of homework to do. On the other hand, using a smartphone too much makes my eyes feel dry and tired. Also, text messages and ads keep me from paying attention to my studies. So I need to use my smartphone intelligently.

25 위 글의 밑줄 친 ⓐright away와 바꿔 쓸 수 <u>없는</u> 말을 <u>모두</u> 고르시오.

① for a moment   ② immediately
③ from time to time   ④ right now
⑤ at once

서답형

26 위 글의 밑줄 친 ⓑThat이 가리키는 것을 본문에서 찾아 영어로 쓰시오.

➡ _____

중요

27 위 글에서 설명하고 있는 스마트폰 사용의 장점을 <u>모두</u> 고르시오.

① 친구들과 즉시 연락할 수 있다.
② SNS로 친구 관계를 잘 유지할 수 있다.
③ 전 세계에 이메일을 바로 보낼 수 있다.
④ 필요로 하는 정보를 쉽게 얻을 수 있다.
⑤ 많은 광고들을 쉽게 접할 수 있다.

[01~02] 다음 글을 읽고 물음에 답하시오.

Seongmin cannot take his hands off his smartphone all day long. ⓐHe does not know that using a smartphone too much can cause health problems. Are you a heavy user of your smartphone like Seongmin? ⓑIf so, here are some tips to protect your health.

01 위 글의 밑줄 친 문장 ⓐ를 다음과 같이 바꿔 쓸 때 빈칸에 알맞은 말을 쓰시오.

➡ He does not know that _____ _____ a smartphone too much can cause health problems.

02 위 글의 밑줄 친 ⓑIf so가 가리키는 내용을 본문의 단어를 사용하여 풀어쓰시오.

➡ _____

_____

[03~05] 다음 글을 읽고 물음에 답하시오.

Watch your neck and back. When you read on your smartphone, you usually ____ⓐ____ your neck. This "text neck" pose increases the pressure on your neck and back. The best way to prevent ⓑthis pressure is to bring the phone up to the level of your eyes. ⓒAnother way is to lift your eyes instead of bending your neck.

03 다음 그림을 참조하여 위 글의 빈칸 ⓐ에 들어갈 알맞은 말을 쓰시오.

 ➡ _____

04 위 글의 밑줄 친 ⓑ가 가리키는 것을 25자 내외의 우리말로 설명하시오.

➡ _____

05 위 글의 밑줄 친 ⓒ에서 흐름상 어색한 부분을 찾아 고치시오.

➡ _____

[06~08] 다음 글을 읽고 물음에 답하시오.

ⓐGive your eyes a break. It makes your eyes feel (A)[tired / tiring] and dry to read small letters on a smartphone for a long time. Using a smartphone in the dark or in a moving car makes this problem worse. To avoid this, give your eyes a break from time to time. Follow ⓑthe 20-20-20 rules: Every 20 (B)[minute / minutes], take a (C)[20-second / 20-seconds] break and look at something at least 20 feet away. Also, blink your eyes often. This will keep your eyes from becoming dry.

06 위 글의 밑줄 친 ⓐ를 3형식으로 고치시오.

➡ _____

07 위 글의 괄호 (A)~(C)에서 어법상 알맞은 낱말을 골라 쓰시오.

➡ (A)_____ (B)_____ (C)_____

08 위 글의 밑줄 친 ⓑthe 20-20-20 rules의 내용을 우리말로 설명하시오.

➡ _____

_____

[09~11] 다음 글을 읽고 물음에 답하시오.

Do you text a lot on your smartphone? Texting for a long time can hurt your fingers and wrists. Try these exercises. They will help reduce the pain in your fingers and wrists.

(1)   (2)

But remember. ⓐThe best tip to prevent these health problems are to use your smartphone less. Give yourself some rest from your smartphone.

09 다음 문장에서 그림 (1)에 대한 설명으로 틀린 부분을 고치시오.

Pull on each wrist of each hand.

➡ _____

10 다음 빈칸 (A)와 (B)에 알맞은 단어를 넣어 그림 (2)에 대한 설명을 완성하시오.

Put the (A) _____ of your hands together with your arms out (B)_____ _____ _____ you.

11 위 글의 밑줄 친 ⓐ에서 어법상 틀린 부분을 찾아 고치시오.

➡ _____

[12~14] 스마트폰 사용으로 생긴 건강 문제를 나타내는 다음 그림을 보고 물음에 답하시오.

12 다음 빈칸 ⓐ~ⓒ에 알맞은 단어를 넣어 위 그림의 문제 A를 해결하는 알맞은 방법을 완성하시오.

The best way to prevent the ⓐ_____ from bending your neck is to bring the phone ⓑ_____ to the level of your eyes and to lower your eyes instead of ⓒ_____ your neck.

13 다음 빈칸 ⓐ~ⓒ에 들어갈 알맞은 단어를 보기에서 골라 넣어 위 그림의 문제 B를 해결하는 방법을 완성하시오.

To avoid making your ⓐ_____ feel tired and dry, give your eyes a ⓑ_____ from time to time by following the 20-20-20 rules and ⓒ_____ your eyes often.

┤ 보기 ├

wrists, open, blow, blink, break, eyes

14 다음 빈칸 ⓐ~ⓒ에 알맞은 단어를 넣어 위 그림의 문제 C를 해결하는 알맞은 방법을 완성하시오.

To reduce the pain in your ⓐ_____ and ⓑ_____, pull on each finger of each hand and put the backs of your hands together ⓒ_____ your arms out in front of you.

구석구석

Before You Read A

1. I use my smartphone <u>when</u> I eat breakfast.
　　　　　　　　　　～할 때(접속사)

2. I use my smartphone <u>in a car</u>.
　　　　　　　　　　차 안에서

3. I use my smartphone when I am <u>walking</u>.
　　　　　　　　　　　　　현재분사

4. I feel <u>uncomfortable</u> when I do not have my smartphone <u>with me</u>.
　감각동사 feel의 보어로 형용사를 써야 함. uncomfortably(×)　　　　　　　～와 함께

5. I use my smartphone in <u>bed</u>.
　　　　　　　　　　a bed(×)

구문해설 • uncomfortable: 불편한, • in bed: 잠자리에서

1. 나는 아침을 먹을 때 스마트폰을 사용한다.
2. 나는 차에서 스마트폰을 사용한다.
3. 나는 걸으면서 스마트폰을 사용한다.
4. 나는 수중에 스마트폰이 없으면 불편함을 느낀다.
5. 나는 잠자리에서 스마트폰을 사용한다.

Before You Read B

Watch Out!
　= Be careful!

Yesterday, Sejin walked into a tree <u>while texting</u> and <u>hurt</u> her head. She needs
　　　　　　　　　　　　　└she was 생략.┘　hurt-hurt-hurt

to avoid <u>using</u> her phone while walking. Also, she should reduce <u>the time she</u>
　avoid는 목적어로 동명사를 씀.　　　　　　　　　　목적격 관계대명사 that[which] 생략

spends <u>using</u> it.
　spend+시간+~ing

구문해설 • watch out: 조심하다, • avoid: 피하다, • reduce: 줄이다

조심해!

어제, 세진이는 문자를 보내다가 나무에 부딪쳐서 머리를 다쳤다. 그녀는 걷는 도중에 전화기를 사용하는 것을 피할 필요가 있다. 또한, 그녀는 그것을 사용하는 데 보내는 시간을 줄여야 한다.

Writing Workshop

A Smartphone & Me

<u>There are</u> <u>both</u> good things <u>and</u> bad things about <u>using</u> a smartphone. First, I
└There are ~: ~가 있다　both A and B: A와 B 둘 다　동명사(전치사 about의 목적어)

can <u>get in touch with</u> my friends <u>right away</u>.
　～와 연락[접촉]하다　　즉시 (= immediately)

Also, I can <u>easily</u> get information I need. <u>That</u> is useful <u>when</u> I have <u>a lot of</u>
　　　동사를 수식하는 부사　앞에 목적격 관계대명사 생략　앞 문장을 가리킨다.　～할 때　　많은 = much

homework to do. <u>On the other hand</u>, <u>using</u> a smartphone too much <u>makes</u> my
앞의 명사 수식(형용사적 용법)　한편, 반면에　동명사 주어　　　　　동명사 주어이므로 단수 동사

eyes <u>feel</u> dry and tired.
　make+목적어+목적격보어(동사원형)

Also, text messages and ads <u>keep</u> me <u>from</u> paying attention to my studies. So I
　　　　　　　　　　keep … from ~ing: …이 ~하는 것을 막다

<u>need to</u> use my smartphone intelligently.
　～할 필요가 있다

구문해설 • get in touch with: ~와 연락[접촉]하다, • right away: 즉시, • easily: 쉽게,
　　　　　• on the other hand: 한편, 반면에, • pay attention to: ~에 유의하다, ~에 주목하다,
　　　　　• intelligently: 현명하게

스마트폰과 나

스마트폰을 사용하는 것에 대해서 좋은 것과 나쁜 것 둘 다 있다. 첫째, 내 친구들과 즉시 연락할 수 있다. 또한, 나는 내가 필요한 정보를 쉽게 얻을 수 있다. 그것은 내가 해야 할 숙제가 많을 때 유용하다. 반면에, 스마트폰을 너무 많이 사용하는 것은 나의 눈을 건조하고 피곤하게 만든다. 또한 메시지를 보내는 것과 광고들은 공부에 집중하는 것을 막는다. 그래서 나는 휴대 전화를 똑똑하게 사용할 필요가 있다.

영역별 핵심문제

01 다음 제시된 단어를 사용하여 자연스러운 문장을 만들 수 없는 것은? (형태 변화 가능)

┌─ 보기 ┐
drop give reduce pay

① Your button has _____ off.
② Small businesses will need to _____ costs in order to survive.
③ We have to _____ down on expenses this month.
④ If you _____ more attention in class, you may actually learn something!
⑤ I'll _____ the keys back to you tomorrow morning.

02 다음 대화의 빈칸 (A)와 (B)에 들어갈 알맞은 단어를 골라 쓰시오.

A: I'm always late (A)[in / for / of / to] school. What should I do?
B: You should (B)[do / have / get / set] an alarm on your smartphone.

➡ _____

03 다음 밑줄 친 부분의 뜻이 잘못된 것은?

① The people are in the hall. (구멍)
② Road safety is taught to young children to avoid road accidents. (피하다)
③ Could you give me some advice about buying a car? (조언)
④ Could you hold my bag for me? (들다)
⑤ I blinked as I came out into the sunlight. ((눈을) 깜빡였다)

04 다음 대화의 밑줄 친 text와 같은 의미를 지닌 문장을 고르시오.

B: Mom, may I sleep over at Jinsu's house?
W: Okay. Make sure you text me when you get to Jinsu's house.

① The text of the song may sing well.
② These books contain fewer pictures and a lot more texts.
③ Type the message text you wish to send.
④ I'll text you the final score.
⑤ She sent me a lot of text messages late last night.

[05~06] 다음 빈칸에 공통으로 들어갈 말을 쓰시오.

05
• Try to _____ a diary every day.
• It's a good idea. I'll _____ it in mind.

06
• You should _____ it to the service center.
• I think you should _____ a walk for about 30 minutes.

07 밑줄 친 단어와 의미가 같은 단어를 모두 고르시오.

The helmet law will reduce injuries in motorcycle accidents.

① cut   ② protect   ③ decrease
④ increase   ⑤ avoid

08 다음 대화의 빈칸에 알맞은 것을 <u>모두</u> 고르시오.

> G: Oh, no! I have dark circles under my eyes.
> B: _____

① I will get more sleep.
② You should get more sleep.
③ I guess I should get more sleep.
④ I think you should get more sleep.
⑤ You'd better get more sleep.

[09~12] 다음 대화를 읽고 물음에 답하시오.

> G: What's the matter, Henry? (①)
> B: Look at my new cellphone.
> G: (②) Did you drop it?
> B: Yes. I dropped it on the way here. (③) I'm so upset!
> G: (④) I think you should get a phone case. It will (A)_____ your phone.
> B: Okay. (⑤) I'll get one.

09 위 대화의 ①~⑤ 중 다음 주어진 말이 들어갈 알맞은 곳은?

> Oh, your phone screen has a crack.

①   ②   ③   ④   ⑤

10 빈칸 (A)에 들어갈 알맞은 말은?

① protect   ② prevent   ③ increase
④ avoid   ⑤ produce

11 다음 영영풀이에 해당하는 단어를 대화에서 찾아 쓰시오.

> to fall suddenly onto the ground or into something

➡ _____

12 위 대화를 읽고 답할 수 있는 질문을 고르시오.

① Why did Henry drop his cellphone?
② Where will Henry get a phone case?
③ Where did Henry buy a new cellphone?
④ How does the phone have a crack?
⑤ Does the girl have a phone case?

13 다음 중 짝지어진 대화가 <u>어색한</u> 것은?

① A: There are no fish in the river.
   B: I think it's because of the trash. We should pick up the trash in the river.
② A: What should I keep in mind?
   B: Make sure you don't run in the hall.
③ A: I'm worried about gaining weight.
   B: I think you should do exercise every day.
④ A: You should turn off the light.
   B: OK. I will.
⑤ A: Can you give me some advice for water activity?
   B: You should not wear your life jacket.

14 괄호 안에 주어진 단어를 이용하여 빈칸에 알맞은 말을 어법에 맞게 쓰시오.

> (1) There are many dresses _____ in the store. (sell)
> (2) There are many sights _____ in Seoul. (see)

15 〈보기〉의 밑줄 친 부분과 같은 용법으로 쓰인 것은?

> ┤ 보기 ├
> I want to have some time to take a rest.

① He is the last man to tell a lie.
② The book is not difficult to read.
③ The thing I want to do is to play online soccer games.
④ Lucy studies very hard to become a teacher.
⑤ Isaac grew up to be a famous scientist.

16 다음 빈칸에 알맞은 말을 쓰시오.

> 그녀의 부모님은 그녀가 그 콘서트에 가게 하지 않으셨다.
> = Her parents did not _____ her go to the concert.

➡ _____

17 다음 두 문장을 to부정사를 이용하여 바꿔 쓸 때 빈칸에 알맞은 말을 쓰시오.

(1) • Kay bought a pen.
　• She will write letters with it.
　= Kay bought a pen _____.
(2) • Sonya is looking for a camera.
　• She will take pictures with it.
　= Sonya is looking for a camera _____.
(3) • Angelina bought a house.
　• She wants to live in the house.
　= Angelina bought a house _____.

18 밑줄 친 부분의 쓰임이 나머지 넷과 다른 것은?

① He had me help him.
② He had his students submit their report the next day.
③ Melanie had her pictures taken at the amusement park.
④ He had no time to meet her.
⑤ Did she have him fix her new computer?

19 다음 빈칸에 알맞은 것은?

> Larry's car is not clean. I'll have it _____.

① wash　② washes
③ washed　④ washing
⑤ to wash

20 다음 빈칸에 들어갈 수 없는 것은?

> Mom _____ me study all day long.

① lets　② gets　③ has
④ makes　⑤ helps

21 다음 중 어법상 어색한 문장은?

① The president didn't have anything to say about the accident.
② Sadly it's time to say good-bye.
③ The reporters had many questions to ask of the K-pop singer.
④ Would you give me anything hot to drink?
⑤ Linda doesn't have any patients to take care.

22 다음 문장 중 어법상 자연스러운 것은?

① My sister often helps me doing my homework.
② They had many options choose about the experiment.
③ I'll have your health check.
④ Please let me go to the concert next weekend.
⑤ He spends a lot of time use his smartphone.

23 다음 〈보기〉의 어휘 중에서 골라 어법에 맞게 빈칸을 채우시오.

┌─── 보기 ───┐
build   turn down   put   produce
└───────────┘

(1) They made the company _____ a factory _____ electricity.

(2) John had me _____ the TV volume because he had his younger brother _____ to bed.

24 다음 답을 보고 물음에 있는 빈칸을 알맞게 채우시오.

Q: What is your topic _____?
A: I want to talk about the environment.

Reading

[25~27] 다음 글을 읽고 물음에 답하시오.

Give your eyes a ⓐbreak. It makes your eyes feel tired and dry to read small letters on a smartphone for a long time. ⓑUsing a smartphone in the dark or in a ⓒmoving car makes this problem worse. To avoid this, give your eyes a break from time to time. Follow the 20-20-20 rules: Every 20 minutes, take a 20-second break and look at something at least 20 feet away. Also, blink your eyes often. This will keep your eyes from becoming dry.

25 위 글의 밑줄 친 ⓐbreak와 같은 의미로 쓰인 것을 고르시오.

① Don't break the law.
② Who will break the news to her?
③ She worked all day without a break.
④ Be careful not to break a window.
⑤ Waves break against the rocks.

26 아래 보기에서 위 글의 밑줄 친 ⓑUsing이나 ⓒmoving과 문법적 쓰임이 같은 것을 각각 고르시오.

┌─── 보기 ───┐
① My dad is watching TV now.
② He is good at playing tennis.
③ I saw her entering the room.
④ The girl helping her mom is pretty.
⑤ Did you finish doing your homework?
└───────────┘

➡ ⓑ와 같은 것: _____
   ⓒ와 같은 것: _____

27 다음 질문에 대한 알맞은 대답을 본문에서 찾아 쓰시오.

Q: According to the paragraph, what makes your eyes feel more tired and drier?

A: _____

[28~29] 다음 글을 읽고 물음에 답하시오.

Watch your neck and back. When you read on your smartphone, you usually bend your neck. This "text neck" pose increases the pressure on your neck and back. The best way to prevent this pressure is to bring the phone up to the level of your eyes. Another way is to lower your eyes instead of ___ⓐ___ your neck.

28 위 글의 빈칸 ⓐ에 bend를 알맞은 형태로 쓰시오.

➡ _____

29 위 글의 내용과 일치하지 <u>않는</u> 것은?

① 스마트폰을 볼 때, 여러분은 보통 목을 구부린다.
② 목을 구부리는 자세를 "거북목" 자세라고 한다.
③ "거북목" 자세는 여러분의 목과 척추에 가해지는 압력을 증가시킨다.
④ 이러한 압력을 예방하는 가장 좋은 방법은 당신의 목을 전화기 쪽으로 숙이는 것이다.
⑤ 또 다른 방법은 목을 구부리는 대신에 시선을 낮추는 것이다.

[30~32] 다음 글을 읽고 물음에 답하시오.

A Smartphone & Me
There are both good things and bad things about using a smartphone. (①) First, ⓐ나는 친구들과 바로 연락할 수 있다. (②) Also, I can easily get information I need. (③) On the other hand, using a smartphone too much makes my eyes feel dry and tired. (④) Also, text messages and ads keep me from paying attention to my studies. (⑤) So I need to use my smartphone ___ⓑ___.

30 위 글의 흐름으로 보아, 주어진 문장이 들어가기에 가장 적절한 곳은?

That is useful when I have a lot of homework to do.

①   ②   ③   ④   ⑤

31 위 글의 밑줄 친 ⓐ의 우리말에 맞게 주어진 어휘를 이용하여 10 단어로 영작하시오.

get in touch, right away

➡ _____

32 위 글의 빈칸 ⓑ에 들어갈 알맞은 말을 고르시오.

① all the time   ② intelligently
③ slowly   ④ immediately
⑤ again and again

[33~34] 다음 글을 읽고 물음에 답하시오.

Seongmin cannot take his hands (A)[on / off] his smartphone all (B)[day / days] long. He does not know that using a smartphone too much can cause health problems. Are you a (C)[heavy / proper] user of your smartphone like Seongmin? If so, here are some ___ⓐ___ to protect your health.

33 위 글의 괄호 (A)~(C)에서 문맥이나 어법상 알맞은 낱말을 골라 쓰시오.

➡ (A)_____ (B)_____ (C)_____

34 주어진 영영풀이를 참고하여 빈칸 ⓐ에 철자 t로 시작하는 단어를 쓰시오.

useful pieces of advice

➡ _____

출제율 90%

01 다음 보기에 짝지어진 두 단어의 관계와 같도록 빈칸에 알맞은 말을 쓰시오.

> ┌ 보기 ┐
> happen : occur

(1) rely on : _____ _____
(2) tip : _____

출제율 95%

02 다음 〈보기〉의 단어를 사용하여 자연스러운 문장을 만들 수 없는 것은?

> ┌ 보기 ┐
> on   from   for

① Stay away _____ the fire.
② Do you still get in touch _____ John ?
③ Fresh fruit and vegetables are good _____ you.
④ They eat lunch in the park _____ time to time.
⑤ Cut down _____ fatty food if you want to lose weight.

출제율 90%

03 다음 밑줄 친 부분의 뜻이 잘못된 것은?

① The <u>rules</u> of the game are quite simple. (규칙)
② The weather was a lot <u>worse</u> this year. (더 나쁜)
③ Debbie was <u>upset</u> that he didn't spend more time with her. (화난)
④ We worked for ten hours without a <u>break</u>. (깨뜨리다)
⑤ Keep your head up and your <u>back</u> straight. (등)

출제율 90%

04 다음 우리말에 맞게 빈칸을 완성하시오.

(1) His _____ injury may _____ _____ _____ in tomorrow's game. (등 부상이 그가 내일 경기를 못하게 할지 모른다.)
(2) What problems _____ I _____ _____ _____ when buying an old house? (오래된 집을 살 때 무슨 문제를 주의해야 하나요?)
(3) _____ _____ _____ _____ school. (나는 학교에 지각했다.)
(4) You probably picked up my keys _____ _____ yours. (네가 아마 네 열쇠 대신에 내 것을 가져갔을 거야.)

[05~06] 다음 대화의 순서를 바르게 배열하시오.

출제율 90%

05
> (A) Yes, she is. What should I do?
> (B) Isn't she your best friend?
> (C) I forgot Jenny's birthday!
> (D) I think you should tell her you're very sorry.

➡ _____

출제율 85%

06
> (A) I think you should cut down on snacks.
> (B) I feel down.
> (C) I put on 5kg this winter. What should I do?
> (D) Why? What's the matter?

➡ _____

[07~08] 다음 대화를 읽고 물음에 답하시오.

B: Oh, no! I didn't bring my science book!
G: Ms. Lee ①won't be happy about that.
B: I know. Umm, ②can I borrow your science book?
G: Okay. Just ③make sure you ④give back it ⑤when you're done.

07 위 대화의 어법상 어색한 문장을 고르시오. *출제율 100%*

① ② ③ ④ ⑤

08 위 대화를 읽고 답할 수 없는 질문을 모두 고르시오. *출제율 90%*

① What book didn't the boy bring?
② How long is the science class?
③ Who can lend the science book to the boy?
④ What subject does Ms. Lee teach?
⑤ Why didn't the boy bring the science book?

[09~11] 다음 대화를 읽고 물음에 답하시오.

G: What does your shirt say?
B: Oh, this? (①)
G: No Cellphone? Why?
B: We depend on our phones too much these days. (②)
G: That's true. How often will you do this?
B: 한 달에 한 번 할 계획이야, but I'm not sure. (③)
G: Try it first. Then, decide how often you should do it. (④)
B: (⑤) Okay. I'm going to keep a diary of what I did without my phone for 24 hours. You should try it, too.
G: I'll think about it. Make sure you keep up with it.
B: I plan to. After I do it, I'll talk about my experience in class.

09 위 대화의 ①~⑤ 중 주어진 말이 들어갈 알맞은 곳은? *출제율 90%*

It says "No Cellphone for 24 Hours."

① ② ③ ④ ⑤

10 밑줄 친 우리말과 의미가 같도록 주어진 단어를 이용해 문장을 완성하시오. *출제율 85%*

➡ _____

(on, a, planning, month)

11 위 대화의 내용과 일치하지 않는 것을 고르시오. *출제율 90%*

① The girl will do what the boy said.
② The boy is going to talk about his one-day experience of not using his cellphone.
③ The girl agrees with his view that people rely on cellphones too much.
④ The boy thinks we use cellphones a lot these days.
⑤ The boy is wearing a shirt with letters.

12 다음 대화의 흐름상 어색한 문장을 고르시오. *출제율 95%*

G: ①Daniel, what are you doing?
B: ②I'm reading a novel on my smartphone.
G: ③Make sure you don't read in the dark. ④It's good for your eyes.
B: ⑤Okay. I'll turn the light on.

① ② ③ ④ ⑤

13 출제율90%

다음 중 어법상 올바른 문장은?

① The best way to preventing this pressure is to bring the phone up to the level of your eyes.

② I had my computer fixed yesterday.

③ Some were really beautiful, but others made me to feel scared.

④ I have something to tell important you.

⑤ I'll get him do the work.

14 출제율95%

어법상 잘못된 부분을 바르게 고쳐 문장을 다시 쓰시오.

(1) My dad didn't let me to go camping.

➡ _____

(2) Emily had her new dress make last week.

➡ _____

(3) There's wrong nothing to correct in this report.

➡ _____

(4) I bought my parents a house to live.

➡ _____

[15~16] 다음 글을 읽고 물음에 답하시오.

ⓐSeongmin cannot take his hands off his smartphone every day long. He does not know that using a smartphone too much can cause health problems. Are you a heavy user of your smartphone ⓑlike Seongmin? If so, here are some tips to protect your health.

15 출제율95%

위 글의 밑줄 친 ⓐ에서 어법상 어색한 것을 고치시오.

➡ _____

16 출제율100%

위 글의 밑줄 친 ⓑlike와 같은 의미로 쓰인 것을 고르시오.

① Which season do you like best?

② He has hobbies like reading and painting.

③ I like playing tennis.

④ He ran like the wind.

⑤ Do you like vegetables?

[17~19] 다음 글을 읽고 물음에 답하시오.

Watch your neck and back. When you read on your smartphone, you usually bend your neck. This "text neck" pose increases the pressure on your neck and back. The best way ⓐto prevent this pressure is to bring the phone up to the level of your eyes. Another way is to lower your eyes ⓑ____ bending your neck.

17 출제율95%

위 글의 밑줄 친 ⓐto prevent와 to부정사의 용법이 같은 것을 모두 고르시오.

① She was happy to get the present.

② I want something to write on.

③ He awoke to find himself famous.

④ He decided to buy new shoes.

⑤ There is no water to drink.

18 출제율100%

위 글의 빈칸 ⓑ에 들어갈 알맞은 말을 고르시오.

① in spite of ② according to

③ because of ④ instead of

⑤ together with

출제율 95%

19 위 글의 요지로 알맞은 것을 고르시오.

① 여러분의 목과 척추를 조심해야 한다.

② 스마트폰을 볼 때 목을 구부리는 것이 편하다.

③ 스마트폰을 사용할 때 "거북목" 자세를 방지해야 한다.

④ "거북목" 자세를 방지하기 위해 스마트폰을 사용하지 말아야 한다.

⑤ 스마트폰을 사용할 때 목을 구부리는 것이 시선을 낮추는 것보다 더 좋다.

출제율 90%

22 위 글의 내용과 일치하지 <u>않는</u> 것은?

① 오랫동안 스마트폰의 작은 글자를 읽는 것은 당신의 머리를 피곤하게 만든다.

② 어두운 곳이나 움직이는 차에서 스마트폰을 사용하는 것은 눈을 더 건조하게 느끼도록 만든다.

③ 눈이 피로해지는 것을 피하기 위해서는 눈을 때때로 쉬게 해야 한다.

④ 20-20-20 규칙을 따라야 한다.

⑤ 눈을 자주 깜빡이는 것은 눈이 건조해지는 것을 막아 준다.

[20~22] 다음 글을 읽고 물음에 답하시오.

Give your eyes a break. It makes your eyes feel tired and dry to read small letters on a smartphone for a long time. Using a smartphone in the dark or in a moving car makes this problem worse. To avoid this, give your eyes a break from time to time. Follow the 20-20-20 rules: Every 20 ⓐ____, take a 20-second ⓑ____ and look at something at least 20 feet ⓒ____. Also, blink your eyes often. This will ⓓ<u>keep</u> your eyes from becoming dry.

[23~24] 다음 글을 읽고 물음에 답하시오.

Do you text (A)[a lot / a lot of] on your smartphone? Texting for a long time can hurt your fingers and wrists. Try these exercises. ⓐ<u>They</u> will help reduce the pain in your fingers and wrists.

Pull on each finger of each hand.

Put the backs of your hands together with your arms out in front of you.

But remember. The best tip to prevent these health problems is to use your smartphone (B)[more / less]. Give (C)[you / yourself] some rest from your smartphone.

출제율 95%

20 다음 그림을 참조하여 위 글의 빈칸 ⓐ~ⓒ에 들어갈 알맞은 말을 쓰시오.

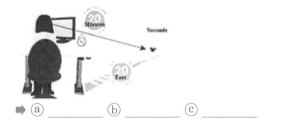

➡ ⓐ _____ ⓑ _____ ⓒ _____

출제율 95%

23 위 글의 괄호 (A)~(C)에서 문맥이나 어법상 알맞은 낱말을 골라 쓰시오.

➡ (A)_____ (B)_____ (C)_____

출제율 90%

21 위 글의 밑줄 친 ⓓ<u>keep</u>과 바꿔 쓸 수 있는 말을 <u>모두</u> 고르시오.

① stop   ② avoid

③ allow   ④ prevent

⑤ provide

출제율 90%

24 위 글의 밑줄 친 ⓐ<u>They</u>가 가리키는 것을 본문에서 찾아 쓰시오.

➡ _____

01 다음 대화의 밑줄 친 부분과 의미가 같도록 주어진 단어를 이용하여 영작하시오.

> A: Can I eat this pizza?
> B: Sure. Just make sure you wash your hands first.

➡ (1) _____ (better)

➡ (2) _____ (forget)

➡ (3) _____
　　 (remember)

02 괄호 안의 단어를 이용하여 우리말을 바르게 영작하시오.

> B: I put on 5kg this winter. What should I do?
> G: 나는 네가 간식을 줄여야 한다고 생각해.

➡ _____
　 (think, cut)

03 다음 대화의 밑줄 친 부분에서 어색한 것을 찾아 고치시오.

> G: ①I forgot Jenny's birthday!
> B: ②Isn't she your best friend?
> G: ③Yes, she is. ④What should I to do?
> B: ⑤I think you should tell her you're very sorry.

➡ _____

04 괄호 안에 주어진 단어를 이용하여 다음을 영작하시오.

(1) Brian은 오늘 해야 할 숙제가 많다. (a lot of, do, 9 단어)

➡ _____

(2) 이름들을 쓸 종이 한 장을 내게 가져다줄래? (will, bring, piece, 12 단어)

➡ _____

(3) 따로 보관할 중요한 어떤 것이 있나요? (there, valuable, keep separately, 7 단어)

➡ _____

(4) 맛있는 식사는 그에게 군침을 흘리게 하였다. (make, delicious, meal, water, 7 단어)

➡ _____

(5) 그들은 그로 하여금 새로운 계약에 서명하도록 했다. (get, sign, contract, 8 단어)

➡ _____

05 〈보기〉와 같이 주어진 두 문장을 한 문장으로 쓰시오.

> ┤ 보기 ├
> • Sharon made.
> • I waited for her.
> → Sharon made me wait for her.

(1) • Julia made.
　 • I did my homework.

➡ _____

(2) • Her mom had Jenny.
　 • Jenny prepared dinner.

➡ _____

(3) • Sam helped me.
　 • I repaired my computer.

➡ _____

[06~08] 다음 글을 읽고 물음에 답하시오.

Watch your neck and back. When you read on your smartphone, you usually bend your neck. This "text neck" pose increases the pressure on your neck and back. The best way to prevent this pressure is to bring the phone ⓐ_____ _____ the level of your eyes. Another way is to lower your eyes instead of bending your neck.

06 본문의 내용과 일치하도록 다음 빈칸 (A)와 (B)에 알맞은 단어를 쓰시오.

> If you bend your neck when reading on your smartphone, the pressure on your (A)_____ and (B)_____ increases because of this posture.

07 다음 그림을 참조하여 위 글의 빈칸 ⓐ에 들어갈 알맞은 말을 쓰시오.

 ➡ _____

08 위 글을 읽고 "거북목" 자세로 인한 압력을 예방할 수 있는 좋은 방법 두 가지를 우리말로 설명하시오.

➡ (1) _____
　 (2) _____

[09~11] 다음 글을 읽고 물음에 답하시오.

Give your eyes a break. ⓐIt makes your eyes to feel tired and dry to read small letters on a smartphone for a long time. Using a smartphone in the dark or in a moving car makes this problem (A)[better / worse]. To avoid this, give your eyes a break from time to time. Follow the 20-20-20 rules: (B)[All / Every] 20 minutes, take a 20-second break and look at something (C)[at last / at least] 20 feet away. Also, blink your eyes often. ⓑ이것은 눈이 건조해지는 것을 막을 것이다.

09 위 글의 밑줄 친 ⓐ에서 어법상 틀린 부분을 찾아 고치시오.

➡ _____

10 위 글의 괄호 (A)~(C)에서 문맥상 알맞은 낱말을 골라 쓰시오.

➡ (A)_____　(B)_____　(C)_____

11 위 글의 밑줄 친 ⓑ의 우리말에 맞게 주어진 어휘를 이용하여 8 단어로 영작하시오.

> keep, becoming

➡ _____

01 친구의 고민에 should를 이용하여 충고하는 말을 3 문장 이상 쓰시오.

> A: I am worried about gaining weight.
> B: _____
> A: I guess I should.

02 주어진 어구를 이용하여 3 문장 이상을 쓰시오.

> make   have   let
> prepare dinner   clean the room   go to the movies   play soccer

(1) _____
(2) _____
(3) _____
(4) _____

03 다음 스마트폰의 장점과 단점을 바탕으로 '스마트폰과 나'를 주제로 말하기 발표 대본을 쓰시오.

> 장점:
> (1) I can get in touch with my friends right away.
> (2) I can easily get information I need.
> 단점:
> (1) My eyes feel dry and tired.
> (2) Text messages and ads keep me from paying attention to my studies.

> A Smartphone & Me
>   There are both good things and bad things about using a smartphone. First, I can get in touch with my friends (A)_____. Also, I can easily get (B)_____ I need. That is useful when I have a lot of homework to do. On the other hand, using a smartphone too much makes my eyes feel (C)_____. Also, text messages and ads (D)_____ me from paying attention to my studies. So I need to use my smartphone (E)_____ .

단원별 모의고사

[01~03] 다음 대화의 빈칸에 알맞은 것을 고르시오.

01

> M: You forgot to turn _____ your radio again today.
> B: Oh, I'm sorry, Mom.

① over   ② into   ③ off
④ to   ⑤ for

02

> W: Jake, you should pay attention _____ the person who talks to you.
> M: Okay, I will.

① by   ② with   ③ for
④ to   ⑤ on

03

> A: Can I _____ this boat?
> B: Sure. Just make sure you wear a life jacket.

① ride on   ② go on   ③ get to
④ come on   ⑤ take on

04 다음 빈칸에 공통으로 들어갈 단어를 쓰시오.

> • I live far _____ from the station.
> • I'll phone him right _____.

[05~06] 다음 대화를 읽고 물음에 답하시오.

> B: Mom, 진수네 집에서 자도 돼요?
> W: Did Jinsu's mom say it was okay?
> B: Yes. Jinsu said she would (A)_____ pizza for us.
> W: Okay. (B)_____ sure you text me when you get to Jinsu's house.

05 위 대화의 밑줄 친 우리말에 맞게 주어진 단어를 이용하여 영어로 쓰시오.

➡ _____

(over, at, may)

06 위 대화의 빈칸 (A)와 (B)에 공통으로 들어갈 알맞은 말을 쓰시오.

➡ _____

07 다음 대화의 괄호 안에 주어진 단어를 알맞게 배열하시오.

> W: _____
>   (by, sure, are, 12:00, make, you, home)
> G: Okay, I will.

[08~09] 다음 대화를 읽고 물음에 답하시오.

> G: What's the matter, Henry?
> B: Look at my new cellphone.
> G: Oh, your phone screen has a crack. Did you drop it?
> B: Yes. I dropped it on the way here. I'm so upset!
> G: I think you should get a phone case. It will protect your phone.
> B: Okay. I'll (A)_____ one.

08 다음 영영풀이에 해당하는 단어를 대화에서 찾아 쓰시오.

> to keep someone or something safe from harm, damage, or illness

➡ _____

09 빈칸 (A)에 알맞은 단어를 대화에서 찾아 쓰시오.

➡ _____

[10~13] 다음 대화를 읽고 물음에 답하시오.

> G: What does your shirt say?
> B: Oh, this? (①) It says "No Cellphone (A)[during / for] 24 Hours."
> G: No Cellphone? Why? (②)
> B: We (B)[depend on / don't depend on] our phones too much these days.
> G: That's true. (③) How ⓐ_____ will you do this?
> B: I'm planning on doing it once a month, but I'm not sure.
> G: (④) Then, decide how ⓑ_____ you should do it.
> B: Okay. (⑤) I'm going to keep a diary of what I did (C)[without / with] my phone for 24 hours. You should try it, too.
> G: I'll think about it. (you, with, make, it, sure, keep, up)
> B: I plan to. After I do it, I'll talk about my experience in class.

10 위 대화의 ①~⑤ 중 주어진 문장이 들어갈 알맞은 곳은?

Try it first.

①   ②   ③   ④   ⑤

11 위 대화의 (A)~(C)에 적절한 말을 골라 쓰시오.

➡ _____

12 위 대화의 ⓐ와 ⓑ에 공통으로 들어갈 단어를 쓰시오.

➡ _____

13 위 대화의 괄호 안에 주어진 단어를 알맞게 배열하시오.

➡ _____

14 다음 대화의 빈칸에 들어갈 말로 알맞은 것은?

> M: What do you need?
> W: I need a chair _____.

① sit   ② sitting
③ to sit   ④ to sit on
⑤ to sitting

15 다음 빈칸에 들어갈 말로 알맞은 것은?

> Margaret had her son _____ his room.

① clean   ② cleans
③ cleaned   ④ to clean
⑤ cleaning

16 다음 중 어법상 어색한 부분을 바르게 고쳐 다시 쓰시오.

(1) It makes your eyes to feel tired and dry to read small letters.

➡ _____

(2) They had a big factory build at the top of the hill.

➡ _____

(3) There was somebody to meet important there.

➡ _____

(4) Olivia has few friends to play.

➡ _____

(5) Mike had his computer steal.

➡ _____

17 다음 중 어법상 어색한 것을 고르시오.

① My mom made me wash the dishes.
② There is a small pool to swim.
③ I want to bring some books to read.
④ My dad wouldn't let me swim in the lake.
⑤ I want to have something spicy to eat.

[18~19] 다음 글을 읽고 물음에 답하시오.

Seongmin cannot take his hands ___ⓐ___ his smartphone all day long. He does not know that using a smartphone too much can cause health problems. Are you a heavy user ___ⓑ___ your smartphone like Seongmin? ⓒ만약 그렇다면, here are some tips to protect your health.

18 위 글의 빈칸 ⓐ와 ⓑ에 들어갈 알맞은 말을 쓰시오.

➡ ⓐ _____ ⓑ _____

19 위 글의 밑줄 친 ⓒ의 우리말을 두 단어로 쓰시오.

➡ _____

[20~21] 다음 글을 읽고 물음에 답하시오.

Watch your neck and back. When you read on your smartphone, you usually bend your neck. This "text neck" pose increases the pressure on your neck and back. The best way to prevent this pressure is ⓐto bring the phone up to the level of your eyes.

20 다음 그림을 참조하여 빈칸 (A)와 (B)에 알맞은 단어를 넣어, 본문의 마지막 부분을 완성하시오.

Another way is to lower your (A)_____ instead of bending your (B)_____.

21 아래 보기에서 위 글의 밑줄 친 ⓐto bring과 to부정사의 용법이 같은 것의 개수를 고르시오.

보기
① It is difficult to know oneself.
② I have no house to live in.
③ I got up early to catch the train.
④ This water is not good to drink.
⑤ He began to read the book.

① 1개 ② 2개 ③ 3개 ④ 4개 ⑤ 5개

[22~23] 다음 글을 읽고 물음에 답하시오.

Give your eyes a break. It makes your eyes feel tired and dry to read small letters on a smartphone for a long time. ⓐUsing a smartphone in the dark or in a moving car makes this problem worse. To avoid this, give your eyes a break from time to time. Follow the 20-20-20 rules: Every 20 minutes, take a 20-second break and look at something at least 20 feet away. Also, blink your eyes often. This will keep your eyes from becoming dry.

22 위 글의 제목으로 알맞은 것을 고르시오.

① How about Giving Your Eyes a Break?
② Read Small Letters on a Smartphone!
③ Don't Use a Smartphone in the Car
④ The Difficulty of Following 20-20-20 Rules
⑤ How to Blink Your Eyes Effectively

23 위 글의 밑줄 친 ⓐ와 문장의 형식이 다른 것을 고르시오.

① She found the box empty.
② You should keep your room clean.
③ The news made her happy.
④ I found this book easily.
⑤ Please leave the door open.

[24~25] 다음 글을 읽고 물음에 답하시오.

Do you text a lot ①on your smartphone? Texting ②for a long time can hurt your fingers and wrists. Try these exercises. They will help reduce the pain ③in your fingers and wrists.
Pull on each finger of each hand.
Put the backs of your hands together ④by your arms out in front of you.

But remember. The best tip to prevent these health problems is to use your smartphone less. Give yourself some rest ⑤from your smartphone.

24 위 글의 밑줄 친 ①~⑤ 중 쓰임이 어색한 전치사를 찾아 고치시오.

➡ _____

25 위 글의 내용과 일치하지 <u>않는</u> 것은?

① 오랫동안 문자 메시지를 보내는 것은 손가락과 손목을 상하게 할 수 있다.
② 손가락과 손목의 통증을 줄이는 데 도움을 주는 운동이 있다.
③ 팔을 여러분 앞에서 벌린 채로 손바닥을 마주 놓아야 한다.
④ 스마트폰으로 인한 건강 문제를 예방하는 가장 좋은 방법은 스마트폰을 덜 사용하는 것이다.
⑤ 자신에게 스마트폰으로부터 약간의 휴식을 주어야 한다.

Lesson

3

The School Club Activity Day

🐦 의사소통 기능

- 능력 여부 묻기
  A: I don't know how to swim. Do you know how to?
  B: Yes, I can teach you.
- 좋아하는 것 표현하기
  A: What do you enjoy doing when you have free time?
  B: I enjoy painting pictures of people in the park.

🐦 언어 형식

- 의문사 + to부정사
  We also teach children **how to play** musical instruments as a service to our community.

- 주격 관계대명사
  Anyone **who** likes to paint can join.

교과서
Words & Expressions

Key Words

- **activity** [æktívəti] 명 활동
- **actually** [ǽktʃuəli] 부 실제로, 사실은
- **bake** [beik] 동 (빵 등을) 굽다
- **bit** [bit] 명 조금, 한 조각[가지], 부분
- **bright** [brait] 형 밝은, 똑똑한
- **clothes** [klouz] 명 옷, 의상
- **club** [klʌb] 명 동아리, 클럽
- **concert** [ká:nsərt] 명 연주회
- **cook** [kuk] 동 요리하다 명 요리사
- **cooking** [kúkiŋ] 명 요리, 음식
- **dolphin** [dálfin] 명 돌고래
- **doughnut** [dóunət] 명 도넛
- **drone** [droun] 명 무인 비행기
- **easy** [í:zi] 형 쉬운
- **elementary school** 초등학교
- **experience** [ikspíəriəns] 명 경험, 경력
- **fly** [flai] 동 (항공기, 우주선, 인공위성 등을) 조종하다, 날게 하다
- **free time** 여가 시간
- **garden** [gá:rdn] 명 정원
- **get** [get] 동 사다, 획득하다
- **grow** [grou] 동 (동식물을) 기르다, 자라다
- **hold** [hould] 동 (모임, 식 등을) 개최하다
- **however** [hauévər] 부 그러나, 하지만

- **interest** [íntərəst] 명 관심 동 ~의 관심[흥미]을 끌다
- **introduce** [intrədjú:s] 동 소개하다
- **join** [dʒɔin] 동 참여하다, 가입하다
- **leader** [lí:dər] 명 지도자, 대표
- **library** [láibrèri] 도서관
- **main gate** 정문
- **musical instrument** 악기
- **neighbor** [néibər] 명 이웃
- **neighborhood** [néibərhùd] 명 동네, (도시 내의 한 단위) 지역
- **note** [nout] 명 음, 음표
- **opportunity** [àpərtjú:nəti] 명 기회
- **orchestra** [ɔ́:rkəstrə] 명 오케스트라, 교향악단
- **own** [oun] 형 (소유격 다음에서 강조어로 쓰여) 자기 자신의
- **practice** [prǽktis] 명 연습 동 연습하다
- **present** [préznt] 명 선물 형 참석한
- **project** [prádʒekt] 명 사업, 계획
- **service** [sɔ́:rvis] 명 봉사, 유익한[전문적인] 활동
- **several** [sévərəl] 형 몇몇의
- **Spanish** [spǽniʃ] 명 스페인어 형 스페인의
- **vegetable** [védʒətəbl] 명 채소
- **volunteer** [vàləntíər] 동 봉사하다
- **walk** [wɔːk] 동 (사람 · 동물을) 걷게 하다

Key Expressions

- **a bit**: 조금
- **a little bit**: 아주 조금
- **as a result**: 결과적으로
- **ask for help**: 도움을 청하다
- **at first**: 처음에
- **at night**: 밤에
- **be good at**: ~을 잘하다
- **change into**: ~로 변화시키다[바꾸다]
- **enjoy+-ing**: ~하는 것을 즐기다
- **fall into**: ~에 빠지다

- **get better**: (병 · 상황 등이) 나아지다
- **have a great time**: 좋은 시간을 보내다
- **how to**+동사원형: ~하는 방법
- **let**+목적어+동사원형: …가 ~하게 하다
- **look at**: ~을 보다
- **look for**: ~을 찾다
- **participate in**: ~에 참여하다
- **thank for**: ~에 대해 감사하다
- **watch out (for)** (~에 대해서) 조심하다
- **would like to** +동사원형: ~하고 싶다

Word Power

※ 서로 반대되는 뜻을 가진 단어
- bright(밝은) ↔ dark(어두운)
- easy(쉬운) ↔ difficult(어려운)

※ 서로 비슷한 뜻을 가진 단어
- actually(실제로, 사실은) : really (정말로, 실제로)
- bright(총명한) : clever(영리한)
- get(사다, 획득하다) : obtain(획득하다), gain(얻다, 입수하다)
- grow((식물을) 재배하다) : farm(경작하다)
- leader(지도자, 대표) : chief(장, 우두머리)
- practice(연습) : training(훈련), exercise(연습)
- project(사업, 계획) : plan(계획)
- several(몇몇의) : a few(약간의), some(조금의)
- foolish(어리석은) : stupid(어리석은)
- join(참여하다, 가입하다) : enter(~에 들어가다)
- opportunity(기회) : chance(기회)
- present(선물) : gift(선물)

English Dictionary

- **a bit** 조금, 약간
  → slightly or to a small degree(= a little)
  약간, 적은 정도로
- **bake** (빵 등을) 굽다
  → to cook something using dry heat, in an oven
  오븐 안에서 건조한 열을 사용하여 무언가를 요리하다
- **bright** 밝은
  → strong and easy to see
  강렬하며 쉽게 보이는
- **club** 동아리
  → organization for people who share a particular interest or enjoy similar activities, or a group of people who meet together to do something they are interested in
  특정한 흥미를 공유하거나 비슷한 활동을 즐기는 사람들을 위한 단체 또는 그들이 관심 있는 무언가를 위해서 같이 만나는 사람들의 모임
- **drone** 무인 비행기
  → aircraft that does not have a pilot, but is operated by radio
  조종사가 없지만 무선으로 작동되는 비행기
- **garden** 정원
  → a part of the area next to a house, which has plants and flowers in it
  집 옆에 식물과 꽃이 있는 지역의 일부
- **grow** 자라다
  → to develop or increase in size or length
  크기나 길이가 발달하거나 증가하다
- **hold** (모임·식 등을) 개최하다
  → to have a meeting, party, election etc in a particular place or at a particular time
  회의, 파티, 선거 등을 특정한 장소 또는 특정한 시간에 가지다
- **join** 참여하다, 가입하다
  → 1. to become a member of an organization, society, or group

조직, 사회 또는 그룹의 구성원이 되다
2. to begin to take part in an activity that other people are involved in
다른 사람들이 관련된 활동에 참여하기 시작하다
- **leader** 지도자, 대표
  → the person who directs or controls a group, organization, country, etc.
  그룹, 조직, 국가 등을 총괄하거나 통제하는 사람
- **musical instrument** 악기
  → something that you use for playing music, such as a piano or guitar
  피아노나 기타와 같은 음악을 연주하기 위해 사용하는 어떤 것
- **neighbor** 이웃
  → someone who lives next to you or near you
  당신의 옆이나 근처에 사는 어떤 사람
- **neighborhood** 인근, 이웃 사람들, 동네
  → the area around you or around a particular place, or the people who live there
  당신 또는 특정한 장소 주변의 지역 또는 거기에 사는 사람들
- **opportunity** 기회
  → a chance to do something or an occasion when it is easy for you to do something
  무엇인가를 할 기회 또는 당신이 무엇인가 하는 것이 쉬운 때
- **orchestra** 오케스트라, 교향악단
  → a large group of musicians playing many different kinds of instruments and led by a conductor
  많은 여러 종류의 악기를 연주하는 음악가들과 지휘자에 의해 지휘되는 큰 규모의 집단
- **practice** 연습하다
  → to do something regularly in order to do it better
  어떤 것을 더 잘하기 위해서 규칙적으로 그것을 하다
- **walk** (동물을) 걷게 하다
  → to take a dog for a walk for exercise
  개를 운동시키기 위해 산책시키다

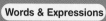

01 다음 짝지어진 두 단어의 관계가 같도록 빈칸에 알맞은 단어를 쓰시오.

> increase : decrease – difficult : _____

① easy   ② hard   ③ different

④ bright   ⑤ early

[02~03] 다음 빈칸에 들어갈 말로 적절한 것은?

02

> I'm _____ some bread in an oven.

① baking   ② eating   ③ biting

④ breaking   ⑤ buying

03

> They use organic methods of _____ vegetables.

① growing   ② flying

③ forgetting   ④ repairing

⑤ falling

04 다음 밑줄 친 부분과 의미가 가장 가까운 것을 고르시오.

> It was a valuable <u>opportunity</u> to see how rich people lived.

① chance   ② experience   ③ effort

④ effect   ⑤ situation

05 서답형 다음 영영 풀이에 해당하는 단어를 주어진 철자로 시작하여 쓰시오.

> someone who lives next to you or near you

➡ n_____

06 서답형 다음 괄호 안의 단어를 문맥에 맞게 알맞은 형태로 고쳐 쓰시오.

> She is the _____ of the most powerful country in Europe. (lead)

07 다음 대화의 빈칸에 들어갈 말로 적절한 것은?

> A: What festival is the most famous in New York?
> B: It is Halloween festival. New York City _____ the largest Halloween parade in the U.S. every year.

① grows   ② finds   ③ falls

④ takes   ⑤ holds

08 다음 중 밑줄 친 부분의 뜻풀이가 바르지 <u>않은</u> 것은?

① What's the most popular free time <u>activity</u> for teenagers? (활동)

② I really miss your <u>cooking</u>. (요리)

③ She doesn't like <u>bright</u> colors. (밝은)

④ He plays the piano perfectly even though he cannot read a single <u>note</u>. (메모)

⑤ Korea has already won <u>several</u> medals. (몇 개의)

09 서답형 다음 우리말에 맞게 빈칸에 알맞은 말을 쓰시오.

> Anyone _____ loves books _____
> _____ our event! (책을 좋아하는 사람은 누구라도 우리의 행사에 참여할 수 있어요!)

01 다음 〈보기〉와 같은 관계가 되도록 빈칸에 주어진 철자로 알맞은 말을 쓰시오.

┌─── 보기 ───
happy – pleased
└────────────

(1) gain – g_____
(2) gift – p_____

[02~03] 다음 빈칸에 공통으로 들어갈 말을 쓰시오. (대·소문자 무시)

02
• The more you _____, the more you want.
• _____ a great time before the new semester begins!

03
• _____ can I join this club?
• I want to learn _____ to do that.

04 다음 빈칸에 알맞은 어구를 〈보기〉에서 골라 쓰시오. (형태 변화 가능)

┌─── 보기 ───
introduce / concert / doughnut / dolphin
└────────────

(1) Let me _____ my friend Caden to you.
(2) I saw many _____ swimming in the sea.
(3) You should fry a _____ for 1 or 2 minutes.
(4) The orchestra held a _____ at Seoul Arts Center to help children in North Korea.

05 다음 괄호 안의 단어를 문맥에 맞게 알맞은 형태로 고쳐 쓰시오.

(1) What kind of club _____ do you like? (act)
(2) This _____ is great for shopping. (neighbor)

06 다음 주어진 우리말에 맞게 빈칸을 채우시오. (철자가 주어진 것도 있음)

(1) 나는 항상 싼 옷을 산다.
   ➡ I always buy cheap c_____.
(2) 어떻게 하면 우리의 제품을 많은 사람들에게 소개할 수 있을까요?
   ➡ How can we _____ our products to a lot of people?
(3) 나는 당신의 기사를 많은 흥미를 가지고 읽었다.
   ➡ I read your article with great _____.
(4) 너는 많은 신선한 과일과 야채를 먹어야 한다.
   ➡ You must eat a lot of fresh fruit and _____.

07 다음 우리말과 같은 뜻이 되도록 주어진 단어를 알맞은 순서로 배열하시오.

┌────────────────────────
내가 이 동아리에 가입한다면, 나는 매우 열심히 연습할 것이다. (if, club, very, join, I, I, this, practice, will, hard)
└────────────────────────

➡ _____

Conversation

교과서

1 능력 여부 묻기

> **A** I don't know how to swim. Do you know how to? 나는 수영하는 법을 알지 못해. 너는 방법을 알고 있니?
>
> **B** Yes, I can teach you. 응. 내가 가르쳐 줄 수 있어.

■ 'how to+동사원형'은 '~하는 방법, 어떻게 ~하는지'의 의미로, 'Do you know how to + 동사원형 ~?' 을 이용해 상대방의 능력이나 무언가를 하는 방법에 대해 물을 수 있다.

능력 여부 묻기

- Do you know how to + 동사원형 ~?
- Can you + 동사원형 ~?

능력 여부 대답하기

- 긍정: Yes, I do[can]./ Of course I do[can].
- 부정: No, I don't./ No, I can't.

■ '의문사+to부정사'는 명사구로 문장에서 주어, 목적어, 보어로 쓰일 수 있다. 여기에 사용될 수 있는 의문사는 what, when, where, how, which, whom 등이 있다.

의문사+to부정사

- what to부정사: 무엇을 ~할지
- where to부정사: 어디에서 ~할지
- how to부정사: 어떻게 ~할지, ~하는 방법
- when to부정사: 언제 ~할지
- which to부정사: 어느 것을 ~할지
- whom to부정사: 누구를 ~할지

■ '의문사+to부정사'는 '의문사+주어+should 동사원형'으로 바꾸어 쓸 수 있다.
  Tell me how to do it. (내가 그것을 어떻게 해야 할지 말해 주세요.)
  = Tell me how I should do it.

핵심 Check

1. 우리말과 일치하도록 빈칸에 알맞은 말을 쓰시오.

   He taught me _____ _____ _____ my new cellphone.

   (그는 나에게 새 휴대 전화를 사용하는 법을 가르쳐 주었다.)

2. 우리말과 일치하도록 주어진 단어를 배열하여 문장을 완성하시오.

   _____ (learn, pictures, I, to, good, want,

   how, take, to) (나는 좋은 사진을 찍는 법을 배우고 싶다.)

2 좋아하는 것 표현하기

> **A** What do you enjoy doing when you have free time? 너는 여가 시간에 뭐 하는 것을 즐기니?
> **B** I enjoy painting pictures of people in the park. 나는 공원에서 사람들을 그리는 것을 즐겨.

■ 'I enjoy 동명사'는 '나는 ~하는 것을 즐긴다.'는 의미로 자신이 좋아하는 것을 나타내는 표현이다. 주로 취미 등을 묻는 'What do you enjoy doing when you have free time?', 'What do you usually do in your free time?' 등에 대한 응답으로 쓰인다.

좋아하는 것 표현하기

- I enjoy 동명사 ~.
- I like 동명사/to부정사 ~.
- I love 동명사/to부정사 ~.

■ 동사를 주어, 목적어, 보어의 자리에 쓰기 위해서 동명사 또는 to부정사를 사용할 수 있다. 하지만, 특정한 동사의 목적어로 동명사나 to부정사가 사용될 때는 그 동사의 종류에 따라 동명사를 사용할지, 아니면 to부정사를 사용할지 잘 선택해야 한다.

■ enjoy는 동명사를 목적어로 사용할 수 있고, want는 to부정사를 목적어로 사용한다. like와 love는 동명사와 to부정사 둘 다 목적어로 사용할 수 있다.

핵심 Check

3. 다음 대화의 우리말과 일치하도록 빈칸에 알맞은 말을 쓰시오.

   A: _____ enjoy _____ when you have _____ ?

   (너는 여가 시간에 뭐 하는 것을 즐기니?)

   B: _____. (나는 음악을 듣는 것을 즐겨.)

4. 다음 그림을 보고, 주어진 단어를 사용하여 빈칸을 완성하시오.

   A: What do you like to do on weekends?

   B: _____. (enjoy)

Listen & Speak 1 A

> G: ❶Do you know ❷how to make a paper cat?
>
> B: Of course. ❸It's easy.

G: 종이 고양이 만드는 법을 알고 있니?
B: 물론이지. 그건 쉬워.

❶ 'Do you know ~?'는 어떤 것을 아는지 질문할 때 사용한다. 비슷한 의미로 'Can you tell me ~?'를 대신 사용할 수 있다.
❷ how to부정사: 어떻게 ~할지, ~하는 방법   ❸ 인칭대명사 It은 how to make a paper cat을 가리킨다.

Check(√) True or False

(1) The boy knows how to make a paper cat. T ☐ F ☐

(2) The way to make a paper cat is not difficult. T ☐ F ☐

 Listen & Speak 1 B-1

> G: I heard ❶you went to Yuna's violin concert yesterday. ❷How was it?
>
> B: It was great. ❸I hope I can play the violin ❹like her someday.
>
> G: I didn't know ❺you knew how to play the violin.
>
> B: I can, but ❻I'm not good at it yet.

G: 어제 유나의 바이올린 콘서트에 갔다고 들었어. 어땠니?
B: 좋았어. 나도 언젠가 그녀처럼 바이올린을 연주할 수 있기를 바라.
G: 나는 네가 바이올린 연주하는 법을 아는지 몰랐어.
B: 할 수 있어. 그러나 아직 잘하지는 못해.

❶ heard와 you 사이에 명사절을 이끄는 접속사 that이 생략되어 있다. 'you went to Yuna's violin concert yesterday'는 heard의 목적어로 사용되었다.
❷ 과거의 경험에 대해 묻고자 할 때 'How was ~?' 표현을 사용한다. 과거의 경험에 대한 답변이 되어야 하므로 대답의 동사도 과거형을 사용한다. 여기서 it은 Yuna's violin concert를 가리킨다.
❸ 'I hope I can 동사원형 ~.'은 자신이 어떤 것을 할 수 있기를 희망하거나 기대를 한다는 표현이다.
❹ like: (전치사) ~처럼, ~와 같이
❺ know와 you 사이에 명사절을 이끄는 접속사 that이 생략되어 있다. how to부정사: 어떻게 ~할지, ~하는 방법
❻ be good at: ~을 잘하다

Check(√) True or False

(3) Yuna is good at playing the violin. T ☐ F ☐

(4) The girl knew that the boy knew how to play the violin. T ☐ F ☐

 Listen & Speak 1 B-2

> G: ❶Look at these pictures. I ❷grew these vegetables ❸myself. I have my ❹own garden.
>
> B: Cool! Do you know how to cook the vegetables you grow, too?
>
> G: Yes, my grandmother ❺taught me.

G: 이 사진들 좀 봐. 나는 이 채소들을 직접 길렀어. 나는 내 정원이 있어.
B: 멋지다! 네가 재배한 채소로 요리하는 법도 아니?
G: 응, 할머니께서 내게 가르쳐 주셨어.

❶ look at: ~을 보다 pictures가 복수형이므로, this가 아닌 these를 사용한다.
❷ grew는 grow의 과거형이다. grow: [식물을] 재배하다
❸ 재귀대명사의 강조 용법으로 주어 'I'를 강조하고 있다.
❹ own은 소유격 다음에서 강조어로 사용한다. own: 자기 자신의, 직접 ~한
❺ taught는 teach의 과거형 동사이다.

Check(√) True or False

(5) In the pictures, there are vegetables. T ☐ F ☐

(6) The girl doesn't know how to cook the vegetables. T ☐ F ☐

Listen & Speak 2 A

A: Do you enjoy ❶looking at the stars at night?

G: Yes, I ❷love doing that.

❶ enjoy는 동명사를 목적어로 취하는 동사이다. look at: ~을 보다 at night: 밤에

❷ love는 목적어로 동명사와 to부정사를 취할 수 있다. love doing it = love to do it / doing that=looking at the stars

Listen & Speak 2 B-1

B: Do you ❶enjoy reading books, Yumi?

G: Yes, I love reading science books. ❷How about you?

B: I love reading books, too.

G: Then, ❸let's go to the library ❹after school today.

❶ enjoy(~을 즐기다)를 사용해서 좋아하는 것을 말할 수 있다. enjoy는 목적어로 동명사를 취하는 동사로 reading을 사용해야 한다.

❷ 'How about you?'는 '너는 어때?'라고 묻는 내용이다. 'What about you?'로 바꿔 쓸 수 있다.

❸ 'Let's+동사원형'은 '~하자'라는 의미로, 제안하는 말을 할 때 쓴다. go to 장소: ~에 가다

❹ after school: 방과 후에

Listen & Speak 2 B-2

G: ❶What did you do on the weekend, Minsu?

B: ❷I made breakfast ❸for my family.

G: Do you enjoy cooking?

B: Yes, I'm a good ❹cook! My family loves my ❺cooking.

❶ 과거에 무엇을 했는지 묻고 싶을 때에는 What did you do?라고 묻는다. 특정한 때를 넣어 어떤 날에 무엇을 했냐고 물을 수도 있다.

❷ 과거에 무엇을 했는지 묻는 질문에 대한 대답이므로, 과거형 동사를 사용해야 한다.

❸ make는 간접목적어를 직접목적어 뒤로 보낼 때 for를 붙인다.

❹ cook: (동) 요리하다 (명) 요리사 / 이 문장에서는 명사로 쓰였다.

❺ cooking: 요리, 음식

Listen & Speak 2 B-3

B: Jiyun, that's a pretty backpack! Where did you ❶get it?

G: My sister made ❷it for me.

B: Wow! She's a really good designer.

G: Yes, she is. And she enjoys making ❸clothes, too.

❶ get: 얻다, 사다

❷ it은 앞에 나온 a backpack을 가리킨다.

❸ clothes: 옷, 의상 cloth: 천, 옷감 cloths: 옷감들

Real-Life Zone A

B: Hello, Kate. I'm Hamin, the ❶leader of the Nanum Orchestra. ❷Thank you for your interest in our club.

G: Hi. Nice to meet you.

B: You play the violin? ❸When did you start playing the violin?

G: I started learning ❹how to play the violin when I was ten.

B: ❺Do you have any experience playing in a group?

G: Yes. Actually, I was a member of an orchestra ❻when I was in elementary school.

B: Great. We also ❼volunteer to teach children. Do you enjoy teaching others?

G: I have no experience teaching others. But I enjoy working with people, so ❽I'd like to try.

B: Good. I think we'll have a great time playing together. Welcome to the Nanum Orchestra.

❶ leader: 지도자, 대표

❷ 'Thank you for ~.'는 감사를 표현하는 말로 for 다음에 감사의 이유나 원인이 나온다. interest: 관심

❸ 'When did you 동사원형 ~?'은 '너 언제 ~했니?'의 의미로, 과거에 언제 어떠한 일을 했는지 묻는 질문이다.

❹ how to부정사: 어떻게 ~할지, ~하는 방법

❺ Do you have any experience~?는 어떤 일을 한 경험이 있는지 물을 때 쓰인다.

❻ when: (접) ~할 때

❼ volunteer: 자원봉사하다

❽ 'I'd'는 'I would'를 줄여서 표현한 것이다. would like to 동사원형: ~하고 싶다

● 다음 우리말과 일치하도록 빈칸에 알맞은 말을 쓰시오.

Listen & Speak 1 A

A: Do you _____ _____ _____ make a paper cat?

B: Of course. It's easy.

Listen & Speak 1 B

1. G: I _____ _____ _____ _____ Yuna's violin concert
   yesterday. _____ was it?

   B: It was great. _____ _____ _____ _____ _____ the
   violin like her someday.

   G: I didn't know you _____ _____ _____ _____
   _____ _____.

   B: I can, but I'm not _____ _____ it yet.

2. G: Look _____ these pictures. I _____ these vegetables
   _____. I have my _____ garden.

   B: Cool! Do you know _____ _____ _____ the vegetables
   you grow, too?

   G: Yes, my grandmother _____ me.

Listen & Speak 2 A

A: Do you enjoy _____ _____ the stars _____ _____?

G: Yes, I love doing that.

Listen & Speak 2 B

1. B: _____ _____ _____ reading books, Yumi?

   G: Yes, I _____ _____ science books. How _____ you?

   B: I love _____ books, too.

   G: Then, let's _____ to _____ _____ after school today.

2. G: _____ _____ _____ _____ on the weekend, Minsu?

   B: I _____ breakfast for my family.

   G: _____ _____ _____ _____ _____?

   B: Yes, I'm a good _____! My family loves my _____.

3. **B:** Jiyun, that's a pretty backpack! _____ did you _____ it?

   G: My sister _____ _____ _____ _____.

   B: Wow! She's a really good _____.

   G: Yes, she is. And she _____ _____ _____, too.

Real-Life Zone A

B: Hello, Kate. I'm Hamin, _____ _____ of the Nanum Orchestra. Thank you for your _____ in our club.

G: Hi. Nice to meet you.

B: You play the violin? _____ _____ _____ _____ _____ _____ the violin?

G: I started learning _____ _____ _____ _____ _____ I was ten.

B: Do you have any _____ _____ in a group?

G: Yes. Actually, I was a member of _____ _____ _____ I was in _____ school.

B: Great. We also _____ _____ _____ children. _____ _____ _____ _____ others?

G: I have no _____ teaching others. But I _____ _____ _____ people, so I'd like to try.

B: Good. I think we'll _____ a great time playing together. Welcome to the Nanum Orchestra.

Wrap Up

B: These cookies _____ so _____. Did you make them?

G: Yes. I _____ _____ _____ yesterday. I enjoy _____. I'm _____ _____ make doughnuts this Saturday.

B: Oh, I _____ _____ _____ _____ _____ _____ doughnuts. Is it difficult?

G: Not _____ all. You can come to my house and join me if you want.

B: Thanks, Bora. What _____ should I come?

G: At 2:00.

B: _____ good. _____ you then.

3. B: 지윤아, 그거 예쁜 배낭이네! 어디서 샀어?
   G: 언니가 내게 만들어 준 거야.
   B: 와! 그녀는 정말 훌륭한 디자이너구나.
   G: 응, 그래. 그리고 그녀는 옷 만드는 것도 즐겨.

B: 안녕, 케이트. 나는 나눔 오케스트라의 대표 하민이야. 우리 동아리에 관심을 가져줘서 고마워.
G: 안녕. 만나서 반가워.
B: 너는 바이올린을 연주하니? 언제 바이올린 연주를 시작했니?
G: 10살 때 바이올린을 연주하는 법을 배우기 시작했어.
B: 그룹에서 연주해 본 경험이 있니?
G: 응. 사실 나는 초등학교 때 오케스트라 단원이었어.
B: 좋아. 우리는 자원봉사로 아이들도 가르쳐. 다른 사람들을 가르치는 것을 즐기니?
G: 나는 다른 사람들을 가르친 경험이 없어. 그러나 나는 사람들과 일하는 것을 즐겨, 그래서 나는 해보고 싶어.
B: 좋아. 나는 우리가 함께 연주하며 좋은 시간을 보낼 것이라고 생각해. 나눔 오케스트라에 온 걸 환영해.

B: 이 쿠키들은 정말 맛있어 보여. 네가 만들었니?
G: 응. 어제 내가 직접 만들었어. 나는 제빵을 즐겨. 이번 주 토요일에 도넛을 만들 예정이야.
B: 오, 나는 도넛 만드는 법을 배우고 싶어. 그건 어렵니?
G: 전혀 아니야. 네가 원한다면 우리 집에 와서 같이 해도 돼.
B: 고마워, 보라야. 내가 몇 시에 가야 해?
G: 2시에.
B: 좋아. 그때 보자.

[01~02] 다음 대화의 빈칸에 알맞은 말은?

01

> A: What do you enjoy doing when you have free time?
> B: _____

① I went shopping.
② I want to have free time.
③ I will go to the movie with my friends.
④ I enjoy painting pictures of people in the park.
⑤ I don't like to play computer games.

02

> A: Do you know _____?
> B: Of course. It's easy.

① how to make a paper cat
② what to make a paper cat
③ making a paper cat
④ how making a paper cat
⑤ that I can make a paper cat

03 다음 주어진 문장과 의미하는 것이 같은 문장을 고르시오.

> Do you know how to make doughnuts?

① Do you want to make doughnuts?
② Are you practicing making doughnuts?
③ Do you mind making doughnuts?
④ Can you make doughnuts?
⑤ Why don't you make doughnuts?

04 다음 문장의 빈칸에 알맞은 것을 모두 고르시오.

> G: Look at these pictures. I grew these vegetables myself. I have
>   my own garden.
> B: Cool! Do you know how to cook the vegetables you grow, too?
> G: (A)_____. My grandmother taught me.

① Yes, I do   ② No, I can't   ③ Of course
④ Not at all   ⑤ Yes, I am

[01~03] 다음 대화를 읽고 물음에 답하시오.

G: I heard you went to Yuna's violin concert yesterday. (①)

B: It was great. (②) I hope I can play the violin (A)like her someday. (③)

G: I didn't know you knew how to play the violin. (④)

B: I can, but I'm not good at it yet. (⑤)

01 위 대화의 ①~⑤ 중 다음 주어진 말이 들어갈 알맞은 곳은?

How was it?

①　　　②　　　③　　　④　　　⑤

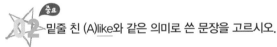 밑줄 친 (A)like와 같은 의미로 쓴 문장을 고르시오.

① I don't know why he doesn't like me.

② I don't like to study English.

③ I could dance like that!

④ Why do you like to climb the mountain?

⑤ She likes to watch TV all day.

03 위 대화의 내용과 일치하지 <u>않는</u> 것은?

① The boy thinks that Yuna's violin concert was great.

② The boy thinks he is good at playing the violin.

③ The boy went to Yuna's violin concert.

④ Yuna's violin concert was held yesterday.

⑤ The boy knows how to play the violin.

04 다음 대화의 빈칸에 알맞은 말은?

A: I don't know how to speak Spanish.
_____
B: Yes, I can teach you.

① Do you know how to?

② Why don't we learn to speak Spanish?

③ What are you going to speak?

④ How do you say this in Spanish?

⑤ What are you good at?

05 다음 중 짝지어진 대화가 <u>어색한</u> 것은?

① A: Do you know how to use the washing machine?
   B: Yes. I do.

② A: Do you know how to play the guitar?
   B: No, I don't.

③ A: What do you do after school?
   B: I enjoy drawing cartoons.

④ A: What do you like to do in your free time?
   B: I enjoy reading books. How about you?

⑤ A: Do you know how to take pictures?
   B: Of course I am.

서답형
06 (A)와 (B)에 주어진 단어를 이용해 빈칸에 들어갈 수 있는 말을 쓰시오.

A: Do you enjoy (A)_____(look) at the stars at night?

G: Yes, I love (B)_____(do) that.

[07~09] 다음 대화를 읽고 물음에 답하시오.

B: Jiyun, that's a pretty backpack! (①)
G: (②) My sister made it for me. (③)
B: Wow! She's a really good designer. (④)
G: (A)_____ (⑤) And she enjoys making clothes, too.

 07 위 대화의 ①~⑤ 중 다음 주어진 말이 들어갈 알맞은 곳은?

> Where did you get it?

①　　②　　③　　④　　⑤

⭐ 중요
08 빈칸 (A)에 알맞은 말을 고르시오.

① Yes, she does.　② Yes, she can.
③ No, she isn't.　④ No, she doesn't.
⑤ Yes, she is.

09 위 대화의 내용과 일치하지 않는 것은?

① Jiyun's sister made her a backpack.
② Jiyun knows how to make a backpack.
③ Jiyun's sister is a good designer.
④ Jiyun's sister enjoys making clothes.
⑤ Jiyun has a sister.

[10~13] 다음 대화를 읽고 물음에 답하시오.

B: Hello, Kate. I'm Hamin, the leader of the Nanum Orchestra. Thank you for your interest in our club.
G: Hi. Nice to meet you.
B: You play the violin? When did you start playing the violin? (①)
G: (the, I, I, ten, started, when, how, learning, was, play, violin, to)

B: Do you have any experience playing (A) [alone / in a group]? (②)
G: Yes. Actually, I was a member of an orchestra when I was in elementary school.
B: Great. (③) Do you enjoy teaching others?
G: I have (B)[no experience / many experiences] teaching others. (④) But I enjoy working with people, so I'd like to try.
B: (⑤) Good. I think we'll have a great time playing together. Welcome to the Nanum Orchestra.

⭐ 중요
10 위 대화의 ①~⑤ 중 다음 주어진 말이 들어갈 알맞은 곳은?

> We also volunteer to teach children.

①　　②　　③　　④　　⑤

서답형
11 (A)~(B)에 들어갈 말로 적절한 것을 고르시오.

➡ (A) _____ (B) _____

서답형
12 괄호 안에 주어진 어휘를 바르게 배열하여 문장을 완성하시오. (로 시작할 것)

➡ _____

13 위 대화의 내용과 일치하지 않는 것을 고르시오.

① Kate will join the Nanum Orchestra after this conversation.
② Kate is a member of an orchestra now.
③ Kate knows how to play the violin.
④ Hamin is the leader of the Nanum Orchestra.
⑤ Kate and Hamin meet for the first time.

[01~02] 주어진 문장 다음에 이어질 대화의 순서를 바르게 배열하시오.

01

Mina, do you enjoy cooking?

(A) Then why don't you join the cooking club?
(B) Hmm, let me think about it.
(C) Sometimes. I know how to make a pizza.

➡ _____

02

Did you buy that drone?

(A) No, I got it as a present from my parents, but I don't know how to use it. Do you know how to?
(B) Then, I will ask her for help.
(C) No, maybe Jina knows how to do it. She enjoys flying drones.

➡ _____

[03~05] 다음 대화를 읽고 물음에 답하시오.

G: Look __(A)__ these pictures. (B)I grew these vegetables me. I have my own garden.
B: Cool! (C)네가 기르는 채소를 요리하는 법을 아니, too?
G: Yes, my grandmother taught me.

03 빈칸 (A)에 알맞는 전치사를 쓰시오.

➡ _____

04 밑줄 친 (B)에서 어색한 것을 찾아 고치시오.

➡ _____

05 (C)의 밑줄 친 우리말을 주어진 단어를 이용해 영작하시오.

➡ _____

(how, vegetables)

06 밑줄 친 부분에서 어색한 것을 찾아 고치시오. (2개)

A: Do you enjoy looking at the stars at night?
B: Yes, I enjoyed do that.

➡ _____

[07~08] 다음 대화를 읽고 물음에 답하시오.

G: I heard you went to Yuna's violin concert yesterday. How was it?
B: It was great. I hope I can play the violin like her someday.
G: (A)나는 네가 바이올린 연주하는 법을 아는지 몰랐어.
B: I can, but (B)(not, at, yet, I'm, good, it).

07 (A)에 주어진 우리말을 영작하시오. (10 단어)

➡ _____

08 괄호 (B) 안에 주어진 어휘를 알맞게 배열하여 문장을 완성하시오.

➡ _____

Grammar

1 의문사 + to부정사

> We also teach children **how to play** musical instruments as a service to our community. 우리는 지역 사회를 위한 봉사로 아이들에게 악기를 연주하는 법도 가르칩니다.
> I don't know **what to do**. 나는 무엇을 해야 할지 모르겠어.

■ '의문사+to부정사'는 문장 속에서 주어, 목적어, 보어 역할을 하는 명사구로 사용되어 '~해야 할지, ~하는 것이 좋을지'라는 뜻을 나타낸다.

• Please tell me **when to go**. (언제 가야 할지 나에게 말해 줘.)

■ what, which, who, whom, how, when, where 등의 의문사가 사용되지만 why는 쓰지 않는다는 점에 주의한다.

형태	의미	예문
how + to부정사	어떻게 ~할지	He doesn't know how to talk politely.
what + to부정사	무엇을 ~할지	Please tell me what to do next.
when + to부정사	언제 ~할지	I also don't know when to ask him.
where + to부정사	어디에 ~할지	I am not sure where to put the key.

■ '의문사+to부정사'는 '의문사+주어+should/can+동사원형'으로 바꾸어 쓸 수 있다.

• She asked me **whom to meet**. (그녀는 내게 누구를 만나야 할지 물었다.)
  = She asked me whom she should meet.

■ 의문사가 의문형용사로 쓰여 to부정사와의 사이에 명사가 올 수 있다.

• The host usually tells the guests **what time to leave**. (주인은 대개 손님들에게 몇 시에 떠나야 하는지를 말해 준다.)

핵심 Check

1. 다음 우리말과 일치하도록 빈칸에 알맞은 말을 쓰시오.

(1) 나는 그녀에게 무슨 말을 해야 할지 모르겠어.

➡ I don't know _____ _____ say to her.

= I don't know _____ _____ _____ say to her.

(2) 이번 주말에 그를 어디서 만날지 내게 말해줘.

➡ Tell me _____ _____ _____ him this weekend.

= Tell me _____ _____ _____ _____ him this weekend.

② 주격 관계대명사

Anyone **who** likes to paint can join. 그림 그리는 것을 좋아하는 사람은 누구나 가입할 수 있습니다.

She has a cat **which** has brown hair. 그녀는 갈색 털을 가진 고양이를 갖고 있다.

■ 관계대명사는 접속사와 대명사의 역할을 한다. 관계대명사절은 명사를 수식해 주는 절의 한 종류로 관계대명사절이 꾸며 주는 말을 선행사라고 하고 관계대명사는 앞의 선행사와 같은 대상을 가리킨다. 관계대명사절이 되기 전의 문장에서 주어로 쓰였으면 주격 관계대명사로, 소유격으로 쓰였으면 소유격 관계대명사로, 목적격으로 쓰였으면 목적격 관계대명사가 된다. 주격 관계대명사는 관계대명사절에서 주어 역할을 하므로 그 다음에는 동사가 온다.

• Mr. Kim is a farmer. He(=Mr. Kim) grows apples.

= Mr. Kim is a farmer **who**[**that**] grows apples. (주격)

• This is the smartphone. She bought it(=the smartphone) at the shop.

= This is the smartphone **which**[**that**] she bought at the shop. (목적격)

• This is the dress. Its color is blue.

= This is the dress **whose** color is blue. (소유격)

■ 관계대명사는 선행사에 따라 다음과 같이 사용되며, 목적격 관계대명사는 생략할 수 있다.

	주격	소유격	목적격
사람	who/that	whose	whom[who]/that
동물, 사물	which/that	whose/of which	which/that

■ 주격 관계대명사절의 동사는 선행사의 인칭과 수에 일치시킨다.

• I have a friend **who**[**that**] helps me a lot. (나는 나를 많이 도와주는 친구가 있다.)

■ 관계대명사 that은 who, whom과 which 대신 사용할 수 있으며 소유격은 없다. 또한 선행사가 '사람+동물[사물]'인 경우에는 반드시 that을 써야 한다.

• There are a boy and his dog **that** are running in the park. 공원에서 뛰고 있는 소년과 그의 개가 있다.

■ '주격 관계대명사 + be동사'는 생략이 가능하다.

• The boy (**who is**) singing on the stage is my brother. (무대에서 노래하고 있는 소년은 내 동생이다.)

핵심 Check

2. 다음 우리말과 일치하도록 빈칸에 알맞은 말을 쓰시오.

(1) 나는 서울에 살고 있는 친구가 있다.

➡ I have a friend _____ lives in Seoul.

(2) 매우 멋있어 보이는 저 옷 좀 봐.

➡ Look at that dress _____ looks very nice.

01 다음 문장에서 어법상 <u>어색한</u> 부분을 바르게 고쳐 쓰시오.

(1) I can't decide what eating.

_____ ➡ _____

(2) Do you know when go?

_____ ➡ _____

(3) There is a man which is waiting for his bag.

_____ ➡ _____

(4) This is the movie who made me laugh a lot.

_____ ➡ _____

02 다음 중 어법상 <u>어색한</u> 문장을 <u>모두</u> 고르시오.

① Marie Curie is the person who first found radium.
② I lost the watch which my father had given to me.
③ I want to show you some pictures who I took a few days ago.
④ Please show me how do it.
⑤ Will you tell me where to stay in Seoul?

03 다음 우리말에 맞게 주어진 단어를 바르게 배열하시오. (필요하면 어형을 바꿀 것)

(1) 그녀는 내게 무엇을 해야 할지 묻지 않았다.

(she / me / what / do / ask / didn't / to)

➡ _____

(2) Mariel은 어디로 가야 할지 몰랐다.

(where / Mariel / go / know / didn't / to)

➡ _____

(3) Degas는 춤추고 있는 무용수를 그리는 것을 좋아했다.

(Degas / dancers / who / liked / dancing / paint / were / to)

➡ _____

(4) 그는 어제 그 소녀에게 짖은 개를 갖고 있다.

(he / that / dog / girl / yesterday / the / the / barked / has / at)

➡ _____

01 다음 빈칸에 알맞은 것은?

I don't know _____ to do it.

① how　　　　　② what
③ that　　　　　④ whom
⑤ why

02 다음 문장의 빈칸에 들어갈 알맞은 것은?

Look at the boy _____ is dancing.

① which　　　　② who
③ whose　　　　④ whom
⑤ what

03 중요 다음 빈칸에 알맞은 말이 바르게 짝지어진 것은?

• She knows _____ to solve the problem. • Molly is reading the message from Kate _____ arrived yesterday.

① what – which　　② what – who
③ how – which　　④ how – who
⑤ that – that

04 서답형 다음 문장에서 어법상 틀린 부분을 찾아 바르게 고쳐 쓰시오.

The painting is about a party who took place in a small town.

_____ ➡ _____

05 중요 다음 중 어법상 어색한 것은?

① I don't know how to make a paper doll.
② Can you tell me whom to wait for here?
③ We asked him when to start.
④ Morri told us where to go after we finished the work.
⑤ I wanted to know what to do it.

06 다음 중 어법상 올바른 것은?

① This is the book who has many exciting stories.
② Anyone which loves books can join our event!
③ I saw a tree who looked like a big elephant.
④ He is the man that lived next door five years ago.
⑤ Amy likes movies who have sad endings.

07 다음 중 어법상 올바른 것은?

① They went to the restaurant who was famous for its traditional Korean food.
② I know a girl who name is Karen.
③ Please let me know how way I should go.
④ Tom has a painting who was drawn by a famous artist.
⑤ The two brothers always argue about how to share their presents.

서답형

08 괄호 안에서 알맞은 것을 고르시오.

(1) This is a sea horse (which / who) lives in the sea.

(2) There lived a girl and her dog (that / which) would play on the grass together.

(3) They enjoyed samgyupsal (that / who) tasted yummy last night.

(4) Let's look at some paintings that (was / were) painted by my aunt.

(5) He is a great novelist (who / which) writes many interesting novels.

(6) This is the boy (who / whom) helped me yesterday.

(7) Paul gave her a bag (which / which was) made in Korea.

서답형

09 다음 우리말을 두 가지로 영작하시오.

나는 무엇을 입을지 결정하지 못하겠어.

➡ _____

➡ _____

서답형

10 다음 중 관계대명사가 들어갈 곳을 고르고 알맞게 쓰시오.

(1) I can't ① remember ② the lady ③ visited ④ me ⑤ last night.

(2) There ① was ② a big house ③ has ④ a beautiful garden ⑤ over there.

➡ (1) _____ (2) _____

서답형

11 괄호 안에서 알맞은 것을 고르시오.

(1) Let me tell you (how / what) to use the machine.

(2) I don't know where (spending / to spend) the holidays.

(3) Jennifer didn't know (what / why) to do, so she just waited for him.

(4) I'm not sure what (I should / I) do after graduation.

(5) At first, he did not know (how he read / how to read) a note.

중요

12 다음 〈보기〉의 밑줄 친 부분과 쓰임이 같은 것은?

보기

These are the animals which live both on the land and in the water.

① Which do you like better, this one or that one?

② That is the dog which barked at me the other day.

③ Can you tell me which one will be good for Harry?

④ The scarf which she is wearing around her neck looks beautiful.

⑤ Let's decide which way to take.

13 다음 빈칸에 적절하지 않은 것을 모두 고르시오.

He didn't tell us _____ to go.

① what   ② where   ③ when

④ how   ⑤ why

14 다음 중 주어진 문장의 밑줄 친 that과 용법이 같은 것은?

> The girl that is talking to Jack over there is very kind.

① Yuna has a cat that likes to hide in boxes.
② Don't forget that small efforts can make big differences.
③ I didn't know that.
④ Look at that big bird.
⑤ I can't understand you when you speak that fast.

15 두 문장의 의미가 같아지도록 빈칸에 알맞은 말을 쓰시오.

(1) We are going to teach them how to do magic.
= We are going to teach them _____ _____ _____ magic.

(2) I can't decide where to put this computer.
= I can't decide _____ _____ _____ _____ this computer.

(3) Please inform me what to do next.
= Please inform me _____ _____ _____ _____ next.

16 다음 빈칸에 공통으로 알맞은 말은?

> • The boy _____ gave me a present is my boyfriend.
> • She has a dog _____ has a short tail.

① who   ② whose
③ whom   ④ which
⑤ that

17

> 아버지는 그 기계를 어떻게 사용해야 하는지 배우셨다.

① My father learned when to use the machine.
② My father learned where to use the machine.
③ My father learned how to use the machine.
④ My father learned what to use the machine.
⑤ My father learned that to use the machine.

18

> 기린은 긴 목을 가진 동물이다.

① A giraffe is an animal who has a long neck.
② A giraffe is an animal whose has a long neck.
③ A giraffe is an animal whom has a long neck.
④ A giraffe is an animal which has a long neck.
⑤ A giraffe is an animal that it has a long neck.

19 우리말과 일치하도록 주어진 어휘를 이용하여 빈칸에 알맞은 말을 쓰시오.

(1) 그는 그것을 어디서 살지 모른다. (buy)
➡ He doesn't know _____ _____ _____ it.

(2) 나는 사진이 많이 들어간 여행 책을 좋아한다. (have)
➡ I like travel books _____ _____ lots of pictures.

01 다음 글에서 어법상 잘못 쓰인 것을 찾아 알맞게 고치시오.
(3개)

> I volunteered at a computer school for old people. I met several old people which want to know about computers. I helped the teacher taught them how using a computer.

➡ _____

02 다음 중 어법상 어색한 것을 바르게 고치시오.

(1) I want to have a toy who can speak.

_____ ➡ _____

(2) The dog is running after the girl has long ears.

_____ ➡ _____

(3) Angie likes to take pictures of old ladies whom are working.

_____ ➡ _____

(4) Look at the people who is standing in line.

_____ ➡ _____

(5) She is the teacher who she teaches us English.

_____ ➡ _____

03 다음 빈칸에 알맞은 것을 쓰시오.

(1) Do you know how to swim?
 = Do you know _____ _____ _____ _____?

(2) Which movie to watch is hard for us to decide.
 = _____ _____ _____ _____ _____ is hard for us to decide.

(3) I did not know whom to thank for the gift.
 = I did not know _____ _____ _____ _____ for the gift.

04 주어진 두 문장을 한 문장으로 바꿔 쓰시오.

(1) • Here are two club leaders.
 • They want students to join their clubs.
 ➡ _____
 _____

(2) • This is the tea.
 • It is good for your health.
 ➡ _____

(3) • The movie was interesting.
 • It was directed by James Cameron.
 ➡ _____
 _____

(4) • There are a boy and his dog.
 • They are running at the playground.
 ➡ _____
 _____

(5) • Do you know the girl?
 • She is dancing on the stage.
 ➡ _____

★5 다음 중 어법상 잘못된 것을 고쳐 문장을 다시 쓰시오.

(1) You need to know how play an instrument to join our club.

➡ _____

_____

(2) The old man didn't know what to use the smartphone.

➡ _____

(3) When I to visit London has to be decided.

➡ _____

(4) I don't know why to go there.

➡ _____

06 다음 중 생략할 수 있는 것을 찾아 쓰시오.

(1) The man who is dancing there lives next door.

➡ _____

(2) These are the pictures which were taken at our field trip in spring.

➡ _____

07 주어진 어구와 to부정사를 이용하여 자신의 문장을 쓰시오.

(1) how, speak

➡ _____

(2) what, say to

➡ _____

(3) where, park

➡ _____

[08~09] 다음 그림을 보고 주어진 어휘를 이용하여 빈칸에 알맞은 말을 쓰시오.

08

A: Do you know the girl _____
_____? (be, read)

B: Oh, she is Sumi.

09

A: Does Minsu know _____
the piano? (play)

B: Of course. He plays the piano very well.

10 다음 우리말을 괄호 안에 주어진 어구를 이용하여 영작하시오.

(1) 어떻게 영어로 이메일을 쓸 수 있는지 나에게 말해 줄 수 있니? (tell, write, an email, in English, 12 단어)

➡ _____

(2) 나는 무엇을 먼저 해야 할지 모르겠어. (know, do, first, 8 단어)

➡ _____

(3) 너는 강을 따라 뛰고 있는 저 남자를 알고 있니? (that, run, along the river, 11 단어)

➡ _____

_____

Reading

Why Don't You Join Our Club?

Participating in club activities is a great way to enjoy your school
life. How about joining a club? Here are two club leaders who want
students to join their clubs. Let's listen to what they say.

The Picasso Art Club

Hi! I am Sora Kang from the Picasso Art Club. As you can guess
from the name of our club, we paint. We also do volunteer work from
time to time. Last summer, our club members participated in the
"Change Our Neighborhood" project. On the dirty old walls of the
buildings in our neighborhood, we painted birds flying high in the sky
and dolphins jumping over blue waves.
As a result, the old neighborhood changed into a bright and beautiful
place. The neighbors were happy to see our work and thanked us. You
don't have to be a good painter. Anyone who likes to paint can join.
Come and be a member of the Picasso Art Club.

join 가입하다
club 동아리
participate in ~에 참여하다
leader 대표, 회장
volunteer 자원봉사자
neighborhood 동네, 이웃
dolphin 돌고래
bright 밝은
as a result 결과적으로

확인문제

● 다음 문장이 본문의 내용과 일치하면 T, 일치하지 않으면 F를 쓰시오.

1 The Picasso Art Club is a painting club. ☐

2 The Picasso Art Club has no interest in volunteer work. ☐

3 This summer, the club members of the Picasso Art Club joined the "Change Our
Neighborhood" project. ☐

4 The old neighborhood changed into a bright and beautiful place. ☐

5 If you aren't a skillful painter, you can't join the Picasso Art Club. ☐

6 If you like to paint, you can join the Picasso Art Club. ☐

The Boram Orchestra

Hi! I am Minsu Jang, the leader of the Boram Orchestra. Did you see
several students playing music at the main gate when you came to
school today? We were those students. We play music for our friends
every morning. You need to know how to play an instrument a little
bit to join our club. But don't worry if you don't play well. We will
practice hard and get better together. We also teach children how to
play musical instruments as a service to our community. I am teaching
an eleven-year-old boy to play the violin. At first, he did not know
how to read a note. Now he can play a simple song. Hearing him play
the violin makes me very happy. By joining our club, you can have an
opportunity to help others. Come and join our club. We are waiting for
you.

orchestra 관현악단, 오케스트라
several 몇몇의
a littel bit 조금, 약간
service 서비스, 봉사
practice 연습하다
community 지역 사회
note 음표
opportunity 기회
wait for ~을 기다리다

 확인문제

- 다음 문장이 본문의 내용과 일치하면 T, 일치하지 않으면 F를 쓰시오.

1 Minsu Jang is the leader of the Boram Orchestra.

2 The members of the Boram Orchestra play music for their friends after school.

3 If you can't play an instrument, you can't join the Boram Orchestra.

4 The members of the Boram Orchestra teach children how to play musical instruments.

5 Minsu is teaching an eleven-year-old boy to play the violin.

6 Hearing the boy play the violin makes Minsu very upset.

Reading 133

• 우리말을 참고하여 빈칸에 알맞은 말을 쓰시오.

1 _____ _____ _____ Join Our Club?

2 _____ _____ club activities is a great way _____ _____ your school life.

3 _____ _____ joining a club?

4 Here are two club leaders _____ _____ students _____ _____ their clubs.

5 Let's listen to _____ they say.

6 The Picasso _____ _____

7 Hi! I am Sora Kang _____ the Picasso Art Club.

8 _____ you can _____ _____ the name of our club, we paint.

9 We also _____ _____ _____ from time to time.

10 Last summer, our club members _____ _____ the "Change Our Neighborhood" project.

11 _____ _____ _____ _____ _____ of the buildings in our neighborhood, we painted birds _____ high in the sky and dolphins _____ over blue waves.

12 _____ _____ _____, the old neighborhood changed _____ a bright and beautiful place.

13 The neighbors were happy _____ _____ our work and _____ us.

14 You _____ _____ _____ be a good painter.

15 _____ _____ likes to paint can join.

---

1 우리 동아리에 가입하는 게 어때?

2 동아리 활동에 참여하는 것은 학교생활을 즐기는 좋은 방법이에요.

3 동아리에 가입하는 게 어떤가요?

4 여기 학생들이 그들의 동아리에 가입하기를 원하는 두 명의 동아리 대표가 있어요.

5 그들이 하는 말을 들어 봅시다.

6 피카소 미술 동아리

7 안녕하세요! 저는 피카소 미술 동아리의 강소라입니다.

8 우리 동아리의 이름에서 추측할 수 있듯이, 우리는 그림을 그립니다.

9 우리는 가끔 자원봉사도 합니다.

10 지난여름, 우리 동아리 회원들은 "우리 마을 바꾸기" 프로젝트에 참여했습니다.

11 우리 마을에 있는 건물의 더럽고 오래된 벽에 하늘 높이 나는 새들과 푸른 파도 위로 점프하는 돌고래들을 그렸습니다.

12 결과적으로, 오래된 마을은 밝고 아름다운 곳으로 바뀌었습니다.

13 이웃들은 우리의 작품을 보고 행복해 했고 고마워했습니다.

14 여러분은 그림을 잘 그릴 필요는 없습니다.

15 그림 그리는 것을 좋아하는 사람은 누구나 가입할 수 있습니다.

16 _____ _____ _____ a member of the Picasso Art Club.

17 The Boram _____

18 Hi! I am Minsu Jang, _____ _____ of the Boram Orchestra.

19 Did you see several students _____ _____ at the main gate when you _____ _____ _____ today?

20 We were _____ students.

21 We _____ _____ _____ our friends every morning.

22 You need to know _____ _____ _____ an instrument _____ _____ _____ to join our club.

23 But _____ _____ if you don't play well.

24 We will _____ _____ and _____ _____ together.

25 We _____ _____ children how to play musical instruments _____ _____ _____ our community.

26 I am teaching _____ _____ _____ to play the violin.

27 _____ _____, he did not know how to _____ _____ _____.

28 Now he can play _____ _____ _____.

29 _____ _____ _____ the violin _____ me very happy.

30 _____ _____ our club, you can _____ _____ _____ to help others.

31 _____ _____ _____ our club.

32 We are waiting _____ you.

16 와서 피카소 미술 동아리의 회원이 되세요.

17 보람 오케스트라

18 안녕하세요! 저는 보람 오케스트라의 회장 장민수입니다.

19 오늘 학교에 왔을 때 정문에서 음악을 연주하는 몇 명의 학생들을 보았습니까?

20 우리가 그 학생들이었습니다.

21 우리는 매일 아침 친구들을 위해 음악을 연주합니다.

22 우리 동아리에 가입하기 위해서는 악기 연주하는 법을 조금 알아야 합니다.

23 그러나 여러분이 연주를 잘 못한다고 해서 걱정하지 마세요.

24 우리는 열심히 연습하고 함께 좋아질 것입니다.

25 우리는 지역 사회에 대한 봉사로 아이들에게 악기를 연주하는 법도 가르칩니다.

26 저는 열한 살 소년에게 바이올린을 가르치고 있습니다.

27 처음에 그는 음표를 읽는 법을 알지 못했습니다.

28 이제는 간단한 노래도 연주할 수 있습니다.

29 그가 바이올린을 연주하는 걸 듣는 것은 저를 매우 행복하게 합니다.

30 우리 동아리에 가입함으로써, 여러분은 다른 사람들을 도울 수 있는 기회를 가질 수 있습니다.

31 와서 우리 동아리에 가입하세요.

32 우리는 여러분을 기다리고 있습니다.

● 우리말을 참고하여 본문을 영작하시오.

1 우리 동아리에 가입하는 게 어때?
➡ _____

2 동아리 활동에 참여하는 것은 학교생활을 즐기는 좋은 방법이에요.
➡ _____

3 동아리에 가입하는 게 어떤가요?
➡ _____

4 여기 학생들이 그들의 동아리에 가입하기를 원하는 두 명의 동아리 대표가 있어요.
➡ _____

5 그들이 하는 말을 들어 봅시다.
➡ _____

6 피카소 미술 동아리
➡ _____

7 안녕하세요! 저는 피카소 미술 동아리의 강소라입니다.
➡ _____

8 우리 동아리의 이름에서 추측할 수 있듯이, 우리는 그림을 그립니다.
➡ _____

9 우리는 가끔 자원봉사도 합니다.
➡ _____

10 지난여름, 우리 동아리 회원들은 "우리 마을 바꾸기" 프로젝트에 참여했습니다.
➡ _____

11 우리 마을에 있는 건물의 더럽고 오래된 벽에 하늘 높이 나는 새들과 푸른 파도 위로 점프하는 돌고래들을 그렸습니다.
➡ _____
_____

12 결과적으로, 오래된 마을은 밝고 아름다운 곳으로 바뀌었습니다.
➡ _____

13 이웃들은 우리의 작품을 보고 행복해 했고 고마워했습니다.
➡ _____

14 여러분은 그림을 잘 그릴 필요는 없습니다.
➡ _____

15 그림 그리는 것을 좋아하는 사람은 누구나 가입할 수 있습니다.
➡ _____

16 와서 피카소 미술 동아리의 회원이 되세요.
➡ _____

17 보람 오케스트라

➡ _____

18 안녕하세요! 저는 보람 오케스트라의 회장 장민수입니다.

➡ _____

19 오늘 학교에 왔을 때 정문에서 음악을 연주하는 몇 명의 학생들을 보았습니까?

➡ _____

20 우리가 그 학생들이었습니다.

➡ _____

21 우리는 매일 아침 친구들을 위해 음악을 연주합니다.

➡ _____

22 우리 동아리에 가입하기 위해서는 악기 연주하는 법을 조금 알아야 합니다.

➡ _____

23 그러나 여러분이 연주를 잘 못한다고 해서 걱정하지 마세요.

➡ _____

24 우리는 열심히 연습하고 함께 좋아질 것입니다.

➡ _____

25 우리는 지역 사회에 대한 봉사로 아이들에게 악기를 연주하는 법도 가르칩니다.

➡ _____

26 저는 열한 살 소년에게 바이올린을 가르치고 있습니다.

➡ _____

27 처음에 그는 음표를 읽는 법을 알지 못했습니다.

➡ _____

28 이제는 간단한 노래도 연주할 수 있습니다.

➡ _____

29 그가 바이올린을 연주하는 걸 듣는 것은 저를 매우 행복하게 합니다.

➡ _____

30 우리 동아리에 가입함으로써, 여러분은 다른 사람들을 도울 수 있는 기회를 가질 수 있습니다.

➡ _____

31 와서 우리 동아리에 가입하세요.

➡ _____

32 우리는 여러분을 기다리고 있습니다.

➡ _____

[01~03] 다음 글을 읽고 물음에 답하시오.

Participating in club activities (A)[is / are] a great way to enjoy your school life. ⓐ How about joining a club? Here are two club leaders who (B)[want / wants] students (C) [joining / to join] their clubs. Let's listen to what ⓑthey say.

서답형

01 위 글의 괄호 (A)~(C)에서 어법상 알맞은 것을 골라 쓰시오.

➡ (A)_____ (B)_____ (C)_____

중요

02 위 글의 밑줄 친 ⓐHow about joining과 바꿔 쓸 수 있는 말을 모두 고르시오.

① What about joining
② How do you join
③ Why don't you join
④ Which about joining
⑤ Why do you join

서답형

03 위 글의 밑줄 친 ⓑthey가 가리키는 것을 본문에서 찾아 쓰시오.

➡ _____

[04~06] 다음 글을 읽고 물음에 답하시오.

The Picasso Art Club

Hi! I am Sora Kang from the Picasso Art Club. ⓐAs you can guess from the name of our club, we paint. We also do volunteer work from time to time. (①) Last summer, our club members participated in the "Change Our Neighborhood" project. (②) On the dirty old walls of the buildings in our neighborhood, we painted birds flying high in the sky and dolphins jumping over blue waves. (③) The neighbors were happy to see our work and thanked us. (④) You don't have to be a good painter. (⑤) Anyone who likes to paint can join. Come and be a member of the Picasso Art Club.

04 위 글의 흐름으로 보아, 주어진 문장이 들어가기에 가장 적절한 곳은?

> As a result, the old neighborhood changed into a bright and beautiful place.

① ② ③ ④ ⑤

중요

05 위 글의 밑줄 친 ⓐAs와 같은 의미로 쓰인 것을 고르시오.

① As he often lies, I don't like him.
② As she grew older, she became wiser.
③ She respects him as a mentor.
④ As you know, Julia is leaving soon.
⑤ He told it to me as we went along.

06 위 글의 피카소 미술 동아리에 대한 설명으로 옳지 않은 것은?

① 그림 동아리이다.
② 가끔 자원봉사도 한다.
③ 지난여름, 동아리 회원들은 "우리 마을 바꾸기" 프로젝트에 참여했다.
④ 이웃 마을에 있는 건물의 더럽고 오래된 벽에 그림을 그렸다.
⑤ 동아리 회원이 되려면 그림을 잘 그려야 한다.

[07~09] 다음 글을 읽고 물음에 답하시오.

The Boram Orchestra

Hi! I am Minsu Jang, the leader of the Boram

Orchestra. ⓐDid you see several students to play music at the main gate when you came to school today? We were those students. We play music for our friends every morning. You need to know ⓑ to play an instrument a little bit to join our club. But don't worry if you don't play well. We will practice hard and get better together. We also teach children how to play musical instruments as a service to our community. I am teaching an eleven-year-old boy to play the violin. At first, he did not know how to read a note. Now he can play a simple song. Hearing him play the violin makes me very happy. By joining our club, you can have an opportunity to help others. Come and join our club. We are waiting for you.

서답형

07 위 글의 밑줄 친 ⓐ에서 어법상 틀린 부분을 찾아 고치시오.

➡ _____

08 위 글의 빈칸 ⓑ에 들어갈 알맞은 말을 고르시오.

① what   ② whom   ③ how
④ when   ⑤ whether

서답형

09 다음 중 보람 오케스트라 동아리에 가입할 수 있는 사람을 고르시오.

지혜: I'm interested in doing volunteer work.
보람: I don't know how to play an instrument at all, but I like music.
선미: I like painting pictures and helping others.
준호: I'm not a skillful pianist, but I practice playing the piano hard.
혜영: I know how to read a note, but I can't play any instrument.

➡ _____

[10~12] 다음 글을 읽고 물음에 답하시오.

Boram Middle School
Club Membership Form
- **Name of Club**: FC Boram
- **Student Name**: Sunho Park
- **Why You Want to Join the Club**: I love soccer and would like to join FC Boram. I am good at passing the ball and running fast. ⓐ , I don't know how to head the ball, so I want to learn how to do that. I want to become a soccer player who can make wonderful heading goals.
- **Your Goals**: ⓑIf I will join this club, I will practice very hard and become a good team player!

10 위 글의 빈칸 ⓐ에 들어갈 알맞은 말을 고르시오.

① Moreover   ② However
③ Therefore   ④ Similarly
⑤ For instance

서답형

11 위 글을 읽고 순호가 잘하는 것과 못하는 것을 우리말로 쓰시오.

➡ 잘하는 것: _____
➡ 못하는 것: _____

서답형

12 위 글의 밑줄 친 ⓑ에서 어법상 틀린 부분을 찾아 고치시오.

➡ _____

[13~15] 다음 글을 읽고 물음에 답하시오.

Participating in club activities is a great way ⓐto enjoy your school life. How about ⓑ joining a club? Here are two club leaders ⓒ want students to join their clubs. Let's listen to what they say.

13 위 글의 밑줄 친 ⓐto enjoy와 to부정사의 용법이 다른 것을 모두 고르시오.

① I have much work to do today.

② He is rich enough to buy the car.

③ I have nothing particular to do today.

④ I don't know what to do next.

⑤ Give me a chair to sit on.

서답형

14 위 글의 밑줄 친 ⓑjoining과 바꿔 쓸 수 있는 말을 본문에서 찾아 쓰시오.

➡ _____

서답형

15 위 글의 빈칸 ⓒ에 들어갈 알맞은 말을 쓰시오.

➡ _____

[16~18] 다음 글을 읽고 물음에 답하시오.

The Picasso Art Club

Hi! I am Sora Kang from the Picasso Art Club. As you can guess ⓐ the name of our club, we paint. We also do volunteer work from time to time. Last summer, our club members participated in the "Change Our Neighborhood" project. On the dirty old walls of the buildings in our neighborhood, we painted birds flying high in the sky and dolphins jumping over blue waves. ⓑ , the old neighborhood changed ⓒ a bright and beautiful place. The neighbors were happy ⓓto see our work and thanked us. You don't have to be a good painter. Anyone who likes to paint can join. Come and be a member of the Picasso Art Club.

16 위 글의 빈칸 ⓐ와 ⓒ에 들어갈 전치사가 바르게 짝지어진 것은?

① from – into　　② by – for

③ in – from　　④ from – on

⑤ for – into

17 위 글의 빈칸 ⓑ에 들어갈 알맞은 말을 고르시오.

① However　　② In addition

③ For example　　④ As a result

⑤ In other words

18 아래 보기에서 위 글의 밑줄 친 ⓓto see와 to부정사의 용법이 같은 것의 개수를 고르시오.

┤ 보기 ├
① He promised not to do it.
② English is difficult to learn.
③ She has many children to take care of.
④ What a fool he is to say such a thing!
⑤ She worked hard to pass the exam.

① 1개　② 2개　③ 3개　④ 4개　⑤ 5개

[19~21] 다음 글을 읽고 물음에 답하시오.

The Boram Orchestra

Hi! I am Minsu Jang, the leader of the Boram Orchestra. Did you see several students playing music at the main gate when you came to school today? We were those students. We play music for our friends every morning. You need to know how to play an instrument a little bit to join our club. But don't worry if you don't play well. We will practice hard and get better together. We also teach children ⓐ musical instruments as a service to our community. I am teaching an eleven-year-old boy to play the violin. At first, he did not know how to read a ⓑnote. Now he can play a simple song. Hearing him play the violin makes me very happy. By joining our club, you can have an opportunity to help others. Come and join our club. We are waiting for you.

서답형
19 위 글의 빈칸 ⓐ에 play를 알맞은 형태로 쓰시오.

➡ _____

20 위 글의 밑줄 친 ⓑnote와 같은 의미로 쓰인 것을 고르시오.

① Please make a <u>note</u> of what I'm saying.
② He is striking a <u>note</u> on a piano.
③ She left a <u>note</u> for Ben on the table.
④ Can I borrow your lecture <u>note</u>?
⑤ You must <u>note</u> that this is essential.

서답형
21 위 글을 읽고 보람 오케스트라 동아리의 활동 두 가지를 우리말로 쓰시오.

➡ (1) _____
   (2) _____

[22~24] 다음 글을 읽고 물음에 답하시오.

Boram Middle School
Club Membership Form
• **Name of Club**: FC Boram
• **Student Name**: Sunho Park
• **Why You Want to Join the Club**: I love soccer and would like ①<u>joining</u> FC Boram. I am good at ②<u>passing</u> the ball and ③<u>running</u> fast. However, I don't know ④<u>how to head</u> the ball, so I want to learn how to do that. I want to become a soccer player ⑤<u>who</u> can make wonderful heading ⓐ<u>goals</u>.
• **Your** ⓑ**Goals**: If I join this club, I will practice very hard and become a good team player!

서답형
22 위 글의 밑줄 친 ①~⑤ 중 어법상 틀린 것을 찾아 고치시오.

➡ _____

23 위 글의 박 순호에 대한 설명으로 옳지 않은 것은?

① FC Boram에 가입하고 싶어 한다.
② 공을 패스하는 것을 잘한다.
③ 빨리 달린다.
④ 공을 헤딩하는 것을 잘한다.
⑤ 멋진 헤딩 골을 만들 수 있는 축구 선수가 되기를 원한다.

서답형
24 위 글의 밑줄 친 ⓐgoals와 ⓑGoals의 뜻을 쓰시오.

➡ ⓐ_____, ⓑ_____

[25~27] 다음 글을 읽고 물음에 답하시오.

Looking For Volunteers
We will ____ⓐ____ a book fair at Nanum Middle School on May 5. We are looking for volunteers who can introduce and sell books to people. Anyone who loves books can join our event! If you are interested, please let us know!

25 위 글의 빈칸 ⓐ에 들어갈 알맞은 말을 고르시오.

① take   ② turn
③ hold   ④ bring
⑤ grow

서답형
26 다음 질문에 대한 알맞은 대답을 영어로 쓰시오. (8 단어)

Q: What will volunteers do at the event?
A: _____

27 위 글을 읽고 전시회에 대해 알 수 <u>없는</u> 것을 고르시오.

① 전시회의 종류   ② 개최 장소
③ 전시회의 규모   ④ 개최일
⑤ 전시회 참가 자격

[01~03] 다음 글을 읽고 물음에 답하시오.

The Picasso Art Club

Hi! I am Sora Kang from the Picasso Art Club. As you can guess from the name of our club, we paint. We also do volunteer work from time to time. Last summer, our club members participated in the "Change Our Neighborhood" project. On the dirty old walls of the buildings in our neighborhood, we painted birds __ⓐ__ high in the sky and dolphins __ⓑ__ over blue waves. As a result, the old neighborhood changed into a bright and beautiful place. The neighbors were happy to see our work and thanked us. You ©don't have to be a good painter. Anyone who likes to paint can join. Come and be a member of the Picasso Art Club.

01 다음 빈칸 (A)~(C)에 알맞은 단어를 넣어 Picasso Art Club 에 대한 소개를 완성하시오. 단, (B)와 (C)에는 같은 단어를 쓰시오.

> The Picasso Art Club is an art club and sometimes does (A)_____ _____, too. Anyone who likes (B)_____ can join it and don't have to be good at (C)_____.

02 위 글의 빈칸 ⓐ와 ⓑ에 fly와 jump를 각각 알맞은 형태로 쓰시오.

➡ ⓐ_____, ⓑ_____

03 위 글의 밑줄 친 ©don't have to와 바꿔 쓸 수 있는 어구를 쓰시오.

➡ _____

[04~06] 다음 글을 읽고 물음에 답하시오.

The Boram Orchestra

Hi! I am Minsu Jang, the leader of the Boram Orchestra. Did you see several students playing music at the main gate when you came to school today? We were those students. We play music for our friends every morning. You need to know how to play an instrument (A)[a few / a little] bit to join our club. But don't worry ⓐif you don't play well. We will practice hard and get better together. ⓑ우리는 지역 사회에 대한 봉사로 아이들에게 악기를 연주하는 법도 가르칩니다(musical instruments / teach / a service / children / to our community / we / how to play / also). I am teaching an (B) [eleven-year-old / eleven-years-old] boy to play the violin. At first, he did not know how to read a note. Now he can play a simple song. Hearing him play the violin makes me very (C)[happy / happily]. By joining our club, you can have an opportunity to help others. Come and join our club. We are waiting for you.

04 위 글의 괄호 (A)~(C)에서 어법상 알맞은 것을 골라 쓰시오.

➡ (A)_____ (B)_____ (C)_____

05 위 글의 밑줄 친 ⓐ를 다음과 같이 바꿔 쓸 때 빈칸에 들어갈 알맞은 말을 쓰시오.

➡ _____ you play well

06 위 글의 밑줄 친 ⓑ의 우리말에 맞게 한 단어를 보충하여, 괄호 안에 주어진 어휘를 알맞게 배열하시오.

➡ _____
_____

[07~09] 다음 글을 읽고 물음에 답하시오.

The Picasso Art Club

Hi! I am Sora Kang from the Picasso Art Club. As you can guess from the name of our club, we paint. We also do volunteer work from time to time. Last summer, our club members participated in the "Change Our Neighborhood" project. On the dirty old walls of the buildings in our neighborhood, we painted birds flying high in the sky and dolphins jumping over blue waves. As a result, the old neighborhood changed into a bright and beautiful place. The neighbors were happy to see our work and thanked us. ⓐ<u>You must not be a good painter.</u> ⓑ<u>그림 그리는 것을 좋아하는 사람은 누구나 가입할 수 있습니다.</u> Come and be a member of the Picasso Art Club.

07 다음 질문에 대한 알맞은 대답을 영어로 쓰시오.

Q: How did Sora Kang's neighborhood change after the "Change Our Neighborhood" project?

A: _____

08 위 글의 밑줄 친 ⓐ에서 흐름상 어색한 부분을 찾아 고치시오.

➡ _____

09 위 글의 밑줄 친 ⓑ의 우리말에 맞게 주어진 어휘를 이용하여 7 단어로 영작하시오.

anyone, who

➡ _____

[10~12] 다음 글을 읽고 물음에 답하시오.

The Boram Orchestra

Hi! I am Minsu Jang, the leader of the Boram Orchestra. Did you see several students playing music at the main gate when you came to school today? We were those students. We play music for our friends every morning. You need to know how to play an instrument a little bit to join our club. But don't worry if you don't play well. We will practice hard and get better together. We also teach children how to play musical instruments as a service to our community. I am teaching an eleven-year-old boy to play the violin. At first, he did not know how to read a note. Now he can play a simple song. ⓐ<u>Hearing him play the violin make me very happy.</u> By joining our club, you can have an opportunity to help others. Come and join our club. We are waiting for you.

10 위 글을 읽고 보람 오케스트라 동아리의 가입 자격을 우리말로 쓰시오.

➡ _____

11 본문의 내용과 일치하도록 다음 빈칸 (A)와 (B)에 들어갈 알맞은 단어를 본문에서 찾아 쓰시오.

Minsu tells the students not to (A)_____ even though they don't play a musical instrument well because they will practice hard and (B)_____ _____ together.

12 위 글의 밑줄 친 ⓐ에서 어법상 틀린 부분을 찾아 고치시오.

➡ _____

After You Read

April 30

Today, <u>Minsu</u>, <u>the leader of the Boram Orchestra</u>, came to community center.
Minsu와 the leader of the Boram Orchestra는 동격이다.

He <u>started</u> teaching me <u>how to play</u> the violin last month. <u>At first</u>, I didn't
start는 명사와 to부정사를 목적어로 취한다.   how to+동사원형: ~하는 방법   처음에는

know how to read a <u>note</u>.
음, 음표

I <u>hope to join</u> the Boram Orchestra and play the violin at the main gate <u>when</u> I
hope는 to부정사를 목적어로 취한다. join: 가입하다   (접) ~할 때

become a middle school student.

구문해설 • commnunity: 지역 사회 • the main gate: 정문

해석

오늘, 보람 오케스트라의 대표인 민수가 지역 주민 회관에 왔다. 그는 지난달에 바이올린을 연주하는 법을 나에게 가르쳐 주기 시작했다. 처음에는 나는 하나의 음표도 읽는 법을 알지 못했다. 나는 보람 오케스트라에 가입하여, 내가 중학생이 될 때 정문에서 바이올린을 연주하기를 희망한다.

Writing Workshop

Boram Middle School
Club Membership Form

• Name of Club: FC Boram

• Student Name: Sunho Park

• <u>Why</u> You Want to Join the Club: I love soccer and <u>would like to join</u> FC
= The reason   ~하고 싶다, ~하는 것을 바라다

Boram. I <u>am good at</u> <u>passing</u> the ball and <u>running</u> fast. However, I don't know
be good at: ~을 잘하다. 동명사   동명사

<u>how to head</u> the ball, <u>so</u> I want to learn how to <u>do that</u>. I want to become a
= how I should head   그래서   =head the ball

soccer player <u>who</u> can make wonderful heading goals.
주격 관계대명사(= that)

• Your Goals: If I <u>join</u> this club, I will practice very <u>hard</u> and become a good
조건의 부사절에서 현재시제가 미래시제를 대신함.   열심히

team player!

구문해설 • be good at: ~을 잘하다, • however: 그러나, • wonderful: 아주 멋진, • goal: 득점, 목표,
• practice: 연습하다

보람중학교 동아리 지원서

동아리 이름: FC Boram

학생 이름: 박순호

가입을 원하는 이유: 나는 축구를 사랑하고 FC Boram에 가입하고 싶다. 나는 공을 패스하는 것을 잘하고 빨리 달린다. 그러나, 나는 공을 헤딩하는 법을 모르기 때문에 그것을 하는 법을 배우고 싶다. 나는 멋진 헤딩 골을 만들 수 있는 축구 선수가 되기를 원한다.

당신의 목표: 만약 내가 이 동아리에 가입하면, 나는 매우 열심히 연습해서 좋은 팀 플레이어가 될 것이다.

Real Life Zone

I <u>would like to</u> introduce <u>our new orchestra member, Kate</u>. She knows <u>how</u>
= want to   동격(콤마로 연결)

<u>to play</u> the violin. She also has <u>lots of</u> experience <u>playing</u> in a group. And she
의문사+to부정사: ~하는 법   = much(양과 수 모두에 쓰임)   동명사(앞에 전치사 in이 생략된 것으로 볼 수 있음)

said she enjoys <u>working</u> with people.
enjoys의 목적어로 쓰인 동명사

Let's <u>all</u> welcome <u>her</u> to the Nanum Orchestra.
모두   = Kate

구문해설 • introduce: 소개하다, experience: 경험

나는 우리의 새로운 오케스트라 회원인 케이트를 소개하고 싶어. 그녀는 바이올린을 연주하는 법을 알아. 그녀는 또한 그룹에서 연주해 본 경험이 많아. 그리고 그녀는 사람들과 일하는 것을 즐긴다고 말했어. 모두 그녀가 나눔 오케스트라에 온 걸 환영하자.

01 다음 짝지어진 낱말의 관계가 나머지 넷과 <u>다른</u> 것은?

① gift – present　　② dark – bright

③ activity – action　④ actually – really

⑤ enter – join

02 다음 빈칸에 알맞은 말이 순서대로 바르게 나열된 것은?

- Are you pretty _____ at using computers?
- We are _____ for volunteers who can introduce books to people.
- I will _____ in the event next time!

① well – starting – participate

② well – looking – enter

③ good – looking – participate

④ good – starting – enter

⑤ good – looking – enter

03 밑줄 친 단어와 의미가 같은 단어를 고르시오.

What should I <u>get</u> them for their wedding gift?

① keep　　② bring　　③ carry

④ buy　　⑤ find

04 다음 빈칸에 공통으로 들어갈 말을 쓰시오.

- You can ask _____ help when you need it.
- Thank you _____ showing your interest.

05 다음 우리말에 맞게 빈칸을 완성하시오. (철자가 주어진 경우, 그 철자로 시작할 것)

(1) 사실 오늘 밤에 나는 나가고 싶지 않다.

➡ A_____, I don't think I want to go out tonight.

(2) 너는 어디서 요리하는 것을 배웠니?

➡ _____ did you learn _____ _____?

(3) 이것은 돈을 절약할 기회이다.

➡ This is an o_____ to save money.

[06~07] 다음 대화를 읽고 물음에 답하시오.

B: Do you enjoy ⓐto read books, Yumi?
G: Yes, I love ⓑreading science books. ⓒ What about you?
B: I love ⓓto read books, too.
G: Then, let's ⓔto go to the library after school today.

06 위 대화의 밑줄 친 ⓐ~ⓔ 중 어법상 틀린 개수를 고르시오.

① 1개　② 2개　③ 3개　④ 4개　⑤ 5개

07 위 대화를 읽고 답할 수 <u>없는</u> 질문을 고르시오.

① What is the boy's hobby?

② What kinds of books does Yumi love reading?

③ Where are they going to go after school?

④ Does Yumi love reading?

⑤ Does the boy love reading?

[08~09] 다음 대화를 읽고 물음에 답하시오.

> G: (A)_____, Minsu?
> B: I made breakfast for my family.
> G: Do you enjoy ⓐ_____?
> B: Yes, I'm a good ⓑ_____! My family loves my ⓒ_____.

08 빈칸 (A)에 들어갈 알맞은 말을 고르시오.

① Where did you go on the weekend
② Where did you get it
③ What are you going to do on the weekend
④ What are you making for your family
⑤ What did you do on the weekend

09 빈칸 ⓐ~ⓒ에 들어갈 알맞은 말을 보기에서 골라 쓰시오.

┌─ 보기 ─┐
cook   cooking   to cook   cooked
└──────┘

➡ ⓐ_____ ⓑ_____ ⓒ_____

[10~12] 다음 대화를 읽고 물음에 답하시오.

> B: Hello, Kate. I'm Hamin, the leader of the Nanum Orchestra. Thank you for your (A)_____ in our club. (①)
> G: Hi. Nice to meet you.
> B: You play ⓐthe violin? ⓑWhen did you start playing the violin?
> G: I started learning how to play the violin ⓒthat I was ten. (②)
> B: Do you have any experience playing in a group?
> G: Yes. Actually, I was a member of an orchestra ⓓwhen I was in elementary school. (③)
> B: Great. We also volunteer ⓔto teach children. Do you enjoy teaching others? (④)
> G: I have no experience teaching others. (⑤)
> B: Good. I think we'll have a great time playing together. Welcome to the Nanum Orchestra.

10 위 대화의 ①~⑤ 중 다음 주어진 말이 들어갈 알맞은 곳은?

> But I enjoy working with people, so I'd like to try.

① ② ③ ④ ⑤

11 빈칸 (A)에 들어갈 알맞은 말을 고르시오.

① interest   ② surprise   ③ event
④ attention   ⑤ effort

12 위 글의 밑줄 친 ⓐ~ⓔ 중 어법상 틀린 것을 고르시오.

① ⓐ   ② ⓑ   ③ ⓒ   ④ ⓓ   ⑤ ⓔ

[13~14] 다음 대화를 읽고 물음에 답하시오.

> A: Do you enioy ⓐlook at the stars at night?
> B: Yes, I love ⓑdoing that.

13 위 대화의 밑줄 친 ⓐ를 알맞은 형으로 고치시오.

➡ _____

14 위 대화의 밑줄 친 ⓑ가 가리키는 것을 영어로 쓰시오.

➡ _____

Grammar

15 다음 빈칸에 알맞은 것을 모두 고르시오.

> Jin is a girl _____ likes to play the piano.

① who   ② whose   ③ whom
④ which   ⑤ that

16 다음 주어진 단어를 이용하여 빈칸에 알맞은 말을 쓰시오.

> 지수는 엄마에게 어디에 가방을 둬야 할지 물어
> 봤다.
> = Jisu asked her mother ＿＿＿＿＿＿＿＿
> 　the bag. (put)

17 밑줄 친 that의 쓰임이 나머지 넷과 다른 것은?

　① A baker is a person that bakes bread.

　② She told me that I should be more careful.

　③ I walked to my school that is three stops away.

　④ I know the very person that will do the job quickly.

　⑤ The girl that is talking on the phone is my sister, Susan.

18 다음 괄호 안에 주어진 단어를 어법에 맞게 빈칸에 쓰시오.

　(1) Do you know how ＿＿＿＿ ＿＿＿＿
　　　＿＿＿＿ to the National Museum? (get)

　(2) I don't know where ＿＿＿＿ ＿＿＿＿
　　　the bus. (take)

　(3) I told him who ＿＿＿＿ ＿＿＿＿ for.
　　　(look)

　(4) You should choose ＿＿＿ dress
　　　＿＿＿＿ ＿＿＿＿ to the party. (wear)

19 빈칸에 알맞은 말을 어법에 맞게 쓰시오. (that은 쓰지 말 것)

> (1) Look at the boy ＿＿＿＿ is playing
> 　　the piano on the street.
> (2) The coat ＿＿＿＿ is black is mine.

20 다음 중 어법상 어색한 문장은?

　① I want to become a soccer player who can make wonderful heading goals.

　② Would you tell me where to park the car?

　③ I have a smartphone that was made in Korea.

　④ Her mother taught her how to make delicious spaghetti.

　⑤ The writer couldn't decide what to write the story.

21 다음은 두 문장을 관계대명사를 사용하여 한 문장으로 쓴 것이다. 빈칸에 다른 한 문장을 쓰시오.

　(1) • ＿＿＿＿＿＿＿＿＿＿＿＿＿＿＿
　　　• They can introduce and sell books to people.
　　　→ We are looking for volunteers who[that] can introduce and sell books to people.

　(2) • My class has some students.
　　　• ＿＿＿＿＿＿＿＿＿＿＿＿＿＿＿
　　　→ My class has some students who[that] are good at English.

　(3) • I have a friend.
　　　• ＿＿＿＿＿＿＿＿＿＿＿＿＿＿＿
　　　→ I have a friend who[that] lives in New Zealand.

　(4) • Angelina loved the present.
　　　• ＿＿＿＿＿＿＿＿＿＿＿＿＿＿＿
　　　→ Angelina loved the present that[which] Chuck gave to her on her birthday.

22 다음 밑줄 친 부분의 쓰임이 나머지 넷과 다른 것은?

① I want to learn how to do that.

② Do you know when to start the performance?

③ He couldn't decide what to do.

④ Julia bought a book to read on the train.

⑤ She asked me where to find the ladies' room.

23 두 문장을 관계대명사를 사용하여 한 문장으로 쓰시오. (that은 사용하지 말 것)

(1) • She wants to see a movie.
 • The movie is interesting.

 ➡ _____

(2) • Rose is Jake's best friend.
 • She works for a bank.

 ➡ _____

(3) • James bought a new computer.
 • The computer is really nice

 ➡ _____

Reading

[24~26] 다음 글을 읽고 물음에 답하시오.

The Boram Orchestra
Hi! I am Minsu Jang, the leader of the Boram Orchestra. Did you see several students playing music at the main gate when you came to school today? We were @those students. We play music for our friends every morning. You need to know how to play an instrument a little bit to join our club. But don't worry if you don't play well. We will practice hard and get better together. We also teach children how to play musical instruments as a service to our community. I am teaching an eleven-year-old boy to play the violin. At first, he did not know how to read a note. Now he can play a simple song. ⓑHearing him play the violin

makes me very happy. By joining our club, you can have an opportunity to help others. Come and join our club. We are waiting for you.

24 위 글의 밑줄 친 @those students가 가리키는 것을 본문에서 찾아 쓰시오.

➡ _____

_____

25 위 글의 밑줄 친 ⓑHearing과 문법적 쓰임이 다른 것을 모두 고르시오.

① Look at the man hearing the lecture.

② He is interested in hearing the lecture.

③ My dream is hearing the lecture.

④ Are they hearing the lecture now?

⑤ I enjoyed hearing the lecture.

26 위 글의 내용과 일치하지 않는 것은?

① 민수는 매일 방과 후에 친구들을 위해 음악을 연주한다.

② 보람 오케스트라 동아리에 가입하려면 악기를 연주하는 법을 조금 알아야 한다.

③ 보람 오케스트라 동아리는 아이들에게 악기를 연주하는 법도 가르친다.

④ 민수는 열한 살 난 소년에게 바이올린을 가르치고 있다.

⑤ 보람 오케스트라 동아리에 가입함으로써 다른 사람들을 도울 수 있는 기회를 가질 수 있다.

[27~29] 다음 글을 읽고 물음에 답하시오.

The Picasso Art Club
Hi! I am Sora Kang from the Picasso Art Club. As you can guess from the name of our club, we paint. We also do volunteer work @from time to time. (A)[Last summer / In last summer], our club members participated

in the "Change Our Neighborhood" project. On the dirty old walls of the buildings in our neighborhood, we painted birds flying (B)[high / highly] in the sky and dolphins jumping over blue waves. As a result, the old neighborhood changed into a bright and beautiful place. The neighbors were happy to see our work and (C)[to thank / thanked] us. You don't have to be a good painter. Anyone who likes ⓑ can join. Come and be a member of the Picasso Art Club.

27 위 글의 밑줄 친 ⓐfrom time to time과 의미가 다른 것을 모두 고르시오.

① once in a while　② always
③ now and then　④ sometimes
⑤ rarely

28 위 글의 괄호 (A)~(C)에서 문맥이나 어법상 알맞은 낱말을 골라 쓰시오.

➡ (A)_____ (B)_____ (C)_____

29 위 글의 빈칸 ⓑ에 들어갈 알맞은 말을 고르시오.

① to change the neighborhood
② to play music
③ to paint
④ to help others
⑤ to play sports

[30~31] 다음 글을 읽고 물음에 답하시오.

Hello, everyone. I'm Jason, the leader of the Abracadabra Club. On May 5, our club members will go to Hanguk Hospital to visit sick children. We are going to show them magic and teach ⓐthem how to do magic.

30 위 글의 밑줄 친 ⓐthem이 가리키는 것을 본문에서 찾아 쓰시오.

➡ _____

31 Abracadabra 동아리에 대한 소개를 완성하도록 다음 빈칸에 공통으로 들어갈 단어를 쓰시오.

The Abracadabra Club is a _____ club. On May 5, its members will go to Hanguk Hospital and show _____ to sick children and teach them how to do _____.

[32~33] 다음 글을 읽고 물음에 답하시오.

We will hold a book ⓐfair at Nanum Middle School on May 5. We are looking ⓑ_____ volunteers who can introduce and sell books ⓒ_____ people. Anyone who loves books can join our event! If you are interested, please let us know!

32 위 글의 밑줄 친 ⓐfair와 같은 의미로 쓰인 것을 고르시오.

① We have to be fair to both players.
② Let's take the kids to the fair.
③ She has long fair hair.
④ A fair number of people came along.
⑤ It was a fair and breezy day.

33 위 글의 빈칸 ⓑ와 ⓒ에 들어갈 전치사가 바르게 짝지어진 것은?

① at – to　② for – of
③ in – on　④ at – or
⑤ for – to

출제율 85%

01 다음 짝지어진 두 단어의 관계가 같도록 주어진 철자로 시작해 빈칸에 쓰시오.

> chief : leader – training : p_____

출제율 95%

02 다음 〈보기〉의 단어를 사용하여 자연스러운 문장을 만들 수 없는 것은?

> ┤ 보기 ├
>
> drone   garden   interest   leader

① He is the _____ of the music club.

② Do you have any _____ in the opera?

③ The house has a _____ with trees and flowers.

④ You can come a little _____ later.

⑤ A _____ is a small remote-controlled helicopter.

[03~06] 다음 대화를 읽고 물음에 답하시오.

B: ⓐThese cookies look so delicious. Did you make ⓑthem?

G: Yes. I made ⓒthem myself yesterday. I enjoy baking. I'm going to make doughnuts this Saturday.

B: Oh, I want to learn how to make ⓓthem. Is it difficult?

G: Not at all. You can come to my house and join me if you want.

B: Thanks, Bora. (A)_____ should I come?

G: At 2:00.

B: Sounds good. See you then.

출제율 90%

03 밑줄 친 ⓐ~ⓓ 중 가리키는 것이 같은 것끼리 짝지어진 것을 고르시오.

① ⓐ, ⓓ   ② ⓑ, ⓓ
③ ⓒ, ⓓ   ④ ⓐ, ⓑ, ⓒ
⑤ ⓐ, ⓑ, ⓒ, ⓓ

출제율 95%

04 빈칸 (A)에 들어갈 말을 쓰시오. (2 단어)

➡ _____

출제율 90%

05 다음 영영풀이에 해당하는 단어를 대화에서 찾아 쓰시오.

> 1. to become a member of an organization, society, or group
> 2. to begin to take part in an activity that other people are involved in

➡ _____

출제율 100%

06 대화를 읽고 답할 수 없는 질문을 고르시오.

① Who made the cookies?

② Where are they going to meet this Saturday?

③ What kinds of food does the boy know how to make?

④ When did the girl make the cookies?

⑤ What will the girl make this Saturday?

07 다음 빈칸에 공통으로 들어갈 말을 쓰시오.

> • I'd like _____ _____ soccer.
>
> • I don't know how _____ _____ the piano or violin.

08 다음 우리말 해석에 맞게 빈칸을 완성하시오.

(1) _____ _____ _____, my team lost. (결과적으로, 우리 팀은 졌다.)

(2) _____ _____, I was very _____ in acting. (처음에, 나는 연기에 아주 관심이 많았다.)

(3) It can _____ _____ different types of chair. (그것은 다른 종류들의 의자로 변할 수 있다.)

(4) P l e a s e _____ _____ _____ _____ _____ do it. (그것을 어떻게 해야 하는지 우리에게 알려주세요.)

[09~10] 주어진 문장 다음에 이어질 대화의 순서를 바르게 배열하시오.

09

> What did you do on the weekend, Minsu?

> (A) Yes, I'm a good cook! My family loves my cooking.
>
> (B) I made breakfast for my family.
>
> (C) Do you enjoy cooking?

➡ _____

10

> Jiyun, that's a pretty backpack! Where did you get it?

> (A) Wow! She's a really good designer.
>
> (B) My sister made it for me.
>
> (C) Yes, she is. And she enjoys making clothes, too.

➡ _____

11 대화의 밑줄 친 우리말을 주어진 단어를 이용해 영작하시오.

> A: 너는 여가 시간에 뭐 하는 것을 즐기니?
>
> B: I enjoy taking pictures of people in the park.

➡ _____

(free, enjoy, have, when)

12 다음 우리말을 주어진 어휘를 이용하여 영작하시오.

(1) Jisu는 그녀의 엄마에게 어디에 가방을 둬야 할지 물어봤다. (where, the bag, put, to)

➡ _____

(2) 너는 다음에 우리가 무엇을 해야 할지 아니? (what, should, next)

➡ _____

(3) 나는 무엇을 요리할지 결정할 수 없었다. (decide, cook, to)

➡ _____

(4) 운동장에서 농구를 하고 있는 소녀들이 몇 명 있다. (there, a few girls, playing, the playground.)

➡ _____
_____

(5) Janet은 재미있는 그림이 많은 책을 아주 좋아한다. (pictures, funny, have, love, many)

➡ _____

(6) 길을 건너던 Linda와 그녀의 개가 부상을 입었다. (crossing the street, injured)

➡ _____

_____

출제율 100%

13 다음 중 어법상 올바른 문장은?

① I know a girl which is good at English.

② I want to buy a bag who is expensive.

③ When to use the model has to be decided.

④ I asked her where putting the baggage.

⑤ We also teach children how play musical instruments as a service to our community.

출제율 90%

14 다음 중 어법상 잘못된 것을 바르게 고치시오.

(1) Can you tell me how get to the subway station?

➡ _____

(2) There are some tips for what to lose weight.

➡ _____

(3) What he to eat is important to him.

➡ _____

(4) I have a friend which likes soccer.

➡ _____

(5) The girl is standing under the tree is waiting for you.

➡ _____

(6) Christel sent a letter to her mom whom missed her a lot.

➡ _____

(7) Mike is wearing shoes that is too small for him.

➡ _____

(8) Peter Pan was a boy who he liked to fly.

➡ _____

[15~16] 다음 글을 읽고 물음에 답하시오.

@Participating in club activities is a great way to enjoy your school life. How about joining a club? Here are two club leaders who want students ⓑ their clubs. Let's listen to what they say.

출제율 95%

15 위 글의 밑줄 친 @Participating과 문법적 쓰임이 같은 것을 모두 고르시오.

① She isn't playing tennis.

② My hobby is taking pictures.

③ I saw him walking with his friends.

④ Look at the man sitting on the bench.

⑤ He is proud of being Korean.

출제율 85%

16 위 글의 빈칸 ⓑ에 join을 알맞은 형태로 쓰시오.

➡ _____

[17~19] 다음 글을 읽고 물음에 답하시오.

The Picasso Art Club

Hi! I am Sora Kang from the Picasso Art Club. As you can guess from the name of our club, we paint. We also do ⓐ work from time to time. Last summer, our club members participated in the "Change Our Neighborhood" project. On the dirty old walls of the buildings in our neighborhood, ⓑ하늘 높이 나는 새들과 푸른 파도 위로 점프하는 돌고래들을 그렸습니다. As a result, the old neighborhood changed into a bright and beautiful place. The neighbors were happy to see our work and thanked us. You don't have to be a good painter. ⓒAnyone who likes to paint can join. Come and be a member of the Picasso Art Club.

17 주어진 영영풀이를 참고하여 빈칸 ⓐ에 철자 v로 시작하는 단어를 쓰시오.

> someone who does work without being paid for it, because they want to do it

➡ _____

18 위 글의 밑줄 친 ⓑ의 우리말에 맞게 한 단어를 보충하여, 주어진 어휘를 알맞게 배열하시오.

> dolphins / in the sky / and / painted / over blue waves / birds / jumping / flying / we

➡ _____
_____

19 위 글의 밑줄 친 ⓒAnyone who와 바꿔 쓸 수 있는 말을 고르시오.

① Whoever   ② Whichever
③ Whatever   ④ However
⑤ Whomever

[20~22] 다음 글을 읽고 물음에 답하시오.

The Boram Orchestra
Hi! I am Minsu Jang, the leader of the Boram Orchestra. (①) Did you see several students playing music at the main gate when you came to school today? (②) We play music for our friends every morning. (③) You need to know how to play an instrument a little bit to join our club. (④) But don't worry if you don't play well. (⑤) We will practice hard and get better together. We also teach children how to play musical instruments ⓐas a service to our community. I am teaching an eleven-year-old

boy to play the violin. ___ⓑ___, he did not know how to read a note. Now he can play a simple song. Hearing him play the violin makes me very happy. By joining our club, you can have an opportunity to help others. Come and join our club. We are waiting for you.

20 위 글의 흐름으로 보아, 주어진 문장이 들어가기에 가장 적절한 곳은?

> We were those students.

①   ②   ③   ④   ⑤

21 위 글의 밑줄 친 ⓐas와 같은 의미로 쓰인 것을 고르시오.

① As she was tired, she soon fell asleep.
② Do as you like.
③ I love you as much as I love her.
④ This box can be used as a chair.
⑤ Her anger grew as she talked.

22 위 글의 빈칸 ⓑ에 들어갈 알맞은 말을 고르시오.

① Finally   ② At first
③ At last   ④ Therefore
⑤ As a result

01 다음 대화의 순서를 바르게 배열하시오.

> (A) Yes, I love reading science books. How about you?
> (B) I love reading books, too.
> (C) Then, let's go to the library after school today.
> (D) Do you enjoy reading books, Yumi?

➡ _____

02 중요 다음 대화의 밑줄 친 부분과 의미가 같도록 조동사를 이용하여 영작하시오.

> A: Do you know how to make a paper cat?
> B: Of course. It's easy.

➡ _____

[03~04] 다음 대화를 읽고 물음에 답하시오.

> G: Did you buy that drone?
> B: No, I got it as a present from my parents, but I don't know how to use it. 어떻게 하는지 아니?
> G: No, maybe Jina knows how to do it. She enjoys flying drones.
> B: Then, (ask, help, will, I, her, for)

03 괄호 안의 단어를 이용하여 밑줄 친 우리말을 바르게 영작하시오. (5 단어)

➡ _____ (how)

04 괄호 안의 단어를 배열하여 문장을 만드시오.

➡ _____

05 중요 다음 두 문장의 의미가 같도록 빈칸을 완성하시오.

(1) Do you know how I can get to the National Museum?
= Do you know _____ _____ _____ to the National Museum?

(2) Brigette taught us how we should make a paper cat.
= Brigette taught us _____ _____ _____ a paper cat.

(3) Tell me when I should wake you up.
= Tell me _____ _____ _____ you up.

(4) Tell the driver where he should stop.
= Tell the driver _____ _____ _____.

(5) I do not know what I should do.
= I do not know _____ _____ _____.

(6) Whom I should meet became the most important to me.
= _____ _____ _____ became the most important to me.

06 두 문장을 관계대명사를 사용하여 한 문장으로 쓰시오. (that은 사용하지 말 것)

(1) • Kay lives in a house.
• The house has a beautiful garden.

➡ _____

(2) • Naomi is standing over there.
• She is very beautiful.

➡ _____

The Picasso Art Club

Hi! I am Sora Kang from the Picasso Art Club. As you can guess from the name of our club, we paint. We also do volunteer work from time to time. Last summer, our club members participated in the "Change Our Neighborhood" project. On the dirty old walls of the buildings in our neighborhood, we painted birds flying high in the sky and dolphins jumping over blue waves. __ⓐ__ a result, the old neighborhood changed into a bright and beautiful place. The neighbors were happy to see our work and thanked us. You don't have to be a good painter. Anyone ⓑwho likes to paint can join. Come and be a member of the Picasso Art Club.

07 다음 질문에 대한 알맞은 대답을 영어로 쓰시오. (8 단어)

Q: What did the members of the Picasso Art Club do last summer?

A: _____

08 위 글의 빈칸 ⓐ에 알맞는 단어를 쓰시오.

➡ _____

09 위 글의 밑줄 친 ⓑwho와 바꿔 쓸 수 있는 단어를 쓰시오.

➡ _____

The Boram Orchestra

Hi! I am Minsu Jang, the leader of the Boram Orchestra. Did you see several students playing music at the main gate when you came to school today? We were (A)[that / those] students. We play music for our friends every morning. You need to know how to play an instrument a little bit to join our club. But don't worry if you don't play well. We will practice (B)[hard / hardly] and get better together. We also teach children ⓐhow to play musical instruments as a service to our community. I am teaching an eleven-year-old boy to play the violin. At first, he did not know how to read a note. Now he can play a simple song. Hearing him (C)[play / to play] the violin makes me very happy. By joining our club, you can have an opportunity to help others. Come and join our club. We are waiting for you.

10 위 글의 괄호 (A)~(C)에서 문맥이나 어법상 알맞은 낱말을 골라 쓰시오.

➡ (A)_____ (B)_____ (C)_____

11 위 글의 밑줄 친 ⓐ를 다음과 같이 바꿔 쓸 때 빈칸에 들어갈 알맞은 말을 쓰시오.

➡ how _____ _____ play

12 위 글의 내용을 다음과 같이 정리하고자 한다. 빈칸 (A)와 (B)에 들어갈 알맞은 단어를 본문에서 찾아 쓰시오.

Minsu Jang is the (A)_____ of the Boram Orchestra and he introduces the activities of his club and tells students to (B)_____ his club.

01 다음 그림을 보고 주어진 〈조건〉에 맞게 문장을 완성하시오.

> 주어진 단어를 사용하고 필요하면 단어의 형태를 변화시킬 것

(1)

➡ I _____. (enjoy, fly)

(2)

➡ We _____. (a pizza, make, want)

02 다음 가입하고 싶은 동아리와 그 이유를 바탕으로 동아리 지원서를 작성하시오.

Club	FC Boram
What I Am Good at	• pass the ball
	• run fast
What I Want to Learn	• head the ball
My Goals	• practice hard
	• become a good team player

Boram Middle School
Club Membership Form
• (A)_____ of Club: FC Boram
• Student Name: Sunho Park
• Why You Want to Join the Club: I love soccer and would like to join (B)_____. I am good at (C)_____ the ball and (D)_____ fast. However, I don't know how to head the ball, so I want to learn how to do that. I want to become a soccer player who can make wonderful (E)_____ goals.
• Your Goals: If I join this club, I will practice very hard and become (F)_____!

03 주어진 어휘와 표현을 이용하여 3 문장 이상을 쓰시오.

what	how	when	where	whom
go	start	play	find	say

(1) _____

(2) _____

(3) _____

(4) _____

(5) _____

단원별 모의고사

[01~02] 다음 대화의 빈칸에 알맞은 단어를 고르시오.

01

> A: What do you enjoy doing when you have free time?
> B: I enjoy _____ my dog in the park.

① making　② getting　③ walking
④ climbing　⑤ knowing

02

> B: Jiyun, that's a pretty backpack! Where did you _____ it?
> G: My sister made it for me.

① get　② see　③ bake
④ grow　⑤ join

03 다음 빈칸에 들어갈 말을 〈보기〉에서 찾아 쓰시오. (형태 변화 가능)

> ┤ 보기 ├
> join　own　neighbor　interest

(1) Ben shows much _____ in learning French.
(2) I decided to _____ the army.
(3) One of the _____ complained about the noise from the party.
(4) Bring your _____ book.

04 다음 영영풀이에 해당하는 단어를 주어진 철자로 시작하여 쓰고, (1), (2), (3)에 알맞는 단어를 쓰시오. (형태 변화 가능)

> • p_____ : to do something regularly in order to do it better
> • h_____ : to have a meeting, party, election, etc in a particular place or at a particular time
> • n_____ : the area around you or around a particular place, or the people who live there

(1) The meeting will be _____ at this hotel.
(2) Is there a good Chinese restaurant in the _____?
(3) I need to _____ playing the guitar.

[05~07] 다음 대화를 읽고 물음에 답하시오.

> B: These cookies look so delicious. Did you make (A)[it / them]? (①)
> G: Yes. I made them myself yesterday. (②) I enjoy baking. (B)[I went / I'm going] to make doughnuts this Saturday.
> B: Oh, I want to learn how to make doughnuts. (③) Is it difficult?
> G: Not at all. (④)
> B: Thanks, Bora. (⑤) What time should I (C)[come / to come]?
> G: At 2:00.
> B: Sounds good. See you then.

05 위 대화의 ①~⑤ 중 다음 주어진 말이 들어갈 알맞은 곳은?

> You can come to my house and join me if you want.

①　　②　　③　　④　　⑤

06 (A), (B), (C)에 적절한 말을 골라 쓰시오.

➡ (A)_____ (B)_____ (C)_____

07 위 대화의 내용과 일치하지 <u>않는</u> 것을 <u>모두</u> 고르시오.

① The boy wants to learn how to make doughnuts.

② The boy went to her house at 2:00.

③ The girl thinks that making doughnuts is not difficult.

④ The boy wants to go to the girl's house to learn how to make cookies.

⑤ The girl enjoys baking.

[08~10] 다음 대화를 읽고 물음에 답하시오.

G: Did you buy that drone? (①)

B: No, I got it as a present from my parents, but I don't know (A)_____ use it. (②) Do you know how to? (③)

G: (④) No, maybe Jina knows (B)_____ do it. (⑤)

B: Then, I will ask her for help.

08 위 대화의 ①~⑤ 중 다음 주어진 말이 들어갈 알맞은 곳은?

She enjoys flying drones.

①   ②   ③   ④   ⑤

09 다음 영영풀이에 해당하는 단어를 대화에서 찾아 쓰시오.

an aircraft that does not have a pilot, but is operated by radio

➡ _____

10 (A)와 (B)에 공통으로 들어갈 말을 대화에서 찾아 쓰시오.

➡ _____

11 다음 대화에서 어색한 부분을 찾아 고치시오.

A: ①Do you know ②how to ③make a paper cat?

B: ④Of course not. ⑤It's easy.

➡ _____

[12~14] 다음 대화를 읽고 물음에 답하시오.

B: Hello, Kate. I'm Hamin, the leader of the Nanum Orchestra. <u>우리 동아리에 관심을 가져줘서 고마워</u>.

G: Hi. Nice to meet you.

B: You play the violin? (A)_____?

G: I started learning how to play the violin when I was ten.

B: (B)_____?

G: Yes. Actually, I was a member of an orchestra when I was in elementary school.

B: Great. We also volunteer to teach children. (C)_____?

G: I have no experience teaching others. But I enjoy working with people, so I'd like to try.

B: Good. I think we'll have a great time playing together. Welcome to the Nanum Orchestra.

12 다음 영영풀이에 해당하는 단어를 대화에서 찾아 쓰시오.

(1)

the person who directs or controls a group, organization, country, etc.

➡ _____

(2)

a large group of musicians playing many different kinds of instruments and led by a conductor

➡ _____

13 밑줄 친 우리말과 의미가 같도록 주어진 단어를 이용해 문장을 완성하시오.

➡ _____

(in, you, your, our)

14 (A)~(C)에 알맞은 질문을 〈보기〉에서 골라 쓰시오.

┌─ 보기 ┐
- Do you know how to play the violin?
- Do you enjoy teaching others?
- What do you enjoy doing when you have free time?
- When did you start playing the violin?
- Do you have any experience playing in a group?

➡ (A) _____
(B) _____
(C) _____

15 다음 빈칸에 들어갈 말로 알맞지 않은 것은? (2개)

He let me know _____ to do it.

① what   ② how   ③ when
④ why   ⑤ where

16 다음 중 어법상 어색한 것을 고르시오.

① I don't know when to start.
② Where are the pictures that it was taken by Gibson?
③ Can you teach me how to play the guitar?
④ Anyone who likes to paint can join our club.
⑤ This is the key which was lost yesterday.

17 다음 중 어법상 어색한 것을 바르게 고쳐 다시 쓰시오.

(1) Tell me how use this computer.

➡ _____

(2) He didn't know what to go.

➡ _____

(3) Do you know how should you to swim?

➡ _____
_____

(4) The doctors are working in this hospital are very kind.

➡ _____
_____

(5) Did you meet the girl that she is wearing sunglasses?

➡ _____

(6) Mary has a cousin which live in Seoul.

➡ _____

(7) Melina took some pictures of her friends whom were on a hiking trip.

➡ _____
_____

[18~20] 다음 글을 읽고 물음에 답하시오.

The Picasso Art Club
Hi! I am Sora Kang from the Picasso Art Club. As you can guess from the name of our club, we paint. We also do volunteer work from time to time. Last summer, our club members ⓐparticipated in the "Change Our Neighborhood" project. On the dirty old walls of the buildings in our neighborhood,

we painted birds ⓑflying high in the sky and dolphins jumping over blue waves. As a result, the old neighborhood changed into a bright and beautiful place. The neighbors were happy to see our work and thanked us. You don't have to be a good painter. Anyone who likes to paint can join. Come and be a member of the Picasso Art Club.

18 위 글의 밑줄 친 ⓐparticipated in과 바꿔 쓸 수 있는 것을 <u>모두</u> 고르시오.

① joined   ② made a plan for
③ prepared for   ④ took part in
⑤ took care of

19 아래 보기에서 위 글의 밑줄 친 ⓑflying과 문법적 쓰임이 <u>다른</u> 것의 개수를 고르시오.

┌─── 보기 ───┐
① She was <u>watching</u> TV in the living room.
② Thank you for <u>visiting</u> our house.
③ <u>Talking</u> behind others' back is not good.
④ He enjoyed <u>listening</u> to her stories.
⑤ Is your hobby <u>playing</u> tennis?
└─────────┘

① 1개   ② 2개   ③ 3개   ④ 4개   ⑤ 5개

20 다음 빈칸 (A)와 (B)에 알맞은 단어를 넣어 피카소 미술 동아리의 가입 조건을 완성하시오.

┌──────────────────────────┐
You can be a member of the Picasso Art Club if you like (A)_____ _____ but there is no need for you to be (B)_____ _____ _____.
└──────────────────────────┘

[21~23] 다음 글을 읽고 물음에 답하시오.

The Boram Orchestra

Hi! I am Minsu Jang, the leader of the Boram Orchestra. Did you see several students playing music at the main gate when you came to school today? We were those students. We play music for our friends every morning. You need to know how to play an instrument a little bit to join our club. But don't worry if you don't play well. We will practice hard and get better together. We also teach children how to play musical instruments   ⓐ   a service to our community. I am teaching an eleven-year-old boy to play the violin. At first, he did not know ⓑhow to read a note. Now he can play a simple song. ⓒ그가 바이올린을 연주하는 걸 듣는 것은 저를 매우 행복하게 합니다.   ⓓ   joining our club, you can have an opportunity to help others. Come and join our club. We are waiting for you.

21 위 글의 빈칸 ⓐ와 ⓓ에 들어갈 전치사가 바르게 짝지어진 것은?

① to – By   ② as – To
③ as – By   ④ at – In
⑤ on – For

22 위 글의 밑줄 친 ⓑhow to read와 to부정사의 용법이 다른 것을 <u>모두</u> 고르시오.

① It is interesting <u>to play</u> tennis.
② Tell me the way <u>to play</u> tennis well.
③ I think it interesting <u>to play</u> tennis.
④ He got up early <u>to play</u> tennis.
⑤ I'm healthy enough <u>to play</u> tennis.

23 위 글의 밑줄 친 ⓒ의 우리말에 맞게 주어진 어휘를 이용하여 9 단어로 영작하시오.

┌──────────────────────────┐
hearing
└──────────────────────────┘

➡ _____

INSIGHT
on the textbook

교과서 파헤치기

※ 다음 영어를 우리말로 쓰시오.

01	favor		22	wash	
02	overcome		23	surprise	
03	detective		24	save	
04	weak		25	book fair	
05	complete		26	Chinese	
06	worry		27	walk	
07	Europe		28	weakness	
08	experience		29	missing	
09	start		30	someday	
10	by		31	pleased	
11	stay		32	fully	
12	right		33	finally	
13	adopt		34	spend	
14	freely		35	take care of	
15	cartoon		36	be willing to 동사원형	
16	writer		37	for a while	
17	goal		38	share A with B	
18	hope		39	ask for help	
19	introduce		40	get into	
20	challenging		41	be ready to 동사원형	
21	draw		42	make an effort	
			43	throw away	

※ 다음 우리말을 영어로 쓰시오.

01 국가의, 국민의 _____

02 콘서트 _____

03 달성하고싶은일들을적은목록 _____

04 드라마 _____

05 악기 _____

06 구하다, 아끼다 _____

07 놀라게 하다 _____

08 씻다 _____

09 탐정, 형사 _____

10 도전적인, 힘든 _____

11 좋아하는 _____

12 쓰다, 소비하다 _____

13 밴드 _____

14 약점 _____

15 축제 _____

16 완전히 _____

17 과목 _____

18 언젠가 _____

19 특별한 _____

20 없어진, 분실한 _____

21 계획; 계획하다 _____

22 기쁜 _____

23 타다 _____

24 마지막으로 _____

25 팔다, 판매하다 _____

26 말하다 _____

27 입양하다 _____

28 걱정하다 _____

29 호의, 친절 _____

30 머무르다, 지내다 _____

31 극복하다 _____

32 경험하다; 경험 _____

33 약한 _____

34 완료하다, 완결하다 _____

35 ~말까지 _____

36 (병·상황 등이) 나아지다 _____

37 ~할 준비가 되다 _____

38 ~을 버리다, ~을 던지다 _____

39 도움을 청하다 _____

40 노력하다 _____

41 잠깐 _____

42 기꺼이 ~하다 _____

43 친구를 사귀다 _____

※ 다음 영영풀이에 알맞은 단어를 <보기>에서 골라 쓴 후, 우리말 뜻을 쓰시오.

1 _____ : completely: _____

2 _____ : exactly in a particular position or place _____

3 _____ : difficult in an interesting or enjoyable way: _____

4 _____ : group of musicians, especially a group that plays popular music: _____

5 _____ : without anyone stopping or limiting something: _____

6 _____ : something that you hope to achieve in the future: _____

7 _____ : to a greater degree or more times than anything else: _____

8 _____ : to successfully control a feeling or problem: _____

9 _____ : to use your money to pay for goods or services: _____

10 _____ : to produce a picture of something using a pencil, pen, etc.: _____

11 _____ : an event at which people or businesses show and sell their books: _____

12 _____ : to make someone or something safe from danger, harm, or destruction: _____

13 _____ : at an unknown time in the future, especially a long time in the future: _____

14 _____ : to finish doing or making something, especially when it has taken a long time: _____

15 _____ : something that you do for someone in order to help them or be kind to them: _____

16 _____ : someone whose job is to discover what has happened in a crime or other situation and to find the people involved: _____

right	save	freely	draw
band	complete	challenging	someday
most	favor	goal	fully
spend	detective	overcome	book fair

※ 다음 우리말과 일치하도록 빈칸에 알맞은 말을 쓰시오.

Listen & Speak 1 A

G: I _____ I _____ _____ _____ this year.

B: You will. _____ _____.

Listen & Speak 1 B

1. B: Hana, _____ _____ _____ today. Happy birthday!

   G: Thank you.

   B: _____ do you _____ _____ your birthday?

   G: _____ _____ _____ a new computer.

2. G: _____ are you _____?

   B: _____ _____ my _____ _____ for the new school year.

   G: That sounds _____! What's _____ _____ thing on your list?

   B: I _____ I _____ _____ _____ _____ new friends.

3. G: _____ was your _____ _____?

   B: _____ _____ fun! We _____ _____ our dreams _____ the future.

   G: Oh, did _____? So _____ me. What's _____?

   B: Well, first, I _____ _____ become a rock star _____.

1. B: 하나야, 오늘은 너의 생일이야. 축하해!
　　G: 고마워.
　　B: 생일 선물로 뭘 원하니?
　　G: 새 컴퓨터를 받길 바라.

2. G: 뭐 하고 있니?
　　B: 나는 새 학년을 맞이하여 소원 목록을 만들고 있어.
　　G: 멋지다! 목록의 첫 번째는 뭐니?
　　B: 나는 새로운 친구들을 많이 사귈 수 있기를 바라.

3. G: 영어 수업은 어땠니?
　　B: 재밌었어! 우리는 미래에 대한 꿈을 적었어.
　　G: 오, 그랬니? 나에게 말해줘. 너의 꿈은 뭐니?
　　B: 음, 우선, 나는 내가 언젠가 록 스타가 되길 바라.

Listen & Speak 1 C

1. A: I _____ _____ _____ _____ to Europe _____ summer.

   B: That _____ great.

2. A: I _____ I _____ my grandmother.

   B: That _____ great.

3. A: I _____ _____ _____ how _____ swim.

   B: That _____ _____.

1. A: 나는 이번 여름에 유럽으로 여행을 할 수 있기를 바라.
　　B: 좋은데.

2. A: 나는 할머니를 뵐 수 있기를 바라.
　　B: 좋은데.

3. A: 나는 수영하는 법을 배울 수 있기를 바라.
　　B: 좋은데.

Everyday English 2. A Function Practice 2

G: _____ _____ _____ _____ _____ do tomorrow?

B: I'm _____ _____ _____ my hair _____.

G: 내일 뭐 할 계획이니?
B: 이발을 할 계획이야.

Everyday English 2 – B Listening Activity

1. B: What are you _____ _____ _____ _____?

   G: _____ _____ to go to the _____ _____ _____ Jimmy.

   Would you _____ _____ _____ us?

   B: Sure. _____ _____ are you _____ _____ _____?

   G: _____ 3:00 _____ _____ _____ the school cafeteria.

2. G: What _____ _____ _____ to do tomorrow?

   B: Well, I'm _____ _____.

   G: Then _____ _____ _____ to a movie _____ me?

   B: That _____ wonderful.

3. G: Jack! _____ you do me _____ _____?

   B: Yes, _____ is it?

   G: I'm planning _____ _____ a new bike _____. Can you

   _____ me _____ _____?

   B: Sure, I'd _____ _____.

1. B: 내일 뭐 할 거니?
   G: 지미랑 도서 박람회에 갈 계획이야. 같이 갈래?
   B: 물론이지. 몇 시에 만날 거니?
   G: 학교 식당 앞에서 3시에.

2. G: 내일 뭐 할 계획이니?
   B: 글쎄, 잘 모르겠어.
   G: 그럼, 나랑 영화 보러 가는 게 어때?
   B: 좋아.

3. G: 잭! 부탁 좀 들어줄래?
   B: 응, 뭔데?
   G: 내일 새 자전거를 살 계획이야. 하나 고르는 걸 도와줄 수 있니?
   B: 좋아. 그러고 싶어.

Listen & Speak 2 C

1. A: What are you planning to _____ _____ the school festival?

   B: I'm _____ _____ _____ snacks.

2. A: What _____ _____ _____ _____ do at the school festival?

   B: I'm _____ _____ _____ _____ _____ _____ show.

3. A: _____ _____ _____ _____ _____ to do at the school festival?

   B: I'm planning _____ _____ _____ _____ _____ _____.

1. A: 학교 축제에서 뭐 할 계획이니?
   B: 간식을 팔 계획이야.

2. A: 학교 축제에서 뭐 할 계획이니?
   B: 마술 쇼를 할 계획이야.

3. A: 학교 축제에서 뭐 할 계획이니?
   B: 그룹으로 춤 출 계획이야.

※ 다음 우리말에 맞도록 대화를 영어로 쓰시오.

해석

Listen & Speak 1 A

G: _____

B: _____

1. G: 난 올해 좋은 성적을 얻길 바라.
   B: 그럴 거야. 걱정하지 마.

Listen & Speak 1 B

1. B: _____
   G: _____
   B: _____
   G: _____

2. G: _____
   B: _____
   G: _____
   B: _____

3. G: _____
   B: _____
   G: _____
   B: _____

1. B: 하나야, 오늘은 너의 생일이야. 축하해!
   G: 고마워.
   B: 생일 선물로 뭘 원하니?
   G: 새 컴퓨터를 받길 바라.

2. G: 뭐 하고 있니?
   B: 나는 새 학년을 맞이하여 소원 목록을 만들고 있어.
   G: 멋지다! 목록의 첫 번째는 뭐니?
   B: 나는 새로운 친구들을 많이 사귈 수 있기를 바라.

3. G: 영어 수업은 어땠니?
   B: 재밌었어! 우리는 미래에 대한 꿈을 적었어.
   G: 오, 그랬니? 나에게 말해줘. 너의 꿈은 뭐니?
   B: 음, 우선, 나는 내가 언젠가 록 스타가 되길 바라.

Listen & Speak 1 C

1. A: _____
   B: _____

2. A: _____
   B: _____

3. A: _____
   B: _____

1. A: 나는 이번 여름에 유럽으로 여행을 할 수 있기를 바라.
   B: 좋은데.

2. A: 나는 할머니를 뵐 수 있기를 바라.
   B: 좋은데.

3. A: 나는 수영하는 법을 배울 수 있기를 바라.
   B: 좋은데.

Everyday English 2. A Function Practice 2

G: _____

B: _____

Everyday English 2 – B Listening Activity

1. B: _____

   G: _____

   B: _____

   G: _____

2. G: _____

   B: _____

   G: _____

   B: _____

3. G: _____

   B: _____

   G: _____

   B: _____

Listen & Speak 2 C

1. A: _____

   B: _____

2. A: _____

   B: _____

3. A: _____

   B: _____

G: 내일 뭐 할 계획이니?
B: 이발을 할 계획이야.

1. B: 내일 뭐 할 거니?
   G: 지미랑 도서 박람회에 갈 계획이야. 같이 갈래?
   B: 물론이지. 몇 시에 만날 거니?
   G: 학교 식당 앞에서 3시에.

2. G: 내일 뭐 할 계획이니?
   B: 글쎄, 잘 모르겠어.
   G: 그럼, 나랑 영화 보러 가는 게 어때?
   B: 좋아.

3. G: 잭! 부탁 좀 들어줄래?
   B: 응, 뭔데?
   G: 내일 새 자전거를 살 계획이야. 하나 고르는 걸 도와줄 수 있니?
   B: 좋아. 그러고 싶어.

1. A: 학교 축제에서 뭐 할 계획이니?
   B: 간식을 팔 계획이야.

2. A: 학교 축제에서 뭐 할 계획이니?
   B: 마술 쇼를 할 계획이야.

3. A: 학교 축제에서 뭐 할 계획이니?
   B: 그룹으로 춤 출 계획이야.

※ 다음 우리말과 일치하도록 빈칸에 알맞은 것을 골라 쓰시오.

1 _____ "Bucket List" for the New _____ _____
   A. Year   B. School   C. my

2 _____, _____.
   A. everyone   B. hi

3 Today is the _____ day of _____ new school _____.
   A. year   B. our   C. first

4 I want to _____ your _____ and hopes for _____ year.
   A. this   B. plans   C. hear

5 _____ do you _____ to do _____?
   A. most   B. want   C. what

6 _____ _____ three _____ you want to do.
   A. things   B. about   C. think

7 And _____, _____ a bucket list and _____ it _____
   your friends.
   A. with   B. share   C. make   D. then

8 Hi! _____ _____.
   A. Jinsu   B. I'm

9 This is _____ bucket _____ for _____ _____.
   A. year   B. this   C. list   D. my

10 _____, I want to go _____ a bike _____ of Jejudo
   this summer.
   A. tour   B. on   C. first

11 I've _____ there before, but I want to _____ the island
   more _____ _____ my bike this time.
   A. on   B. freely   C. experience   D. been

12 My _____ goal is _____ learn _____ to play the guitar.
   A. how   B. to   C. second

13 I _____ the guitar has the _____ beautiful _____ of all
   musical _____.
   A. instruments   B. sound   C. most   D. think

---

1 나의 새 학년 버킷 리스트

2 모두들, 안녕.

3 오늘은 우리 새 학년의 첫날이에요.

4 저는 여러분들의 올해 계획과 희망을 듣고 싶어요.

5 여러분이 가장 원하는 것은 무엇인가요?

6 여러분이 원하는 것 세 가지를 생각해 보세요.

7 그러고 나서 버킷 리스트를 만들어 친구들과 공유해 봐요.

8 안녕하세요! 저는 진수예요.

9 이것은 올해 제 버킷 리스트예요.

10 우선, 저는 이번 여름에 제주도로 자전거 여행을 가고 싶어요.

11 저는 그곳을 전에 가 본 적이 있지만 이번에는 제 자전거를 타고 좀 더 자유롭게 그 섬을 경험해 보고 싶어요.

12 제 두 번째 목표는 기타 연주하는 법을 배우는 거예요.

13 저는 기타가 모든 악기 중에 가장 아름다운 소리를 낸다고 생각해요.

14 I hope I can _____ my favorite song _____ my guitar _____ the _____ of this year.
A. end   B. by   C. on   D. play

15 _____, I want to _____ a good _____ _____ math.
A. in   B. grade   C. get   D. finally

16 Math is my _____ _____.
A. subject   B. weakest

17 This year, I'll _____ more effort _____ studying math to _____ my _____.
A. weakness   B. overcome   C. into   D. put

18 Hi! _____ _____ _____ Somi.
A. is   B. name   C. my

19 First, I want to see a concert of my _____ band _____ in _____ of the _____.
A. stage   B. front   C. right   D. favorite

20 I'm _____ to stand in _____ all night to _____ the front area.
A. enter   B. line   C. willing

21 _____, I want to _____ a _____.
A. puppy   B. adopt   C. second

22 I've _____ _____ a puppy.
A. wanted   B. always

23 I think I'm _____ _____ to take _____ of a pet now.
A. care   B. ready   C. fully

24 My _____ goal is a _____ more _____.
A. challenging   B. little   C. last

25 I'd _____ to read _____ of the Sherlock Holmes _____.
A. stories   B. all   C. like

26 I became a _____ fan of this _____ series last year, _____ I don't want to _____ a single one.
A. miss   B. so   C. detective   D. big

14 올해 말쯤에는 제가 가장 좋아하는 곡을 제 기타로 연주할 수 있으면 좋겠어요.

15 마지막으로 수학에서 좋은 점수를 받고 싶어요.

16 수학은 제가 가장 약한 과목이에요.

17 올해는 제 약점을 극복하기 위해 수학 공부에 좀 더 노력을 기울일 거예요.

18 안녕하세요! 제 이름은 소미예요.

19 우선, 저는 제가 가장 좋아하는 밴드의 공연을 무대 바로 앞에서 보고 싶어요.

20 앞자리에 들어가기 위해 저는 기꺼이 밤새 줄을 서서 기다릴 거예요.

21 두 번째로, 강아지를 입양하고 싶어요.

22 저는 항상 강아지를 원해 왔어요.

23 이제는 제가 애완동물을 돌볼 준비가 완벽히 되었다고 생각해요.

24 제 마지막 목표는 좀 더 도전적이에요.

25 저는 셜록 홈스 이야기들을 모두 읽고 싶어요.

26 저는 작년에 이 탐정 시리즈의 열성 팬이 되었어요. 그래서 저는 단 하나도 놓치고 싶지 않아요.

※ 다음 우리말과 일치하도록 빈칸에 알맞은 말을 쓰시오.

1 My "Bucket List" _____ _____ _____ _____ _____

2 _____, _____.

3 Today is _____ _____ _____ of our _____ _____ _____.

4 I _____ _____ _____ your plans and hopes _____ _____ _____.

5 _____ do you _____ to do _____?

6 _____ _____ three things _____ _____ _____ _____.

7 And then, _____ _____ _____ _____ and _____ it _____ your friends.

8 Hi! _____ Jinsu.

9 _____ _____ my bucket list for _____ _____.

10 First, I want to _____ _____ _____ _____ of Jejudo _____ _____.

11 _____ _____ _____ _____, but I want to experience the island more _____ _____ _____ _____ this time.

12 My _____ _____ is to learn _____ _____ _____ the guitar.

13 I think the guitar has _____ _____ _____ _____ of all _____ _____.

1 나의 새 학년 버킷 리스트

2 모두들, 안녕.

3 오늘은 우리 새 학년의 첫날이에요.

4 저는 여러분들의 올해 계획과 희망을 듣고 싶어요.

5 여러분이 가장 원하는 것은 무엇인가요?

6 여러분이 원하는 것 세 가지를 생각해 보세요.

7 그리고 나서 버킷 리스트를 만들어 친구들과 공유해 봐요.

8 안녕하세요! 저는 진수예요.

9 이것은 올해 제 버킷 리스트예요.

10 우선, 저는 이번 여름에 제주도로 자전거 여행을 가고 싶어요.

11 저는 그곳을 전에 가 본 적이 있지만 이번에는 제 자전거를 타고 좀 더 자유롭게 그 섬을 경험해 보고 싶어요.

12 제 두 번째 목표는 기타 연주하는 법을 배우는 거예요.

13 저는 기타가 모든 악기 중에 가장 아름다운 소리를 낸다고 생각해요.

14 I _____ I _____ _____ my favorite song _____ my guitar _____ _____ _____ _____ this year.

15 _____, I want to _____ _____ _____ _____ in math.

16 Math is my _____ _____.

17 This year, I'll _____ more effort _____ studying math _____ _____ _____ _____ _____.

18 Hi! _____ _____ _____ Somi.

19 First, I _____ _____ _____ a concert of my favorite band _____ _____ _____ _____ the stage.

20 I'm _____ to _____ _____ _____ all night to enter the _____ _____.

21 _____, I want to _____ _____ _____.

22 _____ always _____ a puppy.

23 I think _____ fully _____ _____ _____ _____ _____ a pet now.

24 My _____ _____ is _____ _____ _____ _____ _____.

25 _____ _____ _____ read _____ _____ the Sherlock Holmes stories.

26 I became _____ _____ _____ of this _____ _____ last year, so I don't want to _____ _____ _____ _____.

14 올해 말쯤에는 제가 가장 좋아하는 곡을 제 기타로 연주할 수 있으면 좋겠어요.

15 마지막으로 수학에서 좋은 점수를 받고 싶어요.

16 수학은 제가 가장 약한 과목이에요.

17 올해는 제 약점을 극복하기 위해 수학 공부에 좀 더 노력을 기울일 거예요.

18 안녕하세요! 제 이름은 소미예요.

19 우선, 저는 제가 가장 좋아하는 밴드의 공연을 무대 바로 앞에서 보고 싶어요.

20 앞자리에 들어가기 위해 저는 기꺼이 밤새 줄을 서서 기다릴 거예요.

21 두 번째로, 강아지를 입양하고 싶어요.

22 저는 항상 강아지를 원해 왔어요.

23 이제는 제가 애완동물을 돌볼 준비가 완벽히 되었다고 생각해요.

24 제 마지막 목표는 좀 더 도전적이에요.

25 저는 셜록 홈스 이야기들을 모두 읽고 싶어요.

26 저는 작년에 이 탐정 시리즈의 열성 팬이 되었어요. 그래서 저는 단 하나도 놓치고 싶지 않아요.

※ 다음 문장을 우리말로 쓰시오.

1 My "Bucket List" for the New School Year

➡ _____

2 Hi, everyone.

➡ _____

3 Today is the first day of our new school year.

➡ _____

4 I want to hear your plans and hopes for this year.

➡ _____

5 What do you want to do most?

➡ _____

6 Think about three things you want to do.

➡ _____

7 And then, make a bucket list and share it with your friends.

➡ _____

8 Hi! I'm Jinsu.

➡ _____

9 This is my bucket list for this year.

➡ _____

10 First, I want to go on a bike tour of Jejudo this summer.

➡ _____

11 I've been there before, but I want to experience the island more freely on my bike this time.

➡ _____

12 My second goal is to learn how to play the guitar.

➡ _____

13 I think the guitar has the most beautiful sound of all musical instruments.

➡ _____

14 I hope I can play my favorite song on my guitar by the end of this year.

➡ _____

15 Finally, I want to get a good grade in math.

➡ _____

16 Math is my weakest subject.

➡ _____

17 This year, I'll put more effort into studying math to overcome my weakness.

➡ _____

18 Hi! My name is Somi.

➡ _____

19 First, I want to see a concert of my favorite band right in front of the stage.

➡ _____

20 I'm willing to stand in line all night to enter the front area.

➡ _____

21 Second, I want to adopt a puppy.

➡ _____

22 I've always wanted a puppy.

➡ _____

23 I think I'm fully ready to take care of a pet now.

➡ _____

24 My last goal is a little more challenging.

➡ _____

25 I'd like to read all of the Sherlock Holmes stories.

➡ _____

26 I became a big fan of this detective series last year, so I don't want to miss a single one.

➡ _____

Step4

※ 다음 괄호 안의 단어들을 우리말에 맞도록 바르게 배열하시오.

1 ("Bucket / My / List" / for / New / Year / the / School)
➡ _____

2 (everyone. / hi,)
➡ _____

3 (is / today / first / the / day / of / new / our / year. / school)
➡ _____

4 (want / I / hear / to / plans / your / and / hopes / year. / this / for)
➡ _____

5 (do / you / what / want / to / most? / do)
➡ _____

6 (about / think / things / three / want / do. / you / to)
➡ _____

7 (then, / and / a / make / list / bucket / and / share / with / it / friends. / your)
➡ _____

8 (I'm / Hi! / Jinsu.)
➡ _____

9 (is / this / bucket / my / for / list / year. / this)
➡ _____

10 (I / first, / to / want / on / go / a / tour / bike / Jejudo / of / summer. / this)
➡ _____

11 (been / I've / before, / there / but / want / I / experience / to / the / more / island / freely / my / on / bike / time. / this)
➡ _____

12 (second / my / goal / is / to / how / learn / play / to / guitar. / the)
➡ _____

13 (think / I / guitar / the / has / most / the / sound / beautiful / of / all / instruments. / musical)
➡ _____

1 나의 새 학년 버킷 리스트

2 모두들, 안녕.

3 오늘은 우리 새 학년의 첫날이에요.

4 저는 여러분들의 올해 계획과 희망을 듣고 싶어요.

5 여러분이 가장 원하는 것은 무엇인가요?

6 여러분이 원하는 것 세 가지를 생각해 보세요.

7 그리고 나서 버킷 리스트를 만들어 친구들과 공유해 봐요.

8 안녕하세요! 저는 진수예요.

9 이것은 올해 제 버킷 리스트예요.

10 우선, 저는 이번 여름에 제주도로 자전거 여행을 가고 싶어요.

11 저는 그곳을 전에 가 본 적이 있지만 이번에는 제 자전거를 타고 좀 더 자유롭게 그 섬을 경험해 보고 싶어요.

12 제 두 번째 목표는 기타 연주하는 법을 배우는 거예요.

13 저는 기타가 모든 악기 중에 가장 아름다운 소리를 낸다고 생각해요.

14 (hope / I / can / I / play / favorite / my / song / my / on / guitar / by / end / the / of / year. / this)

➡ _____

15 (I / finally, / to / want / a / get / grade / good / math. / in)

➡ _____

16 (is / math / subject. / weakest / my)

➡ _____

17 (year, / this / put / I'll / effort / more / studying / into / math / overcome / to / weakness. / my)

➡ _____

18 (my / hi! / is / Somi. / name)

➡ _____

19 (I / first, / to / want / a / see / concert / of / favorite / my / right / band / of / front / in / stage. / the)

➡ _____

20 (willing / I'm / stand / to / line / in / night / all / enter / to / area. / front / the)

➡ _____

21 (I / second, / to / want / puppy. / a / adopt)

➡ _____

22 (always / I've / a / wanted / puppy.)

➡ _____

23 (think / I / fully / I'm / to / ready / care / take / now. / of / pet / a)

➡ _____

24 (last / my / goal / is / little / a / challenging. / more)

➡ _____

25 (like / I'd / read / to / of / all / the / Holmes / Sherlock / stories.)

➡ _____

26 (became / I / big / a / fan / detective / of / this / series / year, / last / so / don't / I / want / miss / to / one. / single / a)

➡ _____

14 올해 말쯤에는 제가 가장 좋아하는 곡을 제 기타로 연주할 수 있으면 좋겠어요.

15 마지막으로 수학에서 좋은 점수를 받고 싶어요.

16 수학은 제가 가장 약한 과목이에요.

17 올해는 제 약점을 극복하기 위해 수학 공부에 좀 더 노력을 기울일 거예요.

18 안녕하세요! 제 이름은 소미예요.

19 우선, 저는 제가 가장 좋아하는 밴드의 공연을 무대 바로 앞에서 보고 싶어요.

20 앞자리에 들어가기 위해 저는 기꺼이 밤새 줄을 서서 기다릴 거예요.

21 두 번째로, 강아지를 입양하고 싶어요.

22 저는 항상 강아지를 원해 왔어요.

23 이제는 제가 애완동물을 돌볼 준비가 완벽히 되었다고 생각해요.

24 제 마지막 목표는 좀 더 도전적이에요.

25 저는 셜록 홈스 이야기들을 모두 읽고 싶어요.

26 저는 작년에 이 탐정 시리즈의 열성 팬이 되었어요. 그래서 저는 단 하나도 놓치고 싶지 않아요.

※ 다음 우리말을 영어로 쓰시오.

1 나의 새 학년 버킷 리스트

➡ _____

2 모두들, 안녕.

➡ _____

3 오늘은 우리 새 학년의 첫날이에요.

➡ _____

4 저는 여러분들의 올해 계획과 희망을 듣고 싶어요.

➡ _____

5 여러분이 가장 원하는 것은 무엇인가요?

➡ _____

6 여러분이 원하는 것 세 가지를 생각해 보세요.

➡ _____

7 그러고 나서 버킷 리스트를 만들어 친구들과 공유해 봐요.

➡ _____

8 안녕하세요! 저는 진수예요.

➡ _____

9 이것은 올해 제 버킷 리스트예요.

➡ _____

10 우선, 저는 이번 여름에 제주도로 자전거 여행을 가고 싶어요.

➡ _____

11 저는 그곳을 전에 가 본 적이 있지만 이번에는 제 자전거를 타고 좀 더 자유롭게 그 섬을 경험해 보고 싶어요.

➡ _____

12 제 두 번째 목표는 기타 연주하는 법을 배우는 거예요.

➡ _____

13 저는 기타가 모든 악기 중에 가장 아름다운 소리를 낸다고 생각해요.

➡ _____

14 올해 말쯤에는 제가 가장 좋아하는 곡을 제 기타로 연주할 수 있으면 좋겠어요.

➡ _____

15 마지막으로 수학에서 좋은 점수를 받고 싶어요.

➡ _____

16 수학은 제가 가장 약한 과목이에요.

➡ _____

17 올해는 제 약점을 극복하기 위해 수학 공부에 좀 더 노력을 기울일 거예요.

➡ _____

18 안녕하세요! 제 이름은 소미예요.

➡ _____

19 우선, 저는 제가 가장 좋아하는 밴드의 공연을 무대 바로 앞에서 보고 싶어요.

➡ _____

20 앞자리에 들어가기 위해 저는 기꺼이 밤새 줄을 서서 기다릴 거예요.

➡ _____

21 두 번째로, 강아지를 입양하고 싶어요.

➡ _____

22 저는 항상 강아지를 원해 왔어요.

➡ _____

23 이제는 제가 애완동물을 돌볼 준비가 완벽히 되었다고 생각해요.

➡ _____

24 제 마지막 목표는 좀 더 도전적이에요.

➡ _____

25 저는 셜록 홈스 이야기들을 모두 읽고 싶어요.

➡ _____

26 저는 작년에 이 탐정 시리즈의 열성 팬이 되었어요. 그래서 저는 단 하나도 놓치고 싶지 않아요.

➡ _____

※ 다음 우리말과 일치하도록 빈칸에 알맞은 말을 쓰시오.

Work Together Step 3

1. This is the _____ _____ _____ _____.

2. First, I _____ I _____ meet my favorite _____.

3. _____, I hope I can _____ _____ _____ my role model.

4. _____, I hope I _____ _____ to _____ countries.

5. We _____ ninety dollars _____ _____ these items.

1. 이것은 우리가 산 버킷 리스트이다.
2. 첫째, 나는 내가 좋아하는 배우를 만나기를 바란다.
3. 둘째, 나는 역할 모델과 식사할 수 있기를 바란다.
4. 셋째, 나는 다른 나라를 여행할 수 있기를 바란다.
5. 이것들을 사기 위해 나는 90달러를 사용했다.

Writing Workshop

1. My "Bucket List" for _____ _____

2. _____ _____ my bucket list.

3. _____, I want to learn _____ _____ _____ cookies.

4. I _____ _____ make them _____ _____ my mom.

5. _____, I want _____ _____ a simple _____.

6. I will _____ _____ things _____ I do _____ _____.

7. The _____ _____ is _____ _____ online English _____ every day.

8. _____ _____ _____ of this year, I _____ _____ my problems with my _____ subject, English.

1. 올해의 나의 "버킷 리스트"
2. 여기에 나의 버킷 리스트가 있어.
3. 먼저, 나는 쿠키 만드는 법을 배우고 싶어.
4. 나는 엄마를 놀라게 하기 위해 그것들을 만들고 싶어.
5. 두 번째로, 나는 간소한 삶을 살고 싶어.
6. 나는 필요하지 않은 물건들을 버릴 거야.
7. 마지막 것은 매일 온라인으로 영어 공부를 하는 거야.
8. 올해 말에는 나는 가장 약한 과목인 영어에서의 문제를 극복할 거야.

Solve the Problem

1. Hi, _____ _____ Gijun.

2. I hope I _____ _____ _____ this year, but I sleep too much.

3. Could you _____ me _____ _____?

4. _____ _____ _____ go to bed on time and _____ _____ early?

5. I think you need to _____ _____ _____ _____ and sleep on a regular schedule to _____ _____ _____.

1. 안녕, 나는 기준이야.
2. 나는 올해 좋은 성적을 받길 바라, 하지만 나는 너무 많이 자.
3. 나에게 조언을 좀 해주겠니?
4. 정해진 시간에 자고 일찍 일어나는 게 어떠니?
5. 나는 좋은 성적을 받기 위해서 네가 일찍 자고 규칙적으로 잘 필요가 있다고 생각해.

※ 다음 우리말을 영어로 쓰시오.

Work Together Step 3

1. 이것은 우리가 산 버킷 리스트이다.
   ➡ _____

2. 첫째, 나는 내가 좋아하는 배우를 만나기를 바란다.
   ➡ _____

3. 둘째, 나는 역할 모델과 식사할 수 있기를 바란다.
   ➡ _____

4. 셋째, 나는 다른 나라를 여행할 수 있기를 바란다.
   ➡ _____

5. 이것들을 사기 위해 나는 90달러를 사용했다.
   ➡ _____

Writing Workshop

1. 올해의 나의 "버킷 리스트"
   ➡ _____

2. 여기에 나의 버킷 리스트가 있어.
   ➡ _____

3. 먼저, 나는 쿠키 만드는 법을 배우고 싶어.
   ➡ _____

4. 나는 엄마를 놀라게 하기 위해 그것들을 만들고 싶어.
   ➡ _____

5. 두 번째로, 나는 간소한 삶을 살고 싶어.
   ➡ _____

6. 나는 필요하지 않은 물건들을 버릴 거야.
   ➡ _____

7. 마지막 것은 매일 온라인으로 영어 공부를 하는 거야.
   ➡ _____

8. 올해 말에는 나는 가장 약한 과목인 영어에서의 문제를 극복할 거야.
   ➡ _____

Solve the Problem

1. 안녕, 나는 기준이야.
   ➡ _____

2. 나는 올해 좋은 성적을 받길 바라, 하지만 나는 너무 많이 자.
   ➡ _____

3. 나에게 조언을 좀 해주겠니?
   ➡ _____

4. 정해진 시간에 자고 일찍 일어나는 게 어떠니?
   ➡ _____

5. 나는 좋은 성적을 받기 위해서 네가 일찍 자고 규칙적으로 잘 필요가 있다고 생각해.
   ➡ _____

※ 다음 영어를 우리말로 쓰시오.

01	pose	22	weather
02	bend	23	increase
03	pull	24	pain
04	hall	25	rule
05	advice	26	hurt
06	blink	27	upset
07	avoid	28	pressure
08	tip	29	prevent
09	lean	30	historical
10	back	31	break
11	deserted	32	worse
12	letter	33	crack
13	lower	34	uncomfortable
14	novel	35	be good for
15	check	36	cut down on
16	protect	37	right away
17	service center	38	get in touch with
18	text	39	pay attention to
19	wrist	40	from time to time
20	reduce	41	keep A from B
21	hold	42	depend on
		43	keep in mind

※ 다음 우리말을 영어로 쓰시오.

01 금, 깨진 틈 _____

02 초래하다, 야기하다 _____

03 떨어뜨리다 _____

04 규칙 _____

05 불편한 _____

06 ～ 아래에 _____

07 잡다 _____

08 증가하다 _____

09 역사적인 _____

10 나쁜 _____

11 휴식 _____

12 구명 조끼 _____

13 압력 _____

14 고통 _____

15 날씨 _____

16 줄이다, 감소시키다 _____

17 다치게 하다, 아프다 _____

18 화난 _____

19 예방하다, 막다 _____

20 (눈을) 깜빡이다 _____

21 손목 _____

22 피하다 _____

23 등 _____

24 보호하다 _____

25 당기다 _____

26 자세 _____

27 버려진 _____

28 복도 _____

29 조언, 비법 _____

30 확인하다 _____

31 기대다 _____

32 낮추다 _____

33 문자, 글자 _____

34 충고 _____

35 ～에 주의를 기울이다 _____

36 ～에 늦다 _____

37 ～에 의존하다 _____

38 ～와 연락[접촉]하다 _____

39 ～ 대신에 _____

40 ～을 줄이다 _____

41 적어도 _____

42 돌려주다 _____

43 산책하다 _____

※ 다음 영영풀이에 알맞은 단어를 <보기>에서 골라 쓴 후, 우리말 뜻을 쓰시오.

1 _____ : a helpful piece of advice: _____

2 _____ : to prevent something bad from happening: _____

3 _____ : empty and quiet because no people are there: _____

4 _____ : to fall suddenly onto the ground or into something: _____

5 _____ : to shut and open your eyes quickly: _____

6 _____ : to keep someone or something safe from harm, damage, or illness:

_____

7 _____ : a long written story in which the characters and events are usually

imaginary: _____

8 _____ : to move something down from higher up: _____

9 _____ : to make something smaller or less in size, amount, or price:

_____

10 _____ : a period of time when you stop working in order to rest, eat, etc.:

_____

11 _____ : to make something happen, especially something bad: _____

12 _____ : to send someone a written message on a mobile phone: _____

13 _____ : not feeling physically comfortable, or not making you feel comfortable:

_____

14 _____ : the area just inside the door of a house or other building, that leads to

other rooms: _____

15 _____ : to stop something from happening, or stop someone from doing

something: _____

16 _____ : unhappy and worried because something unpleasant or disappointing has

happened: _____

※ 다음 우리말과 일치하도록 빈칸에 알맞은 말을 쓰시오.

Listen & Speak 1 A

G: Oh, no! I have _____ _____ _____ my eyes.

M: You _____ _____ _____ _____.

1. G: 오, 이런! 눈 밑에 다크서클이 있어요.
   M: 너는 잠을 더 자야 한단다.

Listen & Speak 1 B

1. G: I _____ Jenny's birthday!

   B: _____ she your _____ _____?

   G: _____, she is. _____ _____ _____ _____ _____?

   B: _____ _____ _____ _____ _____ _____ her you're very sorry.

2. B: I _____ _____.

   G: Why? What's the _____?

   B: I _____ _____ 5 kg _____ winter. _____ _____ I do?

   G: I think you _____ _____ _____ _____ snacks.

1. G: 제니의 생일을 잊어버렸어!
   B: 그녀는 너의 가장 친한 친구 아니니?
   G: 응, 맞아. 어떻게 해야 할까?
   B: 나는 네가 그녀에게 정말 미안하다고 말해야 한다고 생각해.

2. B: 기분이 우울해.
   G: 왜? 무슨 일이니?
   B: 이번 겨울에 5kg이 늘었어. 어떻게 해야 할까?
   G: 나는 네가 간식을 줄여야 한다고 생각해.

Listen & Speak 1 C

1. A: I'm _____ _____ _____ school. What _____ _____ do?

   B: You _____ _____ _____ _____ _____ on your smartphone.

2. A: I _____ a _____. _____ _____ do?

   B: You _____ _____ _____ _____ _____.

3. A: My phone _____ _____. _____ _____ _____ _____?

   B: You should _____ it to _____ _____ _____.

1. A: 나는 항상 학교에 늦어. 어떻게 해야 할까?
   B: 너는 스마트폰 알람을 맞춰야 해.
2. A: 두통이 있어. 어떻게 해야 할까?
   B: 너는 좀 쉬어야 해.
3. A: 내 휴대 전화가 작동하지 않아. 어떻게 해야 할까?
   B: 너는 그것을 서비스 센터에 가져가야 해.

Listen & Speak 2 A

W: _____ _____ you are home _____ 12:00.

G: Okay, I _____.

W: 반드시 12까지는 집에 있도록 하세요.
G: 알겠어요, 그럴게요.

Listen & Speak 2 B

1. **B:** Mom, may I _____ _____ _____ Jinsu's house?

   W: Did Jinsu's mom _____ it was _____?

   B: Yes. Jinsu _____ she _____ _____ pizza for us.

   W: Okay. _____ _____ _____ _____ me when you _____ _____ Jinsu's house.

2. **G:** Daniel, _____ are you _____?

   B: I'm _____ a novel _____ my smartphone.

   G: Make sure you _____ _____ _____ _____ _____. It's _____ _____ _____ your eyes.

   B: Okay. I'll _____ the light _____.

3. **B:** Oh, no! I _____ _____ my science book!

   G: Ms. Lee _____ be happy about that.

   B: I know. Umm, can I _____ your science book?

   G: Okay. Just _____ _____ you _____ _____ _____ _____ you're _____.

Listen & Speak 2 C

1. **A:** _____ I _____ this pizza?

   B: Sure. Just _____ _____ _____ wash your hands _____.

2. **A:** _____ _____ use this computer?

   B: Sure. Just make sure you _____ _____ _____ _____ _____.

3. **A:** _____ _____ _____ _____ this boat?

   B: Sure. Just _____ _____ you _____ _____.

1. B: 엄마, 진수네 집에서 자고 와도 돼요?
   W: 진수 엄마가 괜찮다고 하셨니?
   B: 네. 진수는 그녀가 우리를 위해 피자를 만들 것이라고 말했어요.
   W: 알겠어. 진수네 집에 도착하면 반드시 나에게 문자 하렴.
2. G: 다니엘, 뭐 하고 있니?
   B: 스마트폰에서 소설을 읽고 있어.
   G: 반드시 어두운 곳에서 읽지 않도록 해. 너의 눈에 좋지 않아.
   B: 알겠어. 불을 켤게.
3. B: 오, 이런! 과학 책을 가져오지 않았어!
   G: 이 선생님께서 좋아하지 않으실 거야.
   B: 알아. 음, 네 과학 책을 빌릴 수 있을까?
   G: 좋아. 다 사용하면 반드시 다시 돌려주도록 해.

1. A: 이 피자를 먹어도 되나요?
   B: 물론이죠. 반드시 손을 먼저 씻도록 하세요.
2. A: 이 컴퓨터를 사용해도 되나요?
   B: 물론이죠. 사용 후에는 반드시 전원을 끄도록 하세요.
3. A: 이 보트를 타도 되나요?
   B: 물론이죠. 구명조끼를 반드시 입도록 하세요.

※ 다음 우리말에 맞도록 대화를 영어로 쓰시오.

Listen & Speak 1 A

G: _____

M: _____

Listen & Speak 1 B

1. G: _____

   B: _____

   G: _____

   B: _____

2. B: _____

   G: _____

   B: _____

   G: _____

Listen & Speak 1 C

1. A: _____

   B: _____

2. A: _____

   B: _____

3. A: _____

   B: _____

Listen & Speak 2 A

W: _____

G: _____

해석

1. G: 오, 이런! 눈 밑에 다크서클이 있어요.
   M: 너는 잠을 더 자야 한단다.

1. G: 제니의 생일을 잊어버렸어!
   B: 그녀는 너의 가장 친한 친구 아니니?
   G: 응, 맞아. 어떻게 해야 할까?
   B: 나는 네가 그녀에게 정말 미안하다고 말해야 한다고 생각해.

2. B: 기분이 우울해.
   G: 왜? 무슨 일이니?
   B: 이번 겨울에 5kg이 늘었어. 어떻게 해야 할까?
   G: 나는 네가 간식을 줄여야 한다고 생각해.

1. A: 나는 항상 학교에 늦어. 어떻게 해야 할까?
   B: 너는 스마트폰 알람을 맞춰야 해.
2. A: 두통이 있어. 어떻게 해야 할까?
   B: 너는 좀 쉬어야 해.
3. A: 내 휴대 전화가 작동하지 않아. 어떻게 해야 할까?
   B: 너는 그것을 서비스 센터에 가져가야 해.

W: 반드시 12까지는 집에 있도록 하세요.
G: 알겠어요, 그럴게요.

Listen & Speak 2 B

1. B: _____

   W: _____

   B: _____

   W: _____

2. G: _____

   B: _____

   G: _____

   B: _____

3. B: _____

   G: _____

   B: _____

   G: _____

1. B: 엄마, 진수네 집에서 자고 와도 돼요?

   W: 진수 엄마가 괜찮다고 하셨니?

   B: 네. 진수는 그녀가 우리를 위해 피자를 만들 것이라고 말했어요.

   W: 알겠어. 진수네 집에 도착하면 반드시 나에게 문자 하렴.

2. G: 다니엘, 뭐 하고 있니?

   B: 스마트폰에서 소설을 읽고 있어.

   G: 반드시 어두운 곳에서 읽지 않도록 해. 너의 눈에 좋지 않아.

   B: 알겠어. 불을 켤게.

3. B: 오, 이런! 과학 책을 가져오지 않았어!

   G: 이 선생님께서 좋아하지 않으실 거야.

   B: 알아. 음, 네 과학 책을 빌릴 수 있을까?

   G: 좋아. 다 사용하면 반드시 다시 돌려주도록 해.

Listen & Speak 2 C

1. A: _____

   B: _____

2. A: _____

   B: _____

3. A: _____

   B: _____

1. A: 이 피자를 먹어도 되나요?

   B: 물론이죠. 반드시 손을 먼저 씻도록 하세요.

2. A: 이 컴퓨터를 사용해도 되나요?

   B: 물론이죠. 사용 후에는 반드시 전원을 끄도록 하세요.

3. A: 이 보트를 타도 되나요?

   B: 물론이죠. 구명조끼를 반드시 입도록 하세요.

※ 다음 우리말과 일치하도록 빈칸에 알맞은 것을 골라 쓰시오.

1 _____ _____ for Smartphone _____
   A. Users   B. Tips   C. Health

2 Seongmin _____ a _____ of time _____ his smartphone.
   A. using   B. lot   C. spends

3 He _____ the _____ and _____ .
   A. weather   B. checks   C. news

4 He _____ smartphone _____ .
   A. games   B. plays

5 He _____ _____ friends.
   A. his   B. texts

6 He _____ _____ on the _____ .
   A. Internet   B. information   C. finds

7 He reads _____ _____ _____ .
   A. books   B. online   C. comic

8 He _____ _____ .
   A. movies   B. watches

9 Seongmin cannot _____ his hands _____ his smartphone all day _____ .
   A. long   B. take   C. off

10 He does not know that _____ a smartphone _____ much can _____ _____ problems.
   A. health   B. using   C. too   D. cause

11 Are you a _____ _____ of your smartphone _____ Seongmin?
   A. like   B. user   C. heavy

12 If _____ , here are some _____ to _____ your health.
   A. protect   B. so   C. tips

13 _____ your _____ and _____ .
   A. back   B. neck   C. watch

14 _____ you _____ on your smartphone, you _____ _____ your neck.
   A. bend   B. when   C. read   D. usually

15 This " _____ neck" pose _____ the _____ on your neck and _____ .
   A. back   B. text   C. increases   D. pressure

16 The best way to _____ this pressure is to _____ the phone _____ _____ the level of your eyes.
   A. to   B. prevent   C. bring   D. up

---

1 스마트폰 사용자들을 위한 건강 조언

2 성민이는 스마트폰을 사용하는 데 많은 시간을 보냅니다.

3 그는 뉴스와 날씨를 확인합니다.

4 그는 스마트폰 게임을 합니다.

5 그는 친구들에게 문자 메시지를 보냅니다.

6 그는 인터넷에서 정보를 찾습니다.

7 그는 온라인 만화책을 읽습니다.

8 그는 영화를 봅니다.

9 성민이는 하루 종일 스마트폰에서 손을 뗄 수가 없습니다.

10 그는 스마트폰을 너무 많이 사용하는 것이 건강 문제를 일으킬 수 있다는 것을 모릅니다.

11 여러분은 성민이와 같은 스마트폰 과다 사용자인가요?

12 그렇다면, 여기 여러분의 건강을 지켜 줄 몇 가지 조언이 있습니다.

13 여러분의 목과 척추를 조심하세요.

14 스마트폰을 볼 때, 여러분은 보통 목을 구부립니다.

15 이 "거북목" 자세는 여러분의 목과 척추에 가해지는 압력을 증가시킵니다.

16 이러한 압력을 예방하는 가장 좋은 방법은 휴대 전화를 여러분의 눈높이까지 올리는 것입니다.

17 _____ _____ is to lower your eyes _____ of _____ your neck.

    A. bending   B. another   C. way   D. instead

18 _____ your _____ a _____.

    A. break   B. eyes   C. give

19 It _____ your eyes _____ tired and _____ to read small letters on a smartphone _____ a long time.

    A. for   B. makes   C. feel   D. dry

20 _____ a smartphone in the dark or in a _____ car this problem _____.

    A. worse   B. makes   C. moving   D. using

21 To _____ this, give your eyes a break _____ time _____ time.

    A. to   B. from   C. avoid

22 _____ the 20-20-20 rules: _____ 20 minutes, take a 20-second break and look at something at _____ 20 feet _____.

    A. away   B. follow   C. every   D. least

23 Also, _____ your eyes _____.

    A. often   B. blink

24 This will _____ your eyes _____ _____ dry.

    A. becoming   B. from   C. keep

25 Do you _____ a _____ _____ your smartphone?

    A. on   B. text   C. lot

26 _____ for a long time can _____ your fingers and _____.

    A. wrists   B. hurt   C. texting

27 _____ these _____.

    A. exercises   B. try

28 They will _____ _____ the _____ in your fingers and wrists.

    A. pain   B. reduce   C. help

29 _____ _____ each finger of _____ hand.

    A. each   B. on   C. pull

30 _____ the _____ of your hands together _____ your arms _____ in front of you.

    A. out   B. with   C. backs   D. put

31 _____ _____.

    A. remember   B. but

32 The best _____ to _____ these health problems is to _____ your smartphone _____.

    A. less   B. tip   C. prevent   D. use

33 Give _____ some _____ _____ your smartphone.

    A. from   B. rest   C. yourself

17 또 다른 방법은 여러분의 목을 구부리는 대신에 시선을 낮추는 것입니다.

18 눈을 쉬게 하세요.

19 오랫동안 스마트폰의 작은 글자를 읽는 것은 눈이 피곤해지고 건조하게 느끼도록 만듭니다.

20 어두운 곳이나 움직이는 차에서 스마트폰을 사용하는 것은 이러한 문제를 더욱 악화시킵니다.

21 이것을 피하려면, 눈을 때때로 쉬게 하세요.

22 20-20-20 규칙을 따르세요. 20분마다 20초의 휴식을 취하고 적어도 20피트 이상 떨어져 있는 사물을 바라보세요.

23 또한, 눈을 자주 깜박이세요.

24 이것은 여러분의 눈이 건조해지는 것을 막아 줄 것입니다.

25 스마트폰으로 문자 메시지를 많이 보내나요?

26 오랫동안 문자 메시지를 보내는 것은 여러분의 손가락과 손목을 상하게 할 수 있습니다.

27 이런 운동을 해 보세요.

28 그것은 여러분의 손가락과 손목의 통증을 줄이는 것을 도와줄 것입니다.

29 각 손의 각 손가락을 당기세요.

30 팔을 여러분 앞에서 벌린 채로 손등을 마주 놓으세요.

31 그러나 기억하세요.

32 이러한 건강 문제를 예방하는 가장 좋은 방법은 스미트폰을 덜 사용하는 것입니다.

33 여러분 자신에게 스마트폰으로부터 휴식을 주세요.

※ 다음 우리말과 일치하도록 빈칸에 알맞은 말을 쓰시오.

1 _____ _____ for Smartphone _____

2 Seongmin _____ a _____ of time _____ his smartphone.

3 He _____ the _____ and _____ .

4 He _____ smartphone _____ .

5 He _____ _____ _____ .

6 He _____ _____ _____ the _____ .

7 He _____ _____ _____ _____ .

8 He _____ _____ .

9 Seongmin cannot _____ his hands _____ his smartphone _____ _____ _____ .

10 He does not know that _____ a smartphone _____ _____ can _____ _____ _____ .

11 Are you _____ _____ _____ of your smartphone _____ Seongmin?

12 _____ _____ , _____ _____ some tips _____ _____ your health.

13 _____ your _____ and _____ .

14 _____ you read on your smartphone, you _____ _____ your neck.

15 This "_____ _____" _____ _____ the pressure on your neck and back.

16 The best way _____ _____ this pressure is _____ _____ the phone _____ _____ the level of your eyes.

1 스마트폰 사용자들을 위한 건강 조언

2 성민이는 스마트폰을 사용하는 데 많은 시간을 보냅니다.

3 그는 뉴스와 날씨를 확인합니다.

4 그는 스마트폰 게임을 합니다.

5 그는 친구들에게 문자 메시지를 보냅니다.

6 그는 인터넷에서 정보를 찾습니다.

7 그는 온라인 만화책을 읽습니다.

8 그는 영화를 봅니다.

9 성민이는 하루 종일 스마트폰에 서 손을 뗄 수가 없습니다.

10 그는 스마트폰을 너무 많이 사 용하는 것이 건강 문제를 일으 킬 수 있다는 것을 모릅니다.

11 여러분은 성민이와 같은 스마트 폰 과다 사용자인가요?

12 그렇다면, 여기 여러분의 건강 을 지켜 줄 몇 가지 조언이 있습 니다.

13 여러분의 목과 척추를 조심하세요.

14 스마트폰을 볼 때, 여러분은 보 통 목을 구부립니다.

15 이 "거북목" 자세는 여러분의 목과 척추에 가해지는 압력을 증가시킵니다.

16 이러한 압력을 예방하는 가장 좋 은 방법은 휴대 전화를 여러분의 눈높이까지 올리는 것입니다.

17 _____ _____ is _____ _____ your eyes _____ _____ _____ your neck.

18 _____ your eyes _____ _____.

19 It _____ your eyes _____ _____ and dry to read small letters on a smartphone _____ _____ _____ _____.

20 _____ a smartphone _____ _____ _____ or in a moving car _____ this problem _____.

21 _____ _____ this, give your eyes a break _____ _____ _____ _____.

22 _____ the 20-20-20 rules: _____ 20 minutes, take _____ _____ _____ and look at something _____ _____ 20 _____.

23 Also, _____ your eyes _____.

24 This will _____ your eyes _____ _____ dry.

25 Do you _____ a lot _____ _____ _____?

26 _____ for a long time can _____ your fingers and wrists.

27 _____ these _____.

28 They will _____ _____ the pain in your fingers and wrists.

29 _____ _____ each finger of _____ _____.

30 _____ the backs of your hands _____ _____ _____ _____ out _____ _____ _____ you.

31 But _____.

32 _____ _____ _____ _____ these health problems is _____ _____ your smartphone _____.

33 Give yourself _____ _____ your smartphone.

17	또 다른 방법은 여러분의 목을 구부리는 대신에 시선을 낮추는 것입니다.
18	눈을 쉬게 하세요.
19	오랫동안 스마트폰의 작은 글자를 읽는 것은 눈이 피곤해지고 건조하게 느끼도록 만듭니다.
20	어두운 곳이나 움직이는 차에서 스마트폰을 사용하는 것은 이러한 문제를 더욱 악화시킵니다.
21	이것을 피하려면, 눈을 때때로 쉬게 하세요.
22	20-20-20 규칙을 따르세요. 20분마다 20초의 휴식을 취하고 적어도 20피트 이상 떨어져 있는 사물을 바라보세요.
23	또한, 눈을 자주 깜박이세요.
24	이것은 여러분의 눈이 건조해지는 것을 막아 줄 것입니다.
25	스마트폰으로 문자 메시지를 많이 보내나요?
26	오랫동안 문자 메시지를 보내는 것은 여러분의 손가락과 손목을 상하게 할 수 있습니다.
27	이런 운동을 해 보세요.
28	그것은 여러분의 손가락과 손목의 통증을 줄이는 것을 도와줄 것입니다.
29	각 손의 각 손가락을 당기세요.
30	팔을 여러분 앞에서 벌린 채로 손등을 마주 놓으세요.
31	그러나 기억하세요.
32	이러한 건강 문제를 예방하는 가장 좋은 방법은 스마트폰을 덜 사용하는 것입니다.
33	여러분 자신에게 스마트폰으로부터 휴식을 주세요.

※ 다음 문장을 우리말로 쓰시오.

1 Health Tips for Smartphone Users

➡ _____

2 Seongmin spends a lot of time using his smartphone.

➡ _____

3 He checks the news and weather.

➡ _____

4 He plays smartphone games.

➡ _____

5 He texts his friends.

➡ _____

6 He finds information on the Internet.

➡ _____

7 He reads online comic books.

➡ _____

8 He watches movies

➡ _____

9 Seongmin cannot take his hands off his smartphone all day long.

➡ _____

10 He does not know that using a smartphone too much can cause health problems.

➡ _____

11 Are you a heavy user of your smartphone like Seongmin?

➡ _____

12 If so, here are some tips to protect your health.

➡ _____

13 Watch your neck and back.

➡ _____

14 When you read on your smartphone, you usually bend your neck.

➡ _____

15 This "text neck" pose increases the pressure on your neck and back.

➡ _____

16 The best way to prevent this pressure is to bring the phone up to the level of your eyes.

➡ _____

17 Another way is to lower your eyes instead of bending your neck.

➡ _____

18 Give your eyes a break.

➡ _____

19 It makes your eyes feel tired and dry to read small letters on a smartphone for a long time.

➡ _____

20 Using a smartphone in the dark or in a moving car makes this problem worse.

➡ _____

21 To avoid this, give your eyes a break from time to time.

➡ _____

22 Follow the 20-20-20 rules: Every 20 minutes, take a 20-second break and look at something at least 20 feet away.

➡ _____

23 Also, blink your eyes often.

➡ _____

24 This will keep your eyes from becoming dry.

➡ _____

25 Do you text a lot on your smartphone?

➡ _____

26 Texting for a long time can hurt your fingers and wrists.

➡ _____

27 Try these exercises.

➡ _____

28 They will help reduce the pain in your fingers and wrists.

➡ _____

29 Pull on each finger of each hand.

➡ _____

30 Put the backs of your hands together with your arms out in front of you.

➡ _____

31 But remember.

➡ _____

32 The best tip to prevent these health problems is to use your smartphone less.

➡ _____

33 Give yourself some rest from your smartphone.

➡ _____

※ 다음 괄호 안의 단어들을 우리말에 맞도록 바르게 배열하시오.

1 (Tips / Health / Users / Smartphone / for)
➡ _____

2 (spends / Seongmin / lot / a / of / time / smartphone. / his / using)
➡ _____

3 (checks / he / news / the / weather. / and)
➡ _____

4 (plays / he / games. / smartphone)
➡ _____

5 (his / texts / friends. / he)
➡ _____

6 (finds / he / information / on / Internet. / the)
➡ _____

7 (reads / he / books. / comic / online)
➡ _____

8 (movies. / watches / he)
➡ _____

9 (cannot / Seongmin / take / hands / his / off / smartphone / his / long. / day / all)
➡ _____

10 (does / he / know / not / that / using / smartphone / a / much / too / cause / can / problems. / health)
➡ _____

11 (you / are / a / user / heavy / of / smartphone / your / Seongmin? / like)
➡ _____

12 (so, / if / are / here / some / to / tips / protect / health. / your)
➡ _____

13 (your / watch / back. / and / neck)
➡ _____

14 (you / when / read / your / on / smartphone, / usually / you / neck. / your / bend)
➡ _____

15 ("text / this / neck" / increases / pose / pressure / the / your / on / back. / and / neck)
➡ _____

16 (best / the / way / prevent / to / pressure / this / is / bring / to / phone / the / to / up / level / the / of / eyes. / your)
➡ _____

1 스마트폰 사용자들을 위한 건강 조언

2 성민이는 스마트폰을 사용하는 데 많은 시간을 보냅니다.

3 그는 뉴스와 날씨를 확인합니다.

4 그는 스마트폰 게임을 합니다.

5 그는 친구들에게 문자 메시지를 보냅니다.

6 그는 인터넷에서 정보를 찾습니다.

7 그는 온라인 만화책을 읽습니다.

8 그는 영화를 봅니다.

9 성민이는 하루 종일 스마트폰에서 손을 뗄 수가 없습니다.

10 그는 스마트폰을 너무 많이 사용하는 것이 건강 문제를 일으킬 수 있다는 것을 모릅니다.

11 여러분은 성민이와 같은 스마트폰 과다 사용자인가요?

12 그렇다면, 여기 여러분의 건강을 지켜 줄 몇 가지 조언이 있습니다.

13 여러분의 목과 척추를 조심하세요.

14 스마트폰을 볼 때, 여러분은 보통 목을 구부립니다.

15 이 "거북목" 자세는 여러분의 목과 척추에 가해지는 압력을 증가시킵니다.

16 이러한 압력을 예방하는 가장 좋은 방법은 휴대 전화를 여러분의 눈높이까지 올리는 것입니다.

17 (way / another / to / is / lower / eyes / your / of / instead / bending / neck. / your)
➡ _____

18 (eyes / give / your / break. / a)
➡ _____

19 (your / makes / it / feel / eyes / tired / and / to / dry / small / read / letters / on / smartphone / a / long / a / time. / for)
➡ _____
_____

20 (a / using / in / smartphone / dark / the / or / a / in / moving / makes / car / worse. / problem / this)
➡ _____
_____

21 (this, / avoid / to / your / give / eyes / break / a / time / from / time. / to)
➡ _____

22 (the / follow / rules: / 20-20-20 / minutes, / 20 / every / take / 20-second / a / break / and / at / look / something / least / at / away. / feet / 20)
➡ _____
_____

23 (blink / also, / often. / eyes / your)
➡ _____

24 (will / this / keep / eyes / your / from / dry. / becoming)
➡ _____

25 (you / text / do / lot / a / on / smartphone? / your)
➡ _____

26 (for / texting / time / long / a / hurt / can / fingers / your / wrists. / and)
➡ _____

27 (try / exercises. / these)
➡ _____

28 (they / help / will / reduce / pain / the / in / fingers / your / wrists. / and)
➡ _____

29 (on / pull / finger / each / hand. / each / of)
➡ _____

30 (the / put / backs / your / of / hands / together / with / arms / your / in / out / you. / of / front)
➡ _____

31 (remember. / but)
➡ _____

32 (best / the / tip / prevent / to / health / these / problems / to / is / your / use / less. / smartphone)
➡ _____

33 (yourself / rest / give / some / smartphone. / your / from)
➡ _____

17 또 다른 방법은 여러분의 목을 구부리는 대신에 시선을 낮추는 것입니다.

18 눈을 쉬게 하세요.

19 오랫동안 스마트폰의 작은 글자를 읽는 것은 눈이 피곤해지고 건조하게 느끼도록 만듭니다.

20 어두운 곳이나 움직이는 차에서 스마트폰을 사용하는 것은 이러한 문제를 더욱 악화시킵니다.

21 이것을 피하려면, 눈을 때때로 쉬게 하세요.

22 20-20-20 규칙을 따르세요. 20분마다 20초의 휴식을 취하고 적어도 20피트 이상 떨어져 있는 사물을 바라보세요.

23 또한, 눈을 자주 깜박이세요.

24 이것은 여러분의 눈이 건조해지는 것을 막아 줄 것입니다.

25 스마트폰으로 문자 메시지를 많이 보내나요?

26 오랫동안 문자 메시지를 보내는 것은 여러분의 손가락과 손목을 상하게 할 수 있습니다.

27 이런 운동을 해 보세요.

28 그것은 여러분의 손가락과 손목의 통증을 줄이는 것을 도와줄 것입니다.

29 각 손의 각 손가락을 당기세요.

30 팔을 여러분 앞에서 벌린 채로 손등을 마주 놓으세요.

31 그러나 기억하세요.

32 이러한 건강 문제를 예방하는 가장 좋은 방법은 스마트폰을 덜 사용하는 것입니다.

33 여러분 자신에게 스마트폰으로부터 휴식을 주세요.

※ 다음 우리말을 영어로 쓰시오.

1 스마트폰 사용자들을 위한 건강 조언

➡ _____

2 성민이는 스마트폰을 사용하는 데 많은 시간을 보냅니다.

➡ _____

3 그는 뉴스와 날씨를 확인합니다.

➡ _____

4 그는 스마트폰 게임을 합니다.

➡ _____

5 그는 친구들에게 문자 메시지를 보냅니다.

➡ _____

6 그는 인터넷에서 정보를 찾습니다.

➡ _____

7 그는 온라인 만화책을 읽습니다.

➡ _____

8 그는 영화를 봅니다.

➡ _____

9 성민이는 하루 종일 스마트폰에서 손을 뗄 수가 없습니다.

➡ _____

10 그는 스마트폰을 너무 많이 사용하는 것이 건강 문제를 일으킬 수 있다는 것을 모릅니다.

➡ _____

11 여러분은 성민이와 같은 스마트폰 과다 사용자인가요?

➡ _____

12 그렇다면, 여기 여러분의 건강을 지켜 줄 몇 가지 조언이 있습니다.

➡ _____

13 여러분의 목과 척추를 조심하세요.

➡ _____

14 스마트폰을 볼 때, 여러분은 보통 목을 구부립니다.

➡ _____

15 이 "거북목" 자세는 여러분의 목과 척추에 가해지는 압력을 증가시킵니다.

➡ _____

16 이러한 압력을 예방하는 가장 좋은 방법은 휴대 전화를 여러분의 눈높이까지 올리는 것입니다.

➡ _____

17 또 다른 방법은 여러분의 목을 구부리는 대신에 시선을 낮추는 것입니다.

➡ _____

18 눈을 쉬게 하세요.

➡ _____

19 오랫동안 스마트폰의 작은 글자를 읽는 것은 눈이 피곤해지고 건조하게 느끼도록 만듭니다.

➡ _____

20 어두운 곳이나 움직이는 차에서 스마트폰을 사용하는 것은 이러한 문제를 더욱 악화시킵니다.

➡ _____

21 이것을 피하려면, 눈을 때때로 쉬게 하세요.

➡ _____

22 20-20-20 규칙을 따르세요. 20분마다 20초의 휴식을 취하고 적어도 20피트 이상 떨어져 있는 사물을 바라보세요.

➡ _____

23 또한, 눈을 자주 깜박이세요.

➡ _____

24 이것은 여러분의 눈이 건조해지는 것을 막아 줄 것입니다.

➡ _____

25 스마트폰으로 문자 메시지를 많이 보내나요?

➡ _____

26 오랫동안 문자 메시지를 보내는 것은 여러분의 손가락과 손목을 상하게 할 수 있습니다.

➡ _____

27 이런 운동을 해 보세요.

➡ _____

28 그것은 여러분의 손가락과 손목의 통증을 줄이는 것을 도와줄 것입니다.

➡ _____

29 각 손의 각 손가락을 당기세요.

➡ _____

30 팔을 여러분 앞에서 벌린 채로 손등을 마주 놓으세요.

➡ _____

31 그러나 기억하세요.

➡ _____

32 이러한 건강 문제를 예방하는 가장 좋은 방법은 스마트폰을 덜 사용하는 것입니다.

➡ _____

33 여러분 자신에게 스마트폰으로부터 휴식을 주세요.

➡ _____

※ 다음 우리말과 일치하도록 빈칸에 알맞은 말을 쓰시오.

Before You Read A

1. I use my smartphone _____ I _____ _____.

2. I use my smartphone _____ _____ _____.

3. I use my smartphone _____ _____ _____ _____.

4. I _____ _____ when I do _____ _____ my smartphone _____ me.

5. I use my smartphone _____ _____.

1. 나는 아침을 먹을 때 스마트폰을 사용한다.
2. 나는 차에서 스마트폰을 사용한다.
3. 나는 걸으면서 스마트폰을 사용한다.
4. 나는 수중에 스마트폰이 없으면 불편함을 느낀다.
5. 나는 잠자리에서 스마트폰을 사용한다.

Before You Read B

1. _____ _____!

2. Yesterday, Sejin _____ _____ a tree _____ _____ and _____ her head.

3. She needs to _____ _____ her phone _____ _____.

4. Also, she _____ _____ the time _____ _____ it.

1. 조심해!
2. 어제, 세진이는 문자를 보내다가 나무에 부딪쳐서 머리를 다쳤다.
3. 그녀는 걷는 도중에 전화기를 사용하는 것을 피할 필요가 있다.
4. 또한, 그녀는 그것을 사용하는 데 보내는 시간을 줄여야 한다.

Writing Workshop

1. A _____ & _____

2. There _____ _____ good things _____ bad things about _____ a smartphone.

3. First, I can _____ _____ _____ _____ my friends _____ _____.

4. Also, I can easily get _____ _____ _____.

5. That is useful _____ I have a lot of homework _____ _____.

6. _____ _____ _____ _____, using a smartphone too much makes my eyes _____ _____ and _____.

7. Also, text messages and ads _____ me _____ _____ attention to my studies.

8. So I _____ _____ use my smartphone _____.

1. 스마트폰과 나
2. 스마트폰을 사용하는 것에 대해서 좋은 것과 나쁜 것 둘 다 있다.
3. 첫째, 내 친구들과 즉시 연락할 수 있다.
4. 또한, 나는 내가 필요한 정보를 쉽게 얻을 수 있다.
4. 그것은 내가 해야 할 숙제가 많을 때 유용하다.
6. 반면에, 스마트폰을 너무 많이 사용하는 것은 나의 눈을 건조하고 피곤하게 만든다.
7 또한 메시지를 보내는 것과 광고들은 공부에 집중하는 것을 막는다.
8. 그래서 나는 휴대 전화를 똑똑하게 사용할 필요가 있다.

※ 다음 우리말을 영어로 쓰시오.

Before You Read A

1. 나는 아침을 먹을 때 스마트폰을 사용한다.
➡ _____

2. 나는 차에서 스마트폰을 사용한다.
➡ _____

3. 나는 걸으면서 스마트폰을 사용한다.
➡ _____

4. 나는 수중에 스마트폰이 없으면 불편함을 느낀다.
➡ _____

5. 나는 잠자리에서 스마트폰을 사용한다.
➡ _____

Before You Read B

1. 조심해!
➡ _____

2. 어제, 세진이는 문자를 보내다가 나무에 부딪쳐서 머리를 다쳤다.
➡ _____

3. 그녀는 걷는 도중에 전화기를 사용하는 것을 피할 필요가 있다.
➡ _____

4. 또한, 그녀는 그것을 사용하는 데 보내는 시간을 줄여야 한다.
➡ _____

Writing Workshop

1. 스마트폰과 나
➡ _____

2. 스마트폰을 사용하는 것에 대해서 좋은 것과 나쁜 것 둘 다 있다.
➡ _____

3. 첫째, 내 친구들과 즉시 연락할 수 있다.
➡ _____

4. 또한, 나는 내가 필요한 정보를 쉽게 얻을 수 있다.
➡ _____

5. 그것은 내가 해야 할 숙제가 많을 때 유용하다.
➡ _____

6. 반면에, 스마트폰을 너무 많이 사용하는 것은 나의 눈을 건조하고 피곤하게 만든다.
➡ _____

7. 또한 메시지를 보내는 것과 광고들은 공부에 집중하는 것을 막는다.
➡ _____

8. 그래서 나는 휴대 전화를 똑똑하게 사용할 필요가 있다.
➡ _____

※ 다음 영어를 우리말로 쓰시오.

01 concert _____

02 grow _____

03 actually _____

04 bit _____

05 clothes _____

06 opportunity _____

07 bright _____

08 dolphin _____

09 elementary school _____

10 musical instrument _____

11 cook _____

12 free time _____

13 hold _____

14 join _____

15 easy _____

16 neighbor _____

17 main gate _____

18 orchestra _____

19 introduce _____

20 own _____

21 garden _____

22 vegetable _____

23 library _____

24 present _____

25 volunteer _____

26 experience _____

27 several _____

28 note _____

29 activity _____

30 leader _____

31 interest _____

32 practice _____

33 neighborhood _____

34 cooking _____

35 as a result _____

36 enjoy+동사ing _____

37 look for _____

38 would like to+동사원형 _____

39 participate in _____

40 change into _____

41 ask for help _____

42 be good at _____

43 how to+동사원형 _____

※ 다음 우리말을 영어로 쓰시오.

01 도넛

02 경험, 경력

03 무인 비행기

04 선물, 참석한

05 연습; 연습하다

06 활동

07 요리, 음식

08 관심

09 날게 하다

10 봉사, 유익한 활동

11 몇몇의

12 동네

13 ~을 사다, ~을 획득하다

14 지도자, 대표

15 도서관

16 동아리

17 그러나, 하지만

18 봉사하다

19 음, 음표

20 사업, 계획

21 스페인어

22 (사람·동물을) 걷게 하다

23 실제로, 사실은

24 기회

25 (모임·식 등을) 개최하다

26 소개하다

27 실제로, 사실은

28 밝은

29 옷, 의상

30 (동식물을) 기르다

31 (모임·식 등을) 개최하다

32 이웃

33 정문

34 채소

35 ~로 변화시키다[바꾸다]

36 아주 조금

37 ~에 빠지다

38 결과적으로

39 ~에 참여하다

40 (병·상황 등이) 나아지다

41 ~에 대해 감사하다

42 도움을 청하다

43 (~에 대해서) 조심하다

※ 다음 영영풀이에 알맞은 단어를 <보기>에서 골라 쓴 후, 우리말 뜻을 쓰시오.

1 _____ : strong and easy to see: _____

2 _____ : to develop or increase in size or length: _____

3 _____ : slightly or to a small degree(=a little): _____

4 _____ : to do something regularly in order to do it better: _____

5 _____ : to take a dog for a walk for exercise: _____

6 _____ : to cook something using dry heat, in an oven: _____

7 _____ : aircraft that does not have a pilot, but is operated by radio: _____

8 _____ : to become a member of an organization, society, or group: _____

9 _____ : someone who lives next to you or near you: _____

10 _____ : a part of the area next to a house, which has plants and flowers in it: _____

11 _____ : something that you use for playing music, such as a piano or guitar: _____

12 _____ : the person who directs or controls a group, organization, country, etc.: _____

13 _____ : a chance to do something or an occasion when it is easy for you to do something: _____

14 _____ : to have a meeting, party, election etc in a particular place or at a particular time: _____

15 _____ : a large group of musicians playing many different kinds of instruments and led by a conductor: _____

16 _____ : organization for people who share a particular interest or enjoy similar activities, or a group of people who meet together to do something they are interested in: _____

보기			
join	drone	opportunity	bake
bright	hold	orchestra	walk
a bit	musical instrument	grow	leader
neighbor	club	practice	garden

※ 다음 우리말과 일치하도록 빈칸에 알맞은 말을 쓰시오.

Listen & Speak 1 A

A: Do you _____ _____ _____ _____ a paper cat?

B: Of _____ . It's _____ .

Listen & Speak 1 B

1. G: I _____ _____ _____ _____ Yuna's violin concert yesterday. _____ was it?

   B: It was great. _____ _____ _____ _____ _____ the violin _____ _____ _____ .

   G: I didn't know you _____ _____ .

   B: I can, but I'm _____ _____ _____ it _____ .

2. G: _____ _____ these pictures. I _____ these vegetables _____ . I have my _____ _____ .

   B: Cool! Do you know _____ _____ _____ the vegetables you _____ , _____ ?

   G: Yes, my grandmother _____ _____ .

Listen & Speak 2 A

A: Do you enjoy _____ _____ the stars _____ _____ ?

G: Yes, I _____ _____ that.

Listen & Speak 2 B

1. B: _____ _____ _____ _____ books, Yumi?

   G: Yes, I _____ _____ science books. How _____ you?

   B: I love _____ books, _____ .

   G: Then, _____ _____ to _____ _____ after school today.

2. G: _____ _____ _____ _____ on the weekend, Minsu?

   B: I _____ _____ for my family.

   G: _____ _____ _____ _____ ?

   B: Yes, I'm a _____ _____ ! My family loves my _____ .

해석

G: 종이 고양이 만드는 법을 알고 있니?
B: 물론이지. 그건 쉬워.

1. G: 어제 유나의 바이올린 콘서트에 갔다고 들었어. 어땠니?
   B: 좋았어. 나도 언젠가 그녀처럼 바이올린을 연주할 수 있기를 바라.
   G: 나는 네가 바이올린 연주하는 법을 아는지 몰랐어.
   B: 할 수 있어, 그러나 아직 잘하지는 못해.
2. G: 이 사진들 좀 봐. 나는 이 채소를 직접 길렀어. 나는 내 자신의 정원이 있어.
   B: 멋지다! 네가 기르는 채소로 요리하는 법도 아니?
   G: 응, 할머니께서 내게 가르쳐 주셨어.

B: 너는 밤에 별을 보는 것을 즐기니?
G: 응, 나는 별을 보는 것을 아주 좋아해.

1. B: 유미야, 너는 책 읽는 것을 즐기니?
   G: 응, 나는 과학 책을 읽는 것을 좋아해. 너는 어때?
   B: 나도 책 읽는 것을 좋아해.
   G: 그럼 오늘 방과 후에 도서관 가자.
2. G: 민수야, 주말에 뭐 했니?
   B: 가족을 위해 아침을 만들었어.
   G: 너는 요리를 즐기니?
   D: 응, 나는 훌륭한 요리사야! 우리 가족은 내 요리를 좋아해.

3. **B:** Jiyun, that's a pretty backpack! _____ did you _____ it?

 G: My sister _____ _____ _____ _____.

 B: Wow! She's a _____ _____ _____.

 G: Yes, she is. And she _____ _____ _____, _____.

Real-Life Zone A

B: Hello, Kate. I'm Hamin, _____ _____ of the Nanum Orchestra. _____ you _____ _____ _____ in our club.

G: Hi. Nice _____ _____ you.

B: You play the violin? _____ _____ _____ _____ the violin?

G: I started learning _____ _____ _____ _____ _____ I was ten.

B: Do you have any _____ _____ in a group?

G: Yes. _____, I was a member of _____ _____ _____ I was in _____ _____.

B: Great. We also _____ _____ _____ children. _____ _____ _____ _____ _____?

G: I have no _____ teaching others. But I _____ _____ _____ people, so I'd _____ _____ _____.

B: Good. I think we'll _____ a great time _____ together. _____ _____ the Nanum Orchestra.

Wrap Up

B: These cookies _____ so _____. Did you make them?

G: Yes. I _____ _____ _____ yesterday. I enjoy _____. I'm _____ _____ make doughnuts _____ _____.

B: Oh, I _____ _____ _____ _____ _____ _____ _____ _____ doughnuts. _____ it _____?

G: Not _____ _____. You can come to my house and _____ _____ if you want.

B: Thanks, Bora. _____ _____ _____ I come?

G: _____ 2:00.

B: _____ good. _____ you _____.

3. **B:** 지윤아, 그거 예쁜 배낭이네! 어디서 샀어?
 G: 언니가 내게 만들어 준 거야.
 B: 와! 그녀는 정말 훌륭한 디자이너구나.
 G: 응, 그래. 그리고 그녀는 옷 만드는 것도 즐겨.

B: 안녕, 케이트. 나는 나눔 오케스트라의 대표 하민이야. 우리 동아리에 관심을 가져줘서 고마워.
G: 안녕, 만나서 반가워.
B: 너는 바이올린을 연주하니? 언제 바이올린 연주를 시작했니?
G: 10살 때 바이올린을 연주하는 법을 배우기 시작했어.
B: 그룹에서 연주해 본 경험이 있니?
G: 응. 사실 나는 초등학교 때 오케스트라 단원이었어.
B: 좋아. 우리는 자원봉사로 아이들도 가르쳐. 다른 사람들을 가르치는 것을 즐기니?
G: 나는 다른 사람들을 가르친 경험이 없어. 그러나 나는 사람들과 일하는 것을 즐겨, 그래서 나는 해보고 싶어.
B: 좋아. 나는 우리가 함께 연주하며 좋은 시간을 보낼 것이라고 생각해. 나눔 오케스트라에 온 걸 환영해.

B: 이 쿠키들은 정말 맛있어 보여. 네가 만들었니?
G: 응. 어제 내가 직접 만들었어. 나는 제빵을 즐겨. 이번 주 토요일에 도넛을 만들 예정이야.
B: 오, 나는 도넛 만드는 법을 배우고 싶어. 그건 어렵니?
G: 전혀 아니야. 네가 원한다면 우리 집에 와서 같이 해도 돼.
B: 고마워, 보라야. 내가 몇 시에 가야 해?
G: 2시에.
B: 좋아. 그때 보자.

※ 다음 우리말에 맞도록 대화를 영어로 쓰시오.

Listen & Speak 1 A

A: _____

B: _____

G: 종이 고양이 만드는 법을 알고 있니?
B: 물론이지. 그건 쉬워.

Listen & Speak 1 B

1. G: _____

   B: _____

   G: _____

   B: _____

2. G: _____

   B: _____

   G: _____

1. G: 어제 유나의 바이올린 콘서트에
      갔다고 들었어. 어땠니?
   B: 좋았어. 나도 언젠가 그녀처럼 바
      이올린을 연주할 수 있기를 바라.
   G: 나는 네가 바이올린 연주하는 법
      을 아는지 몰랐어.
   B: 할 수 있어, 그러나 아직 잘하지는
      못해.
2. G: 이 사진들 좀 봐. 나는 이 채소를
      직접 길렀어. 나는 내 자신의 정원
      이 있어.
   B: 멋지다! 네가 기르는 채소로 요리
      하는 법도 아니?
   G: 응, 할머니께서 내게 가르쳐 주셨
      어.

Listen & Speak 2 A

A: _____

G: _____

B: 너는 밤에 별을 보는 것을 즐기니?
G: 응, 나는 별을 보는 것을 아주 좋아
   해.

Listen & Speak 2 B

1. B: _____

   G: _____

   B: _____

   G: _____

2. G: _____

   B: _____

   G: _____

   B: _____

1. B: 유미야, 너는 책 읽는 것을 즐
      기니?
   G: 응, 나는 과학 책을 읽는 것을
      좋아해. 너는 어때?
   B: 나도 책 읽는 것을 좋아해.
   G: 그럼 오늘 방과 후에 도서관 가
      자.
2. G: 민수야, 주말에 뭐 했니?
   B: 가족을 위해 아침을 만들었어.
   G: 너는 요리를 즐기니?
   B: 응, 나는 훌륭한 요리사야! 우
      리 가족은 내 요리를 좋아해.

3. B: _____

   G: _____

   B: _____

   G: _____

Real-Life Zone A

B: _____
_____

G: _____

B: _____

G: _____

B: _____

G: _____

B: _____

G: _____
_____

B: _____

Wrap Up

B: _____

G: _____

B: _____

G: _____

B: _____

G: _____

B: _____

---

3. B: 지윤아, 그거 예쁜 배낭이네! 어디서 샀어?

   G: 언니가 내게 만들어 준 거야.

   B: 왜! 그녀는 정말 훌륭한 디자이너구나.

   G: 응, 그래. 그리고 그녀는 옷 만드는 것도 즐겨.

B: 안녕, 케이트. 나는 나눔 오케스트라의 대표 하민이야. 우리 동아리에 관심을 가져줘서 고마워.

G: 안녕. 만나서 반가워.

B: 너는 바이올린을 연주하니? 언제 바이올린 연주를 시작했니?

G: 10살 때 바이올린을 연주하는 법을 배우기 시작했어.

B: 그룹에서 연주해 본 경험이 있니?

G: 응. 사실 나는 초등학교 때 오케스트라 단원이었어.

B: 좋아. 우리는 자원봉사로 아이들도 가르쳐. 다른 사람들을 가르치는 것을 즐기니?

G: 나는 다른 사람들을 가르친 경험이 없어. 그러나 나는 사람들과 일하는 것을 즐겨, 그래서 나는 해보고 싶어.

B: 좋아. 나는 우리가 함께 연주하며 좋은 시간을 보낼 것이라고 생각해. 나눔 오케스트라에 온 걸 환영해.

B: 이 쿠키들은 정말 맛있어 보여. 네가 만들었니?

G: 응. 어제 내가 직접 만들었어. 나는 제빵을 즐겨. 이번 주 토요일에 도넛을 만들 예정이야.

B: 오, 나는 도넛 만드는 법을 배우고 싶어. 그건 어렵니?

G: 전혀 아니야. 네가 원한다면 우리 집에 와서 같이 해도 돼.

B: 고마워, 보라야. 내가 몇 시에 가야 해?

G: 2시에.

B: 좋아. 그때 보자.

※ 다음 우리말과 일치하도록 빈칸에 알맞은 것을 골라 쓰시오.

1 _____ _____ You _____ Our Club?
   A. Join   B. Don't   C. Why

2 _____ in club activities is a great _____ to enjoy your school _____.
   A. life   B. participating   C. way

3 _____ about _____ a club?
   A. joining   B. how

4 Here _____ two club _____ _____ want students to _____ their clubs.
   A. join   B. who   C. are   D. leaders

5 _____ listen _____ _____ they say.
   A. what   B. to   C. let's

6 The Picasso _____ _____
   A. Club   B. Art

7 Hi! I am Sora Kang _____ the Picasso _____ _____.
   A. Club   B. from   C. Art

8 _____ you can _____ _____ the name of our club, we _____.
   A. paint   B. as   C. guess   D. from

9 We also do _____ _____ from time _____ time.
   A. to   B. work   C. volunteer

10 _____ summer, our club members _____ _____ the "_____ Our Neighborhood" project.
   A. in   B. change   C. participated   D. last

11 On the _____ old walls of the buildings in our neighborhood, we painted birds _____ high in the sky and dolphins _____ over blue _____.
   A. waves   B. dirty   C. flying   D. jumping

12 _____ a result, the old neighborhood changed _____ a _____ and beautiful _____.
   A. bright   B. into   C. place   D. as

13 The _____ were happy _____ see our work and _____ us.
   A. thanked   B. to   C. neighbors

14 You _____ _____ be a good painter.
   A. to   B. have   C. don't

15 _____ who likes to _____ can _____.
   A. join   B. paint   C. anyone

1 우리 동아리에 가입하는 게 어때?

2 동아리 활동에 참여하는 것은 학교생활을 즐기는 좋은 방법이 에요.

3 동아리에 가입하는 게 어떤가요?

4 여기 학생들이 그들의 동아리에 가입하기를 원하는 두 명의 동아리 대표가 있어요.

5 그들이 하는 말을 들어 봅시다.

6 피카소 미술 동아리

7 안녕하세요! 저는 피카소 미술 동아리의 강소라입니다.

8 우리 동아리의 이름에서 추측할 수 있듯이, 우리는 그림을 그립니다.

9 우리는 가끔 자원봉사도 합니다.

10 지난여름, 우리 동아리 회원들은 "우리 마을 바꾸기" 프로젝트에 참여했습니다.

11 우리 마을에 있는 건물의 더럽고 오래된 벽에 하늘 높이 나는 새들과 푸른 파도 위로 점프하는 돌고래들을 그렸습니다.

12 결과적으로, 오래된 마을은 밝고 아름다운 곳으로 바뀌었습니다.

13 이웃들은 우리의 작품을 보고 행복해 했고 고마워했습니다.

14 여러분은 그림을 잘 그릴 필요는 없습니다.

15 그림 그리는 것을 좋아하는 사람은 누구나 가입할 수 있습니다.

16 _____ and _____ a _____ of the Picasso Art Club.
A. member   B. be   C. come

17 The _____ _____
A. Orchestra   B. Boram

18 Hi! I am Minsu Jang, the _____ _____ the Boram _____.
A. Orchestra   B. of   C. leader

19 Did you see _____ students _____ music at the _____ _____ when you came to school today?
A. gate   B. playing   C. main   D. several

20 We _____ _____ students.
A. those   B. were

21 We _____ music _____ our friends _____ morning.
A. every   B. for   C. play

22 You _____ to know _____ to play an instrument a _____ _____ to join our club.
A. bit   B. how   C. need   D. little

23 But don't _____ _____ you don't _____ well.
A. play   B. if   C. worry

24 We will _____ hard and _____ _____ together.
A. better   B. get   C. practice

25 We also teach children how to play _____ _____ as a _____ to our _____.
A. community   B. service   C. instruments   D. musical

26 I am _____ an _____ boy to _____ the violin.
A. how   B. teaching   C. eleven-year-old

27 _____ first, he did not know _____ to read a _____.
A. note   B. note   C. at

28 Now he _____ play a _____ _____.
A. song   B. simple   C. can

29 _____ him _____ the violin _____ me very happy.
A. makes   B. play   C. hearing

30 _____ _____ our club, you can have an _____ to help _____.
A. joining   B. opportunity   C. others   D. by

31 _____ and _____ our _____.
A. club   B. join   C. come

32 We are _____ you.
A. for   B. waiting

16 와서 피카소 미술 동아리의 회원이 되세요.

17 보람 오케스트라

18 안녕하세요! 저는 보람 오케스트라의 회장 장민수입니다.

19 오늘 학교에 왔을 때 정문에서 음악을 연주하는 몇 명의 학생들을 보았습니까?

20 우리가 그 학생들이었습니다.

21 우리는 매일 아침 친구들을 위해 음악을 연주합니다.

22 우리 동아리에 가입하기 위해서는 악기 연주하는 법을 조금 알아야 합니다.

23 그러나 여러분이 연주를 잘 못한다고 해서 걱정하지 마세요.

24 우리는 열심히 연습하고 함께 좋아질 것입니다.

25 우리는 지역 사회에 대한 봉사로 아이들에게 악기를 연주하는 법도 가르칩니다.

26 저는 열한 살 소년에게 바이올린을 가르치고 있습니다.

27 처음에 그는 음표를 읽는 법을 알지 못했습니다.

28 이제는 간단한 노래도 연주할 수 있습니다.

29 그가 바이올린을 연주하는 걸 듣는 것은 저를 매우 행복하게 합니다.

30 우리 동아리에 가입함으로써. 여러분은 다른 사람들을 도울 수 있는 기회를 가질 수 있습니다.

31 와서 우리 동아리에 가입하세요.

32 우리는 여러분을 기다리고 있습니다.

※ 다음 우리말과 일치하도록 빈칸에 알맞은 말을 쓰시오.

1 ＿＿＿＿＿ ＿＿＿＿＿ ＿＿＿＿＿ ＿＿＿＿＿ Our Club?

2 ＿＿＿＿＿ ＿＿＿＿＿ ＿＿＿＿＿ ＿＿＿＿＿ is a great way ＿＿＿＿＿ ＿＿＿＿＿ your school life.

3 ＿＿＿＿＿ ＿＿＿＿＿ ＿＿＿＿＿ a club?

4 ＿＿＿＿＿ ＿＿＿＿＿ two club leaders ＿＿＿＿＿ ＿＿＿＿＿ students ＿＿＿＿＿ ＿＿＿＿＿ their clubs.

5 ＿＿＿＿＿ listen ＿＿＿＿＿ ＿＿＿＿＿ they say.

6 The Picasso ＿＿＿＿＿ ＿＿＿＿＿

7 Hi! I am Sora Kang ＿＿＿＿＿ the Picasso ＿＿＿＿＿ ＿＿＿＿＿.

8 ＿＿＿＿＿ you ＿＿＿＿＿ ＿＿＿＿＿ ＿＿＿＿＿ the name of our club, we ＿＿＿＿＿.

9 We also ＿＿＿＿＿ ＿＿＿＿＿ ＿＿＿＿＿ time ＿＿＿＿＿ time.

10 ＿＿＿＿＿ summer, our club members ＿＿＿＿＿ ＿＿＿＿＿ the "＿＿＿＿＿ Our ＿＿＿＿＿" project.

11 ＿＿＿＿＿ ＿＿＿＿＿ ＿＿＿＿＿ ＿＿＿＿＿ ＿＿＿＿＿ of the buildings in our neighborhood, we ＿＿＿＿＿ birds ＿＿＿＿＿ high in the sky and dolphins ＿＿＿＿＿ ＿＿＿＿＿ ＿＿＿＿＿ ＿＿＿＿＿.

12 ＿＿＿＿＿ ＿＿＿＿＿ ＿＿＿＿＿, the old neighborhood ＿＿＿＿＿ ＿＿＿＿＿ a bright and ＿＿＿＿＿ ＿＿＿＿＿.

13 The neighbors ＿＿＿＿＿ ＿＿＿＿＿ ＿＿＿＿＿ ＿＿＿＿＿ ＿＿＿＿＿ our work and ＿＿＿＿＿ us.

14 You ＿＿＿＿＿ ＿＿＿＿＿ ＿＿＿＿＿ be a good ＿＿＿＿＿.

15 ＿＿＿＿＿ ＿＿＿＿＿ ＿＿＿＿＿ ＿＿＿＿＿ paint can ＿＿＿＿＿.

1 우리 동아리에 가입하는 게 어때?

2 동아리 활동에 참여하는 것은 학교생활을 즐기는 좋은 방법이에요.

3 동아리에 가입하는 게 어떤가요?

4 여기 학생들이 그들의 동아리에 가입하기를 원하는 두 명의 동아리 대표가 있어요.

5 그들이 하는 말을 들어 봅시다.

6 피카소 미술 동아리

7 안녕하세요! 저는 피카소 미술 동아리의 강소라입니다.

8 우리 동아리의 이름에서 추측할 수 있듯이, 우리는 그림을 그립니다.

9 우리는 가끔 자원봉사도 합니다.

10 지난여름, 우리 동아리 회원들은 "우리 마을 바꾸기" 프로젝트에 참여했습니다.

11 우리 마을에 있는 건물의 더럽고 오래된 벽에 하늘 높이 나는 새들과 푸른 파도 위로 점프하는 돌고래들을 그렸습니다.

12 결과적으로, 오래된 마을은 밝고 아름다운 곳으로 바뀌었습니다.

13 이웃들은 우리의 작품을 보고 행복해 했고 고마워했습니다.

14 여러분은 그림을 잘 그릴 필요는 없습니다.

15 그림 그리는 것을 좋아하는 사람은 누구나 가입할 수 있습니다.

16 _____ _____ _____ a member of the Picasso Art Club.

17 The Boram _____

18 Hi! I am Minsu Jang, _____ _____ _____ the Boram Orchestra.

19 Did you _____ several students _____ _____ at the _____ _____ when you _____ _____ _____ today?

20 We _____ _____ students.

21 We _____ _____ _____ our friends every morning.

22 You need to know _____ _____ _____ an instrument _____ _____ _____ _____ our club.

23 But _____ _____ _____ you _____ play well.

24 We will _____ _____ and _____ together.

25 We _____ _____ children _____ play musical instruments _____ _____ _____ our community.

26 I am _____ _____ to play the violin.

27 _____ _____, he did not know _____ _____ _____ _____ _____.

28 Now he _____ _____ _____ _____ _____.

29 _____ _____ _____ the violin makes me very _____.

30 _____ _____ our club, you can _____ _____ _____ _____ _____.

31 _____ _____ our club.

32 We are _____ _____ you.

16 와서 피카소 미술 동아리의 회원이 되세요.

17 보람 오케스트라

18 안녕하세요! 저는 보람 오케스트라의 회장 장민수입니다.

19 오늘 학교에 왔을 때 정문에서 음악을 연주하는 몇 명의 학생들을 보았습니까?

20 우리가 그 학생들이었습니다.

21 우리는 매일 아침 친구들을 위해 음악을 연주합니다.

22 우리 동아리에 가입하기 위해서는 악기 연주하는 법을 조금 알아야 합니다.

23 그러나 여러분이 연주를 잘 못한다고 해서 걱정하지 마세요.

24 우리는 열심히 연습하고 함께 좋아질 것입니다.

25 우리는 지역 사회에 대한 봉사로 아이들에게 악기를 연주하는 법도 가르칩니다.

26 저는 열한 살 소년에게 바이올린을 가르치고 있습니다.

27 처음에 그는 음표를 읽는 법을 알지 못했습니다.

28 이제는 간단한 노래도 연주할 수 있습니다.

29 그가 바이올린을 연주하는 걸 듣는 것은 저를 매우 행복하게 합니다.

30 우리 동아리에 가입함으로써, 여러분은 다른 사람들을 도울 수 있는 기회를 가질 수 있습니다.

31 와서 우리 동아리에 가입하세요.

32 우리는 여러분을 기다리고 있습니다.

※ 다음 문장을 우리말로 쓰시오.

1 Why Don't You Join Our Club?

➡ _____

2 Participating in club activities is a great way to enjoy your school life.

➡ _____

3 How about joining a club?

➡ _____

4 Here are two club leaders who want students to join their clubs.

➡ _____

5 Let's listen to what they say.

➡ _____

6 The Picasso Art Club

➡ _____

7 Hi! I am Sora Kang from the Picasso Art Club.

➡ _____

8 As you can guess from the name of our club, we paint.

➡ _____

9 We also do volunteer work from time to time.

➡ _____

10 Last summer, our club members participated in the "Change Our Neighborhood" project.

➡ _____

11 On the dirty old walls of the buildings in our neighborhood, we painted birds flying high in the sky and dolphins jumping over blue waves.

➡ _____

12 As a result, the old neighborhood changed into a bright and beautiful place.

➡ _____

13 The neighbors were happy to see our work and thanked us.

➡ _____

14 You don't have to be a good painter.

➡ _____

15 Anyone who likes to paint can join.

➡ _____

16 Come and be a member of the Picasso Art Club.

➡ _____

17 The Boram Orchestra

➡ _____

18 Hi! I am Minsu Jang, the leader of the Boram Orchestra.

➡ _____

19 Did you see several students playing music at the main gate when you came to school today?

➡ _____

20 We were those students.

➡ _____

21 We play music for our friends every morning.

➡ _____

22 You need to know how to play an instrument a little bit to join our club.

➡ _____

23 But don't worry if you don't play well.

➡ _____

24 We will practice hard and get better together.

➡ _____

25 We also teach children how to play musical instruments as a service to our community.

➡ _____

26 I am teaching an eleven-year-old boy to play the violin.

➡ _____

27 At first, he did not know how to read a note.

➡ _____

28 Now he can play a simple song.

➡ _____

29 Hearing him play the violin makes me very happy.

➡ _____

30 By joining our club, you can have an opportunity to help others.

➡ _____

31 Come and join our club.

➡ _____

32 We are waiting for you.

➡ _____

※ 다음 괄호 안의 단어들을 우리말에 맞도록 바르게 배열하시오.

1 (Don't / Why / Join / You / Club? / Our)
➡ _____

2 (in / participating / activities / club / is / great / a / to / way / enjoy / your / life. / school)
➡ _____

3 (about / how / club? / a / joining)
➡ _____

4 (are / here / two / leaders / club / who / students / want / clubs. / their / join / to)
➡ _____

5 (listen / let's / what / to / say. / they)
➡ _____

6 (Picasso / Club / The / Art)
➡ _____

7 (hi! // am / I / Kang / Sora / from / Picasso / Club. / Art / the)
➡ _____

8 (you / as / guess / can / from / name / the / of / club, / our / paint. / we)
➡ _____

9 (also / do / we / work / volunteer / to / time / from / time.)
➡ _____

10 (summer, / last / club / our / members / in / participated / the / Our / "Change / project. / Neighborhood")
➡ _____

11 (the / on / old / dirty / walls / the / of / buildings / our / in / neighborhood, / painted / we / flying / birds / high / the / in / sky / and / dolphins / over / jumping / waves. / blue)
➡ _____

12 (a / as / result, / old / the / neighborhood / into / changed / a / beautiful / and / place. / bright)
➡ _____

13 (neighbors / the / happy / were / see / to / work / our / and / us. / thanked)
➡ _____

14 (don't / have / you / be / to / painter. / good / a)
➡ _____

15 (who / anyone / likes / to / join. / can / paint)
➡ _____

16 (and / come / be / member / a / of / the / Club. / Art / Picasso)
➡ _____

1 우리 동아리에 가입하는 게 어때?

2 동아리 활동에 참여하는 것은 학교생활을 즐기는 좋은 방법이에요.

3 동아리에 가입하는 게 어떤가요?

4 여기 학생들이 그들의 동아리에 가입하기를 원하는 두 명의 동아리 대표가 있어요.

5 그들이 하는 말을 들어 봅시다.

6 피카소 미술 동아리

7 안녕하세요! 저는 피카소 미술 동아리의 강소라입니다.

8 우리 동아리의 이름에서 추측할 수 있듯이, 우리는 그림을 그립니다.

9 우리는 가끔 자원봉사도 합니다.

10 지난여름, 우리 동아리 회원들은 "우리 마을 바꾸기" 프로젝트에 참여했습니다.

11 우리 마을에 있는 건물의 더럽고 오래된 벽에 하늘 높이 나는 새들과 푸른 파도 위로 점프하는 돌고래들을 그렸습니다.

12 결과적으로, 오래된 마을은 밝고 아름다운 곳으로 바뀌었습니다.

13 이웃들은 우리의 작품을 보고 행복해 했고 고마워했습니다.

14 여러분은 그림을 잘 그릴 필요는 없습니다.

15 그림 그리는 것을 좋아하는 사람은 누구나 가입할 수 있습니다.

16 와서 피카소 미술 동아리의 회원이 되세요.

17 (Boram / The / Orchestra)
➡ _____

18 (hi! // am / I / Jang, / Minsu / leader / the / of / the / Orchestra. / Boram)
➡ _____

19 (you / did / several / see / students / playing / music / the / at / gate / main / when / you / to / came / today? / school)
➡ _____
_____

20 (were / students. / we / those)
➡ _____

21 (play / we / for / music / our / morning. / every / friends)
➡ _____

22 (need / you / know / to / how / play / to / an / instrument / little / a / bit / join / to / club. / our)
➡ _____

23 (don't / but / worry / you / if / play / well. / don't)
➡ _____

24 (will / practice / we / hard / and / together. / better / get)
➡ _____

25 (we / teach / also / children / to / how / play / instruments / musical / as / service / a / to / coummunity. / our)
➡ _____
_____

26 (I / teaching / am / an / boy / eleven-year-old / play / violin. / the / to)
➡ _____

27 (first, / at / did / he / know / not / to / how / read / note. / a)
➡ _____

28 (he / now / play / can / song. / simple / a)
➡ _____

29 (him / hearing / play / violin / the / me / makes / happy. / very)
➡ _____

30 (joining / by / club, / our / can / you / have / opportunity / an / others. / help / to)
➡ _____

31 (join / and / come / club. / our)
➡ _____

32 (are / we / waiting / you. / for)
➡ _____

17 보람 오케스트라

18 안녕하세요! 저는 보람 오케스트라의 회장 장민수입니다.

19 오늘 학교에 왔을 때 정문에서 음악을 연주하는 몇 명의 학생들을 보았습니까?

20 우리가 그 학생들이었습니다.

21 우리는 매일 아침 친구들을 위해 음악을 연주합니다.

22 우리 동아리에 가입하기 위해서는 악기 연주하는 법을 조금 알아야 합니다.

23 그러나 여러분이 연주를 잘 못한다고 해서 걱정하지 마세요.

24 우리는 열심히 연습하고 함께 좋아질 것입니다.

25 우리는 지역 사회에 대한 봉사로 아이들에게 악기를 연주하는 법도 가르칩니다.

26 저는 열한 살 소년에게 바이올린을 가르치고 있습니다.

27 처음에 그는 음표를 읽는 법을 알지 못했습니다.

28 이제는 간단한 노래도 연주할 수 있습니다.

29 그가 바이올린을 연주하는 걸 듣는 것은 저를 매우 행복하게 합니다.

30 우리 동아리에 가입함으로써, 여러분은 다른 사람들을 도울 수 있는 기회를 가질 수 있습니다.

31 와서 우리 동아리에 가입하세요.

32 우리는 여러분을 기다리고 있습니다.

※ **다음 우리말을 영어로 쓰시오.**

1   우리 동아리에 가입하는 게 어때?
➡ _____

2   동아리 활동에 참여하는 것은 학교생활을 즐기는 좋은 방법이에요.
➡ _____

3   동아리에 가입하는 게 어떤가요?
➡ _____

4   여기 학생들이 그들의 동아리에 가입하기를 원하는 두 명의 동아리 대표가 있어요.
➡ _____

5   그들이 하는 말을 들어 봅시다.
➡ _____

6   피카소 미술 동아리
➡ _____

7   안녕하세요! 저는 피카소 미술 동아리의 강소라입니다.
➡ _____

8   우리 동아리의 이름에서 추측할 수 있듯이, 우리는 그림을 그립니다.
➡ _____

9   우리는 가끔 자원봉사도 합니다.
➡ _____

10   지난여름, 우리 동아리 회원들은 "우리 마을 바꾸기" 프로젝트에 참여했습니다.
➡ _____

11   우리 마을에 있는 건물의 더럽고 오래된 벽에 하늘 높이 나는 새들과 푸른 파도 위로 점프하는 돌고래들을 그렸습니다.
➡ _____
_____

12   결과적으로, 오래된 마을은 밝고 아름다운 곳으로 바뀌었습니다.
➡ _____

13   이웃들은 우리의 작품을 보고 행복해 했고 고마워했습니다.
➡ _____

14   여러분은 그림을 잘 그릴 필요는 없습니다.
➡ _____

15   그림 그리는 것을 좋아하는 사람은 누구나 가입할 수 있습니다.
➡ _____

16   와서 피카소 미술 동아리의 회원이 되세요.
➡ _____

17 보람 오케스트라

➡ _____

18 안녕하세요! 저는 보람 오케스트라의 회장 장민수입니다.

➡ _____

19 오늘 학교에 왔을 때 정문에서 음악을 연주하는 몇 명의 학생들을 보았습니까?

➡ _____

20 우리가 그 학생들이었습니다.

➡ _____

21 우리는 매일 아침 친구들을 위해 음악을 연주합니다.

➡ _____

22 우리 동아리에 가입하기 위해서는 악기 연주하는 법을 조금 알아야 합니다.

➡ _____

23 그러나 여러분이 연주를 잘 못한다고 해서 걱정하지 마세요.

➡ _____

24 우리는 열심히 연습하고 함께 좋아질 것입니다.

➡ _____

25 우리는 지역 사회에 대한 봉사로 아이들에게 악기를 연주하는 법도 가르칩니다.

➡ _____

26 저는 열한 살 소년에게 바이올린을 가르치고 있습니다.

➡ _____

27 처음에 그는 음표를 읽는 법을 알지 못했습니다.

➡ _____

28 이제는 간단한 노래도 연주할 수 있습니다.

➡ _____

29 그가 바이올린을 연주하는 걸 듣는 것은 저를 매우 행복하게 합니다.

➡ _____

30 우리 동아리에 가입함으로써, 여러분은 다른 사람들을 도울 수 있는 기회를 가질 수 있습니다.

➡ _____

31 와서 우리 동아리에 가입하세요.

➡ _____

32 우리는 여러분을 기다리고 있습니다.

➡ _____

※ 다음 우리말과 일치하도록 빈칸에 알맞은 말을 쓰시오.

After You Read

1. Today, Minsu, the _____ of the Boram Orchestra, came to _____ _____.

2. He _____ _____ me _____ _____ _____ the violin last month.

3. At first, I didn't know _____ _____ _____ _____ _____.

4. I _____ _____ _____ the Boram Orchestra and play the violin at the _____ _____ when I become a middle school student.

1. 오늘, 보람 오케스트라의 대표인 민수가 지역 주민회관에 왔다.
2. 그는 지난달에 바이올린을 연주하는 법을 나에게 가르쳐 주기 시작했다.
3. 처음에는 나는 하나의 음표도 읽는 법을 알지 못했다.
4. 나는 보람 오케스트라에 가입하여, 내가 중학생이 될 때 정문에서 바이올린을 연주하기를 희망한다.

Writing Workshop

1. Boram _____ _____ _____ Membership Form

2. • _____ of Club: FC Boram

3. • _____ _____ : Sunho Park

4. • Why You Want _____ _____ the Club: I love soccer and _____ _____ _____ join FC Boram.

5. I am _____ _____ _____ the ball and _____ fast.

6. However, I don't know _____ _____ _____ the ball, _____ I want to learn how to do that.

7. I want to _____ a soccer player _____ can make wonderful heading goals.

8. • Your _____ : If I _____ this club, I will _____ very _____ and become a good team player!

1. 보람중학교 동아리 지원서
2. 동아리 이름: FC Boram
3 학생 이름: 박순호
4. 가입을 원하는 이유: 나는 축구를 사랑하고 FC Boram에 가입하고 싶다.
5. 나는 공을 패스하는 것을 잘하고 빨리 달린다.
6. 그러나, 나는 공을 헤딩하는 법을 모르기 때문에 그것을 하는 법을 배우고 싶다.
7. 나는 멋진 헤딩 골을 만들 수 있는 축구 선수가 되기를 원한다.
8. 당신의 목표: 만약 내가 이 동아리에 가입하면, 나는 매우 열심히 연습해서 좋은 팀 플레이어가 될 것이다.

Real Life Zone

1. I _____ _____ to introduce our new orchestra member, Kate.

2. She knows _____ _____ _____ the violin.

3. She also has _____ _____ experience _____ in a group.

4. And she said she _____ _____ with people.

5. _____ all _____ her _____ the Nanum Orchestra.

1. 나는 우리의 새로운 오케스트라 회원인 케이트를 소개하고 싶어.
2. 그녀는 바이올린을 연주하는 법을 알아.
3. 그녀는 또한 그룹에서 연주해 본 경험이 많아.
4. 그리고 그녀는 사람들과 일하는 것을 즐긴다고 말했어.
5. 모두 그녀가 나눔 오케스트라에 온 걸 환영하자.

※ 다음 우리말을 영어로 쓰시오.

After You Read

1. 오늘, 보람 오케스트라의 대표인 민수가 지역 주민회관에 왔다.
➡ _____

2. 그는 지난달에 바이올린을 연주하는 법을 나에게 가르쳐 주기 시작했다.
➡ _____

3. 처음에는 나는 하나의 음표도 읽는 법을 알지 못했다.
➡ _____

4. 나는 보람 오케스트라에 가입하여, 내가 중학생이 될 때 정문에서 바이올린을 연주하기를 희망한다.
➡ _____
_____

Writing Workshop

1. 보람중학교 동아리 지원서
➡ _____

2. 동아리 이름: FC Boram
➡ _____

3. 학생 이름: 박순호
➡ _____

4. 가입을 원하는 이유: 나는 축구를 사랑하고 FC Boram에 가입하고 싶다.
➡ _____

5. 나는 공을 패스하는 것을 잘하고 빨리 달린다.
➡ _____

6. 그러나, 나는 공을 헤딩하는 법을 모르기 때문에 그것을 하는 법을 배우고 싶다.
➡ _____

7. 나는 멋진 헤딩 골을 만들 수 있는 축구 선수가 되기를 원한다.
➡ _____

8. 당신의 목표: 만약 내가 이 동아리에 가입하면, 나는 매우 열심히 연습해서 좋은 팀 플레이어가 될 것이다.
➡ _____

Real Life Zone

1. 나는 우리의 새로운 오케스트라 회원인 케이트를 소개하고 싶어.
➡ _____

2. 그녀는 바이올린을 연주하는 법을 알아.
➡ _____

3. 그녀는 또한 그룹에서 연주해 본 경험이 많아.
➡ _____

4. 그리고 그녀는 사람들과 일하는 것을 즐긴다고 말했어.
➡ _____

5. 모두 그녀가 나눔 오케스트라에 온 걸 환영하자.
➡ _____

MEMO

영어 기출 문제집

적중100

1학기

정답 및 해설

시사 | 송미정

중 2

적중100

영어 기출 문제집

적중100

1학기

정답 및 해설

시사 | 송미정

중 2

적중100

My Bucket List

시험대비 실력평가   p.08

01 ①	02 ②	03 ④	04 (1) for
(2) in	05 ①	06 ④	07 (1) a

favor (2) shared, with them

01 ① 입양하다 ② 맞추다, 조정하다 ③ 동반하다 ④ 인정하다 ⑤ 획득하다 / 그들은 개들을 애완동물 가게에서 사는 대신에 동물 보호소에서 입양하는 것을 추천받았다.

02 ② 중국의, 나머지 보기는 중국어의 뜻을 가진다. ① Mike는 중국어를 배우기를 원한다. ② 이 중국 음식은 치킨 수프와 잘 어울린다. ③ 중국어를 가르치는 학교의 숫자는 늘고 있다. ④ 그의 이름은 중국어로 '오렌지'의 의미이다. ⑤ 나는 밤낮으로 중국어를 공부한다.

03 ① introduce ② band ③ bucket list ④ adopted ⑤ overcome

04 (1) for a while: 잠깐 (2) stand in line: 줄을 서서 기다리다

05 ① right: 바로

06 aim: 목적, 목표 ① effort: 노력 ② turn: 차례 ③ cause: 원인 ④ goal: 목표 ⑤ result: 결과

07 (1) do a favor: 호의를 베풀다 (2) share A with B: A를 B와 나누다[공유하다]

서술형 시험대비   p.09

01 (1) make (2) taking (3) gets (4) ask

02 hope your, gets

03 (1) I fully accept what he says.
   (2) The house is right in front of you.
   (3) It was used only on special situations.
   (4) Poor light produces weak plants.

04 (f)reely

05 (c)hallenging

06 to

07 (1) exercise (2) experience

01 (1) make an effort: 노력하다 (2) take care of: ~을 돌보다 (3) get interested in: ~에 관심을 갖다 (4) ask for help: 도움을 청하다

02 hope: 희망하다, 바라다 get better: (병·상황 등이) 나아지다

03 (1) fully: 완전히 (2) right: 바로, in front of: ~의 앞에 (3) special: 특별한 (4) weak: 약한

04 freely: 자유롭게 / 어떤 것을 멈추거나 제한하는 사람 없이

05 challenging: 도전적인 / 흥미롭거나 재미있는 방식으로 어려운

06 be willing to 동사원형: 기꺼이 ~하다, be ready to 동사원형: ~할 준비가 되다

07 (1) exercise: 운동하다; 운동 (2) experience: 경험하다;경험

교과서 Conversation

핵심 Check   p.10~11

1 hope, I can read / I hope I get good grades this

2 I hope I can learn how to swim. / I hope that you finish it soon.

3 I'm planning to play games with friends.

4 Where are they planning to meet?

교과서 대화문 익히기

Check(√) True or False   p.12

(1) T (2) T (3) F (4) F

교과서 확인학습   p.14~15

Listen & Speak 1 A

hope, get / worry

Listen & Speak 1 B

1 it's / What, want for / I hope I get

2 What / I'm making / the first / hope, make

3 How / It was, wrote, for / tell, yours / hope I, someday

Listen & Speak 1 C

1 hope I, this / sounds

2 sounds

3 hope I can learn, to

Everyday English 2. A Function Practice 2

What are you planning to / planning to get

Everyday English 2 – B Listening Activity

1 planning to do tomorrow / I'm planning, book fair with, like to / What time / At, in front of

2 are you planning / not / about going, with

3 Can, a favor / to buy, tomorrow, help, choose one

1 do at / to sell

2 are you planning to / to do a magic

3 What are you planning / to dance in a group

시험대비 기본평가 p.16

01 ④ 02 ① 03 ③, ⑤ 04 ②

01 be planning to 동사원형: ~할 계획이다

02 남자아이의 질문 다음에 새 컴퓨터를 받기를 바란다고 여자아이가 대답했으므로, 생일 선물로 무엇을 원하는지 질문하는 것이 어울린다.

03 ③ hope는 to부정사만을 목적어로 받을 수 있다. ⑤ '나는 네가 새로운 컴퓨터를 얻기를 원한다'의 의미로 밑줄 친 문장과 다른 뜻이다.

04 학교 축제에서 무엇을 할 계획인지 묻고 대답하는 표현이다. be planning to 동사원형: ~할 계획이다. festival: 축제

시험대비 실력평가 p.17~18

01 ③ 02 ③ 03 (1) making → to make / (that) I make (2) lot of → a lot of / lots of / many
04 (B) → (C) → (D) → (A) 05 ①
06 ⑤ your → yours
07 I hope (that) I become a rock star someday.
08 ② 09 I'm planning to study one new Chinese word every day.
10 (B) what (C) studying 11 ④
12 두 번째: do 다섯 번째: for 13 ②, ③

01 이번 주 계획을 묻고 있는 말에, (B) 할머니 댁을 방문할 계획이라고 대답하며, 할머니가 편찮으시다는 말을 덧붙인다. (C) 이에 유감을 표하고, 그녀가 나아지길 바란다는 말에 (A) 고맙다고 대답하며 상대방의 계획을 묻는다.

02 (A) What are you doing?: '너 뭐 하는 중이니?'로 현재 하고 있는 것을 물어보는 표현으로 대답도 현재진행형(be동사의 현재형+동사ing)으로 하는 것이 어울린다. (B) sound는 2형식 동사로 보어(형용사)를 받을 수 있다.

03 (1) hope는 목적어로 that절이나 to부정사를 받을 수 있다. (2) a lot of+명사: 많은(= lots of+명사), friend는 셀 수 있는 명사로 many(많은)의 수식을 받는다.

04 (B) 내일의 계획에 대해 묻는 질문에 (C) 도서 박람회에 Jimmy랑 같이 간다고 대답하며 같이 가자고 제안하자, (D) 상대방이 동의하고 언제 만날지 질문한다. (A) 이에 시간과 장소를 대답한다.

05 대답의 It이 가리키는 것이 질문에 나와야 한다. 과거시제로 대답했으므로 과거의 일을 질문하는 것이 어울린다. ① 영어 수업은 어땠니? ② 너는 무엇이 되고 싶니? ③ 너의 꿈을 적을 거니? ④ 너의 목록을 만들었니? ⑤ 영어 수업을 듣는 것은 어때?

06 your: 너의, yours: 너의 것 / 여기서 yours는 너의 꿈을 가리킨다.

07 hope: 희망하다, 바라다 become: ~이 되다 someday: 언젠가

08 주어진 말은 언제 중국어 공부를 시작했는지 묻고 있다. 이에 '겨우 지난달에.'라는 대답이 어울리므로 ②에 들어가는 것이 적절하다.

09 be planning to 동사원형: ~할 계획이다, Chinese: 중국의; 중국어, every day: 매일

10 (B) 그들이 말하고 있는 것의 뜻으로, what이 어울린다. (C) keep+동사ing: 계속 ~하다

11 과목마다 좋은 성적을 얻는 것으로 대답하였으므로, 금년 계획에 대해 묻는 ④번이 어울린다. ① 좋은 성적을 얻었니? ② 계획을 세울 거니? ③ 지난달의 계획이 무엇이었니? ④ 올해 계획이 무엇이니? ⑤ 너는 어디를 갈 계획이니?

12 What do you want for your birthday? / what: 무엇 want: 원하다

13 ① Hana의 생일은 오늘이다. ④ Hana의 생일이다. ⑤ 여자아이는 생일 선물로 새 컴퓨터를 받기를 바란다. ② 남자아이가 받기를 바라는 것은 무엇이니? ③ Hana의 생일 선물로 남자아이가 사려고 계획한 것은 무엇이니?

서술형 시험대비 p.19

01 (1) I'm planning to dance in a group
(2) I hope I can travel to Europe this summer.
02 take pictures with your favorite singer
03 go → to go, concert → concerts
04 ② words → word
05 I didn't know you were interested in Chinese.
06 is planning, word, to study, last, now, herself in

01 (1) be planning to 동사원형: ~할 계획이다 dance: 춤추다 in a group: 그룹으로, 단체로
(2) hope: 희망하다, 바라다 travel to: ~으로 여행가다 this summer: 이번 여름에

02 (A)가 가리키고 있는 것은 앞 문장의 'take pictures with my favorite singer'이다. my가 your로 바뀌는 것에 유의해야 한다.

03 be planning to 동사원형: ~할 계획이다, one of+복수명사: ~ 중의 하나

04 one(하나)의 수식을 받고 있으므로 word는 단수형을 쓰는 것이 적절하다

05 be interested in: ~에 관심을 갖다 Chinese: 중국어

06 be interested in: ~에 관심을 갖다, start to 동사원형: ~하는 것을 시작하다 last month: 지난달 introduce: 소개하다 in Chinese: 중국어로

3

핵심 Check   p.20~21

1 (1) the tallest   (2) longest   (3) the coolest

2 (1) to say   (2) to do   (3) to write

3 He studies science very hard to be a scientist.

 시험대비 기본평가   p.22

01 (1) highest → the highest   (2) most small → smallest

(3) being → to be   (4) to not → not to

02 (1) the thinnest/cheapest   (2) the most boring

(3) the cheapest/thinnest   (4) to meet   (5) in order to be

03 (1) Alice is the prettiest of the three sisters.

(2) When is the busiest day of the year?

(3) He studies Korean hard so as to watch Korean TV dramas.

(4) I got up early in order not to miss the first train.

01 (1) 형용사의 최상급 앞에는 the를 붙인다. (2) small의 최상급은 smallest이다. (3) to be로 '목적'을 나타내는 것이 적절하다. (4) to부정사의 부정은 not을 to 앞에 붙인다.

시험대비 실력평가   p.23~25

01 ⑤   **02** ④   **03** ②

04 He is the fastest swimmer in my team.

05 (1) the most   (2) in   (3) to celebrate   (4) to go

(5) to be   (6) to be   **06** ①   **07** ②

08 the prettiest   **09** ②   **10** the saddest

11 ①, ④   **12** ②, ③

13 (1) I want to win first prize to surprise my mom.

(2) Jack used a compass to find the right direction.

(3) I visited the museum to see the works of Gogh.

(4) Tom and Judy went to the restaurant so as to have lunch.

14 ③, ⑤   **15** (1) to play basketball   (2) opened, to study   (3) turned on, to watch   (4) the coldest   (5) the cleverest   (6) the worst of

16 ⑤   **17** (1) to be a math teacher   (2) to buy a dress   (3) not to be late

18 most brightest → brightest

01 뒤에 of my blouses가 있으므로 최상급이 적절하다.

02 ④ most와 최상급을 겹쳐서 쓰지 않는다.

03 silly와 valuable의 최상급은 silliest와 most valuable이며 형용사의 최상급 앞에는 the를 붙인다.

04 형용사의 최상급 앞에는 the를 붙인다.

05 (1) 형용사의 최상급 앞에는 the를 붙인다. (2) 최상급에서 보통 'of+복수 명사', 'in+단수 명사'가 쓰인다. (3), (4) 부사적 용법의 '목적' (5), (6) 부사적 용법의 '결과'이다.

06 ①번은 time을 수식하는 형용사적 용법이지만 <보기>와 나머지는 모두 부사적 용법의 '목적'이다.

07 부사적 용법의 '목적'의 뜻을 보다 분명하게 하기 위하여 to부정사 앞에 in order나 so as를 쓰기도 한다.

08 that I've ever seen으로 보아 최상급이 적절하다.

09 부사적 용법의 '목적'을 이용한다.

10 in this village가 있으므로 최상급이 적절하다.

11 ① 형용사적 용법 ② 부사적 용법의 '목적' ③ 부사적 용법의 '결과' ④ 명사적 용법(목적격 보어) ⑤ 부사적 용법의 '원인'

12 to부정사는 to 다음에 동사원형이 온다.

13 (1) 부사적 용법의 '목적'으로 쓰는 것이 적절하다. (2) 접속사 없이 동사가 두 개 나올 수 없으므로 found를 '~하기 위하여'라는 뜻의 to부정사의 부사적 용법으로 고치는 것이 적절하다. (3) to부정사는 to 다음에 동사원형이 나온다. (4) 목적의 뜻을 보다 분명하게 하기 위하여 to부정사 앞에 in order나 so as를 쓰기도 한다. *compass: 나침반

14 ① The biggest fruit in this shop is that watermelon. ② The light bulb is one of the most famous inventions of the 19th century. ④ The wisest man in the world was Gandhi.

15 (1), (2), (3) '~하기 위하여'라는 뜻의 to부정사의 부사적 용법(목적)을 이용한다. (4), (5), (6) 형용사의 최상급 앞에는 the를 붙인다. bad의 최상급은 worst이다.

16 flamingo가 키와 몸무게 모두 가장 작다.

17 '~하기 위하여'라는 뜻의 to부정사의 부사적 용법의 '목적'을 이용한다.

18 most와 최상급을 겹쳐 쓰지 않는다.

서술형 시험대비   p.26~27

01 heaviest → the lightest

02 (1) in order to

(2) so as to

(3) in order that, could[might]

03 (1) heavier than, bag

(2) No, heavier than

(3) No, as[so] heavy

04 (1) Arthur was pleased to get a good grade in science.

(2) Sue went out at night to buy some water.

(3) Brenda went to Paris to study art.

05 (1) This is the largest room in my house.

(2) John is the tallest of the boys in his class.

(3) Marilyn studies English hard to get good grades.

(4) I want to use my computer to find the information on the Internet.

(5) The most famous scientist, Isaac Newton, lived to be 74.

06 (1) to buy   (2) to have[eat]   (3) not to be late

07 (1) Mom went to the store to buy my dress.

(2) She used a hairbrush to brush her daughter's hair.

(3) Tom was disappointed to find that she loved Mike.

(4) Solomon was one of the wisest men in the world.

(5) This book is the most useful of all the books that I have.

08 (1) wears the brightest

(2) the heaviest

(3) has the darkest

09 (1) the prettiest/nicest, to give

(2) the nicest, to make

(3) the longest, to get

10 (1) to study hard   (2) to use the Internet better

01 문맥상 가벼운 신발이 적절하며 형용사의 최상급에는 the를 붙인다.

02 부사적 용법의 '목적'을 나타내는 to부정사는 (1) 'in order to부정사', (2) 'so as to부정사', (3) 'in order that 주어+can[may] ~'으로 바꿔 쓸 수 있다.

03 최상급 = 비교급 than+any other+단수 명사 = 부정 주어+비교급 than = 부정 주어+as[so] 원급 as

04 (1)은 to부정사의 부사적 용법의 '(감정의) 원인'을, (2)와 (3)은 '목적'을 나타내는 to부정사를 쓴다.

05 (1) most와 최상급을 겹쳐 쓰지 않는다. (2) 형용사의 최상급 앞에는 the를 붙인다. (3), (4) '~하기 위하여'라는 뜻의 to부정사의 부사적 용법의 '목적'을 이용한다. (5) to be 74가 동사 lived의 결과를 나타내는 to부정사의 부사적 용법의 '결과'를 이용한다.

06 부정사의 부사적 용법의 '목적'을 이용한다. 또한 부정사의 부정은 not을 to부정사 앞에 붙인다는 것에 유의한다.

07 (1), (2) 부정시의 부사적 용법의 '목적'을 이용한다. (3) 부사적 용법의 '감정의 원인'을 이용한다. (4) one of the+최상급+복수명사: 가장 ~한 …들 중의 하나 (5) '~ 중에서'는 'of+복수 명사'를 이용한다. the books that I have: 내가 갖고 있는 책들

08 형용사의 최상급 앞에는 the를 붙인다.

09 to부정사의 부사적 용법의 '목적'을 이용하고 형용사의 최상급 앞에는 the를 붙인다.

10 부정사의 부사적 용법의 목적으로 어법에 맞게 쓰면 정답임.

Reading

확인문제   p.28

1 T   2 F   3 F   4 T

확인문제   p.29

1 T   2 F   3 T   4 F

확인문제   p.29

1 T   2 F   3 F   4 T

교과서 확인학습 A   p.30~31

01 for the New School Year   02 Hi

03 the first day   04 for this year   05 most

06 you want to do   07 make a bucket list, share, with

08 I'm

09 This is   10 go on a bike tour

11 I've been there before, on my bike

12 how to play   13 the most beautiful sound

14 on, by the end of   15 Finally

16 weakest subject   17 put, into, to overcome

18 My name is   19 right in front of

20 willing, stand in line   21 adopt a puppy

22 I've, wanted   23 I'm, ready to

24 a little more challenging   25 I'd like to

26 a big fan, a single one

교과서   p.32~33

1 My "Bucket List" for the New School Year

2 Hi, everyone.

3 Today is the first day of our new school year.

4 I want to hear your plans and hopes for this year.

5 What do you want to do most?

6 Think about three things you want to do.

7 And then, make a bucket list and share it with your friends.

8 Hi! I'm Jinsu.

9 This is my bucket list for this year.

10 First, I want to go on a bike tour of Jejudo this summer.

11 I've been there before, but I want to experience the island more freely on my bike this time.

12 My second goal is to learn how to play the guitar.

13 I think the guitar has the most beautiful sound of all musical instruments.

14 I hope I can play my favorite song on my guitar by the end of this year.

15 Finally, I want to get a good grade in math.

16 Math is my weakest subject.

17 This year, I'll put more effort into studying math to overcome my weakness.

18 Hi! My name is Somi.

19 First, I want to see a concert of my favorite band right in front of the stage.

20 I'm willing to stand in line all night to enter the front area.

21 Second, I want to adopt a puppy.

22 I've always wanted a puppy.

23 I think I'm fully ready to take care of a pet now.

24 My last goal is a little more challenging.

25 I'd like to read all of the Sherlock Holmes stories.

26 I became a big fan of this detective series last year, so I don't want to miss a single one.

시험대비 실력평가
p.34~37

01 ④　　02 ①, ③　　03 a bucket list

04 ②, ⑤　　05 (A) this　(B) weakest　(C) weakness

06 by the end of this year　07 ②　　08 stand in line　09 ②　　10 ⑤

11 (A) them (B) last　(C) every day　　12 ④

13 ⑤　　14 ①　　15 ③, ⑤　　16 ③

17 ①　　18 willing　　19 ③

20 (A) First　(B) Second (C) Third 또는 Finally나 Lastly

21 other　　22 most famous　　23 ③

24 ④　　25 ②　　26 What is the first thing on your list?

01 ④번 다음 문장의 then에 주목한다. 주어진 문장의 내용을 받고 있으므로 ④번이 적절하다.

02 ⓐ와 ②, ④, ⑤는 명사적 용법, ① 형용사적 용법, ③ 부사적 용법

03 '버킷 리스트'를 가리킨다.

---

04 ⓐ와 ②, ⑤는 경험 용법, ①과 ④ 계속 용법, ③ 결과 용법

05 (A) '올해의' 버킷 리스트라고 해야 하므로 this가 적절하다. last year: 작년, (B) 수학은 제가 '가장 약한' 과목이라고 해야 하므로 weakest가 적절하다. (C) '약점'을 극복하기 위해라고 해야 하므로 weakness가 적절하다.

06 by는 '완료'를 나타내는 전치사이다.

07 ② 진수는 전에 제주도에 가 본 적이 '있다.'

08 stand in line: 일렬로 서다

09 ⓑ와 ② 이미 나온 가산 명사의 반복을 피하여 씀. ① 하나의, ③ (강조의 의미로 쓰여) 유일한, ④ [another, the other와 대조적으로] 한쪽의, 한편의, ⑤ 사람, 세상 사람

10 위 글은 소미의 올해 버킷 리스트를 소개하는 글이므로, 제목으로는 ⑤ '소미가 올해 하고 싶어 하는 것'이 적절하다.

11 (A) 'cookies'를 가리키므로 them이 적절하다. (B) '마지막 것은'이라고 해야 하므로 last가 적절하다. latest: 최근의, 최신의, (C) '매일'이라고 해야 하므로 every day가 적절하다. everyday: 일상의

12 동족목적어를 가지는 동사는 have로 바꿔 쓸 수 있다.

13 ⑤는 접속사이고, ⓑ와 나머지는 다 관계대명사이다.

14 위 글은 진수의 올해 버킷 리스트를 소개하는 글이므로, 제목으로는 ① '진수의 올해 버킷 리스트'가 적절하다.

15 finally와 lastly: 순서상 '끝으로', '마지막으로', ① 결국, 마침내, ② 게다가, ④ 그러므로

16 ⓑ와 ②, ⑤는 부사적 용법(목적), ①과 ③ 형용사적 용법, ④ 명사적 용법

17 ⓐ와 ① 정확히, 바로(부사), ② 옳은, 올바른, ③ 맞는[알맞은], 제대로 된, ④ 권리(명사), ⑤ 오른쪽의

18 be willing to: 기꺼이 ~하다, 어떤 일을 강요받아서라기 보다는 자신이 하기를 원하기 때문에 꽤 열심히 하는

19 ③ 소미가 어떻게 애완동물을 돌볼 준비가 완벽히 될 수 있었는지는 대답할 수 없다. ① A concert of her favorite band. ② A puppy. ④ To read all of the Sherlock Holmes stories. ⑤ Last year.

20 순서를 표현할 때 First, Second, Third(Finally나 Lastly)로 쓰는 것이 적절하다.

21 another+단수명사, 뒤에 복수명사인 countries가 있으므로 other로 고치는 것이 적절하다.

22 famous는 규칙변화를 하는 형용사이며, 최상급은 most famous이다.

23 for: (이유·원인) ~ 때문에, ~으로 (인하여)

24 부사적 용법(목적)의 to부정사 = in order[so as] to 동사원형 = that[so that/in order that] ~ may[can]

25 ② 소미의 버킷 리스트가 실현될지는 알 수 없다. ① Yes, she did. ③ To see her favorite band in a concert, standing in front of the stage. ④ No, she doesn't. ⑤ It is a bike tour of Jejudo.

26 What about you?: 너는 어때?, 진수의 첫 번째 버킷 리스트가 무엇인지 물어보는 말이다.

01 Today is the first day of our new school year.

02 thinking about three things you want to do

03 bucket list

04 play guitar → play the guitar

05 I think the guitar has the most beautiful sound of all musical instruments.

06 (A) to get a good grade 또는 getting a good grade (B) weakest subject

07 unwilling → willing

08 care for 또는 look after

09 one

10 I've been there before

11 I should

12 musical instrument

13 (A) night (B) to take (C) to read

14 she became a big fan of this detective series last year

15 (1) 가장 좋아하는 밴드의 공연을 무대 바로 앞에서 보기

(2) 강아지를 입양하기

(3) 셜록 홈스 이야기들을 모두 읽기

---

01 서수 first 앞에 the를 써야 한다. new school year: 새 학년

02 'And then(그리고 나서)'은 '여러분이 원하는 것 세 가지를 생각해 보고 나서'라는 뜻이다.

03 bucket list: 버킷 리스트, 사람들이 죽기 전에 경험하거나 성취하기를 원하는 것들의 목록, 'kick the bucket(죽다)'에서 유래하였다.

04 악기 이름 앞에는 the를 붙여야 한다.

05 형용사의 최상급 앞에 'the'를 보충하면 된다.

06 수학은 진수가 '가장 약한 과목'이기 때문에, 그의 마지막 목표는 수학에서 '좋은 점수를 받는 것'이다.

07 소미는 앞 자리에 들어가기 위해 '기꺼이' 밤새 줄을 서서 기다릴 것이다. unwilling: 꺼리는

08 take care of = care for = look after: ~을 돌보다

09 one은 이미 나온 가산 명사의 반복을 피할 때 쓰는 대명사이다.

10 have been to: ~에 가 본 적이 있다. / 부사인 there 앞에는 to를 쓰지 않는 것이 적절하다.

11 의문사+to부정사 = 의문사+주어+should+동사원형

12 '비교급 than any other 단수명사'로 최상급의 의미를 표현할 수 있다.

13 (A) all night: 밤새도록, 하룻밤 내내, (B) be ready to부정사: ~할 준비가 되다, (C) like는 목적어로 동명사와 to부정사를 둘 다 쓸 수 있지만, would like는 to부정사만 쓸 수 있다. would like to부정사 = want to부정사

14 작년에 이 탐정 시리즈의 열성팬이 되었기 때문이다.

15 소미의 버킷 리스트는 '가장 좋아하는 밴드의 공연을 무대 바로 앞에서 보기', '강아지를 입양하기', '셜록 홈스 이야기들을 모두 읽기'이다.

---

01 weakness 02 ③ 03 make

04 go 05 by 06 (1) goal (2) overcome

07 (1) The dogs can run more quickly to save people.

(2) This is my first visit to Europe.

(3) The bookstore is right next to my company.

08 ④ 09 ④ 10 planning

11 (1) happy → sorry (B) got → gets[will get] 12 ④

13 I'm planning to go to the book fair with Jimmy.

14 to go, the book fair with, tomorrow, joining them, will, at, in front of 15 ② 16 ③

17 ⑤ 18 ④ 19 ③

20 (1) Brian was pleased to meet Scarlet yesterday.

(2) Emily went to bed early to take the first train.

(3) Audrey grew up to be an actress.

(4) Wendy went to Seoul never to return.

21 the most important

22 (1) Ann wants to go to Korea to learn the Korean language.

(2) Jane is planning to dance at the school festival to show her friends how well she dances.

23 ③ 24 ① 25 (A) freely (B) how (C)studying 26 second 27 the most beautiful sound 28 ⑤ 29 the Sherlock Holmes stories 30 ③ 31 standing 32 first

33 ①, ④ 34 No.

---

01 주어진 보기는 반의어의 관계이다. outside: 바깥쪽 inside: 안쪽 strength: 힘, 강점 weakness: 약함, 약점

02 ③ full → fully: 완전히 / 그 식당은 이번 주말에 완전히 예약되었다. ① challenging: 도전적인, 힘든, 간단하지 않은 / 어린 아이들을 가르치는 것은 도적적이며 보람된 일이다. ② missing: 없어진, 분실한 / 그들은 없어진 아이를 찾는 중이다. ④ complete: 완료하다, 완결하다 / 그 건물은 완성되는데 2년이 걸렸다. ⑤ bucket list: 버킷 리스트, 달성하고 싶은 목표 목록 / 나는 네가 정말 좋은 버킷 리스트를 만들었기를 바란다.

03 make a friend: 친구를 사귀다 make an effort: 노력하다

04 go back to ~: ~로 돌아가다 go on a tour: 여행을 가다

05 be p.p. by 행위자: …에 의해서 ~되다 by the end of ~: ~ 말까지는

06 (1) goal: 목표, 미래에 달성하기를 바라는 어떤 것 (2) overcome: 극복하다, 감정이나 문제를 성공적으로 통제하다

07 (1) save: 구하다, 살리다 (2) Europe: 유럽, 유럽 대륙 (3) right: 바로

08 좋은 성적을 얻기를 바란다는 말에 네가 좋은 성적을 받을 거니까 걱정하지 말라는 말이 어울린다. ① 그 말을 들으니 유감이야. ② 너는 어때? 너의 계획은 무엇이니? ③ 음, 나는 확실하지 않아. ⑤ 응, 뭔데?

7

09 Brian이 소민이의 계획을 먼저 묻고 이에 대답했다. 이어서 소민이가 Brian의 계획을 묻는 표현이 들어가야 한다. Brian이 자신의 계획은 개를 목욕시키는 것이라고 대답했으므로 ④가 적절하다.

10 Are you planning to 동사원형: ~할 계획이니?

11 (1) 할머니가 아프다는 말에 그 말을 들어 기쁘다는 표현은 어색하다. 그러므로 happy를 sorry로 바꾸는 것이 적절하다. I'm sorry to hear that: 유감이야. (2) 곧 나아지기를 바란다는 말이므로 과거형 got은 어울리지 않는다.

12 ④ 소민이는 이번 주말에 할머님을 방문할 것이다. this Friday → this weekend

13 be planning to 동사원형: ~할 계획이다 book fair: 도서 박람회

14 be planning to 동사원형: ~할 계획이다 suggest: 제안하다 join: 함께 하다, 합류하다 will+동사원형: ~할 것이다 at+시간: ~(시)에 in front of: ~ 앞에서

15 happy의 최상급은 happiest이다.

16 <보기>와 ③번은 부사적 용법의 '목적' ① 명사적 용법 ② 목적어로 쓰인 명사적 용법 ④ 보어로 쓰인 명사적 용법 ⑤ 형용사적 용법

17 뒤에서 in 이하로 한정되고 있으며 '~에서'를 의미하므로 최상급이 적절하고 형용사의 최상급 앞에는 the를 붙인다.

18 ① I want to get a good grade in math. ② I'll put more effort into studying math to overcome my weakness. ③ Arnold saved plenty of money to buy a car. ⑤ William Shakespeare lived to be fifty two.

19 ③ Emma is the kindest girl in her school.

20 (1) 부정사의 부사적 용법의 '감정의 원인'을, (2) 부사적 용법의 '목적'을, (3), (4) 부사적 용법의 '결과'를 이용한다. never to부정사: 결코 ~하지 못하다

21 부정 주어+비교급+than = 최상급

22 부정사의 부사적 용법의 '목적'을 이용한다.

23 '저는 여러분들의 올해 계획과 희망을 듣고 싶어요. 여러분이 가장 원하는 것은 무엇인가요?'라는 두 문장 사이의 '학생들이 더 높은 학년으로 올라가면, 그들은 훨씬 더 많은 시간을 공부하는 데 보낸다.'라는 ③번 문장은 전체 글의 흐름에서 벗어난다.

24 ⓐ for: (정해진 날짜나 시간을 나타내어) ~에[일자의], for this year: 올해의, ⓑ share A with B: B와 A를 공유하다

25 (A) 동사 experience를 수식하므로 부사 freely가 적절하다. (B) '기타 연주하는 법'이라고 해야 하므로 how가 적절하다. (C) 전치사 다음이므로 동명사 studying이 적절하다.

26 제 '두 번째' 목표라고 해야 하므로 second가 적절하다.

27 '부정주어 + 비교급 than'은 최상급의 의미를 지닌다.

28 ⓐ와 ⑤ 부사적 용법(형용사 수식), ① 부사적 용법(목적), ② 부사적 용법(원인), ③ 부사적 용법(결과), ④ 부사적 용법(판단의 근거)

29 '셜록 홈스 이야기'를 가리킨다.

30 ③ 소미는 이제는 애완동물을 돌볼 준비가 '완벽히 되었다'고 생각한다.

31 현재분사를 사용하여 동시동작을 나타내는 분사구문으로 고치는 것이 적절하다.

32 the first thing = the top thing

33 선행사가 사물이므로 관계대명사 which나 that이 적절하다.

34 글쓴이의 가장 약한 과목이 영어이므로, 글쓴이는 영어를 '잘하지 못한다.'

단원별 예상문제
p.46~49

01 (1) (c)omplete (2) (f)amous (3) (a)fter (4) (m)issing
02 ④　　03 ④　　04 ①
05 (D) → (C) → (A) → (B)　　06 (A) → (C) → (B) → (D)
07 ⑤　　08 (A) When did you start studying Chinese? (B) How did you get so into Chinese?
09 ③　　10 I hope I can soon watch them in Chinese and understand what they are saying.
11 ②　　12 ④　　13 (1) healthiest (2) best
14 so as not to get wet　15 (1) He is the best student in my class. (2) Naomi is the smartest girl of them all.　16 (1) I used my smartphone to call Melanie. (2) Karen was glad to see him again tonight.
17 I want to go on a bike tour　18 ⑤
19 weakest　20 (A) willing (B) adopt (C) challenging
21 ④　　22 ②　　23 cookies
24 surprise　25 ③

01 (1) 시작하다 : 시작하다 = finish (끝내다) : complete (완료하다, 완결하다) (2) 처음의, 초기의 : 첫, 처음의 = well-known (유명한, 잘 알려진) : famous (유명한, 잘 알려진) (3) 안에 : 밖으로 = before (~ 전에) : after (~ 후에) (4) 똑똑한 : 똑똑한 = lost (잃은, 행방불명의) : missing (없어진, 분실한)

02 be willing to 동사원형: 기꺼이 ~하다 be ready to 동사원형: ~할 준비가 되다

03 선물로 무엇을 받기를 원하는지 묻는 질문에, 새로운 컴퓨터를 얻기를 바란다고 대답한다. ① 너는 그럴 거야. 걱정하지 마. ② 그거 좋겠다. ③ 나는 새 컴퓨터를 살 계획이다. ④ 나는 새 컴퓨터를 받기를 희망해. ⑤ 나는 네가 새 컴퓨터를 받기를 희망해.

04 ① overcome: 극복하다 / 나는 네가 어려움들을 극복하길 바란다. ② learn: 배우다 / 언어를 배우는 최상의 방법이 무엇이니? ③ surprise: 놀라게 하다 / 그들이 말하고 있는 것은 나를 놀라게 하지 않는다. ④ ride: 타다 / 그는 결코 자전거 타는 것을 배운 적이 없다. ⑤ plan: 계획; 계획하다 / 우리는 시내 근처에 새로운 사무실을 열 계획이다.

05 (D) 부탁을 하는 말에, (C) 좋다고 대답하고. 부탁의 내용을 묻는다. (A) 새 자전거를 사는데 하나 골라 달라고 말하자 (B) 좋

다고 대답한다.

06 (A) 내일의 계획을 묻자 (C) 잘 모르겠다고 대답한다. (B) 그러면 영화 보러 가자고 제안하고 (D) 좋다고 대답한다.

07 새 학년을 위한 특별한 계획에 대해 얘기하는 중이다.

08 (A)의 답이 '지난달'이라는 시간의 정보이기 때문에 When으로 시작된 의문문이 어울린다. 중국어는 공부할 예정이 아니라 이미 공부하고 있기에 과거시제가 들어간 'When did you start studying Chinese?'이 어울린다. (B) It's because라고 답하고 있으므로 이유를 묻는 질문이 적절하다.

09 주어와 목적어가 같기 때문에 재귀대명사를 사용해야 한다. me 대신에 myself를 사용해야 적절하다.

10 I hope I can 동사원형 ~: 내가 ~할 수 있기를 바란다[희망한다] soon: 곧 in Chinese: 중국어로 understand: 이해하다

11 ① Sumi is the tallest in my class. ③ A rabbit is one of the fastest animals. ④ Bill is the hungriest boy in this restaurant. ⑤ Steve is the richest of the three gentlemen.

12 ④번은 부사적 용법의 '원인'이고 나머지는 '목적'이다.

13 (1), (2) 뒤에 in her class와 in his school이라는 비교 집단이 있고 앞에 the가 있으므로 최상급이 적절하다.

14 목적의 뜻을 보다 분명하게 하기 위하여 to부정사 앞에 so as를 쓰기도 한다.

15 (1) 비교급은 '비교급+than+비교 대상'으로 쓰지만 최상급은 'the+최상급'으로 쓴다. (2) most와 최상급을 겹쳐서 쓰지 않는다.

16 (1) 부정사의 부사적 용법의 '목적'을 이용한다. (2) 부정사의 부사적 용법의 '원인'을 이용한다.

17 want는 to부정사를 목적어로 가진다.

18 ⑤ subject는 (논의 등의) 주제[대상/화제], 과목, ⓑ와 나머지는 다 성취하고자 하는 '목표'를 나타낸다.

19 weak은 규칙변화를 하는 형용사이며, 최상급은 weakest이다.

20 (A) '기꺼이' 밤새 줄을 서서 기다릴 것이라고 해야 하므로 willing이 적절하다. unwilling: 꺼리는, (B) 강아지를 '입양하고' 싶다고 해야 하므로 adopt가 적절하다. adopt: 입양하다, adapt: 맞추다[조정하다], 적응하다, (C) 마지막 목표는 셜록 홈스 이야기를 다 읽는 것이라서 약간 '도전적'이라고 해야 하므로 challenging이 적절하다. challenging: 도전적인, 도전 의식을 북돋우는, relaxing: 마음을 느긋하게 해 주는, 편한

21 ④ 작년에 그녀가 셜록 홈스 이야기를 몇 권 읽었는지는 알 수 없다. ① Right in front of the stage. ② A puppy. ③ Yes, she is. ⑤ Because she became a big fan of this detective series last year.

22 ⓑ와 ② (못 보거나 못 듣고) 놓치다, (관심을 안 두고) 지나치다, ① 피하다, 면하다, ③ 그리워하다, ④ (있어야 할 것이) 없다는 것을 알다[눈치 체다], ⑤ 실수, 실패(명사), 조금이건 1마일이건 빗나간 것은 마찬가지다(오십보백보)

23 '쿠키'를 가리킨다.

24 엄마를 '놀라게' 하기 위해 쿠키를 만들고 싶어 한다.

25 ③ 필요하지 않은 물건들을 버릴 것이다.

---

01 I will go to a movie with Toby. / I'm going to go to a movie with Toby.

02 (1) I hope I can travel to Japan next year.
(2) Next year, I hope I can become the winner.
(3) I'm planning to study all day to get good grades.

03 ① Its → It's, ② special anything → anything special, ⑤ How is your plan? → What's[What is] your plan?

04 (1) to play (2) to send

05 (1) bridge → bridges
(2) popularest → the most popular
(3) buying → to buy
(4) stayed → to stay

06 (1) higher than any other mountain
(2) No, more beautiful

07 learning

08 greet → overcome 또는 get over

09 (1) 이번 여름에 제주도로 자전거 여행을 가기
(2) 기타 치는 법을 배우기
(3) 수학에서 좋은 점수를 받기

10 challenged → challenging

11 to read

12 (A) second (B) ready

---

01 계획을 말할 때, I'm planning to 동사원형 ~.(나는 ~할 계획이야.) I'm going to 동사원형 ~.(나는 ~할 거야.) I'll 동사원형 ~.(나는 ~할 거야.)을 사용할 수 있다.

02 (1) I hope (that) 주어 can 동사원형 ~. 주어가 할 수 있기를 바란다. (2) next year: 내년(에) winner: 승자 (3) be planning to 동사원형: ~할 계획이다 all day: 하루 종일 grade: 성적

03 ① 요일을 나타내기 위해 비인칭 주어 it을 사용한다. ② -thing으로 끝나는 anything, nothing, something 등은 형용사가 뒤에 온다. (후치 수식) ⑤ 계획에 대해 남자아이가 대답하고 있으므로, What을 이용해 계획이 무엇인지 물어봐야 한다.

04 부정사의 부사적 용법의 '목적'을 이용한다.

05 (1) one of the+최상급+복수명사: 가장 ~한 …들 중의 하나 (2) popular의 최상급은 most popular이고 형용사의 최상급 앞에는 the를 붙인다. (3), (4) '~하기 위하여'라는 뜻의 to부정사의 부사적 용법을 이용하는 것이 적절하다.

06 최상급 = 비교급 than+any other+단수 명사 = 부정 주어+비교급 than = 부정 주어+as[so] 원급 as

07 보어로 쓰인 to부정사를 동명사로 바꿀 수 있다.

08 나의 약점을 '극복하기' 위해 나는 수학 공부에 더 많은 노력을 기울일 것이라고 하는 것이 적절하다. greet: 맞다, 환영하다,

9

overcome = get over: 극복하다

09 진수의 버킷 리스트는 '이번 여름에 제주도로 자전거 여행을 가기', '기타 치는 법을 배우기', '수학에서 좋은 점수를 받기'이다.

10 challenge의 형용사형 challenging이 알맞다.

11 like는 목적어로 동명사와 to부정사를 둘 다 쓸 수 있지만, would like는 to부정사만 쓸 수 있다. would like to부정사 = want to부정사

12 소미의 '두 번째' 버킷리스트는 강아지를 입양하는 것이다. 사실 그녀는 항상 강아지를 원해 왔고 이제 애완동물을 돌볼 '준비가 완전히 되어 있다'고 생각한다

창의사고력 서술형 문제　　　　　p.52

[모범답안]

01 (A) planning to do
   (B) to visit the museum, What are you
   (A) to go swimming

02 (1) I study math very hard to become a math teacher.
   (2) I practice singing very hard to be a singer.

03 (A) bought   (B) my favorite actor   (C) my role model   (D) can travel   (E) to buy

단원별 모의고사　　　　　p.53~56

01 ③　　02 (1) of　(2) into　(3) away　(4) on

03 ②　　04 (i)nstrument

05 (c)omplete　06 ⓑ to see　ⓒ standing

07 The top thing on my list is a bike tour to Jejudo.

08 ④　　09 do you have any special plans for the new school year?

10 ⓐ in　ⓑ in　ⓒ into　　11 ③　　12 ①, ③

13 What are you planning to do this weekend?

14 ①, ④　　15 (f)avor　　16 help you choose one

17 ②　　18 ②　　19 No, as[so] high

20 (1) Sarah took the subway to go to school.
   (2) I sat under a tree to take a rest.
   (3) Amy woke up to find her cellphone on the bed.

21 ③번, in → of　　22 ②　　23 get over　　24 ④　　25 ③　　26 for

27 completed my bucket list for this year

28 How about you?

01 be planning to 동사원형: ~할 계획이다 get one's hair cut: ~의 머리를 자르다

02 (1) take care of: 돌보다 (2) put effort into: ~에 노력을 들이다, 힘들이다 (3) throw away: 버리다, 던지다 (4) go on a

tour: 관광하다, 여행을 떠나다

03 plan: 계획; 계획하다 / 그의 계획은 한 달에 두 권의 책을 읽는 것이다. 언제 유럽으로 갈 거니?

04 instrument: 기계, 기구 musical instrument: 악기

05 complete: 완료하다, 완결하다 / 특히 긴 시간이 걸릴 때 무엇인가를 하거나 만드는 행위를 끝내다

06 ⓑ want는 to부정사가 목적어로 올 수 있다. ⓒ standing은 접속사와 주어가 생략된 분사구문이다.

07 top: 꼭대기의, 위의 list: 목록 bike tour: 자전거 여행

08 ④ 소미가 좋아하는 밴드가 무엇인지는 나와 있지 않다. ① 소미는 좋아하는 밴드가 있다. ② 금년에 진수는 제주도에 자전거 여행을 가고 싶어 한다. ③ 그들은 금년의 버킷 리스트(하고 싶은 일)에 대해 얘기하는 중이다. ⑤ 소미는 콘서트에서 무대 앞에서 보기를 원한다.

09 special: 특별한 plan: 계획; 계획하다

10 ⓐ be interested in: ~에 관심을 갖다 ⓑ in Chinese: 중국어로 ⓒ get into: ~에 빠지게 되다

11 ③ not sure를 sure로 바꿔야 적절하다.

12 ① 맨 마지막 대화에, 보통 때처럼 과목마다 좋은 성적을 얻기를 원한다는 것으로 보아 남자아이는 보통 좋은 성적을 받는다. ② Kate는 중국어로 자신을 소개할 수 있다. ③ Kate는 중국어 공부를 지난달부터 시작했다. ④ Kate는 금년에 매일 새로운 중국어 단어를 외울 계획을 가지고 있다. ⑤ Kate가 중국 드라마의 열렬한 팬이다.

13 be planning to 동사원형: ~할 계획이다 this weekend: 이번 주말에

14 have[get]+목적어+p.p.: 목적어가 p.p.되도록 하다

15 favor: 친절, 호의

16 새로운 자전거를 찾는 것을 도와주려고 한다.

17 dirty와 wet의 최상급은 각각 dirtiest와 wettest이다.

18 Diana was at a restaurant to have lunch.

19 최상급 = 비교급 than+any other+단수 명사 = 부정 주어+비교급 than = 부정 주어+as[so] 원급 as

20 (1), (2) 부정사의 부사적 용법의 '목적'을 이용한다. (3) 부정사의 부사적 용법의 '결과'를 이용한다.

21 최상급 구문을 쓸 때 '~ 중에서'는 보통 'of+복수명사', 'in+단수 집합체'로 표현하는 것이 적절하다.

22 ⓐ와 ②는 과목, ① 지배를 받는, ③ 주제[대상/화제], ④ (그림•사진 등의) 대상[소재], ⑤ 연구[실험] 대상

23 overcome = get over: 극복하다

24 ④번 다음의 문장들이 주어진 문장의 내용을 설명하는 것이므로 ④번이 적절하다.

25 부사적 용법(목적)의 to부정사 = in order[so as] to동사원형 = that[so that/in order that] ~may[can]

26 be ready to부정사 = be ready for 동명사[명사]: ~할 준비가 되어 있다

27 '올해 나의 버킷 리스트를 완성했다.'

28 What about you? = How about you?: 너는 어때?

Let's Be Smart Smartphone Users

시험대비 실력평가 p.60

01 increase	02 ④	03 ②	04 ①
05 ②	06 ⑤	07 ⑤	08 ③
09 (p)revent			

01 둘은 반의어 관계이다. pull: 당기다 push: 밀다 increase: 증가하다 decrease: 감소하다

02 in front of: ~ 앞에 instead of: ~ 대신에

03 crack: 금, 깨진 틈

04 advice: 충고

05 service center: 서비스 센터, 수리소

06 뉴욕 시는 5년 안에 최소한 20%까지 소금 섭취량을 줄일 것을 계획하고 있다. ⑤ 줄이다, 감소시키다

07 낡은 규칙이 새로운 규칙으로 바뀌었다 ⑤ rule: 규칙

08 ③ 등/등 부상을 피하기 위해서, 무거운 물체를 들 때, 항상 무릎을 구부려라. ① 그 소설은 그것의 역사적인 배경에서 보는 것이 중요하다. ② 아무 말도 하지 마, 너는 상황을 더 악화시킬 뿐이야. ④ 미스터리를 해결할 수 있는 첫 번째 법칙은 사실을 확인하는 것이다. ⑤ 10분 동안 휴식 시간을 갖자.

09 (p)revent: 예방하다. 막다.

서술형 시험대비 p.61

01 (1) worse (2) behind

02 always late for

03 from

04 (1) leaning (2) lower (3) hurt (4) Bend

05 (1) (g)et in touch (2) give it back (3) do warm up[warm–up] exercise (4) paying attention to

06 (1) at / At (2) on

01 주어진 보기는 반의어 관계이다. (1) better: 더 좋은 worse: 더 나쁜 (2) in front of: ~ 앞에 behind: ~ 뒤에

02 be late for: ~에 늦다

03 keep A from B: A를 B로부터 막다 / 연극이 너무 지루해서 나는 잠드는 것을 참을 수 없었다. from time to time: 가끔, 이따금 / 너는 가끔 휴식할 필요가 있다.

04 (1) lean: 기대다 (2) lower: 낮추다 (3) hurt: 다치게 하다,

아프다 (4) bend: 구부리다

05 (1) get in touch with: ~와 연락[접촉]하다 (2) give back: 돌려주다 (3) do warm up[warm-up] exercise: 준비운동을 하다 (4) pay attention to: ~에 주의를 기울이다

06 (1) at+시간: ~시에, at least: 적어도 (2) put on: ~을 늘리다, 더하다 have a ride on: ~을 타다

교과서 Conversation

핵심 Check p.62~63

1 (B) You should study tonight.
  (B) You'd better keep him warm.

2 (B) better eat
  (B) You'd better study

3 (B) Make sure you, for
  (A) Make sure you don't touch
  (B) I won't

4 (B) Make sure you drink a lot of warm water.

교과서 대화문 익히기

Check(√) True or False p.64

[1] F [2] T [3] F [4] T [5] F [6] T

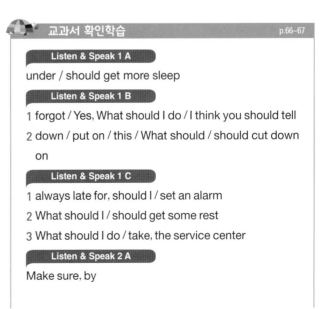

교과서 확인학습 p.66~67

Listen & Speak 1 A

under / should get more sleep

Listen & Speak 1 B

1 forgot / Yes, What should I do / I think you should tell

2 down / put on / this / What should / should cut down on

Listen & Speak 1 C

1 always late for, should I / set an alarm

2 What should I / should get some rest

3 What should I do / take, the service center

Listen & Speak 2 A

Make sure, by

Listen & Speak 2 B

1 sleep over at / make / Make sure you text, get to

2 what / reading / don't read in the dark, good for / turn, on

3 bring / won't / borrow / make sure / give it back

Listen & Speak 2 C

1 make sure you, first

2 Can I / turn it off after using it

3 Can I ride on, a life jacket

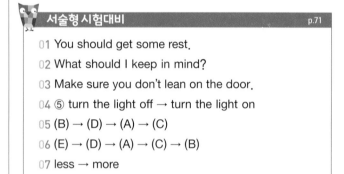

시험대비 기본평가 p.68

01 ② 02 ④ 03 (C) → (A) → (B) → (D)

04 ③ 05 ⑤

01 'You should + 동사원형'을 사용해 충고하는 말을 할 수 있다.

02 'Make sure ~'에 대해서 응답을 할 때, 'Make sure ~' 다음에 대해 긍정이면 'OK. I will.'로 답하고, 부정이면 'OK. I won't.'로 답한다.

03 (C) 진수네 집에서 자는 것을 허락받기 위해서 질문을 하자, (A) 진수의 엄마가 허락을 했는지 물어본다. (B) 허락을 했고, 그녀가 피자를 만들어 줄 것이라고 대답하자, (D) 진수네 집에서 자는 것을 허락하고, 진수의 집에 도착하면 문자를 보내 연락할 것을 당부한다.

04 부정의문문의 질문에 대답할 때, 대답하는 내용이 긍정이면 Yes로 대답한다. No, she is. → Yes, she is.

05 ⑤ Jenny의 생일이 지난 것만 언급되어 있고, 정확히 언제 생일인지는 언급되지 않았다.

시험대비 실력평가 p.69~70

01 ③ 02 ② 03 ② 04 ③

05 ① 06 make sure you take a walk for about 30 minutes 07 ②, ④

08 ④ 09 Just make sure you give it back when you're done. 10 ③ 11 crack

12 ④

01 feel down: 우울하다 ① 실망한 ② 신난 ③ 우울한 ④ 불안한 ⑤ 당황스러운

02 put on: ~을 늘리다, 더하다 cut down on: ~을 줄이다

03 ② 과학책을 빌려줄 수 있느냐는 질문에, 안된다고 말하고 나서, 사용하고 나면 돌라달라는 말은 어색하다.

04 피자를 먹을 수 있는지 물어보는 질문에, 손을 먼저 씻으라는 당부를 하고 있다.

05 잠자기 전에 따뜻한 우유를 마시고, 30분 동안 걸으라는 것은 잠을 자지 못하는 사람에게 해 줄 수 있는 충고이다.

06 make sure ~.: 꼭 하도록 해. take a walk: 산책하다 about: 약

07 당부할 때 사용할 수 있는 표현은 Make sure ~.(꼭 하도록 해.), You had better ~. (~하는 것이 좋겠다.), Don't forget to ~. (~할 것을 잊지 마.), Remember to ~.(~할 것을 기억해라.) 등이 있다.

08 (A) 남자아이가 책을 안 가져와서 (B) 여자아이에게 책을 빌리는 대화이다. bring: 가져오다 borrow: 빌리다 lend: 빌려주다 rent: (땅·집 등을) 빌리다[빌려주다]

09 Make sure ~: 반드시 ~하도록 하다, ~을 확실히 하다 give back: 돌려주다 be done: 끝나다

10 'Did you drop it?(그것을 떨어뜨렸니?)'라는 질문에 주어진 문장인 '여기 오는 길에 떨어뜨렸어.'라는 말이 어울리므로 ③이 적절하다.

11 crack 금, 깨진 틈 / 어떤 것이 깨졌지만 실제로 분리되지는 않았을 때 표면에 생긴 얇은 선

12 ④ Henry가 새로운 휴대 전화를 사용하는 방법을 모른다는 내용은 언급되어 있지 않다. ① 휴대 전화 케이스는 휴대 전를 보호해 준다. ② Henry는 그의 휴대 전화 화면이 깨져서 행복하지 않다. ③ Henry는 휴대 전화 케이스를 살 것이다. ⑤ Henry는 최근에 휴대 전화를 샀다.

서술형 시험대비 p.71

01 You should get some rest.

02 What should I keep in mind?

03 Make sure you don't lean on the door.

04 ⑤ turn the light off → turn the light on

05 (B) → (D) → (A) → (C)

06 (E) → (D) → (A) → (C) → (B)

07 less → more

01 should+동사원형: ~해야 한다(충고하기)

02 should+동사원형: ~해야 한다(충고하기) keep in mind: 명심하다

03 make sure: 반드시 ~하도록 하다, ~을 확실히 하다 lean on: ~에 기대다

04 휴대 전화로 소설을 읽고 있는 남자아이에게, 여자아이는 어두운 데서 읽지 말라고 당부하고 있으므로, 이 당부의 말에 '불을 끌 것이다.'는 어울리지 않는다. turn off: (불·라디오·텔레비전 등을) 끄다 turn on: (불·라디오·텔레비전 등을) 켜다

05 (B) 과학책을 가져오지 않았다는 말에, (D) 상대방은 선생님이 좋아하지 않을 것이라고 말한다. (A) 상대방에게 과학책을 빌려도 되는지 묻자 (C) 허락하며 꼭 돌려달라는 당부의 말을 한다.

06 무슨 일인지 묻는 질문에, (E) 휴대 전화를 보라고 얘기한다. (D) 휴대 전화 화면이 깨진 것을 보고, 떨어뜨렸는지 질문한다. (A) 여기 오는 길에 떨어뜨렸다고 답한다. (C) 이에 휴대 전화를 보호해 주는 휴대 전화 케이스에 대해 말하자, (B) 하나 살 것이라고 말한다.

07 눈 밑에 다크서클이 생겼다는 사람에게 좀 덜 자라는 충고가 아니라 좀 더 자라는 충고가 어울린다.

1 (1) to drink   (2) to teach
    (3) to eat with   (4) curious to ask
2 (1) laugh   (2) repaired
    (3) to do   (4) to paint

01 (1) write → write on   (2) looking → look
    (3) play → to play   (4) doing → (to) do
02 ④
03 (1) He made everyone work late.
    (2) Autumn is the season to harvest.
    (3) He helped me carry the heavy box.
    (4) I had a lot of work to do last night.

01 (1) to부정사가 형용사 역할을 할 때 수식받는 명사가 전치사의 목적어로 사용되었으면 전치사를 생략하면 안 된다. (2) 사역동사의 목적격보어로 동사원형이 적절하다. (3) to play로 time을 수식하는 것이 적절하다. (4) help는 준사역동사로 목적격보어로 동사원형이나 to부정사가 온다.
02 get은 to부정사가 목적격보어로 와야 한다.
03 사역동사는 목적격보어로 동사원형이 온다. (help는 to부정사도 가능) to부정사의 형용사적 용법을 이용하여 앞의 명사를 수식한다.

01 ⑤   **02** ①   **03** ⑤
04 to wear nice → nice to wear
05 (1) smile   (2) painted   (3) to find   (4) to walk   (5) to check   (6) to take care of   (7) wrong to correct
06 ②   **07** ③, ④   **08** ⑤   **09** ②
10 ①   **11** ③
12 (1) I want to make it happen during the school festival.
    (2) Is there anyone funny to bring to the party?
    (3) I'll have all the files copied for the meeting.
    (4) Dominick bought his daughter a doll to play with.
    (5) Amy got her sister to do her homework by herself.
13 ①   **14** ⑤   **15** ③
16 Susan wants a comfortable T-shirt to wear during the hiking.
17 I am looking for something nice to make me look

good.
18 (1) to become   (2) do   (3) to give, to make
    (4) finished   (5) to talk with   (6) to work

01 put on gloves와 같이 쓰므로 전치사 on이 있어야 하며 gloves를 수식해야 하므로 to부정사 형태가 적절하다.
02 사역동사는 목적격보어로 동사원형이 온다.
03 첫 문장에서는 사역동사의 목적격보어로 능동의 의미가 필요하므로 동사원형이 적절하다. 두 번째 문장에서는 something을 수식하는 형용사 역할을 하는 to부정사가 적절하다.
04 to부정사가 -thing, -body, -one으로 끝나는 부정대명사를 형용사와 함께 수식할 때는 '대명사+형용사+to부정사'의 어순이다.
05 (1) 사역동사는 목적격보어로 동사원형이 나온다. (2) 사역동사의 목적격보어로 수동의 의미가 필요하므로 과거분사가 적절하다. (3) help는 준사역동사로 목적격보어로 동사원형이나 to부정사가 나온다. (4) get은 to부정사가 목적격보어로 나와야 한다. (5) time을 수식하는 to check가 적절하다. (6) take care of two daughters와 같이 쓰므로 전치사 of가 있어야 한다. (7) to부정사가 -thing으로 끝나는 부정대명사를 형용사와 함께 수식할 때 '대명사+형용사+to부정사'의 어순이다.
06 ②번은 부사적 용법의 '결과'이지만 <보기>와 나머지는 모두 형용사적 용법이다.
07 ①, ②, ⑤ 형용사적 용법 ③ 부사적 용법의 '원인' ④ 명사적 용법(목적격보어) run into: ~을 우연히 만나다
08 사역동사 make의 목적격보어로 동사원형이 나와야 한다.
09 help는 목적격보어로 동사원형이나 to부정사가 나온다. emails를 수식하는 형용사 용법의 to부정사가 적절하다.
10 allowed는 목적격보어로 to부정사가 나와야 한다.
11 사역동사 let의 목적격보어로 동사원형이 적절하다.
12 (1) 사역동사의 목적격보어로 동사원형이 적절하다. (2) to부정사가 -one으로 끝나는 부정대명사를 형용사와 함께 수식할 때는 '대명사+형용사+to부정사'의 어순이다. (3) 사역동사의 목적격보어로 수동의 의미가 필요하므로 과거분사가 적절하다. (4) 인형을 노는 것이 아니라 인형을 갖고 노는 것이므로 with가 필요하다. play a doll (×) play with a doll (○) (5) get은 사역동사의 의미로 쓰일 수 있지만 목적격보어로 to부정사가 나와야 한다.
13 get은 목적격보어로 to부정사가 나와야 한다.
14 live in a house로 써야 하므로 in을 빠뜨리면 안 된다.
15 주어진 문장과 ③번의 make는 사역동사로 그 쓰임이 같다.
16 to를 보충하여 형용사적 용법으로 T-shirt를 수식하도록 한다.
17 '어떤 멋진 것'은 something nice로 쓰고 to make가 이것을 수식하도록 하고 사역동사 make의 목적격보어로 동사원형 look이 오도록 문장을 만든다.
18 (1) to become이 a chance를 수식하는 형용사적 용법으로 쓴다. (2) 사역동사 make의 목적격보어로 동사원형을 쓴다. (3) to give로 a present를 수식하게 하고 to make로 부사적 용

법(목적)으로 쓴다. (4) 사역동사의 목적격보어로 수동의 의미가 필요하므로 과거분사 finished가 적절하다. (5) to부정사가 -one으로 끝나는 부정대명사를 형용사와 함께 수식할 때는 '명사+형용사+to부정사'의 어순이다. with를 빠뜨리지 않도록 주의한다. (6) get은 사역동사의 의미로 쓰일 수 있지만 목적격보어로 to부정사인 to work가 나와야 한다.

01 achieving → to achieve

02 (1) Angie has twin sisters to take care of.

  (2) Allen knows many silly jokes to make us laugh.

03 (1) Marilyn won't let her daughter sleep over at her friend's.

  (2) I don't know how she got him to say yes.

  (3) I asked him to have my computer repaired.

  (4) He helped her (to) carry her things.

04 (1) I want to have the ability to speak English well.

  (2) She took the chance to become an actress.

  (3) Is there a way to solve the problem? 등 어법에 맞게 쓰면 정답

05 taken

06 (1) to decide

  (2) to talk about

  (3) to remember

07 to eat → eat, feeling → (to) feel

08 (1) to protecting → to protect

  (2) look → look after

  (3) write → write on

  (4) important something to tell → something important to tell

09 (1) Our teacher made us hand in our report by tomorrow.

  (2) The police officer made them leave immediately.

  (3) My mom made me come home early today.

10 (1) Our teacher made us use only English in class.

  (2) When he went to Paris, there was nobody to depend on.

  (3) Simon had his computer checked.

  (4) They needed a teacher to teach them English.

  (5) I helped Mom to prepare dinner last night.

11 (1) to clean   (2) repaired

01 goals를 수식하는 형용사적 용법의 to achieve가 적절하다.

02 형용사적 용법의 to부정사를 이용한다.

03 (1) 사역동사의 목적격보어로 동사원형이 적절하다. (2) get은 사

역동사의 의미로 쓰일 수 있지만 목적격보어로 to부정사가 나온다. (3) 사역동사의 목적격보어로 수동의 의미가 필요하므로 과거분사가 적절하다. (4) help는 목적격보어로 동사원형이나 to부정사가 나온다.

04 앞에 나오는 명사를 수식하는 형용사 용법의 to부정사를 이용한다.

05 사역동사의 목적격보어로 '개가 동물 병원으로 데려가지는' 수동의 의미가 필요하므로 과거분사가 적절하다.

06 앞에 나오는 명사를 수식하는 to부정사의 형용사적 용법을 이용한다. (2)번에서 talk topics가 아니라 talk about topics이므로 about을 빠뜨리면 안 된다.

07 사역동사의 목적격보어로 동사원형이 적절하며 help는 목적격보어로 동사원형이나 to부정사가 나온다.

08 (1) to protect가 tips를 수식하는 형용사적 용법이 적절하다. (2) look after는 두 단어가 하나의 타동사 역할을 하는 것이므로 after를 생략하면 안 된다. (3) to부정사가 형용사 역할을 할 때 수식받는 명사가 전치사의 목적어로 사용되었으면 전치사를 생략하면 안 된다. (4) to부정사가 -thing으로 끝나는 부정대명사를 형용사와 함께 수식할 때는 '대명사+형용사+to부정사'의 어순이다.

09 사역동사 make의 목적격보어로 동사원형이 적절하다.

10 (1) 사역동사의 목적격보어로 동사원형을 쓴다. (2) to부정사의 형용사적 용법을 이용한다. depend on의 on을 빠뜨리지 않도록 조심한다. (3) 컴퓨터가 검사를 받는 수동의 의미이므로 목적격보어로 과거분사를 써야 한다. (4) '가르칠 선생님'이므로 to teach가 a teacher를 수식하도록 한다. (5) help는 목적격보어로 동사원형이나 to부정사가 나온다. 단어 수에 맞춰 to부정사를 이용한다.

11 (1) get은 사역동사의 의미로 쓰일 수 있지만 목적격보어로 to부정사가 나와야 한다. (2) 자전거가 수리되는 것이므로 과거분사 repaired가 적절하다. mechanic: (기계) 수리공, 정비사

교과서

Reading

확인문제   p.80

1 T   2 F   3 F   4 T

확인문제   p.81

1 T   2 F   3 T   4 T   5 F

확인문제   p.81

1 T   2 F   3 F   4 T

01 Health Tips   02 spends, using

03 checks   04 plays, games   05 texts

06 finds information   07 online comic

   books   08 watches   09 take, off

10 cause health problems   11 a heavy user

12 If so, to protect   13 Watch

14 usually bend   15 text neck pose

16 to prevent, up to   17 Another way,

   instead of bending   18 a break

19 feel tired, for a long time   20 in the dark,

   worse   21 To avoid, from time to time

22 Every, a 20-second break, feet away

23 blink, often   24 keep, from becoming

25 on your smartphone   26 Texting, hurt

27 Try   28 help reduce   29 Pull on

30 Put, together with your arms   31 remember

32 The best tip, to use, less

33 some rest from

1 Health Tips for Smartphone Users

2 Seongmin spends a lot of time using his smartphone.

3 He checks the news and weather.

4 He plays smartphone games.

5 He texts his friends.

6 He finds information on the Internet.

7 He reads online comic books.

8 He watches movies.

9 Seongmin cannot take his hands off his smartphone all day long.

10 He does not know that using a smartphone too much can cause health problems.

11 Are you a heavy user of your smartphone like Seongmin?

12 If so, here are some tips to protect your health.

13 Watch your neck and back.

14 When you read on your smartphone, you usually bend your neck.

15 This "text neck" pose increases the pressure on your neck and back.

16 The best way to prevent this pressure is to bring the phone up to the level of your eyes.

17 Another way is to lower your eyes instead of bending your neck.

18 Give your eyes a break.

19 It makes your eyes feel tired and dry to read small letters on a smartphone for a long time.

20 Using a smartphone in the dark or in a moving car makes this problem worse.

21 To avoid this, give your eyes a break from time to time.

22 Follow the 20–20–20 rules: Every 20 minutes, take a 20–second break and look at something at least 20 feet away

23 Also, blink your eyes often.

24 This will keep your eyes from becoming dry.

25 Do you text a lot on your smartphone?

26 Texting for a long time can hurt your fingers and wrists.

27 Try these exercises.

28 They will help reduce the pain in your fingers and wrists.

29 Pull on each finger of each hand.

30 Put the backs of your hands together with your arms out in front of you.

31 But remember.

32 The best tip to prevent these health problems is to use your smartphone less.

33 Give yourself some rest from your smartphone.

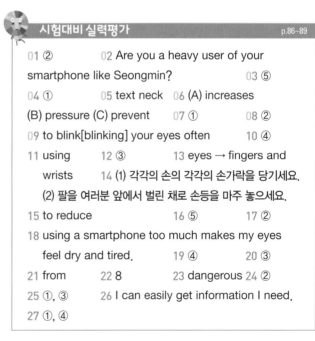

01 ②   02 Are you a heavy user of your smartphone like Seongmin?   03 ⑤

04 ①   05 text neck   06 (A) increases

(B) pressure (C) prevent   07 ①   08 ②

09 to blink[blinking] your eyes often   10 ④

11 using   12 ③   13 eyes → fingers and wrists   14 (1) 각각의 손의 각각의 손가락을 당기세요.

(2) 팔을 여러분 앞에서 벌린 채로 손등을 마주 놓으세요.

15 to reduce   16 ⑤   17 ②

18 using a smartphone too much makes my eyes feel dry and tired.   19 ④   20 ③

21 from   22 8   23 dangerous 24 ②

25 ①, ③   26 I can easily get information I need.

27 ①, ④

01 본문 끝에 여기 여러분의 '건강'을 지켜 줄 몇 가지 조언이 있습니다라는 말이 나오므로 빈칸에는 'health'가 적절하다. ④ posture: 자세, ⑤ grade: 성적

02 a heavy user: 과다 사용자

03 '여기 여러분의 건강을 지켜 줄 몇 가지 조언이 있다'는 말로 본문이 끝나므로, 뒤에는 '스마트폰 사용 시 여러분의 건강을 지켜 줄 몇 가지 조언'이 나온다고 하는 것이 적절하다.

04 read on your smartphone: 스마트폰을 보다, the pressure on: ~에 가해지는 압력

05 text neck: 거북목 증후군, 거북처럼 목이 앞으로 구부러진 자세, 손에 든 장치를 지나치게 보거나 문자를 보내는 것으로 인해서 목에 반복되는 스트레스, 부상 그리고 통증을 묘사하는 단어

06 (A) 압력을 '증가시킨다'고 해야 하므로 increases가 적절하다. decrease: 줄이다, 감소시키다, (B) '압력'을 증가시킨다고 해야 하므로 pressure가 적절하다. pressure: 압력, 압박, pleasure: 기쁨, 즐거움, (C) '예방'하는 가장 제일 좋은 방법이라고 해야 하므로 prevent가 적절하다. protect: 보호하다

07 ①번 다음 문장의 this problem이 주어진 문장의 내용을 받고 있으므로 ①번이 적절하다.

08 ② 드물게, ⓐ와 나머지는 다 '가끔'

09 '눈을 자주 깜빡이는 것'을 가리킨다.

10 many+복수명사, a lot of = lots of = plenty of: 수나 양이 많을 때 사용, ⑤ much = a great deal of: 양이 많을 때 사용

11 spend+시간+~ing: ~하는 데 시간을 보내다

12 스마트폰으로 친구들에게 '문자 메시지를 보낸다.'

13 오랫동안 문자 메시지를 보내는 것은 '손가락'과 '손목'을 상하게 할 수 있다. do harm to: ~에 해를 끼치다

14 본문의 마지막에 설명되어 있다.

15 help 다음에는 원형부정사와 to부정사 둘 다 올 수 있다.

16 위 글은 스마트폰 사용의 좋은 점들과 나쁜 점들에 관한 글이므로, 제목으로는 '스마트폰의 장점과 단점'이 적합하다.

17 앞에 나오는 내용과 상반되는 내용이 뒤에 이어지므로 ②번 On the other hand(한편, 반면에)가 가장 적절하다. ① 게다가, ③ 그러므로, ④ 예를 들면, ⑤ 비슷하게

18 'using'을 보충하면 된다.

19 위 글은 스마트폰을 사용할 때의 눈 문제를 예방하는 법에 관한 글이다.

20 ⓐ와 ③ 가주어, ① 비인칭주어, ② 그것(앞에 이미 언급되었거나 현재 이야기되고 있는 사물·동물을 가리킴), ④ 사람의 신분을 나타낼 때 씀, ⑤ 가목적어

21 keep A from ~ing: ~가 …하는 것을 막다

22 1번 항목 2점 + 2번 항목 1점 + 3번 항목 1점 + 4번 항목 2점 + 5번 항목 2점 = 총 8점

23 7-10점이 'Danger!'인데, 글쓴이는 8점이므로 'dangerous'한 상황에 처해 있다고 할 수 있다.

24 차에서는 스마트폰을 '때때로' 사용한다.

25 ⓐ와 ②, ④, ⑤는 즉시, ① 잠시 동안, ③ 가끔

26 '내가 필요로 하는 정보를 쉽게 얻을 수 있다.'는 것을 가리킨다.

27 ②, ③은 언급되어 있지 않고, ⑤는 단점에 설명되어 있다.

01 to use
02 If you are a heavy user of your smartphone like Seongmin
03 bend
04 "거북목 증후군" 자세 때문에 당신의 목과 척추에 증가된 압력
05 lift → lower
06 Give a break to your eyes
07 (A) tired (B) minutes (C) 20–second
08 20분마다 20초의 휴식을 취하고 적어도 20피트 이상 떨어져 있는 사물을 바라보는 것
09 wrist → finger
10 (A) backs (B) in front of
11 are → is
12 ⓐ pressure ⓑ up ⓒ bending
13 ⓐ eyes ⓑ break ⓒ blink
14 ⓐ fingers ⓑ wrists ⓒ with

01 주어 자리에 동명사와 to부정사를 쓸 수 있다.

02 '만약 여러분이 성민이와 같은 스마트폰 과다 사용자라면'이라는 뜻이다.

03 스마트폰을 볼 때, 여러분은 보통 목을 '구부린다.'

04 앞 문장의 내용을 가리킨다.

05 목을 구부리는 대신에 시선을 '낮추는' 것이라고 하는 것이 적절하다. lift: 들어 올리다

06 give는 'to'를 사용하여 3형식으로 고친다.

07 (A) 눈이 '피곤해진' 것이므로 tired가 적절하다. tiring: 피곤하게 만드는, (B) '20분마다'라고 해야 하므로 minutes가 적절하다. every+기수+복수명사: ~마다, (C) 'a'와 명사 'break' 사이에서 형용사 역할을 하고 있는데, 이런 경우에는 단수로 써야 하므로 20-second가 적절하다.

08 바로 뒤에 나오는 설명을 쓰면 된다.

09 '손목'이 아니라 '손가락'을 당기고 있다.

10 팔을 여러분 '앞에서' 벌린 채로 '손등'을 마주 놓으세요.

11 주어가 The best tip이므로 'is'로 고치는 것이 적절하다.

12 당신의 목을 구부린 것으로 인한 '압력'을 예방할 수 있는 제일 좋은 방법은 휴대 전화를 여러분의 눈높이까지 '올리고' 목을 '구부리는' 대신에 시선을 낮추는 것이다.

13 여러분의 '눈'이 피곤해지고 건조하게 느끼도록 만드는 것을 피하기 위해 20-20-20 규칙을 따르면서 눈을 때때로 '쉬게' 하고 눈을 자주 '깜빡여라'.

14 '손가락'과 '손목'의 통증을 줄이기 위해서 각 손의 각 손가락을 당기고 팔을 여러분 앞에서 벌린 채로 손등을 마주 놓으세요.

| 01 ③ | 02 A) for (B) set | 03 ① |
| 04 ④ | 05 keep | 06 take | 07 ①, ③ |

| 08 ②, ④, ⑤ | 09 ② | 10 ① | 11 drop |

12 ④   13 ⑤   14 (1) to sell (2) to see

15 ①   16 make, have, let 중의 하나를 쓰면 정답

17 (1) to write letters with (2) to take pictures with

(3) to live in   18 ④   19 ③

20 ②   21 ⑤   22 ④

23 (1) build, to produce (2) turn down, to put

24 to talk about   25 ③

26 ⓑ와 같은 것: ②, ⑤ ⓒ와 같은 것: ①, ③, ④

27 Using a smartphone in the dark or in a moving car.

28 bending   29 ④   30 ③

31 I can get in touch with my friends right away.

32 ②   33 (A) off (B) day (C) heavy   34 tips

01 ① dropped, drop: 떨어지다 ② reduce, reduce: 줄이다, 감소시키다 ③ cut, cut down on: ~을 줄이다 ④ pay, pay attention to: ~에 주의를 기울이다 ⑤ give, give back: 돌려주다

02 be late for: ~에 늦다 set an alarm: 자명종 시계를 맞추다

03 ① hall: 복도

04 대화에서는 text가 '(휴대 전화로) 문자를 보내다'의 의미로 쓰였다. ①가사/그 노래의 가사는 노래 부르기가 좋을 것이다. ② 본문, 글/이 책들은 삽화가 적고 글이 훨씬 많이 적혀 있다. ③ 문자/보낼 메시지 문자를 입력하세요. ④ (휴대 전화로) 문자를 보내다/내가 최종 득점을 네게 문자로 보내 줄게. ⑤ 문자/그녀는 어젯밤에 나한테 문자를 엄청 보냈어.

05 keep a diary: 일기를 쓰다 keep in mind: 명심하다

06 take: 가져가다 take a walk: 산책하다

07 reduce: 줄이다, 감소시키다 cut: 줄이다, 삭감하다 decrease: 감소하다

08 충고할 때 쓸 수 있는 표현은 'You'd better+동사원형', '(I think) You should 동사원형 ~.', 'Maybe you should 동사원형 ~.', 'Why don't you ~?' 등이 있다.

09 휴대 전화를 보라는 대답에 '네 휴대 전화 화면에 금이 갔어.'가 들어가는 것이 적절하다.

10 ① protect: 보호하다 ② prevent: 예방하다, 막다 ③ increase: 증가하다 ④ avoid: 피하다 ⑤ produce: 만들다, 생산하다

11 갑자기 땅이나 어떤 것에 떨어지다 / drop: 떨어지다

12 ④ 휴대 전화를 떨어뜨려서 휴대 전화 화면에 금이 갔다.

13 물놀이 활동에 대한 조언을 요청했는데 구명조끼를 입어서는 안 된다는 말은 어색하다.

14 (1) dresses와 (2) sights를 뒤에서 수식하는 형용사적 용법의 to부정사로 쓴다.

15 <보기>와 ①번은 형용사적 용법 ② 부사적 용법의 형용사 수식 ③ 보어로 쓰인 명사적 용법 ④ 부사적 용법의 '목적' ⑤ 부사적 용법의 '결과'

16 목적격보어로 동사원형이 나왔으므로 사역동사가 적절하다. 내용상 동사원형이 올 수 있는 help는 적절하지 않다.

17 to부정사의 형용사적 용법을 이용한다. 수식받는 명사가 전치사의 목적어로 사용되었으므로 전치사를 생략하면 안 된다.

18 ④번은 사역동사가 아니지만 나머지는 모두 사역동사로 쓰였다. ③ have[get]+목적어+과거분사: 목적어가 ~되도록 하다

19 사역동사의 목적격보어로 수동의 의미가 필요하므로 과거분사가 적절하다.

20 get은 사역동사의 의미로 쓰일 수 있지만 목적격보어로 to부정사가 나와야 한다.

21 ⑤ Linda doesn't have any patients to take care of.

22 ① My sister often helps me (to) do my homework. ② They had many options to choose about the experiment. ③ I'll have your health checked. ⑤ He spends a lot of time using his smartphone. option: 선택권, 옵션

23 사역동사의 목적격보어로 동사원형을 쓰고, to부정사의 형용사적 용법을 이용한다. put somebody to bed: 누군가를 재우다

24 to부정사의 형용사적 용법을 이용한다.

25 ⓐ와 ③ (작업 중의) 휴식 (시간), ① (법, 약속 등을) 어기다, ② ~에게 (안 좋은) 소식을 알리다, ④ 깨(뜨리)다, 부수다, ⑤ (파도가) 부서지다

26 ⓑ와 ②, ⑤는 동명사, ⓒ와 ①, ③, ④는 현재분사

27 눈이 더 피곤하고 더 건조하게 느끼도록 만드는 것(즉, 눈 문제를 악화시키는 것)은 '어두운 곳이나 움직이는 차에서 스마트폰을 사용하는 것'이다.

28 전치사 뒤에 '동명사'로 써야 한다.

29 ④ 이러한 압력을 예방하는 가장 좋은 방법은 휴대 전화를 여러분의 눈높이까지 올리는 것이다.

30 주어진 문장의 That에 수복한다. ③번 앞 문장의 내용을 받고 있으므로 ③번이 적절하다.

31 get in touch with: ~와 연락[접촉]하다, right away: 바로

32 ② 스마트폰을 사용하는 데에는 좋은 점들과 나쁜 점들이 둘 다 있기 때문에, 스마트폰을 '똑똑하게' 사용할 필요가 있다. ① 항상, ④ 즉시, ⑤ 되풀이하여

33 (A) 하루 종일 스마트폰에서 '손을 뗄 수가 없다.'고 해야 하므로 off가 적절하다. take one's hands off ~: ~에서 손 떼다, (B) all day long: 하루 종일, 온종일, (C) 스마트폰의 '과다' 사용자인가?라고 해야 하므로 heavy가 적절하다. proper: 적절한

34 tip: 조언, 유용한 충고, 동사 are에 맞춰 복수로 쓰는 것이 적절하다

단원별 예상문제
p.98·101

01 (1) depend on (2) advice   02 ②

03 ④   04 (1) back, prevent him from playing

(2) should, watch out for (3) I was late for

17

(4) instead of 05 (C) → (B) → (A) → (D)

06 (B) → (D) → (C) → (A) 07 ④ 08 ②, ⑤

09 ① 10 I'm planning on doing it once a

month. 11 ① 12 ④ 13 ②

14 (1) My dad didn't let me go camping.

(2) Emily had her new dress made last week.

(3) There's nothing wrong to correct in this report.

(4) I bought my parents a house to live in.

15 every → all 16 ④ 17 ②, ⑤ 18 ④

19 ③ 20 ⓐ minutes ⓑ break ⓒ away

21 ①, ④ 22 ① 23 (A) a lot (B) less

(C) yourself 24 these exercises

---

01 보기의 단어는 동의어 관계이다. happen: 일어나다, 발생하다 occur: 발생하다 (1) rely on: ~에 의지[의존]하다 depend on: ~에 의존하다 (2) tip: 조언, 충고 advice: 조언, 충고

02 ① from, away from: ~에서 떨어져서 ② with, get in touch with: ~와 연락[접촉]하다 ③ for, be good for: ~에 좋다 ④ from, from time to time: 가끔, 이따금 ⑤ on, cut down on: ~을 줄이다

03 ④ break: 휴식

04 (1) back: 등 prevent 목적어 from Ving: 목적어가 ~하는 것을 막다 (2) watch out (for): (~에 대해서) 조심하다 (3) be late for: ~에 늦다 (4) instead of: ~ 대신에

05 (C) Jenny의 생일을 잊었다는 말에, (B) 상대방은 Jenny가 가장 친한 친구가 아니냐고 질문한다. (A) 맞다고 대답하고, 어떻게 해야 할지 충고를 부탁하는 말을 하자, (D) 정말 미안하다고 Jenny에게 말하라고 충고해 준다.

06 (B) 기분이 우울하다는 말에, (D) 이유를 물어보니 (C) 겨울에 5킬로그램이 쪘다고 말한다. 어떻게 해야 하는지 질문을 하자, (A) 간식을 줄이라는 충고를 해준다.

07 ④ give back it → give it back 'give back'은 이어동사인데, '동사+부사'의 이어동사인 경우 목적어가 대명사이면 그 목적어를 반드시 동사와 부사 사이에 써야 한다.

08 ② 과학 수업을 얼마나 오래 하는지 나와 있지 않다. ⑤ 왜 남자아이가 과학책을 가져오지 않았는지는 언급되어 있지 않다.

09 티셔츠에 쓰여 있는 글을 설명하고 있다. 그러므로 티셔츠에 쓰여 있는 글의 내용을 묻는 질문 다음에 들어가야 적절하다.

10 be planning on ~ing: ~할 계획이다 once a month: 한 달에 한 번

11 24시간 동안 휴대 전화를 사용하지 않는 것을 생각해 보겠다고 했다.

12 ④ It's good for your eyes. → It's not good for your eyes.

13 ① The best way to prevent this pressure is to bring the phone up to the level of your eyes. ③ Some were really beautiful, but others made me feel scared. ④ I have

---

something important to tell you. ⑤ I'll get him to do the work.

14 (1) 사역동사의 목적격보어로 동사원형이 적절하다. (2) 사역동사의 목적격보어로 수동의 의미가 필요하므로 과거분사가 적절하다. (3) to부정사가 -thing, -body, -one으로 끝나는 부정대명사를 형용사와 함께 수식할 때는 '대명사+형용사+to부정사'의 어순이다. (4) to부정사가 형용사 역할을 할 때 수식받는 명사가 전치사의 목적어로 사용되었으면 전치사를 생략하면 안 된다.

15 all day long: 하루 종일

16 ⓐ와 ④ ~처럼, ①, ③, ⑤ 좋아하다, ② ~와 같은(such as)

17 ⓐ와 ②, ⑤는 형용사적 용법, ① 부사적 용법(원인), ③ 부사적 용법(결과), ④ 명사적 용법

18 목을 구부리는 '대신에'라고 해야 하므로 instead of가 적절하다. ① ~에도 불구하고, ② ~에 따르면, ③ ~ 때문에, ⑤ ~와 함께

19 ③ 위 글은 '스마트폰을 사용할 때 "거북목" 자세를 방지해야 한다'는 내용의 글이다.

20 20-20-20 규칙은 20'분'마다 20초의 '휴식'을 취하고 적어도 20피트 이상 '떨어져 있는' 사물을 바라보는 것이다. ⓑ rest도 break와 같은 뜻이지만, 일관성을 주기 위해 본문의 시작과 중간에서 사용한 break로 답하는 것이 적절하다.

21 keep[stop/prevent] … from ~ing: …이 ~하지 못하게 막다[방해하다]

22 ① '머리'가 아니라 '눈'을 피곤해지고 건조하게 느끼도록 만든다.

23 (A) 문자 메시지를 '많이' 보내나요?라고 해야 하므로 a lot이 적절하다. a lot of 뒤에는 명사가 나와야 한다. (B) 가장 좋은 방법은 스마트폰을 '덜' 사용하는 것이라고 해야 하므로 less가 적절하다. (C) 주어와 목적어가 같을 때는 재귀대명사를 써야 하므로 yourself가 적절하다.

24 '이런 운동들'을 가리킨다.

서술형 실전문제 p.102~103

01 (1) You had better wash your hands first.

(2) Don't forget to wash your hands first.

(3) Remember to wash your hands first.

02 I think you should cut down on snacks.

03 ④What should I to do? → What should I do?

04 (1) Brian has a lot of homework to do today.

(2) Will you bring me a piece of paper to write names on?

(3) Is there anything valuable to keep separately?

(4) A delicious meal made his mouth water.

(5) They got him to sign a new contract.

05 (1) Julia made me do my homework.

(2) Her mom had Jenny prepare dinner.

(3) Sam helped me (to) repair my computer.

(D) keep

(E) intelligently

01 should+동사원형: ~해야 한다 exercise: 운동하다
vegetables: 야채 cut down on: ~을 줄이다

---

01 당부할 때, Make sure ~. (꼭 ~하도록 해.), You had better
~. (~하는 것이 좋겠다.), Don't forget to ~. (~하는 것을 잊
지 마.), Remember to ~.(~하는 것을 기억해라.)를 사용할 수
있다.

02 should+동사원형: ~해야 한다 cut down on: ~을 줄이다

03 should+동사원형: ~해야 한다

04 (1), (2), (3) 부정사의 형용사적 용법을 이용한다. 수식받는 명사
가 전치사의 목적어로 사용되었으면 전치사를 생략하면 안 된다는
것과 -thing으로 끝나는 부정대명사를 형용사와 함께 수식할 때는
'대명사+형용사+to부정사'의 어순임에 유의한다. (4) made가 사
역동사, water가 목적격 보어이다. (5) get은 사역동사의 의미로
쓰일 수 있지만 목적격보어로 to부정사가 나와야 한다.

05 사역동사의 목적격보어로 동사원형이 나오며 help는 목적격보어
로 동사원형이나 to부정사가 나온다.

06 당신이 스마트폰을 볼 때 목을 구부리면, 이 자세 때문에 당신의
'목'과 '척추'에 압력이 증가한다.

07 압력을 예방하는 가장 좋은 방법은 휴대 전화를 여러분의 눈높
이'까지' 올리는 것이다.

08 두 가지 방법은 다 목을 구부리지 않고 스마트폰을 볼 수 있는 방
법이다.

09 사역동사 make+목적어+원형부정사

10 (A) 문제를 '악화'시킬 수 있다고 해야 하므로 worse가 적절
하다. (B) 20분'마다'라고 해야 하므로 Every가 적절하다.
every+기수+복수명사: ~마다, (C) '적어도' 20피트 이상 떨어
져 있는 사물이라고 해야 하므로 at least가 적절하다. at least:
적어도, at last: 마침내

11 keep … from ~ing: …이 ~ 하는 것을 막다[방해하다]

01 I think you should exercise every day. / You
should eat more vegetables. / I think you should
cut down on the fat in your diet.

02 (1) Mom made me prepare dinner.

(2) Mom had me clean the room.

(3) Mom let me go to the movies.

(4) Mom let me play soccer.

03 (A) right away

(B) information

(C) dry and tired

---

01 turn off: ~을 끄다

02 pay attention to: ~에 주의를 기울이다

03 ride on: ~을 타다

04 away from: ~에서 떨어져서/나는 역에서 멀리 떨어진 곳에 산
다. right away: 당장/나는 당장 그에게 전화할 것이다.

05 sleep over at: (남의 집에서) 자다

06 make: 만들다 make sure: 반드시 ~하도록 하다, ~을 확실히
하다

07 make sure: 반드시 ~하도록 하다, ~을 확실히 하다 by+시간:
~까지는

08 누군가 또는 무엇인가를 해, 손상, 질병으로부터 안전하게 유지
하다/protect: 보호하다

09 get: 구하다, 사다

10 'Try it first.'는 '시험 삼아 먼저 해봐.'라는 의미로, 한 번 해보
고, 얼마나 자주 할지는 그 이후에 결정하라는 말이 어울리므로
④가 적절하다.

11 for+숫자+시간 단위: ~ 동안 during+기간 명사: ~ 동안
depend on: ~에 의존하다

12 how often: 얼마나 자주

13 make sure ~: 반드시 ~하도록 하다, ~을 확실히 하다 keep
up with: ~을 따르다, ~에 뒤지지 않다

14 to부정사가 형용사 역할을 할 때 수식받는 명사가 전치사의 목적어로 사용되었으면 전치사를 생략하면 안 된다.

15 사역동사의 목적격보어로 동사원형이 적절하다.

16 (1) 사역동사의 목적격보어로 동사원형이 적절하다. (2) 공장이 세워지는 수동의 의미이므로 목적격보어로 과거분사가 적절하다. (3) to부정사가 -body로 끝나는 부정대명사를 형용사와 함께 수식할 때는 '대명사+형용사+to부정사'의 어순이다. (4) to 부정사가 형용사 역할을 할 때 수식받는 명사가 전치사의 목적어로 사용되었으면 전치사를 생략하면 안 된다. (5) 컴퓨터가 훔치는 것이 아니라 도난당한 것으로 수동의 의미이므로 목적격보어로 과거분사가 적절하다.

17 ② There is a small pool to swim in. to부정사가 형용사 역할을 할 때 수식받는 명사가 전치사의 목적어로 사용되었으면 전치사를 생략하면 안 된다.

18 ⓐ 하루 종일 스마트폰에서 '손을 뗄 수가 없다.'고 해야 하므로 off가 적절하다. take one's hands off ~: ~에서 손 떼다, ⓑ of: (목적격 관계) ~을, ~의

19 '만약 여러분이 성민이와 같은 스마트폰 과다 사용자라면'이라는 뜻이다.

20 또 다른 방법은 '목'을 구부리는 대신에 '시선'을 낮추는 것이다.

21 ⓐ와 ①, ⑤는 명사적 용법, ② 형용사적 용법, ③ 부사적 용법(목적), ④ 부사적 용법(형용사 수식)

22 이 글은 '여러분의 눈에 휴식을 주라'는 내용의 글이므로, 제목으로는 '여러분의 눈을 쉬게 하는 게 어때?'가 적절하다.

23 ④번은 3형식 문장이고, ⓐ와 나머지는 다 5형식 문장이다.

24 with + 목적어 + 목적격보어: ~을 …한 채로

25 ③ '손바닥'이 아니라 '손등'을 마주 놓아야 한다.

Lesson
3

The School Club Activity Day

시험대비 실력평가　　p.112

01 ①	02 ①	03 ①	04 ①
05 (n)eighbor	06 leader	07 ⑤	08 ④
09 who, can join			

01 둘은 반의어 관계이다. increase: 증가하다 decrease: 감소하다 difficult: 어려운 easy: 쉬운

02 bake: (빵 등을) 굽다 oven: 오븐 / 나는 오븐에 빵을 굽고 있다.

03 grow: (동식물을) 기르다 vegetables: 채소 / 그들은 채소를 재배하는 데 있어 유기농 방식을 사용한다.

04 opportunity: 기회 chance: 가능성, 기회 / 그것은 부유한 사람들이 어떻게 사는지 보여주는 귀중한 기회였다.

05 neighbor: 이웃 / 당신의 옆이나 근처에 사는 어떤 사람

06 leader: 지도자, 대표 / 그녀는 유럽에서 가장 강력한 국가의 지도자이다.

07 hold: (모임·식 등을) 개최하다

08 ① 십대들에게 가장 인기 있는 여가 시간 활동이 무엇입니까? ② 나는 정말 너의 요리가 그립다. ③ 그녀는 밝은 색들을 좋아하지 않는다. ④ note: 음, 음표 / 그는 단 하나의 음표도 읽지 못하지만, 피아노를 완벽하게 연주한다. ⑤ 한국은 이미 몇 개의 메달을 획득했다.

09 join: 참여하다, 가입하다

서술형 시험대비　　p.113

01 (1) (g)et　(2) (p)resent
02 have / Have
03 How / how
04 (1) introduce　(2) dolphins　(3) doughnut　(4) concert
05 (1) activity　(2) neighborhood
06 (1) (c)lothes　(2) introduce　(3) interest　(4) vegetables
07 If I join this club, I will practice very hard.

01 주어진 보기는 동의어 관계이다. happy: 행복한 pleased: 기쁜 (1) gain: 얻다, 입수하다 get: 얻다, 획득하다, 사다 (2) gift: 선물 present: 선물

02 have: 가지다 / 가지면 가질수록 더 갖고 싶다. have a great

time: 좋은 시간을 보내다 / 새 학기가 시작하기 전에 즐거운 시간을 보내라!

03 how: 어떻게 / 어떻게 제가 이 동아리에 가입할 수 있나요? how to+동사원형: ~하는 방법 / 나는 그것을 하는 방법을 배우고 싶다.

04 (1) introduce: 소개하다 (2) dolphin: 돌고래 (3) doughnut: 도넛 (4) concert: 연주회

05 (1) activity: 활동 / 어떤 종류의 동아리 활동을 좋아하세요? (2) neighborhood: 동네, (도시 내의 한 단위) 지역 / 이 근처 지역은 쇼핑하기에 아주 좋다.

06 (1) clothes: 옷, 의상 (2) introduce: 소개하다 (3) interest: 관심 (4) vegetables: 채소

07 join: 참여하다, 가입하다 club: 동아리 practice: 연습하다

Conversation 교과서

핵심 Check p.114~115

1 how to use
2 I want to learn how to take good pictures.
3 What do you, doing, free time / I enjoy listening to music
4 I enjoy riding a bike

교과서 대화문 익히기

Check(√) True or False p.116

[1] T [2] T [3] T [4] F [5] T [6] F

교과서 확인학습 p.118~119

Listen & Speak 1 A
know how to

Listen & Speak 1 B
1 heard you went to, How / I hope I can play / knew how to play the violin / good at
2 at, grew, myself, own / how to cook / taught

Listen & Speak 2 A
looking at, at night

Listen & Speak 2 B
1 Do you enjoy / love reading, about / reading / go,

the library
2 What did you do / made / Do you enjoy cooking / cook, cooking
3 Where, get / made it for me / designer / enjoys making clothes

Real-Life Zone A
the leader, interest / When did you start playing / how to play the violin when / experience playing / an orchestra when, elementary / volunteer to teach / Do you enjoy teaching / experience, enjoy working with / have

Wrap Up
look, delicious / made them myself, baking, going to / want to learn how to make / at / time / Sounds, See

시험대비 기본평가 p.120
01 ④   02 ①   03 ④   04 ①

01 여가 시간에 무엇을 즐기는지 묻고 대답하고 있다. 'I enjoy 동명사 ~.'를 사용해서 자신이 좋아하는 것을 표현할 수 있다.

02 종이 고양이를 만들 수 있는지 여부를 묻고 대답하고 있다. how to+동사원형: ~하는 방법, 어떻게 ~하는지

03 'Do you know how to+동사원형~?'을 이용해 상대방의 능력이나 무언가를 하는 방법에 대해 물을 수 있다.

04 할머니에게서 배웠다는 내용이 나왔으므로, 여자아이는 요리를 하는 방법을 알고 있다.

시험대비 실력평가 p.121~122
01 ①   02 ③   03 ②   04 ①
05 ⑤   06 (A) looking   (B) doing[to do]
07 ①   08 ⑤   09 ②   10 ③
11 (A) in a group (B) no experience
12 I started learning how to play the violin when I was ten.   13 ②

01 'How was it?'은 과거의 경험에 대한 느낌을 묻는 표현으로, 여기서는 유나의 바이올린 콘서트에 대한 느낌을 묻고 있고, 이에 대한 대답 'It was great.'으로 이어진다.

02 대화에서 (A)와 ③은 '~처럼'의 의미로 사용되었다. 이외의 보기는 '좋아하다'의 의미이다.

03 ② 남자아이는 자신이 바이올린을 잘 연주하지 못한다고 생각한다.

04 Do you know how to ~?: 어떻게 ~하는지 하니? how to+

동사원형: ~하는 방법, 어떻게 ~하는지. 스페인어를 하는 방법을 모른다는 말에, 상대방이 'Yes'라고 하고, 가르쳐 줄 수 있다고 말하므로, 상대방에게 스페인어를 말하는 법을 아느냐고 질문하는 것이 적절하다.

05 ⑤ Of course I am. → Of course I do.

06 enjoy는 동명사를 목적어로 취할 수 있고, love는 동명사와 to부정사를 둘 다 목적어로 취할 수 있다.

07 get: ~을 사다, ~을 얻다. 주어진 말의 it이 a pretty backpack을 가리키므로 ①이 적절하다.

08 문장의 끝에 오는 too는 '또한'의 의미로, 내용상 그녀는 훌륭한 디자이너이고, 또한 옷 만드는 것을 즐긴다는 말이 나와야 하므로, 'Yes, she is (a really good designer).'의 의미를 가진 ⑤가 적절하다.

09 ② 지윤이 가방을 만드는 방법을 안다는 내용은 언급되지 않았다.

10 주어진 문장의 We는 나눔 오케스트라를 의미하며, 자원봉사로 아이들을 가르친다는 내용이 나온 후, 다른 사람들을 가르치는 것을 즐기는지 묻는 것이 어울린다.

11 (A)가 있는 질문의 대답이 오케스트라의 멤버였다고 말하고 있으므로, 그룹으로 연주한 경험이 있느냐고 질문해야 한다. (B)가 있는 문장 다음에 But이라는 접속사가 있으므로 뒤의 내용과 반대 또는 대조되는 내용이 나와야 어울린다.

12 start+동명사 또는 to부정사: ~하는 것을 시작하다 how to+동사원형: ~하는 방법, 어떻게 ~하는지

13 케이트는 지금이 아니라 초등학교 때 오케스트라의 구성원이었다.

서술형 시험대비 p.123

01 (C) → (A) → (B)

02 (A) → (C) → (B)

03 at

04 me → myself

05 Do you know how to cook the vegetables (that) you grow

06 enjoyed do → enjoy doing

07 I didn't know you knew how to play the violin.

08 I'm not good at it yet

01 요리하기를 즐기는지 묻는 질문에 (C) 가끔 요리하기를 즐기고, 피자 만드는 법을 알고 있다고 대답한다. (A) 이에 상대방이 요리 동아리에 가입하는 것을 권유하자 (B) 생각해 보겠다고 대답한다.

02 드론을 샀는지 질문하자 (A) 사지는 않았고, 선물로 받았다고 대답하면서 드론을 사용하는 방법을 모른다고 얘기하며 상대방이 방법을 아는지 질문하자 (C) 모르지만 지나가 알 것이라고 대답한다. (B) 그러면, 지나에게 물어보겠다고 말한다.

03 look at: ~을 보다

04 grow의 목적어로 these vegetables가 왔으므로 목적어의 자리

에 들어갈 수 있는 me는 어울리지 않는다. 여기서는 내가 했다는 것을 강조하는 재귀대명사가 어울린다.

05 how to+동사원형: ~하는 방법, 어떻게 ~하는지 cook: 요리하다 grow: 기르다

06 'Do you ~?'로 질문하고 있으므로 현재형의 동사를 사용해야 한다. 또한, enjoy는 동명사를 목적어로 취한다.

07 know 다음에 접속사 that이 생략되었다. play the 악기 이름: ~을 연주하다

08 be good at: ~을 잘하다

교과서
Grammar

핵심 Check p.124~125

1 (1) what to / what I should
  (2) where to meet / where I should meet
2 (1) who[that]   (2) which[that]

시험대비 기본평가 p.126

01 (1) eating → to eat   (2) go → to go
  (3) which → who[that]   (4) who → which[that]

02 ③, ④

03 (1) She didn't ask me what to do.
  (2) Mariel didn't know where to go.
  (3) Degas liked to paint dancers who were dancing.
  (4) He has the dog that barked at the girl yesterday.

01 (1), (2) '의문사+to부정사'가 문장 속에서 decide와 know의 목적어 역할을 하고 있다. (3) a man이 선행사이므로 which가 아니라 who나 that이 적절하다. (4) the movie가 선행사이므로 who가 아니라 which나 that이 적절하다.

02 ③ some pictures가 선행사이므로 who가 아니라 which나 that이 적절하다. ④ 'how to do'가 show의 목적어로 쓰여야 한다.

03 주격 관계대명사는 선행사가 사람이면 who나 that을 쓰고 사물이나 동물이면 which나 that을 쓴다.

시험대비 실력평가 p.127~129

01 ①   02 ②   03 ③   04 who →
which 또는 that   05 ⑤   06 ④
07 ⑤   08 (1) which   (2) that   (3) that   (4) were

(5) who (6) who (7) which was

09 I can't decide what to wear. / I can't decide what I should wear.

10 (1) ③, who[that] (2) ③, which[that]

11 (1) how (2) to spend (3) what (4) I should
(5) how to read　　　12 ②　　　13 ①, ⑤

14 ①　　　15 (1) how they should[can] do
(2) where I should put (3) what I should do

16 ⑤　　　17 ③　　　18 ④

19 (1) where to buy (2) which[that] have

---

01 do it이 나와 있으므로 목적어로 쓰일 수 있는 것은 적절하지 않으며 'why+to부정사'는 쓰지 않는다.

02 사람을 선행사로 하는 주격 관계대명사로는 that이나 who를 쓴다.

03 첫 문장에서는 the problem이 solve의 목적어이므로 what이나 that은 적절하지 않다. 두 번째 문장에서는 the message from Kate가 선행사이므로 which나 that이 적절하다.

04 a party가 선행사이므로 who가 아니라 which나 that이 적절하다.

05 목적어 it이 있으므로 what이 아니라 how나 where 등이 나와야 한다.

06 주격 관계대명사는 선행사가 사람이면 who나 that을 쓰고 사물이나 동물이면 which나 that을 쓴다.

07 ① They went to the restaurant which[that] was famous for its traditional Korean food. ② I know a girl whose name is Karen. ③ Please let me know which way I should go. which가 way를 수식하도록 해야 한다. ④ Tom has a painting which was drawn by a famous artist.

08 (1) 선행사가 사물이므로 which가 적절하다. (2) 선행사가 '사람+동물[사물]'인 경우에는 반드시 관계대명사 that을 써야 한다. (3) 선행사가 사물이므로 that이 적절하다. (4) 주격 관계대명사의 선행사가 복수이므로 복수 동사가 적절하다. (5) a great novelist가 선행사로 사람이므로 who가 적절하다. (6) who를 목적격 whom 대신 쓸 수 있지만 whom을 who 대신 쓰지는 않는다. (7) 주격 관계대명사는 생략할 수 없으나 뒤에 분사나 부사구가 오는 경우 '주격 관계대명사+be동사'를 생략할 수 있으므로 which was를 쓰거나 which was를 생략한 형태로 써야 한다.

09 의문사+to부정사 = 의문사+주어+should+동사원형, what to wear: 무엇을 입을지

10 주격 관계대명사는 다음에 동사가 나오며 선행사가 사람이면 who나 that을, 사물이나 동물이면 which나 that을 쓴다.

11 (1) the machine이 목적어로 나와 있으므로 how가 적절하다. (2) '의문사+to부정사'가 적절하다. (3) why는 '의문사+to부정사'로 쓰이지 않는다. (4), (5) '의문사+to부정사'나 '의문사+

주어+should+동사원형'이 적절하다.

12 주어진 문장과 ②번은 주격 관계대명사로 그 쓰임이 같다. ④번은 목적격 관계대명사이다.

13 go는 자동사로 목적어가 필요 없으므로 what은 적절하지 않고 'why+to부정사'는 쓰지 않는다.

14 주어진 문장과 ①번의 that은 주격 관계대명사이다. ② 접속사 ③ 지시대명사 ④ 지시형용사 ⑤ 지시부사

15 '의문사+to부정사'는 '의문사+주어+should/can+동사원형'으로 바꾸어 쓸 수 있다.

16 선행사가 사람이나 사물 또는 동물일 경우 모두 쓰일 수 있는 것은 that이다.

17 how to use: 어떻게 ~할지

18 an animal이 선행사이므로 which나 that을 써야 한다. ⑤번에서는 주격 관계대명사 that을 썼으므로 관계사절에서 주어로 쓰인 it을 삭제해야 한다.

19 (1) where to buy: 어디에서 살지 (2) 선행사가 사물이므로 which나 that을 쓴다.

🦉 서술형 시험대비　　　p.130~131

01 which → who[that], taught → (to) teach, using → to use

02 (1) who → which[that]
(2) is running → (which[that] is) running
(3) whom → who
(4) is → are
(5) who she teaches → who teaches

03 (1) how you should swim
(2) Which movie we should watch
(3) whom I should thank

04 (1) Here are two club leaders who[that] want students to join their clubs.
(2) This is the tea which[that] is good for your health.
(3) The movie which[that] was directed by James Cameron was interesting.
(4) There are a boy and his dog that are running at the playground.
(5) Do you know the girl (who is) dancing on the stage?

05 (1) You need to know how to play an instrument to join our club.
(2) The old man didn't know how to use the smartphone.
(3) When I should visit London has to be decided.
(4) I don't know why I should go there.

06 (1) who is

23

(2) which were

07 (1) We must learn how to speak English.

(2) I don't know what to say to her.

(3) Tell me where to park the car. 등 어법에 맞게
쓰면 정답

08 who[that] is reading a book

09 how to play

10 (1) Can you tell me how I can write an email in
English?

(2) I do not know what to do first.

(3) Do you know that man who[that] is running
along the river?

---

01 선행사가 people이므로 who나 that이 되어야 하며 helped
의 목적격보어로 to부정사나 동사원형이 나와야 하고, '의문사
(how)+to부정사'가 문장 속에서 teach의 직접목적어 역할을
하도록 하는 것이 적절하다.

02 (1) 선행사가 사물이므로 which나 that이 적절하다. (2) 주격
관계대명사는 생략할 수 없으나 뒤에 분사나 부사구가 오는 경
우 '주격 관계대명사+be동사'를 생략할 수 있다. (3) 주격 관계
대명사가 나와야 하므로 who나 that이 적절하다 who를 목적
격 whom 대신 쓸 수 있지만 whom을 who 대신 쓰지는 않는
다. (4) 주격 관계대명사절의 동사는 선행사의 수에 일치시킨다.
(5) 관계대명사가 접속사와 대명사의 역할을 하므로 주어로 쓰인
she를 삭제해야 한다.

03 '의문사+to부정사'는 '의문사+주어+should/can+동사원형'으로
바꾸어 쓸 수 있다. 또한 의문사가 의문형용사로 쓰여 to부정사와
의 사이에 명사가 올 수 있다.

04 선행사가 사람이면 who나 that을, 사물이나 동물이면 which
나 that을, '사람+동물[사물]'이면 반드시 that을 쓴다. 주격 관
계대명사는 생략할 수 없으나 뒤에 분사나 부사구가 오는 경우
'주격 관계대명사+be동사'를 생략할 수 있다.

05 (1) '의문사+to부정사'가 적절하다. (2) the smartphone이
목적어로 나와 있으므로 how가 적절하다. (3) '의문사+주어
+should+동사원형'이 적절하다. (4) 'why+to부정사'는 쓰지
않는다.

06 주격 관계대명사는 생략할 수 없으나 뒤에 분사나 부사구가 오는
경우 '주격 관계대명사+be동사'를 생략할 수 있다.

07 '의문사+to부정사'는 문장 속에서 주어, 목적어, 보어 역할을 하
는 명사구로 사용되어 '~해야 할지, ~하는 것이 좋을지'라는 뜻
을 나타낸다.

08 the girl이 선행사이므로 who나 that을 이용한다.

09 피아노를 잘 친다는 대답으로 보아 'how to play the piano(피
아노 치는 법)'가 적절하다.

10 (1) how+to부정사: 어떻게 ~할지 (2) what + to부정사: 무
엇을 ~할지 (3) 주격 관계대명사는 선행사가 사람이면 who나
that을 쓴다.

Reading

확인문제   p.132

1 T   2 F   3 F   4 T   5 F   6 T

확인문제   p.133

1 T   2 F   3 T   4 T   5 T   6 F

교과서 확인학습 A   p.134~135

01 Why Don't You   02 Participating
in, to enjoy   03 How about   04 who want, to
join   05 what   06 Art Club

07 from   08 As, guess from

09 do volunteer work   10 participated in

11 On the dirty old walls, flying, jumping

12 As a result, into   13 to see,
thanked   14 don't have to   15 Anyone who

16 Come and be 17 Orchestra   18 the leader

19 playing music, came to school 20 those

21 play music for 22 how to play, a little bit

23 don't worry   24 practice hard, get better

25 also teach, as a service to

26 an eleven-year-old boy

27 At first, read a note

28 a simple song

29 Hearing him play, makes

30 By joining, have an opportunity

31 Come and join

32 for

교과서 확인학습 B   p.136~137

1 Why Don't You Join Our Club?

2 Participating in club activities is a great way to
enjoy your school life.

3 How about joining a club?

4 Here are two club leaders who want students to
join their clubs.

5 Let's listen to what they say.

6 The Picasso Art Club

7 Hi! I am Sora Kang from the Picasso Art Club.

8 As you can guess from the name of our club, we
paint.

9 We also do volunteer work from time to time.

10 Last summer, our club members participated in the "Change Our Neighborhood" project.

11 On the dirty old walls of the buildings in our neighborhood, we painted birds flying high in the sky and dolphins jumping over blue waves.

12 As a result, the old neighborhood changed into a bright and beautiful place.

13 The neighbors were happy to see our work and thanked us.

14 You don't have to be a good painter.

15 Anyone who likes to paint can join.

16 Come and be a member of the Picasso Art Club.

17 The Boram Orchestra

18 Hi! I am Minsu Jang, the leader of the Boram Orchestra.

19 Did you see several students playing music at the main gate when you came to school today?

20 We were those students.

21 We play music for our friends every morning.

22 You need to know how to play an instrument a little bit to join our club.

23 But don't worry if you don't play well.

24 We will practice hard and get better together.

25 We also teach children how to play musical instruments as a service to our community.

26 I am teaching an eleven-year-old boy to play the violin.

27 At first, he did not know how to read a note.

28 Now he can play a simple song.

29 Hearing him play the violin makes me very happy.

30 By joining our club, you can have an opportunity to help others.

31 Come and join our club.

32 We are waiting for you.

시험대비 실력평가
p.138~141

01 (A) is (B) want (C) to join　02 ①, ③　03 two club leaders　04 ③　05 ④

06 ⑤　07 to play → playing 또는 play

08 ③　09 준호　10 ②

11 잘하는 것: 공을 패스하는 것과 빨리 달리기
못하는 것: 공을 헤딩하는 것

12 will join → join　13 ②, ④

14 participating in　15 who 또는 that

16 ①　17 ④　18 ③

19 how to play 또는 to play　20 ②

21 (1) 매일 아침 친구들을 위해 음악을 연주한다. (2) 지역 사회를 위해 아이들에게 악기를 연주하는 법을 가르친다.

22 ① joining → to join　23 ④　24 ⓐ 득점, ⓑ 목표　25 ③　26 They will introduce and sell books to people.　27 ③

01 (A) 동명사 'Participating'이 주어이므로 is가 적절하다. (B) 선행사가 'two club leaders'이므로 want가 적절하다. (C) want+목적어+to부정사이므로 to join이 적절하다.

02 How about ~ing? = What about ~ing? = Why don't you 동사원형?: ~하는 게 어때?

03 '두 명의 동아리 대표'를 가리킨다.

04 주어진 문장의 As a result에 주목한다. ③번 앞 문장의 결과를 가리키므로 ③번이 적절하다.

05 ⓐ와 ④번은 ~하다시피[~이듯이], ① 이유, ② (비례) ~함에 따라, ③ (자격 기능 등이) ~로(서), ⑤ (때) ~하고 있을 때, ~하면서

06 ⑤그림 그리는 것을 좋아하는 사람은 누구라도 피카소 미술 동아리의 회원이 될 수 있다.

07 지각동사 see의 목적격보어 자리에 to부정사를 쓸 수 없다.

08 동아리에 가입하려면 악기를 연주하는 '법'을 조금 알아야 한다고 하는 것이 적절하다.

09 보람 오케스트라 동아리에 가입하려면 악기를 연주하는 법을 조금 알아야 한다고 했기 때문에, '능숙한 피아니스트는 아니지만 열심히 피아노를 연습하는 준호'가 가입할 수 있다.

10 앞에 나오는 내용과 상반되는 내용이 뒤에 이어지므로 However가 가장 적절하다. ① 게다가, 더욱이, ③ 그러므로, ④ 비슷하게, ⑤ 예를 들어

11 '공을 패스하는 것'을 잘하고 '빨리 달린다.' 그러나, 나는 '공을 헤딩하는 법'을 모른다고 했다.

12 조건의 부사절에서는 현재시제가 미래시제를 대신한다.

13 ⓐ와 ①, ③, ⑤는 형용사적 용법, ② 부사적 용법, ④ 명사적 용법

14 participating만 쓰면 틀림. join = participate in: ~에 참석하다

15 선행사가 사람(two club leaders)이고 주어 자리이므로 주격 관계대명사 who 또는 that이 적절하다.

16 ⓐ from: (판단의 근거) ~로 (보아), ⓒ into: 상태의 변화를 나타냄

17 ④ 이웃 마을에 있는 건물들의 더럽고 오래된 벽에 그림을 그린 '결과', 오래된 마을이 밝고 아름다운 곳으로 바뀌었다고 하는 것이 적절하다. ② 게다가, ⑤ 즉, 다시 말해

18 ⓓ와 ②, ④, ⑤번은 부사적 용법, ① 명사적 용법, ③ 형용사적 용법

19 'teach+목적어+to부정사' 또는 'teach+목적어+의문사+to부정사'

20 ⓑ와 ②번은 음, 음표, strike a note on a piano: 피아노로 어

25

떤 음을 치다, ① (기억을 돕기 위한) 메모, 기록 ③ (격식을 차리지 않은 짧은) 편지, 쪽지, ④ 공책, ⑤ 주의하다, 유념하다, 주목하다

21 (1) 매일 아침 친구들을 위해 음악을 연주한다고 했다. (2) 민수가 열한 살 소년에게 바이올린을 가르치고 있는 것처럼, 지역 사회를 위해 아이들에게 악기를 연주하는 법을 가르친다

22 would like to부정사: ~하고 싶다

23 ④ 박 순호는 공을 헤딩하는 법을 모른다.

24 ⓐ make a goal: 득점하다, ⓑ goal(=aim, end, purpose): 목표

25 hold: 개최하다

26 사람들에게 책을 소개하고 팔 것이다.

27 ③ 전시회의 규모는 알 수 없다. ① 도서 전시회, ② 나눔중학교, ④ 5월 5일 ⑤ 책을 사랑하는 사람

서술형 시험대비 p.142~143

01 (A) volunteer work (B) painting (C) painting
02 ⓐ flying ⓑ jumping
03 need not 또는 don't need to
04 (A) a little (B) eleven–year–old (C) happy
05 unless
06 We also teach children how to play musical instruments as a service to our community.
07 It changed into a bright and beautiful place.
08 must not → don't have to 또는 need not
09 Anyone who likes to paint can join.
10 **악기를 연주하는 법을 조금 알아야 한다.**
11 (A) worry (B) get better
12 make → makes

01 피카소 미술 동아리는 미술 동아리이고 가끔 '자원봉사'도 한다. '그림 그리는 것'을 좋아하는 사람은 누구나 동아리에 가입할 수 있고 '그림을 잘 그릴' 필요는 없다.

02 각각 뒤에서 앞의 명사를 수식하는 현재분사로 고치는 것이 적절하다.

03 don't have to = need not = don't need to: ~할 필요가 없다

04 (A) a little: '양'이나 '정도'가 조금, a few: '수'가 조금, a bit: '정도'가 조금, (B) eleven-year-old가 boy를 수식하는 형용사 역할을 하기 때문에 year에 s를 붙이지 않는 것이 적절하다. (C) 목적격보어이므로 부사를 쓸 수 없고 형용사를 써야 한다.

05 if ~ not = unless

06 'as'를 보충하면 된다.

07 밝고 아름다운 곳으로 변했다.

08 여러분은 그림을 잘 그릴 '필요는 없다'고 해야 하므로 don't have to나 need not으로 고치는 것이 적절하다. must not은 '금지'를 나타낸다.

09 anyone who: ~인 사람은 누구나

10 우리 동아리에 가입하기 위해서는 '악기 연주하는 법을 조금 알

아야 합니다.'라고 했다.

11 민수는 학생들에게 연주를 잘 못해도 그들이 열심히 연습하고 함께 '좋아질 것'이기 때문에 '걱정하지' 말라고 말한다.

12 동명사 Hearing이 주어이므로 단수 취급하여 makes로 고치는 것이 적절하다.

영역별 핵심문제 p.145~149

01 ②   02 ③   03 ④
04 for   05 (1) (A)ctually (2) Where, to cook
(3) (o)pportunity   06 ②   07 ①
08 ⑤   09 ⓐ cooking ⓑ cook ⓒ cooking
10 ⑤   11 ①   12 ③   13 looking
14 looking at the stars   15 ①, ⑤
16 where to put   17 ②   18 (1) I can
get (2) to take (3) to look (4) which, to wear
19 (1) who (2) which   20 ⑤
21 (1) We are looking for volunteers.
   (2) They are good at English.
   (3) The friend lives in New Zealand.
   (4) Chuck gave the present to her on her birthday.
22 ④
23 (1) She wants to see a movie which is interesting.
   (2) Rose who works for a bank is Jake's best friend.
   (3) James bought a new computer which is really nice.
24 several students playing music at the main gate
   when you came to school today   25 ①, ④
26 ①   27 ②, ⑤   28 (A) Last summer
(B) high (C) thanked   29 ③
30 sick children   31 magic   32 ②
33 ⑤

01 ②번은 반의어 관계이고 나머지는 동의어 관계이다. ① gift: 선물 present: 선물 ② dark: 어두운 bright: 밝은 ③ activity: 활동 action: 행동, 활동, 실행 ④ actually:실제로, 사실은 really: 정말로, 실제로 ⑤ enter: ~에 들어가다 join: 참여하다, 가입하다

02 be good at: ~을 잘하다 look for: ~을 찾다 participate in: ~에 참여하다

03 그 사람들 결혼 선물로 뭘 사줘야 할까요? get: ~을 사다, ~을 획득하다

04 ask for help: 도움을 청하다 thank for: ~에 대해 감사하다

05 (1) actually: 실제로, 사실은 (2) cook: 요리하다 (3) opportunity: 기회

06 enjoy는 동명사를 목적어로 사용할 수 있고, love는 동명사와 to부정사 둘 다 목적어로 사용할 수 있다. ⓐ to read → reading ⓔ to go → go 제안하는 말을 할 때 'Let's 동사원형 ~.'을 사용한다.

07 ① 소년의 취미가 무엇인지는 언급되지 않았다. ② 유미는 무슨

종류의 책을 읽기를 좋아하니? ③ 방과 후에 그들은 어디에 갈 계획입니까? ④ 유미는 읽는 것을 좋아하니? ⑤ 남자아이는 읽는 것을 좋아하니?

08 질문에 대한 대답에 made를 사용하였으므로, 과거의 일을 물어보는 질문이 어울린다. breakfast: 아침식사

09 ⓐ enjoy는 동명사를 목적어로 취한다. ⓑ cook: 요리사,; 요리하다 ⓒ cooking: 요리, 음식

10 but은 '그러나', '하지만'이라는 뜻으로 반대 또는 대조되는 말이 나와야 한다. 사람들과 일하는 것을 즐기며, 해보고 싶다는 말이므로, ⑤번이 어울린다.

11 interest: 관심

12 ⓒ that → when 여기서 when은 접속사로 '~할 때'의 의미이다.

13 enjoy는 동명사를 목적어로 취한다.

15 사람을 선행사로 하는 주격 관계대명사는 that이나 who를 쓴다.

16 where to put: 어디에 두어야 할지

17 ②번은 명사절을 이끄는 접속사이고 나머지는 모두 주격 관계대명사이다.

18 (1)~(3) 의문사+to부정사 = 의문사+주어+should/can+동사원형 (4) 의문대명사 which가 의문형용사로 쓰여 to부정사와의 사이에 명사가 올 수 있다.

19 선행사가 사람이면 who, 사물이면 which를 쓴다.

20 ⑤ the story가 목적어로 나와 있으므로 what을 how나 when, where 등으로 고치거나 the story를 삭제해야 한다.

21 관계대명사는 두 문장의 공통되는 명사나 대명사와 접속사의 역할을 하는 것이므로 관계사절에 공통되는 (대)명사를 원래대로 써준다.

22 ④번은 부정사의 형용사적 용법이고 나머지는 모두 명사적 용법으로 '의문사+to 부정사'로 쓰였다.

23 주격 관계대명사는 선행사가 사람이면 who나 that을 쓰고 사물이나 동물이면 which나 that을 쓴다.

24 '여러분들이 오늘 학교에 왔을 때 정문에서 음악을 연주하고 있던 몇 명의 학생들'을 가리킨다.

25 ⓑ와 ②, ③, ⑤번은 동명사, ①, ④번은 현재분사

26 '매일 아침' 연주한다.

27 ⓐ와 ①, ③, ④: 가끔, ② 항상 ⑤: 거의 ~ 않다

28 (A) '여름에'는 in summer라고 하지만, '지난여름에'는 전치사 in 없이 last summer라고 한다. (B) 하늘 '높이' 나는 새들이라고 해야 하므로 high가 적절하다. high: 높은; 높이, highly: 매우, 대단히, (C) were와 병렬구문을 이루도록 thanked라고 하는 것이 적절하다.

29 ③ Picasso Art Club은 그림 동아리이므로 '그림 그리는 것'을 좋아하는 사람은 누구나 가입할 수 있다고 하는 것이 적절하다.

30 '아픈 어린이들'을 가리킨다

31 Abracadabra 동아리는 '마술' 동아리이다. 5월 5일에 회원들이 한국 병원을 방문하여 아픈 어린이들에게 '마술'을 보여주고 '마술'하는 법을 가르쳐줄 것이다.

32 ⓐ와 ②번은 축제 마당, 풍물 장터, book fair: 도시 진시회, ① 공정한, ③ 금발의, ④ (수, 크기, 양이) 상당한, 제법 큰[많은], ⑤ (날씨가) 맑은 breezy: 산들바람이 부는

33 ⓑ look for: ~을 찾다, ⓒ sell은 'to'를 사용하여 3형식으로 고친다.

01 (p)ractice   02 ④   03 ④   04 What time   05 join   06 ③   07 to play

08 (1) As a result   (2) At first, interested   (3) change into   (4) let us know how to

09 (B) → (C) → (A)   10 (B) → (A) → (C)

11 What do you enjoy doing when you have free time?

12 (1) Jisu asked her mother where to put the bag.

(2) Do you know what we should do next?

(3) I couldn't decide what to cook.

(4) There are a few girls who[that] are playing basketball on the playground.

(5) Janet loves books which[that] have many funny pictures.

(6) Linda and her dog that were crossing the street were injured.   13 ③

14 (1) get → to get

(2) what → how

(3) What he to eat → What to eat 또는 What he should eat

(4) which → who[that]

(5) is standing → (who[that] is) standing

(6) whom → who[that]

(7) is → are

(8) who he liked → who liked

15 ②, ⑤   16 to join   17 volunteer

18 we painted birds flying high in the sky and dolphins jumping over blue waves   19 ①   20 ②

21 ④   22 ②

01 주어진 단어는 동의어 관계이다. chief: 장, 우두머리 leader: 지도자, 대표 training: 훈련 practice: 연습

02 ① leader: 지도자, 대표 / 그는 음악 클럽의 지도자이다. ② interest: 관심 / 오페라에 관심 있어요? ③ garden: 정원 / 그 집은 나무와 꽃이 있는 정원이 있다. ④ a little bit: 아주 조금 / 너는 조금 더 늦게 와도 된다.⑤ drone: 무인 비행기 / 무인비행기(드론)는 작은 원격 조정의 헬리콥터이다.

03 ⓐ, ⓑ, ⓒ는 cookies를 가리키며, ⓓ는 doughnuts를 가리킨다.

04 'At 2:00(2시에)'라는 시간 정보가 나왔으므로, What time(몇 시에)이 어울린다.

05 join: 참여하다, 가입하다 / 1. 조직, 사회, 그룹의 구성원이 되다 2. 다른 사람이 관련된 활동에 참여하기 시작하다. 위의 대화에서는 2번의 의미로 사용되었다.

06 ①, ④ 여자아이는 어제 쿠키를 만들었다. ② 그들은 이번 주 토요일에 여자아이 집에서 만날 것이다. ③ 남자아이가 무슨 음식을 만들 수 있는지는 언급되지 않았다. ⑤ 여자아이는 이번 주 토요일에 도넛을 만들 것이다.

07 would like to+동사원형: ~하고 싶다 how to+동사원형: ~하는 방법, 어떻게 ~하는지 play the 악기 이름: ~을 연주하다

27

08 (1) as a result: 결과적으로 (2) at first: 처음에 interested: 관심[흥미]이 있는 (3) change into: ~로 변화하다[바뀌다] (4) let+목적어+동사원형: …가 ~하게 하다

09 주말에 무엇을 했는지 질문하자, (B) 가족을 위해 아침식사를 만들었다고 대답한다. (C) 이어서 요리를 즐기는지 질문하자 (A) 요리를 즐기며, 자신은 좋은 요리사이고 가족들이 자신의 요리를 좋아한다고 대답한다.

10 예쁜 가방을 보고, 어디서 샀는지 질문하자 (B) 여동생이 만들어 주었다고 대답한다. (A) 여동생이 좋은 디자이너라고 칭찬하자, (C) 동의하며, 옷을 만드는 것도 즐긴다고 말한다.

11 enjoy+동명사: ~하는 것을 즐기다 free time: 여가 시간 when:(접) ~할 때

12 (1)~(3) '의문사+to부정사'는 문장 속에서 주어, 목적어, 보어 역할을 하는 명사구로 사용된다. (4)~(6) 주격 관계대명사는 선행사가 사람이면 who나 that을 쓰고 사물이나 동물이면 which나 that을 쓴다. 선행사가 '사람+동물[사물]'인 경우에는 반드시 관계대명사 that을 써야 한다.

13 ③ '의문사+to부정사'가 주어 역할을 하고 있다.

14 (1) '의문사+to부정사'가 적절하다. (2) weight가 목적어로 나와 있으므로 how가 적절하다. (3) '의문사+to부정사'나 '의문사+주어+should+동사원형'이 적절하다. (4) 선행사가 사람이므로 who나 that이 적절하다. (5) 주격 관계대명사는 생략할 수 없으나 뒤에 분사나 부사구가 오는 경우 '주격 관계대명사+be동사'를 생략할 수 있다. (6) 주격 관계대명사가 나와야 하므로 who나 that이 적절하다. who를 목적격 whom 대신 쓸 수 있지만 whom을 who 대신 쓰지는 않는다. (7) 주격 관계대명사절의 동사는 선행사(shoes)의 수에 일치시킨다. (8) 관계대명사가 접속사와 대명사의 역할을 하므로 주어로 쓰인 he를 삭제해야 한다.

15 ⓐ와 ②, ⑤번은 동명사, 나머지는 다 현재분사

16 want+목적어+to부정사

17 volunteer: 자원봉사자, 그 일을 하기 원하기 때문에 그 일에 대한 보수 없이 일을 하는 사람

18 'high'를 보충하면 된다.

19 ① anyone who = whoever: ~인 사람은 누구나

20 주어진 문장의 those students에 주목한다. ②번 앞 문장의 several students를 받고 있으므로 ②번이 적절하다.

21 ⓐ와 ④ ~으로, ~로서, ① ~이므로, ~이기 때문에, ② ~하는대로, ③ [보통 as … as ~로 형용사·부사 앞에서] ~와 같은 정도로, ⑤ ~함에 따라, ~할수록

22 ② '처음에' 그는 음표를 읽는 법을 몰랐지만 이제 그는 간단한 노래를 연주할 수 있다고 하는 것이 적절하다. ① ③ 마침내, ④ 그러므로, ⑤ 그 결과

🦊 서술형 실전문제   p.154~155

01 (D) → (A) → (B) → (C)

02 Can you make a paper cat?

03 Do you know how to?

04 I will ask her for help.

05 (1) how to get (2) how to make (3) when to wake

(4) where to stop (5) what to do (6) Whom to meet

06 (1) Kay lives in a house which has a beautiful garden.

(2) Naomi who is standing over there is very beautiful.

07 They participated in the "Change Our Neighborhood" project.

08 As   09 that

10 (A) those   (B) hard   (C) play

11 they should

12 (A) leader   (B) join

01 (D) 유미에게 책을 읽는 것을 즐기는지 질문하자, (A) 과학 책을 읽는 것을 좋아한다고 대답하면서 상대방은 어떤지 질문한다. (B) 상대방도 책을 읽는 것을 좋아한다고 대답하자 (C) 방과 후에 도서관에 가자고 제안한다.

02 'Do you know how to+동사원형 ~?' 또는 'Can you+동사원형 ~?'을 이용해 상대방의 능력이나 무언가를 하는 방법에 대해 물을 수 있다.

03 know: 알다 how to+동사원형: ~하는 방법, 어떻게 ~하는지 / 여기서 how to 뒤에 use it이 생략되어 있다.

04 will+동사원형: ~할 것이다 ask for help: 도움을 청하다

05 '의문사+to부정사'는 '의문사+주어+should/can+동사원형'으로 바꾸어 쓸 수 있다.

06 주격 관계대명사는 선행사가 사람이면 who나 that을 쓰고 사물이나 동물이면 which나 that을 쓴다.

07 피카소 미술 동아리 회원들은 지난여름 "우리 마을 바꾸기" 프로젝트에 참여했다.

08 as a result: 그 결과

09 주격 관계대명사 that이 적절하다.

10 (A) 뒤에 나오는 명사가 복수(students)이므로 지시형용사도 복수형인 those를 쓰는 것이 적절하다. (B) '열심히' 연습할 것이라고 해야 하므로 hard가 적절하다. hard: 열심히, hardly: 거의 ~않는, (C) 지각동사 hearing의 목적격보어 자리에 to부정사를 쓸 수 없으므로 play가 적절하다.

11 '의문사+to부정사'는 '의문사+주어+should+동사원형'으로 바꿔 쓸 수 있다. 아이들에게 악기를 연주하는 법을 가르치는 것이므로 they should로 고치는 것이 적절하다.

12 장 민수는 보람 오케스트라의 '회장'이고 동아리의 활동을 소개하면서 학생들에게 동아리에 '가입할' 것을 권한다.

🐰 창의사고력 서술형 문제   p.156

|모범답안|

01 (1) enjoy flying a drone

(2) want to make a pizza

02 (A) Name (B) FC Boram (C) passing (D) running

(E) heading (F) a good team player

03 (1) I don't know how to play the computer games.

(2) What to say is important to you.

(3) I'd like to know when to start.

(4) Let me know where to go.

(5) Tell me whom to find.

01 (1) enjoy는 동명사를 목적어로 사용한다. fly: (항공기·우주선·인공위성을) 조종하다, 날게 하다 drone: 무인 비행기 (2) want는 to부정사를 목적어로 사용한다. make: 만들다

01 ③　　　02 ①　　　03 (1) interest (2) join
(3) neighbors (4) own

04 (p)ractice (h)old (n)eighborhood
(1) held (2) neighborhood (3) practice　　05 ④

06 (A) them (B) I'm going (C) come　　07 ②, ④

08 ⑤　　　09 drone　　10 how to

11 ④ Of course not. → Of course.

12 (1) leader (2) orchestra　　13 Thank you for your interest in our club.

14 (A) When did you start playing the violin?
(B) Do you have any experience playing in a group?
(C) Do you enjoy teaching others?　　15 ①, ④

16 ②

17 (1) Tell me how to use this computer.
(2) He didn't know where[when/how] to go.
(3) Do you know how to swim? 또는 Do you know how you should swim?
(4) The doctors (who[that] are) working in this hospital are very kind.
(5) Did you meet the girl that is wearing sunglasses?
(6) Mary has a cousin who[that] lives in Seoul.
(7) Melina took some pictures of her friends who were on a hiking trip.　　18 ①, ④

19 ④　　　20 (A) to paint　(B) a good painter

21 ③　　　22 ②, ④, ⑤

23 Hearing him play the violin makes me very happy.

01 walk: (사람·동물을) 걷게 하다

02 get: ~을 사다, ~을 획득하다.

03 (1) interest: 관심 (2) join: 참여하다, 가입하다 (3) neighbor: 이웃 one of 복수명사: ~ 중의 하나 (4) own: (소유격 다음에서 강조어로서) 자기 자신의, 직접 ~한

04 (1) hold: (모임·식 등을) 개최하다 / 회의, 파티, 선거 등을 특정한 장소 또는 특정한 시간에 갖다 / 그 회의가 이 호텔에서 개최될 것이다. (2) neighborhood: 동네, (도시 내의 한 단위) 지역 / 당신 주변의 지역이나 특정한 지역의 근처 또는 거기에 사는 사람들 / 이 동네에 좋은 중국집이 있나요? (3) practice: 연습; 연습하다 / 더 잘하기 위해서 규칙적으로 무언가를 하다

/ 나는 기타 연주를 연습할 필요가 있다.

05 주어진 문장에서 '네가 원한다면 우리 집에 와서 같이 해도 돼.'라는 내용이 나왔으므로, 남자아이가 도넛을 만드는 방법을 배우고 싶다고 하는 말 다음에 주어진 문장이 오고, 이후 시간 약속을 하는 말이 나오는 것이 흐름상 적절하다.

06 (A) 복수명사 cookies를 받기 때문에 them을 사용해야 한다. (B) this Saturday는 미래에 관한 시간 정보이기 때문에 'be going to 동사원형(~할 예정이다)'을 사용해야 한다. (C) should+동사원형: ~해야 한다

07 ② went → will go ④ cookies → doughnuts로 바꿔야 대화의 내용과 일치한다.

08 주어진 문장에서 She는 지나를 의미하므로 '아마도 지나는 어떻게 하는지 알 거야.'라는 문장 다음에 나와야 적절하다.

09 drone: 무인 비행기 / 조종사가 없지만 무선으로 작동되는 비행기

10 how to+동사원형: ~하는 방법, 어떻게 ~하는지

11 종이 고양이를 만드는 방법이 쉽다고 말하고 있으므로, 종이 고양이를 만드는 법을 알고 있다고 대답해야 적절하다.

12 (1) leader: 지도자, 대표 / 그룹, 조직, 국가 등을 총괄하거나 통제하는 사람 (2) orchestra: 오케스트라, 교향악단 / 많은 다른 종류의 악기를 연주하는 음악가와 지휘자에 의해 지휘되는 큰 규모의 집단

13 thank for: ~에 대해 감사하다 interest: 흥미

14 (A) when: 언제 start: 시작하다 play the 악기 이름: ~을 연주하다 (B) experience: 경험, 경력 (C) enjoy: 즐기다 teach: 가르치다

15 ① do의 목적어 it이 있으므로 what을 쓸 수 없다. ④ 'why+to부정사'는 사용하지 않는다.

16 Where are the pictures that were taken by Gibson? 주격 관계대명사의 선행사가 복수이므로 복수 동사를 써야 하며 '접속사+(대)명사의 역할을 하므로 주어로 쓰인 it을 삭제해야 한다.

17 (1) '의문사+to부정사'가 적절하다. (2) go는 자동사이므로 what과는 어색하며 how나 where 또는 when 등이 적절하다. (3) '의문사+to부정사'나 '의문사+주어+should+동사원형'이 적절하다. (4) 주격 관계대명사는 생략할 수 없으나 뒤에 분사나 부사구가 오는 경우 '주격 관계대명사+be동사'를 생략할 수 있다. (5) 관계대명사가 접속사와 대명사의 역할을 하므로 주어로 쓰인 she를 삭제해야 한다. (6) 주격 관계대명사절의 선행사가 사람이므로 who나 that을 써야 하며 동사는 선행사(a cousin)의 수에 일치시킨다. (7) 주격 관계대명사가 나와야 하므로 who나 that이 적절하다. who를 목적격 whom 대신 쓸 수 있지만 whom을 who 대신 쓰지는 않는다.

18 ⓐ와 ①, ④: 참가했다, ② 계획을 짰다, ③ 준비했다, ⑤ 돌보았다

19 ⓑ와 ①번은 현재분사, 나머지는 다 동명사이다. ② 전치사의 목적어, ③ 주어, talk behind somebody's back 남의 험담을 하다, ④ 목적어, ⑤ 보어

20 만약 당신이 '그림 그리는 것'을 좋아한다면 피카소 미술 동아리의 회원이 될 수 있지만 '그림을 잘 그릴' 필요는 없다.

21 ⓐ as: ~으로, ~로서 ⓓ By ~ing: ~함으로써

22 ⓑ와 ①, ③은 명사적 용법, ② 형용사적 용법, ④ 부사적 용법(목적), ⑤ 부사적 용법(정도)

23 동명사 Hearing을 주어로 사용하여 영작하면 된다.

교과서 파헤치기

Lesson 1

1 fully, 완전히   2 right, 바로   3 challenging, 도전적인
4 band, 밴드   5 freely, 자유롭게   6 goal, 목표
7 most, 가장   8 overcome, 극복하다
9 spend, 쓰다, 소비하다   10 draw, 그리다
11 book fair, 도서 박람회   12 save, 구하다, 살리다
13 someday, 언젠가   14 complete, 완료하다, 완결하다
15 favor, 호의. 친절   16 detective, 탐정

단어 TEST Step 1 p.02

01 호의, 친절   02 극복하다   03 탐정, 형사
04 약한   05 완료하다, 완결하다
06 걱정하다   07 유럽, 유럽 대륙   08 경험하다; 경험
09 시작하다   10 ~까지(는)   11 머무르다, 지내다
12 바로   13 입양하다   14 자유롭게
15 만화   16 작가   17 목표
18 희망하다, 바라다; 희망   19 소개하다
20 도전적인, 힘든, 간단하지 않은   21 그리다
22 씻다   23 놀라게 하다   24 구하다, 아끼다
25 도서 박람회   26 중국어; 중국의
27 걷게 하다, 데리고 가다   28 약점
29 없어진, 분실한   30 언젠가   31 기쁜
32 완전히   33 마지막으로   34 쓰다, 소비하다
35 ~을 돌보다   36 기꺼이 ~하다   37 잠깐
38 A를 B와 나누다[공유하다]   39 도움을 청하다
40 ~에 흥미를 갖게 되다   41 ~할 준비가 되다
42 노력하다   43 ~을 버리다, ~을 던지다

대화문 TEST Step 1 p.05~06

Listen & Speak 1 A

hope, get good grades / Don't worry

Listen & Speak 1 B

1 it's your birthday / What, want for / I hope I get /
2 What, doing / I'm making, wish list / cool, the first /
hope, make a lot of
3 How, English class / It was, wrote down, for / you,
tell, yours / hope I, someday

Listen & Speak 1 C

1 hope I can travel, this / sounds
2 hope, can see / sounds
3 hope I can learn, to / sounds great

Everyday English 2. A Function Practice 2

What are you planning to / planning to get, cut

Everyday English 2. B Listening Activity

1 planning to do tomorrow / I'm planning, book fair
with / like to join / What time, going to meet / At,
in front of
2 are you planning / not sure / how about going,
with / sounds
3 Can, a favor / what / to buy, tomorrow, help,
choose one / love to

Listen & Speak 2 C

1 do at / planning to sell
2 are you planning to / planning to do a magic
3 What are you planning / to dance in a group

단어 TEST Step 2 p.03

01 national   02 concert   03 bucket list
04 drama   05 musical instrument
06 save   07 surprise   08 wash
09 detective   10 challenging   11 favorite
12 spend   13 band   14 weakness
15 festival   16 fully   17 subject
18 someday   19 special   20 missing
21 plan   22 pleased   23 ride
24 finally   25 sell   26 talk
27 adopt   28 worry   29 favor
30 stay   31 overcome   32 experience
33 weak   34 complete   35 by the end of ~
36 get better   37 be ready to 동사원형
38 throw away   39 ask for help   40 make an effort
41 for a while   42 be willing to 동사원형
43 make a friend

대화문 TEST Step 2 p.07~08

Listen & Speak 1 A

G: I hope I get good grades this year.
B: You will. Don't worry.

Listen & Speak 1 B

1 B: Hana, it's your birthday today. Happy birthday!
G: Thank you.

B: What do you want for your birthday?

G: I hope I get a new computer.

2 G: What are you doing?

B: I'm making my wish list for the new school year.

G: That sounds cool! What's the first thing on your list?

B: I hope I make a lot of new friends.

3 G: How was your English class?

B: It was fun! We wrote down our dreams for the future.

G: Oh, did you? So tell me. What's yours?

B: Well, first, I hope I become a rock star someday.

Listen & Speak 1 C

1 A: I hope I can travel to Europe this summer.

B: That sounds great.

2 A: I hope I can see my grandmother.

B: That sounds great.

3 A: I hope I can learn how to swim.

B: That sounds great.

Everyday English 2. A Function Practice 2

G: What are you planning to do tomorrow?

B: I'm planning to get my hair cut.

Everyday English 2. B Listening Activity

1 B: What are you planning to do tomorrow?

G: I'm planning to go to the book fair with Jimmy. Would you like to join us?

B: Sure. What time are you going to meet?

G: At 3:00 in front of the school cafeteria.

2 G: What are you planning to do tomorrow?

B: Well, I'm not sure.

G: Then how about going to a movie with me?

B: That sounds wonderful. 3

3 G: Jack! Can you do me a favor?

B: Yes, what is it?

G: I'm planning to buy a new bike tomorrow. Can you help me choose one?

B: Sure, I'd love to.

Listen & Speak 2 C

1 A: What are you planning to do at the school festival?

B: I'm planning to sell snacks.

2 A: What are you planning to do at the school festival?

B: I'm planning to do a magic show.

3 A: What are you planning to do at the school festival?

B: I'm planning to dance in a group.

본문 TEST Step 1   p.09~10

01 My, School Year   02 Hi, everyone

03 first, our, year 04 hear, plans, this

05 What, want, most

06 Think about, things

07 then, make, share, with   08 I'm Jinsu

09 my, list, this year   10 First, on, tour

11 been, experience, freely on

12 second, to, how

13 think, most, sound, instruments

14 play, on, by, end

15 Finally, get, grade in

16 weakest subject

17 put, into, overcome, weakness   18 My name is

19 favorite, right, front, stage

20 willing, line, enter

21 Second, adopt, puppy

22 always wanted

23 fully ready, care

24 last, little, challenging

25 like, all, stories

26 big, detective, so, miss

본문 TEST Step 2   p.11~12

01 for the New School Year   02 Hi, everyone

03 the first day, new school year

04 want to hear, for this year

05 What, want, most

06 Think about, you want to do

07 make a bucket list, share, with   08 I'm

09 This is, this year

10 go on a bike tour, this summer

11 I've been there before, freely on my bike

12 second goal, how to play

13 the most beautiful sound, musical instruments

14 hope, can play, on, by the end of

15 Finally, get a good grade

16 weakest subject

17 put, into, to overcome my weakness

18 My name is   19 want to see, right in front of

20 willing, stand in line, front area

21 Second, adopt a puppy

22 I've, wanted   23 I'm, ready to take care of

24 last goal, a little more challenging

25 I'd like to, all of

26 a big fan, detective series, miss a single one

1 나의 새 학년 버킷 리스트

2 모두들, 안녕.

3 오늘은 우리 새 학년의 첫날이에요.

4 저는 여러분들의 올해 계획과 희망을 듣고 싶어요.

5 여러분이 가장 원하는 것은 무엇인가요?

6 여러분이 원하는 것 세 가지를 생각해 보세요.

7 그리고 나서 버킷 리스트를 만들어 친구들과 공유해 봐요.

8 안녕하세요! 저는 진수예요.

9 이것은 올해 제 버킷 리스트예요.

10 우선, 저는 이번 여름에 제주도로 자전거 여행을 가고 싶어요.

11 저는 그곳을 전에 가 본 적이 있지만 이번에는 제 자전거를 타고 좀 더 자유롭게 그 섬을 경험해 보고 싶어요.

12 제 두 번째 목표는 기타 연주하는 법을 배우는 거예요.

13 저는 기타가 모든 악기 중에 가장 아름다운 소리를 낸다고 생각해요.

14 올해 말쯤에는 제가 가장 좋아하는 곡을 제 기타로 연주할 수 있으면 좋겠어요.

15 마지막으로 수학에서 좋은 점수를 받고 싶어요.

16 수학은 제가 가장 약한 과목이에요.

17 올해는 제 약점을 극복하기 위해 수학 공부에 좀 더 노력을 기울일 거예요.

18 안녕하세요! 제 이름은 소미예요.

19 우선, 저는 제가 가장 좋아하는 밴드의 공연을 무대 바로 앞에서 보고 싶어요.

20 앞자리에 들어가기 위해 저는 기꺼이 밤새 줄을 서서 기다릴 거예요.

21 두 번째로, 강아지를 입양하고 싶어요.

22 저는 항상 강아지를 원해 왔어요.

23 이제는 제가 애완동물을 돌볼 준비가 완벽히 되었다고 생각해요.

24 제 마지막 목표는 좀 더 도전적이에요.

25 저는 셜록 홈스 이야기들을 모두 읽고 싶어요.

26 저는 작년에 이 탐정 시리즈의 열성 팬이 되었어요, 그래서 저는 단 하나도 놓치고 싶지 않아요.

1 My "Bucket List" for the New School Year

2 Hi, everyone.

3 Today is the first day of our new school year.

4 I want to hear your plans and hopes for this year.

5 What do you want to do most?

6 Think about three things you want to do.

7 And then, make a bucket list and share it with your friends.

8 Hi! I'm Jinsu.

9 This is my bucket list for this year.

10 First, I want to go on a bike tour of Jejudo this summer.

11 I've been there before, but I want to experience the island more freely on my bike this time.

12 My second goal is to learn how to play the guitar.

13 I think the guitar has the most beautiful sound of all musical instruments.

14 I hope I can play my favorite song on my guitar by the end of this year.

15 Finally, I want to get a good grade in math.

16 Math is my weakest subject.

17 This year, I'll put more effort into studying math to overcome my weakness.

18 Hi! My name is Somi.

19 First, I want to see a concert of my favorite band right in front of the stage.

20 I'm willing to stand in line all night to enter the front area.

21 Second, I want to adopt a puppy.

22 I've always wanted a puppy.

23 I think I'm fully ready to take care of a pet now.

24 My last goal is a little more challenging.

25 I'd like to read all of the Sherlock Holmes stories.

26 I became a big fan of this detective series last year, so I don't want to miss a single one.

Work Together Step 3

1. bucket list we bought

2. hope, can, actor

3. Second, have dinner with

4. Third, can travel, other

5. spent, to buy

My Writing Portfolio

1. This Year

2. Here is

3. First, how to make

4. want to, to surprise

5. Second, to live, life

6. throw away, that, not need

7. last thing, to study, lessons

8. At the end, will overcome, weakest

Culture Link

1. I am

2. get good grades

3. give, some advice

4. Why don't you, wake up

5. go to bed early, get better grades

구석구석지문 TEST Step 2   p.20

Work Together Step 3

1. This is the bucket list we bought.

2. First, I hope I can meet my favorite actor.

3. Second, I hope I can have dinner with my role model.

4. Third, I hope I can travel to other countries.

5. We spent ninety dollars to buy these items.

My Writing Portfolio

1. My "Bucket List" for This Year

2. Here is my bucket list.

3. First, I want to learn how to make cookies.

4. I want to make them to surprise my mom.

5. Second, I want to live a simple life.

6. I will throw away things that I do not need.

7. The last thing is to study online English lessons every day.

8. At the end of this year, I will overcome my problems with my weakest subject, English.

Culture Link

1. Hi, I am Gijun.

2. I hope I get good grades this year, but I sleep too much.

3. Could you give me some advice?

4. Why don't you go to bed on time and wake up early?

5. I think you need to go to bed early and sleep on a regular schedule to get better grades.

Lesson 2

단어 TEST Step 1   p.21

01 자세	02 구부리다	03 당기다
04 복도	05 충고	06 (눈을) 깜빡이다
07 피하다	08 조언, 비법	09 기대다
10 등	11 버려진	12 문자, 글자
13 낮추다	14 소설	15 확인하다
16 보호하다	17 서비스 센터, 수리소	
18 (휴대 전화로) 문자를 보내다		19 손목
20 줄이다, 감소시키다		21 잡다
22 날씨	23 증가하다	24 고통
25 규칙	26 다치게 하다, 아프다	
27 화난	28 압력	29 예방하다, 막다
30 역사적인	31 휴식	32 나쁜
33 금, 깨진 틈	34 불편한	35 ~에 좋다
36 ~을 줄이다	37 당장	
38 ~와 연락[접촉]하다		
39 ~에 주의를 기울이다		40 가끔, 이따금
41 A를 B로부터 막다		42 ~에 의존하다
43 명심하다		

단어 TEST Step 2   p.22

01 crack	02 cause	03 drop
04 rule	05 uncomfortable	06 under
07 hold	08 increase	09 historical
10 worse	11 break	12 life jacket
13 pressure	14 pain	15 weather
16 reduce	17 hurt	18 upset
19 prevent	20 blink	21 wrist
22 avoid	23 back	24 protect
25 pull	26 pose	27 deserted
28 hall	29 tip	30 check
31 lean	32 lower	33 letter
34 advice	35 pay attention to	
36 be late for	37 depend on	
38 get in touch with		39 instead of
40 cut down on	41 at least	42 give back
43 take a walk		

단어 TEST Step 3   p.23

1 tip, 조언, 비법   2 avoid, 피하다   3 deserted, 버려진

4 drop, 떨어지다   5 blink, (눈을) 깜빡이다

6 protect, 보호하다   7 novel, 소설

8 lower, 낮추다   9 reduce, 줄이다, 감소시키다

10 break, 휴식   11 cause, 초래하다, 야기하다

12 text, (휴대 전화로) 문자를 보내다

13 uncomfortable, 불편한   14 hall, 복도

15 prevent, 예방하다, 막다   16 upset, 화난

대화문 TEST Step 1 p.24~25

Listen & Speak 1 A

dark circles under / should get more sleep

Listen & Speak 1 B

1 forgot / Isn't, best friend / Yes, What should I do / I think you should tell

2 feel down / matter / put on, this, What should / should cut down on

Listen & Speak 1 C

1 always late for, should I / should set an alarm

2 have, headache. What should I / should get some rest

3 doesn't work, What should I do / take, the service center

Listen & Speak 2 A

Make sure, by / will

Listen & Speak 2 B

1 sleep over at / say, okay / said, would make / Make sure you text , get to

2 what, doing / reading, on / don't read in the dark, not good for / turn, on

3 didn't bring / won't / borrow / make sure, give it back when, done

Listen & Speak 2 C

1 Can, eat / make sure you, first

2 Can I / turn it off after using it

3 Can I ride on / make sure, wear a life jacket

대화문 TEST Step 2 p.26~27

Listen & Speak 1 A

G: Oh, no! I have dark circles under my eyes.

M: You should get more sleep.

Listen & Speak 1 B

1 G: I forgot Jenny's birthday!

B: Isn't she your best friend?

G: Yes, she is. What should I do?

B: I think you should tell her you're very sorry.

2 B: I feel down.

G: Why? What's the matter?

B: I put on 5kg this winter. What should I do?

G: I think you should cut down on snacks.

Listen & Speak 1 C

1 A: I'm always late for school. What should I do?

B: You should set an alarm on your smartphone.

2 A: I have a headache. What should I do?

B: You should get some rest.

3 A: My phone doesn't work. What should I do?

B: You should take it to the service center.

Listen & Speak 2 A

W: Make sure you are home by 12:00.

G: Okay, I will.

Listen & Speak 2 B

1 B: Mom, may I sleep over at Jinsu's house?

W: Did Jinsu's mom say it was okay?

B: Yes. Jinsu said she would make pizza for us.

W: Okay. Make sure you text me when you get to Jinsu's house.

2 G: Daniel, what are you doing?

B: I'm reading a novel on my smartphone.

G: Make sure you don't read in the dark. It's not good for your eyes.

B: Okay. I'll turn the light on.

3 B: Oh, no! I didn't bring my science book!

G: Ms. Lee won't be happy about that.

B: I know. Umm, can I borrow your science book?

G: Okay. Just make sure you give it back when you're done.

Listen & Speak 2 C

1 A: Can I eat this pizza?

B: Sure. Just make sure you wash your hands first.

2 A: Can I use this computer?

B: Sure. Just make sure you turn it off after using it.

3 A: Can I ride on this boat?

B: Sure. Just make sure you wear a life jacket.

본문 TEST Step 1 p.28~29

01 Health Tips, Users

02 spends, lot, using

03 checks, news, weather   04 plays, games

05 texts his   06 finds information, Internet

07 online comic books

08 watches movies   09 take, off, long

10 using, too, cause health

11 heavy user, like　　　　　　12 so, tips, protect

13 Watch, neck, back

14 When, read, usually bend

15 text, increases, pressure, back

16 prevent, bring, up to

17 Another way, instead, bending

18 Give, eyes, break

19 makes, feel, dry, for

20 Using, moving, makes, worse　　21 avoid, from, to

22 Follow, Every, least, away　　23 blink, often

24 keep, from becoming　　25 text, lot on

26 Texting, hurt, wrists　　27 Try, exercises

28 help reduce, pain　　29 Pull on, each

30 Put, backs, with, out　　31 But remember

32 tip, prevent, use, less

33 yourself, rest from

본문 TEST Step 2　　p.30~31

01 Health Tips, Users

02 spends, lot, using

03 checks, news, weather　　04 plays, games

05 texts his friends

06 finds information on, Internet

07 reads online comic books

08 watches movies

09 take, off, all day long

10 using, too much, cause health problems

11 a heavy user, like

12 If so, here are, to protect

13 Watch, neck, back

14 When, usually bend

15 text neck, pose increases

16 to prevent, to bring, up to

17 Another way, to lower, instead of bending

18 Give, a break

19 makes, feel tired, for a long time

20 Using, in the dark, makes, worse

21 To avoid, from time to time

22 Follow, Every, a 20-second　break, at least, feet
　　away　　23 blink, often

24 keep, from becoming

25 text, on your smartphone　　26 Texting, hurt

27 Try, exercises 28 help reduce

29 Pull on, each hand

30 Put, together with your arms, in front of

31 remember

---

32 The best tip to prevent, to use, less

33 some rest from

본문 TEST Step 3　　p.32~33

1 스마트폰 사용자들을 위한 건강 조언

2 성민이는 스마트폰을 사용하는 데 많은 시간을 보냅니다.

3 그는 뉴스와 날씨를 확인합니다.

4 그는 스마트폰 게임을 합니다.

5 그는 친구들에게 문자 메시지를 보냅니다.

6 그는 인터넷에서 정보를 찾습니다.

7 그는 온라인 만화책을 읽습니다.

8 그는 영화를 봅니다.

9 성민이는 하루 종일 스마트폰에서 손을 뗄 수가 없습니다.

10 그는 스마트폰을 너무 많이 사용하는 것이 건강 문제를
　일으킬 수 있다는 것을 모릅니다.

11 여러분은 성민이와 같은 스마트폰 과다 사용자인가요?

12 그렇다면, 여기 여러분의 건강을 지켜 줄 몇 가지 조언이 있습니다.

13 여러분의 목과 척추를 조심하세요.

14 스마트폰을 볼 때, 여러분은 보통 목을 구부립니다

15 이 "거북목" 자세는 여러분의 목과 척추에 가해지는 압력을
　증가시킵니다.

16 이러한 압력을 예방하는 가장 좋은 방법은 휴대 전화를
　여러분의 눈높이까지 올리는 것입니다.

17 또 다른 방법은 여러분의 목을 구부리는 대신에 시선을
　낮추는 것입니다.

18 눈을 쉬게 하세요.

19 오랫동안 스마트폰의 작은 글자를 읽는 것은 눈이
　피곤해지고 건조하게 느끼도록 만듭니다.

20 어두운 곳이나 움직이는 차에서 스마트폰을 사용하는 것은
　이러한 문제를 더욱 악화시킵니다.

21 이것을 피하려면, 눈을 때때로 쉬게 하세요.

22 20-20-20 규칙을 따르세요. 20분마다 20초의 휴식을 취하고
　적어도 20피트 이상 떨어져 있는 사물을 바라보세요.

23 또한, 눈을 자주 깜박이세요.

24 이것은 여러분의 눈이 건조해지는 것을 막아 줄 것입니다.

25 스마트폰으로 문자 메시지를 많이 보내나요?

26 오랫동안 문자 메시지를 보내는 것은 여러분의 손가락과
　손목을 상하게 할 수 있습니다.

27 이런 운동을 해 보세요.

28 그것은 여러분의 손가락과 손목의 통증을 줄이는 것을 도와줄 것입니다.

29 각 손의 각 손가락을 당기세요.

30 팔을 여러분 앞에서 벌린 채로 손등을 마주 놓으세요.

31 그러나 기억하세요.

32 이러한 건강 문제를 예방하는 가장 좋은 방법은 스마트폰을 덜
　사용하는 것입니다.

33 여러분 자신에게 스마트폰으로부터 휴식을 주세요.

1 Health Tips for Smartphone Users.

2 Seongmin spends a lot of time using his smartphone.

3 He checks the news and weather.

4 He plays smartphone games.

5 He texts his friends.

6 He finds information on the Internet.

7 He reads online comic books.

8 He watches movies.

9 Seongmin cannot take his hands off his smartphone all day long.

10 He does not know that using a smartphone too much can cause health problems.

11 Are you a heavy user of your smartphone like Seongmin?

12 If so, here are some tips to protect your health.

13 Watch your neck and back.

14 When you read on your smartphone, you usually bend your neck.

15 This "text neck" pose increases the pressure on your neck and back.

16 The best way to prevent this pressure is to bring the phone up to the level of your eyes.

17 Another way is to lower your eyes instead of bending your neck.

18 Give your eyes a break.

19 It makes your eyes feel tired and dry to read small letters on a smartphone for a long time.

20 Using a smartphone in the dark or in a moving car makes this problem worse.

21 To avoid this, give your eyes a break from time to time.

22 Follow the 20-20-20 rules: Every 20 minutes, take a 20-second break and look at something at least 20 feet away.

23 Also, blink your eyes often.

24 This will keep your eyes from becoming dry.

25 Do you text a lot on your smartphone?

26 Texting for a long time can hurt your fingers and wrists.

27 Try these exercises.

28 They will help reduce the pain in your fingers and wrists.

29 Pull on each finger of each hand.

30 Put the backs of your hands together with your arms out in front of you.

31 But remember.

32 The best tip to prevent these health problems is to use your smartphone less.

33 Give yourself some rest from your smartphone.

Before You Read A

1. when, eat breakfast

2. in a car

3. when I am walking

4. feel uncomfortable, not have, with

5. in bed

Before You Read B

1. Watch Out

2. walked into, while texting, hurt

3. avoid using, while walking

4. should reduce, she spends using

Writing Workshop

1. Smartphone, Me

2. are both, and, using

3. get in touch with, right away

4. information I need

5. when, to do

6. On the other hand, feel dry, tired

7. keep, from paying

8. need to, intelligently

Before You Read A

1. I use my smartphone when I eat breakfast.

2. I use my smartphone in a car.

3. I use my smartphone when I am walking.

4. I feel uncomfortable when I do not have my smartphone with me.

5. I use my smartphone in bed.

Before You Read B

1. Watch Out!

2. Yesterday, Sejin walked into a tree while texting and hurt her head.

3. She needs to avoid using her phone while walking.

4. Also, she should reduce the time she spends using it.

Writing Workshop

1. A Smartphone & Me

2. There are both good things and bad things about using a smartphone.

3. First, I can get in touch with my friends right away.

4. Also, I can easily get information I need.

5. That is useful when I have a lot of homework to do.

6. On the other hand, using a smartphone too much makes my eyes feel dry and tired.

7. Also, text messages and ads keep me from paying attention to my studies.

8. So I need to use my smartphone intelligently.

Lesson **3**

6 bake, (빵 등을) 굽다   7 drone, 무인 비행기
8 join, 가입하다   9 neighbor, 이웃   10 garden, 정원
11 musical instrument, 악기   12 leader, 지도자, 대표
13 opportunity, 기회   14 hold, (모임·식 등을) 개최하다
15 orchestra, 오케스트라, 교향악단   16 club, 동아리

단어 TEST Step 1   p.40

01 연주회   02 (동식물을) 기르다, 자라다
03 실제로, 사실은   04 조금, 한 조각(가지), 부분
05 옷, 의상   06 기회   07 밝은, 똑똑한
08 돌고래   09 초등학교   10 악기
11 요리하다; 요리사 12 여가 시간
13 (모임·식 등을) 개최하다   14 참여하다, 가입하다
15 쉬운   16 이웃   17 정문
18 오케스트라, 교향악단   19 소개하다
20 자기 자신의   21 정원   22 채소
23 도서관   24 선물; 참석한   25 봉사하다
26 경험, 경력   27 몇몇의   28 음, 음표
29 활동   30 지도자, 대표
31 관심; ~의 관심[흥미]을 끌다   32 연습; 연습하다
32 동네, (도시 내의 한 단위) 지역   33 요리, 음식
34 결과적으로   35 ~하는 것을 즐기다
36 ~을 찾다   37 ~하고 싶다   38 ~에 참여하다
39 ~로 변화시키다[바꾸다]   40 도움을 청하다
41 ~을 잘하다   42 ~하는 방법

단어 TEST Step 2   p.41

01 doughnut   02 experience   03 drone
04 present   05 practice   06 activity
07 cooking   08 interest   09 fly
10 service   11 several   12 neighborhood
13 get   14 leader   15 library
16 club   17 however   18 volunteer
19 note   20 project   21 Spanish
22 walk   23 actually   24 opportunity
25 hold   26 introduce   27 actually
28 bright   29 clothes   30 grow
31 hold   32 neighbor   33 main gate
34 vegetable   35 change into   36 a little bit
37 fall into   38 as a result   39 participate in
40 get better   41 thank for   42 ask for help
43 watch out (for)

단어 TEST Step 3   p.42

1 bright, 밝은   2 grow, 자라다   3 a bit, 조금, 약간
4 practice, 연습하다   5 walk, (동물을) 걷게 하다

대화문 TEST Step 1   p.43~44

Listen & Speak 1 A
know how to make / course, easy

Listen & Speak 1 B
1 heard you went to, How / I hope I can play, like her someday / knew how to play the violin / not good at, yet
2 Look at, grew, myself, own garden / how to cook, grow, too / taught me

Listen & Speak 2 A
looking at, at night / love doing

Listen & Speak 2 B
1 Do you enjoy reading / love reading, about / reading, too / let's go, the library
2 What did you do / made breakfast / Do you enjoy cooking / good cook, cooking
3 Where, get / made it for me / really good designer / enjoys making clothes, too

Real-Life Zone A
the leader, Thank, for your interest / to meet / When did you start playing / how to play the violin when / experience playing / Actually, an orchestra when, elementary school / volunteer to teach, Do you enjoy teaching others / experience, enjoy working with, like to try / have, playing, Welcome to

Wrap Up
look, delicious / made them myself, baking, going to, this Saturday / want to learn how to make, Is, difficult / at all, join me / What time should / At / Sounds, See, then

대화문 TEST Step 2   p.45~46

Listen & Speak 1 A
A: Do you know how to make a paper cat?
B: Of course. It's easy.

Listen & Speak 1 B
1 G: I heard you went to Yuna's violin concert yesterday. How was it?

37

B: It was great. I hope I can play the violin like her someday.

G: I didn't know you knew how to play the violin

B: I can, but I'm not good at it yet.

2 G: Look at these pictures. I grew these vegetables myself. I have my own garden.

B: Cool! Do you know how to cook the vegetables you grow, too?

G: Yes, my grandmother taught me.

Listen & Speak 2 A

A: Do you enjoy looking at the stars at night?

G: Yes, I love doing that.

Listen & Speak 2 B

1 B: Do you enjoy reading books, Yumi?

G: Yes, I love reading science books. How about you?

B: I love reading books, too.

G: Then, let's go to the library after school today.

2 G: What did you do on the weekend, Minsu?

B: I made breakfast for my family.

G: Do you enjoy cooking ?

B: Yes, I'm a good cook ! My family loves my cooking.

3 B: Jiyun, that's a pretty backpack! Where did you get it?

G: My sister made it for me.

B: Wow! She's a really good designer.

G: Yes, she is. And she enjoys making clothes, too .

Real-Life Zone A

B: Hello, Kate. I'm Hamin, the leader of the Nanum Orchestra. Thank you for your interest in our club.

G: Hi. Nice to meet you.

B: You play the violin? When did you start playing the violin?

G: I started learning how to play the violin when I was ten.

B: Do you have any experience playing in a group?

G: Yes. Actually, I was a member of an orchestra when I was in elementary school.

B: Great. We also volunteer to teach children. Do you enjoy teaching others?

G: I have no experience teaching others. But I enjoy working with people, so I'd like to try.

B: Good. I think we'll have a great time playing together. Welcome to the Nanum Orchestra.

Wrap Up

B: These cookies look so delicious. Did you make them?

G: Yes. I made them myself yesterday. I enjoy baking. I'm going to make doughnuts this Saturday.

B: Oh, I want to learn how to make doughnuts. Is it difficult?

G: Not at all. You can come to my house and join me if you want.

B: Thanks, Bora. What time should I come?

G: At 2:00.

B: Sounds good. See you then.

본문 TEST Step 1   p.47~48

01 Why Don't, Join

02 Participating, way, life   03 How, joining

04 are, leaders who, join   05 Let's, to what

06 Art Club   07 from, Art Club

08 As, guess from, paint

09 volunteer work, to

10 Last, participated in, Change

11 dirty, flying, jumping, waves

12 As, into, bright, place

13 neighbors, to, thanked   14 don't have to

15 Anyone, paint, join

16 Come, be, member

17 Boram Orchestra

18 leader of, Orchestra

19 several, playing, main gate   20 were those

21 play, for, every

22 need, how, little bit   23 worry if, play

24 practice, get better

25 musical instruments, service, community

26 teaching, eleven-year-old, play 27 At, how, note

28 can, simple song

29 Hearing, play, makes

30 By joining, opportunity, others

31 Come, join, club   32 waiting for

본문 TEST Step 2   p.49~50

01 Why Don't You Join

02 Participating in club activities, to enjoy

03 How about joining

04 Here are, who want, to join   05 Let's, to what

06 Art Club   07 from, Art Club

08 As, can guess from, paint

09 do volunteer work from, to

10 Last, participated in, Change, Neighborhood

11 On the dirty old walls, painted, flying, jumping over blue waves

12 As a result, changed into, beautiful place

13 were happy to see, thanked

14 don't have to, painter

15 Anyone who likes to, join

16 Come and be   17 Orchestra

18 the leader of

19 see, playing music, main gate, came to school

20 were those   21 play music for

22 how to play, a little bit to join

23 don't worry if, don't

24 practice hard, get better

25 also teach, how to, as a service to

26 teaching an eleven-year-old boy

27 At first, how to read a note

28 can play a simple song

29 Hearing him play, happy

30 By joining, have an opportunity, to help others

31 Come and join   32 waiting for

17 보람 오케스트라

18 안녕하세요! 저는 보람 오케스트라의 회장 장민수입니다.

19 오늘 학교에 왔을 때 정문에서 음악을 연주하는 몇 명의 학생들을 보았습니까?

20 우리가 그 학생들이었습니다.

21 우리는 매일 아침 친구들을 위해 음악을 연주합니다.

22 우리 동아리에 가입하기 위해서는 악기 연주하는 법을 조금 알아야 합니다.

23 그러나 여러분이 연주를 잘 못한다고 해서 걱정하지 마세요.

24 우리는 열심히 연습하고 함께 좋아질 것입니다.

25 우리는 지역 사회에 대한 봉사로 아이들에게 악기를 연주하는 법도 가르칩니다.

26 저는 열한 살 소년에게 바이올린을 가르치고 있습니다.

27 처음에 그는 음표를 읽는 법을 알지 못했습니다.

28 이제는 간단한 노래도 연주할 수 있습니다.

29 그가 바이올린을 연주하는 걸 듣는 것은 저를 매우 행복하게 합니다.

30 우리 동아리에 가입함으로써, 여러분은 다른 사람들을 도울 수 있는 기회를 가질 수 있습니다.

31 와서 우리 동아리에 가입하세요.

32 우리는 여러분을 기다리고 있습니다.

1 우리 동아리에 가입하는 게 어때?

2 동아리 활동에 참여하는 것은 학교생활을 즐기는 좋은 방법이에요.

3 동아리에 가입하는 게 어떤가요?

4 여기 학생들이 그들의 동아리에 가입하기를 원하는 두 명의 동아리 대표가 있어요.

5 그들이 하는 말을 들어 봅시다.

6 피카소 미술 동아리

7 안녕하세요! 저는 피카소 미술 동아리의 강소라입니다.

8 우리 동아리의 이름에서 추측할 수 있듯이, 우리는 그림을 그립니다.

9 우리는 가끔 자원봉사도 합니다.

10 지난여름, 우리 동아리 회원들은 "우리 마을 바꾸기" 프로젝트에 참여했습니다.

11 우리 마을에 있는 건물의 더럽고 오래된 벽에 하늘 높이 나는 새들과 푸른 파도 위로 점프하는 돌고래들을 그렸습니다.

12 결과적으로, 오래된 마을은 밝고 아름다운 곳으로 바뀌었습니다.

13 이웃들은 우리의 작품을 보고 행복해 했고 고마워했습니다.

14 여러분은 그림을 잘 그릴 필요는 없습니다.

15 그림 그리는 것을 좋아하는 사람은 누구나 가입할 수 있습니다.

16 와서 피카소 미술 동아리의 회원이 되세요.

1 Why Don't You Join Our Club?

2 Participating in club activities is a great way to enjoy your school life.

3 How about joining a club?

4 Here are two club leaders who want students to join their clubs.

5 Let's listen to what they say.

6 The Picasso Art Club

7 Hi! I am Sora Kang from the Picasso Art Club.

8 As you can guess from the name of our club, we paint.

9 We also do volunteer work from time to time.

10 Last summer, our club members participated in the "Change Our Neighborhood" project.

11 On the dirty old walls of the buildings in our neighborhood, we painted birds flying high in the sky and dolphins jumping over blue waves.

12 As a result, the old neighborhood changed into a bright and beautiful place.

13 The neighbors were happy to see our work and thanked us.

14 You don't have to be a good painter.

15 Anyone who likes to paint can join.

16 Come and be a member of the Picasso Art Club.

17 The Boram Orchestra

18 Hi! I am Minsu Jang, the leader of the Boram Orchestra.

19 Did you see several students playing music at the main gate when you came to school today?

20 We were those students.

21 We play music for our friends every morning.

22 You need to know how to play an instrument a little bit to join our club.

23 But don't worry if you don't play well.

24 We will practice hard and get better together.

25 We also teach children how to play musical instruments as a service to our community.

26 I am teaching an eleven-year-old boy to play the violin.

27 At first, he did not know how to read a note.

28 Now he can play a simple song.

29 Hearing him play the violin makes me very happy.

30 By joining our club, you can have an opportunity to help others.

31 Come and join our club.

32 We are waiting for you.

After You Read

1. leader, community center

2. started teaching, how to play

3. how to read a note

4. hope to join, main gate

Writing Workshop

1. Middle School Club

2. Name

3. Student Name

4. to Join, would like to

5. good at passing, running

6. how to head, so

7. become, who

8. Goals, join, practice, hard

Real Life Zone

1. would like

2. how to play

3. lots of, playing

4. enjoys working

5. Let's, welcome, to

After You Read

1. Today, Minsu, the leader of the Boram Orchestra, came to community center.

2. He started teaching me how to play the violin last month.

3. At first, I didn't know how to read a note.

4. I hope to join the Boram Orchestra and play the violin at the main gate when I become a middle school student.

Writing Workshop

1. Boram Middle School Club Membership Form

2. • Name of Club: FC Boram

3. • Student Name: Sunho Park

4. • Why You Want to Join the Club: I love soccer and would like to join FC Boram.

5. I am good at passing the ball and running fast.

6. However, I don't know how to head the ball, so I want to learn how to do that.

7. I want to become a soccer player who can make wonderful heading goals.

8. • Your Goals: If I join this club, I will practice very hard and become a good team player!

Real Life Zone

1. I would like to introduce our new orchestra member, Kate.

2. She knows how to play the violin.

3. She also has lots of experience playing in a group.

4. And she said she enjoys working with people.

5. Let's all welcome her to the Nanum Orchestra.

적중100

영어 기출 문제집

정답 및 해설

시사 | 송미정